Contemporary Debates in Moral Theory

Contemporary Debates in Philosophy

In teaching and research, philosophy makes progress through argumentation and debate. *Contemporary Debates in Philosophy* presents a forum for students and their teachers to follow and participate in the debates that animate philosophy today in the western world. Each volume presents pairs of opposing viewpoints on contested themes and topics in the central subfields of philosophy. Each volume is edited and introduced by an expert in the field, and also includes an index, bibliography, and suggestions for further reading. The opposing essays, commissioned especially for the volumes in the series, are thorough but accessible presentations of opposing points of view.

1 Contemporary Debates in Philosophy of Religion *edited by Michael L. Peterson and Raymond J. VanArragon*
2 Contemporary Debates in Philosophy of Science *edited by Christopher Hitchcock*
3 Contemporary Debates in Epistemology *edited by Matthias Steup and Ernest Sosa*
4 Contemporary Debates in Applied Ethics *edited by Andrew I. Cohen and Christopher Heath Wellman*
5 Contemporary Debates in Aesthetics and the Philosophy of Art *edited by Matthew Kieran*
6 Contemporary Debates in Moral Theory *edited by James Dreier*

Forthcoming *Contemporary Debates* are in:

Cognitive Science *edited by Robert Stainton*
Metaphysics *edited by Ted Sider, Dean Zimmerman, and John Hawthorne*
Philosophy of Mind *edited by Brian McLaughlin and Jonathan Cohen*
Social Philosophy *edited by Laurence Thomas*
Political Philosophy *edited by Thomas Christiano*
Philosophy of Language *edited by Ernie Lepore and Kent Bach*

Contemporary Debates in Moral Theory

Edited by

James Dreier

Blackwell Publishing

© 2006 by Blackwell Publishing Ltd

BLACKWELL PUBLISHING
350 Main Street, Malden, MA 02148–5020, USA
9600 Garsington Road, Oxford OX4 2DQ, UK
550 Swanston Street, Carlton, Victoria 3053, Australia

The right of James Dreier to be identified as the Author of the Editorial Material in this Work has been asserted in accordance with the UK Copyright, Designs, and Patents Act 1988.

First published 2006 by Blackwell Publishing Ltd

1   2006

Library of Congress Cataloging-in-Publication Data

Contemporary debates in moral theory / edited by James Dreier.
    p. cm. – (Contemporary debates in philosophy)
  Includes bibliographical references and index.
  ISBN-13: 978-1-4051-0178-3 (hardcover : alk. paper)
  ISBN-10: 1-4051-0178-4 (hardcover : alk. paper)
  ISBN-13: 978-1-4051-0179-0 (pbk. : alk. paper)
  ISBN-10: 1-4051-0179-2 (pbk. : alk. paper)
 1. Ethics.   I. Dreier, James.   II. Series.

  BJ1012.C6572 2005
  171 – dc22

                                        2005009843

A catalogue record for this title is available from the British Library.

Set in 10 on 12.5 pt Rotif Serif
by SNP Best-set Typesetter Ltd, Hong Kong
Printed and bound in India
by Replika Press

The publisher's policy is to use permanent paper from mills that operate a sustainable forestry policy, and which has been manufactured from pulp processed using acid-free and elementary chlorine-free practices. Furthermore, the publisher ensures that the text paper and cover board used have met acceptable environmental accreditation standards.

For further information on
Blackwell Publishing, visit our website:
www.blackwellpublishing.com

Contents

PART III MORAL FACTS AND EXPLANATIONS   197

Notes on Contributors

Robert Audi works in ethics and related philosophical fields. His books include *Action, Intention, and Reason*, *The Structure of* Justification, *Moral Knowledge and Ethical Character*, *Religious Commitment and Secular Reason*, *The Architecture of Reason*, and *The Good in the Right: A Theory of Intuition and Intrinsic Value*.

Simon Blackburn is Professor of Philosophy at the University of Cambridge. He has taught at Oxford and the University of North Carolina at Chapel Hill. His books include *Spreading the Word*, the *Oxford Dictionary of Philosophy*, *Ruling Passions*, *Think*, and *Being Good*.

James Dreier is Professor of Philosophy at Brown University. He works mainly in metaethics, and has published articles on relativism, expressivism, moral realism, practical rationality, decision theory, and the structure of normative theories.

Julia Driver is Professor of Philosophy at Dartmouth College. She works in normative ethical theory. She is the author of *Uneasy Virtue* and is currently working on a book tentatively entitled "The Greatest Happiness Principle."

Samuel Freeman is Steven F. Goldstone Term Professor of Philosophy and Law at the University of Pennsylvania. He has published articles on a variety of subjects in moral and political philosophy, including contractarianism, deliberative democracy, liberalism and libertarianism, deontology, constitutional interpretation, public reason, and most recently on distributive justice and the Law of Peoples. He is completing a book on John Rawls.

Terry Horgan is Professor of Philosophy at the University of Arizona. He has published work in metaphysics, philosophy of mind, philosophy of psychology, philosophy of language, epistemology, and metaethics. He often collaborates, and virtually all his work in metaethics has been collaborative with Mark Timmons

Rosalind Hursthouse is Professor of Philosophy in her home department at the University of Auckland, New Zealand. Her publications include *On Virtue Ethics* and a couple of textbooks on abortion and the ethics of our treatment of the other animals for the Open University, UK. Currently she has returned to struggling with Aristotle's ethics.

Samuel J. Kerstein is Associate Professor of Philosophy at the University of Maryland, College Park. He is working on a defense of the Kantian view that central to morality is the idea of humanity's being an end in itself.

Mark Norris Lance is Professor of Philosophy and Professor of Justice and Peace at Georgetown University, as well as an activist working with a number of grassroots movements resisting US imperialism. He is currently writing articles or books on logic, semantics, set theory, pragmatism, freedom, and anarchist theory.

Margaret Olivia Little is Associate Professor, Philosophy Department, and Senior Research Scholar, Kennedy Institute of Ethics, at Georgetown University. Her research interests are broadly clustered around ethics, from metaethical questions about morality's standing to applied questions of public policy.

Alastair Norcross is Associate Professor of Philosophy at Rice University. His articles on ethics and applied ethics have appeared in such journals as the *Philosophical Review*, the *Journal of Philosophy*, and *Philosophy & Public Affairs*. He has also co-edited (with Bonnie Steinbock) *Killing and Letting Die*.

Philip Pettit teaches political theory and philosophy at Princeton, where he is the L. S. Rockefeller University Professor of Politics and Human Values. His recent books include *Republicanism: A Theory of Freedom and Government, A Theory of Freedom: From the Psychology to the Politics of Agency*, a collection of his essays, *Rules, Reasons and Norms*, and two collaborations: *The Economy of Esteem: An Essay on Civil and Political Society* with Geoffrey Brennan, and the collection *Mind, Morality and Explanation: Selected Collaborations* with Frank Jackson and Michael Smith.

Peter Railton is the Perrin Professor of Philosophy at the University of Michigan. He is the author of numerous articles in ethics and metaethics, some of which have recently been collected in *Facts, Values, and Norms*.

William H. Shaw is Professor of Philosophy at San José State University, where he was Chair of the Philosophy Department for 11 years. In addition to essays in a variety of professional journals, Bill has edited or co-edited five books and is the author of *Marx's Theory of History, Moore on Right and Wrong: The Normative Ethics of G. E. Moore, Contemporary Ethics: Taking Account of Utilitarianism, Business Ethics*, and (with Vincent Barry) *Moral Issues in Business*.

Nicholas Sturgeon is Professor of Philosophy at Cornell University. He has written on contemporary issues on the foundations of ethics, and on the history of eighteenth-century ethical theories.

Sigrún Svavarsdóttir is Assistant Professor of Philosophy at Ohio State University. She is the author of *Thinking in Moral Terms* and articles on moral motivation, objectivity in ethics, and practical rationality.

Mark Timmons is Professor of Philosophy at the University of Arizona and author of *Morality without Foundations* and *Moral Theory: An Introduction.*

Peter Vallentyne is Florence G. Kline Professor of Philosophy at the University of Missouri-Columbia. He writes on issues of liberty and equality – and left-libertarianism in particular. He edited *Equality and Justice* (6 volumes) and *Contractarianism and Rational Choice: Essays on David Gauthier's Morals by Agreement*, and, with Hillel Steiner, *The Origins of Left Libertarianism: An Anthology of Historical Writings* and *Left Libertarianism and Its Critics: The Contemporary Debate.*

R. Jay Wallace is Professor of Philosophy at the University of California, Berkeley. He is the author of *Responsibility and the Moral Sentiments*, editor of *Reason, Emotion and Will* and *The Practice of Value*, and co-editor of *Reason and Value*. A selection of his papers on moral psychology and practical reason, *Normativity and the Will*, is forthcoming from Oxford University Press.

Nick Zangwill teaches philosophy at St Anne's College, Oxford. He has published on moral philosophy, aesthetics and philosophy of mind. His book *The Metaphysics of Beauty* was published by Cornell University Press in 2001.

Introduction

James Dreier

This book includes debates on some of the most controversial and significant issues in contemporary ethical theory. All of the included papers were commissioned and written for this volume. There are debates on eight topics, and all of them but the first are presented as two-sided. Of course, this is inevitably something of an over-simplification, but where there seemed to be more than two sides to an issue I generally separated the issue into two, as for example the question of what is the most suitable organizing strategy for grounding a moral theory is divided into more specific debates over contractualism, virtue ethics, and consequentialism. The format suggests another simplification that the volume does not, in fact, respect: when there seem to be two opposing sides, often it is much more common (and fruitful) to find philosophers adopting a kind of accommodating position. When that happens here, though, we at least find the interlocutors on different sides of *some* watershed question or other.

The topics range over issues traditionally assigned to normative ethical theory, some that are counted as metaethical issues, and some that roam the borderlands between, and the chapters are arranged more or less beginning with the topics toward the normative theory end of the spectrum and finishing with those more squarely in metaethics.

Consequentialism

The first three essays are about consequentialism. Why three in this one case? There are really two closely related topics at issue. One is whether consequentialism is true; whether, that is to say, what one ought to do is always a matter of what will have the best consequences. The other question can in principle be asked about non-consequentialist conceptions of morality, but has tended to focus on consequentialism.

It is the question of whether a given moral theory is *too demanding*. How could a theory be too demanding? Consequentialist theories insist that we do what is best. That leaves us no wiggle room, no 'moral freedom' as it's sometimes called. There seems to be no such thing, according to consequentialist theories, as having finished your duties and getting a little time and a few resources to worry about your own, non-moral affairs. This is *too* demanding, some philosophers have thought, because it is not plausible that morality should completely control our every decision, and also because if it is insisted that it does, then it will be doubtful that we have sufficient reason to defer to its demands. Why sacrifice everything (else) I care about for the sake of morality, even if I grant that moral considerations must be given some serious weight? William Shaw explains consequentialism and provides a general defense against popular objections. Then Alastair Norcross and Peter Vallentyne focus on the issues surrounding demandingness.

What is consequentialism?

The concept of consequentialism is, I think it's fair to say, an abstraction from utilitarianism. To many philosophers, the problem with utilitarian morality is not merely that it has the wrong account of value, but further that its structure is somehow misconceived. Even given some measure of value, why should morality always insist on maximizing it? Aren't we sometimes permitted to do something other than the value-maximizing act – are we even sometimes *forbidden* from maximizing value, as for instance when so doing would violate someone's rights?

As Shaw explains, consequentialism is the general idea that right action is action with best consequences. We need to clarify: 'best' is defined independently of right, as Rawls (1971) stipulated in his distinction between teleological and deontological theories. There are a number of loose ends to tidy up, but fortunately I can leave them to Shaw, who also explains several distinctions between kinds of consequentialism. There is the agent-neutral kind, for instance, as distinct from a broader sort that allows for agent-centered goods (like the good of *caring for one's own children*); there is the kind that grounds rightness in the *actual* consequences and the kind that grounds it in the *expected* consequences; and there is act consequentialism contrasted with various two-level varieties. Shaw assembles and deploys a number of defenses, some fairly well known, against the most common objections to consequentialism. For instance, he notes that some acts that strike us as wrong, even though consequentialism implies they are right, might seem wrong because they ought not to be blamed (which could be true even if they really are wrong).

Peter Vallentyne's worries about consequentialism can all be seen as addressing its maximizing structure. Some are explicitly about that structure: he urges that a better account of moral permissibility would have a "satisficing" structure; that is, in the context of consequentialism, the permissible would be the "good enough," not the best.

The other part of his objection redevelops Rawls's famous complaint (directed specifically at utilitarianism) that "standard" consequentialism does not respect the separateness of persons. But one could see Vallentyne's criticism rather as insisting that *respecting* certain values is different from and sometimes just as important as *promoting* values (as in Pettit 1989). Promoting truth, for example, means trying to get as much truth told as possible, *even if that might involve lying*! (Maybe someone asks me what will happen to her if she doesn't tell the truth, and I lie and say that the consequences for her will be dire.) *Respecting* truth, on the other hand, involves telling the truth. Similarly, respecting other people's autonomy, for example, does not mean seeking to maximize the amount of autonomy that others have. It means refraining from interfering with (certain of) their powers and the free exercise thereof. Promoting always has a maximizing structure, but respecting does not seem to have one at all. In any case, Vallentyne's own suggestion is that the failure to respect the normative separateness of persons can be cured by incorporating into a theory some constraints that have the form of claims, or rights. The idea is that among the constraints on our actions that there might be, some will be "impersonal," not particularly owed to anyone – these could include a duty never to kill under any circumstances – while others will be personal, as for example the obligation to return what is owed, which may be claimed or waived by the creditor. These personal constraints, Vallentyne argues, can't be accommodated by consequentialism, not exactly because of its concern with consequences, but because of its assimilation of all sorts of reasons to reasons to *promote.*

Alastair Norcross's basic idea, to put it somewhat crudely, is to respond to the demandingness objection by performing a demandectomy on the theory. Consequentialism, Norcross suggests, tells us only which acts are better than which, and doesn't really have any place for the notions of 'right' and 'wrong'. Norcross seems to say that there are no significant lines to be drawn on the goodness scale, but he needn't say that. There might be plenty. For example, there is often a certain amount that I can contribute that counts as my "fair share," and though pure consequentialists will have no truck with free-standing obligations of fairness, they can still recognize the special significance that the line between doing one's fair share and failing to do it might have (compare Murphy 1997). There is also the line Norcross mentions himself between good and bad (if there is any such line – compare Broome 1999), and there could be lots of others. Norcross's real point, I think, is that having noted that various lines have their own sort of significance, what *else* might one be saying by adding that the line below which an action is 'wrong' is right here?

A similar question has been asked in connection with the idea of supererogation. To use Norcross's example, think of a doctor who could, at significant risk, inconvenience, and cost to himself, move to a town stricken by a terrible disease so as better to help the victims, or instead set up a much safer (for him) out-of-town clinic and treat victims there. To move to the stricken town is better, but it is not *wrong* to set up the clinic instead; the doctor is under no *duty* or *obligation*; it is *permissible* to perform the less good act, in this case. But what exactly is that supposed to mean? The more difficult act is better. There is, no doubt, moral reason to do it instead of the safer, less onerous one. (If the doctor did decide bravely to move to the stricken town, it would be absurd to say that he did what he had no moral reason to do.) Then what do we add by adding, "but morality doesn't demand that he do that"?

Maybe consequentialism should reject the whole idea of the supererogatory, and good riddance, on the grounds that presupposed the notion of the demands of morality, in the guise of 'requirements', 'wrong', 'duty', and so forth. Instead, the job of moral theory is to say what moral *reasons* people have. Goodness, with its dimension of weight, is better suited to 'underwriting reasons' than to 'grounding requirements'.

If Norcross is right, then it looks as if consequentialism has a new, surprising answer to the charge that it is too demanding, namely, that it cannot be too demanding since it makes no demands of any kind. Let me say a word or two about the independent plausibility of the idea of "scalar morality."

It's plenty plausible, to my mind. One way of seeing this is to start off with an analogy. Because it has a built-in aim, chess provides a conceptually unproblematic notion of 'better' and 'worse' moves (conceptually unproblematic – in practice, of course, it may be reasonably disputed which move is best). In any given position, which move *ought* one to make? Which one is *right*? The best move is right. The others are wrong. Some may not be too badly wrong, and still pretty good moves, but after analysis, the experts will say that the pretty good move was wrong, since there was an even better one available. There is no room for dispute here: the *best* move is automatically also the *right* one. It is the one that the player *ought* to have chosen; if she didn't, then she made a *mistake*. The evaluations are connected very tightly to the deontic notions.

How, we might ask Norcross, could the case be very different when we turn to morality? If we have found the best action of all available ones, how can we deny that it is also right, and all the inferior alternatives wrong? The answer might be something like this. It is very unusual for chess considerations to compete with other considerations. If it happens at all, it happens only in very artificial "cooked-up" situations. Sometimes I have a reason to make an inferior chess move – I am teaching my son, for example, and want to see if he can spot a definite flaw in my position. But even in that case, it isn't as if didactic reasons *compete* with chess reasons. Rather, my teaching plan changes the landscape of reasons, so that 'reasons of chess' no longer count as reasons in favor of a certain move (they may even count against it) in my planning scheme. Moral reasons, on the other hand, very often do compete with non-moral reasons. Giving a huge contribution to a deserving charity competes with my lifelong devotion to NBA basketball (since those season tickets are expensive) and the possibility of sending my children to private school. So letting the moral reasons stand with their element of weight is important; it would be a mistake to let that dimension get swallowed up in a summary or verdict of wrongness, and in any case, it is that weight that matters when moral reasons come to compete with others outside the moral sphere. A good extension of the chess analogy might be to think of little "subgames" as it were within chess: maybe I first determine what is the best way to promote a pawn, then what is the best way to prevent my opponent from doing the same thing; then what is the best way to tie up his major pieces, and so on. It would be a mistake to summarize each conclusion simply with the "right" move for the purpose. I will have to balance the considerations later. So I need a ranking, and if possible a weighting. Norcross can be seen as suggesting that we think of morality in that way.

Contract Theory

Seeking the foundations of moral principles in the idea of free, rational, unforced agreement is a strategy that runs from Plato's *Republic* through the early modern political theorists Hobbes, Locke, and Rousseau, and to our own time most famously in the work of John Rawls, Thomas Scanlon, and David Gauthier. Samuel Freeman distinguishes two broad forms of contract theory and several senses in which it might be thought to be 'foundational'. One form, which Freeman finds in Hobbes and Gauthier, attempts to justify adherence to moral principles on the basis of self-interest. In reply to the question, "Why should I care about these moral principles?" the 'reductionist' contract theorist replies that complying is in some sense in accord with the things that matter to you independently (self-interest proper, for Hobbes, or one's non-moral preferences, according to Gauthier). The other form, the one that Freeman takes as his main subject, is "right-based." The aim of this form is not to reduce morality to (or justify it in terms of) self-interest, but to "elucidate its structure" from within. A right-based contract theorist takes the subject of morality to be respect for others and the importance of being able to justify one's actions to those whom one affects. As Freeman puts it:

> To respect another as a person is to give a justification for actions and institutions that she can accept in her capacity as a moral agent. It is to address oneself to those capacities of persons by virtue of which they are responsible moral agents with conceptions of the good that are worthy of pursuit. It is in this regard that moral contractarianism seeks to depict morality as involving mutual recognition and respect for persons.

So Freeman's contractarianism asks what reasonable people could agree to, insofar as they were in search of principles to regulate their interpersonal relations. The contract then can be thought of as a "foundation" in the sense that their being the sorts of principles that free and equal people could agree to explains why certain principles are the principles of morality.

Freeman contrasts the contractarian model of people making demands on each other with the consequentialist one of the moral world making demands on us. I'm not sure this is quite fair. The moral world might demand that we respect each other in certain ways, so contractarian morality doesn't logically distinguish itself in that way; and consequentialists can also think of the source of moral demands as the importance of other people, rather than something as impersonal as "the world." Still, Freeman could rest on a different way of making what may be the same point: contractarianism is more "personal" in that it tells us that it is other people who are supposed to be our main objects of concern, rather than the sub-personal happiness, utility, or preferences of other persons. This feature of utilitarianism, that it values the utility rather than its bearer, is related to the criticism (mentioned also by Vallentyne) that it fails to take seriously the "separateness of persons." The usual explanation is that for utilitarians, the location of goodness is not important but only its aggregate sum. Now this may seem a very unfair charge against utilitarianism. Consider the analogous charge against democracy: democrats do not care about the boundaries between voters, but only about the net sum of votes for each candidate. The obvious reply is that the democrat insists that each citizen's vote count the same as every other, and also that a system be positively responsive to votes in the sense that a winning option cannot be made to lose by *adding* votes, and that these conditions are what motivate the aggregation rule. Similarly, utilitarians may defend themselves against the familiar charge by noting that they insist on a kind of positive responsiveness to the welfare of persons along with Bentham's egalitarian "each to count for one and none for more than one," and that these principles underwrite the utilitarian aggregation.

Freeman stresses other, related differences between contractualism and utilitarianism. For one thing, the reasons that appear as moral reasons in contractualism are, he claims, reasons that real people have and act on, whereas the one and only utilitarian moral reason, that a certain action would maximize aggregate happiness, is a reason that no real person ever has. For another, contractualism's reasons are essentially *public* and *shared*, and addressed by citizens to citizens, while utilitarianism could be secret, esoteric, addressed to each by the moral order itself.

Philip Pettit thinks contractualism (he is thinking mainly of T. M. Scanlon's version, closely akin to Freeman's) threatens to collapse to a kind of consequentialism, so that the idea of the best consequences will in the end be what explains what makes actions right or justifiable. Pettit charitably *defends* contractualism against one version of this charge. It might be thought that whatever reasons the contracting parties have to accept or reject various proposed rules would themselves be the ultimate moral reasons. Suppose we reject a certain rule or policy on grounds of fairness, or favor another on grounds of equality; then surely it is the goodness of fairness or equality that ultimately matters. But Pettit notes that there is another possibility: in deciding what to accept, the contracting parties might appeal to their more parochial, centered interests and reasons. Those couldn't be moral reasons (or anyway, they need not), and it would be the way those reasons fit together under the guise of the contract that explained the character of rightness, rather than any antecedently discernible pattern of goodness.

Still, Pettit thinks that contractualism may best be understood as delivering a "practice-relative" notion of right and wrong. We have many practice-relative normative notions. Castling might be "the right move" in a chess game, it is "wrong" to play Beethoven's *Appassionata* in F major, and "Him and I wasn't going" is incorrect English. In each case, right or wrong are relativized to some rules or standards that a person might, but might not, accept or take an interest in. Contractualist rules, Pettit suggests, might be best understood as relativized to rules for "deliberative exchange," namely, the practice of conversing, reasoning together, committing ourselves to what we say. Now Pettit himself thinks that deliberative exchange is very important, that it has great impartial value. But for any practice-relative notion of right and wrong the question always arises whether and why one ought to conform to (or engage in) the practice at all. Pettit's thought is that there may be a very good consequentialist answer to this question in the case of the constituting rules of deliberative exchange, but if so, doesn't that mean it turns out that the great goodness of deliberation is what explains the normative bite of contractualist morality?

Virtue

Virtue ethics is commonly understood as the attempt to ground ethical concepts in the idea of the virtues, so that the virtues have a kind of priority in moral understanding, or its conceptual structure. But Rosalind Hursthouse objects to the 'reductionist' strain in contemporary normative theory, which she attributes to the influence of Rawls. Reductionism seeks to identify one ethical concept as fundamental deriving, or defining the others from the fundamental one. Hursthouse herself takes the following biconditional to be true and central:

An action is right iff it is what a virtuous agent would, characteristically, (i.e. acting in character) do in the circumstances.

This, along with her interesting device of 'v-rules' (which I'll explain in a moment) form the core of virtue ethics – or it might be better to say that this is Hursthouse's version of virtue ethics' account of right action.

One challenge that Hursthouse recognizes is Robert Louden's "application problem." Louden asked whether a biconditional like Hursthouse's could ever really help anybody in practice. For if you are already a virtuous agent, you are not going to need help (and it isn't very helpful to tell you to do what you yourself would do in the circumstances!), and if you aren't entirely virtuous then what you want to know is what a virtuous person would do, after all. Hursthouse suggests supplementary v-rules like 'Do what is courageous, not cowardly', which press virtues into rule form for practical consumption.

A second issue has to do with supererogation (which, remember, Alastair Norcross suggested that we jettison). The question for virtue theorists (or anyone who accepts Hursthouse's biconditional) is whether to think that a virtuous person would always do the supererogatory act, or whether she would sometimes do the merely obligatory when a supererogatory act is available. If the virtuous agent would always do the *best*, even when that was well beyond the call of duty, then how is a virtue ethicist to explain the notion of what is obligatory? On the other hand, if the virtuous agent would always do what is obligatory but not always do what is absolutely the best, then how is a virtue ethicist to explain in what way that "best" action is better?

Hursthouse follows Philippa Foot in disentangling two ways in which a virtuous action might be "difficult" for someone to perform. It might be especially difficult because of the circumstances, in which case it is *more* virtuous and admirable than it would otherwise be; whereas if it is difficult for the person because of flaws in his character, then it is *less* virtuous. Actions of the first type, according to Hursthouse, are supererogatory when they are especially difficult.

I said that Hursthouse explicitly rejects the reductionist approach to ethics according to which we are supposed to derive or define all of our ethical concepts using one primitive one. But definition and derivation aside, there is a serious question about direction of *explanation* here. Suppose we provisionally accept the biconditional that Hursthouse endorses. The question remains whether an action's being the one that a virtuous person would (characteristically) do explains its being the right one, or whether instead its being the right thing to do explains why the virtuous person would do it. While it is not the only question that can interest a virtue theorist (or critic), this is certainly a central philosophical question. (Needless to say, there is another possibility: that some third thing explains both why a virtuous person would perform the action and why it is right, with neither of these explaining the other. And, of course, the biconditional may well be false.) Julia Driver doubts that the explanation could really run from virtue to rightness.

In any case, is the biconditional true? Here is a worry raised by Driver. Sometimes an imperfectly virtuous person might find herself in a situation in which her own lack of virtue means that she really ought *not* to do precisely what a virtuous person ought to do. For instance, she might have an irrational fear of water, so there is no point in her jumping into the lake to save the drowning victim, even though a virtuous person (with no fear of water) would not hesitate. There are some things, it seems, that are wrong for you to do even though a fully virtuous person would do them, precisely because of the differences between you and a fully virtuous person. Making the account relative to circumstance can help. In your circumstance, perhaps, a fully virtuous person wouldn't jump in the lake either, because your circumstance includes your phobia. Can a fully virtuous person share a phobia, or are phobias contrary to the idea of virtue? Hursthouse defends the biconditional on the ground that a phobia is not a virtue or a vice at all. This leaves open the question of whether there are other differences between me and a fully virtuous person that might make a certain action right for the virtuous person to perform, but wrong for me to do.

Reason and Motivation

Do moral obligations stem from reason, or from the sentiments? Here we make the transition from normative theory and its structure to more metaethical considerations, and this is the question that many have taken to divide Hume from Kant, and Humeans from Kantians. Samuel Kerstein defends the Kantian view, which he thinks of as captured by a collection of theses about the rational inescapability of morality, from a sentimentalist challenge.

As Kerstein sees it, sentimentalists (like Hume, or Blackburn) take obligations to others to be grounded in the moral feelings we have toward those others. If that's so, then none of the imperatives of morality can be categorical. Kerstein writes:

> A foreign office knave who does not take the common point of view and who thus has no displeasing sentiment towards treating strangers outside of his group unjustly would, according to sentimentalism, (at least sometimes) have no obligation to act in accordance with the principle 'Do not treat strangers unjustly'. Sentimentalism would therefore not allow this principle to stand as a categorical imperative.

But this consequence, that no moral obligation is categorical, that all of them are conditional on the possession of moral feelings, is inconsistent with the *content* of common-sense moral thinking. Thus, what is intended as a metaethical thesis turns out to be rejectable for first-order normative moral reasons.

But Simon Blackburn claims that Kerstein's arguments misfire. The sentimentalist, Blackburn insists, is in no way committed to the thought that our obligations are conditional on the presence of certain sentiments. Rather, the point is that when we announce or argue about or just endorse in thought the existence of various moral obligations, we do so *by means of* our sentiments. To judge that someone has an obligation, according to sentimentalists, is to express a moral sentiment; thinking through our obligations is sentimental thinking.

It may be that it takes two distinct but related Humean theses to trap sentimentalism into the rejection of the common-sense categoricity of morality. Suppose, with Blackburn, that we do not come by moral motivations purely in virtue of our practical rationality. It's plausible that whenever a person is under a moral requirement, that person has thereby a *reason* to act (in accordance with the requirement). Add a second Humean element, then: nobody can have a reason that cannot motivate her. Then reasons, and so moral requirements, must be contingent on the motivations that people happen to have. As R. Jay Wallace puts it:

> Judgments about what one has reason to do give rise to corresponding motivations to action in agents who are not irrational. So if moral considerations constitute normative reasons, they will be motivating in those agents who are reasoning correctly.

Now, Sigrún Svavarsdóttir poses a challenge to the thesis, generally called 'internalism', that genuine moral judgment is conceptually, logically linked to motivation. She presents an example, spelled out in some detail, of Patrick, who uses the language of moral judgment with apparent sincerity and understanding, but seems to remain unmotivated. Why is it not an open possibility, she asks, that things are, in fact, as they seem, that Patrick is a counterexample to the internalist thesis? The burden, Svavarsdóttir argues, is on internalists to show how that possibility is ruled out.

Svavarsdóttir's own view of moral motivation is, to oversimplify, that people ordinarily have a desire with a distinctively moral content. The thought that something is morally required ordinarily carries with it a novel motivational force just because we contingently but reliably do care about right and wrong, justice and virtue, under those particularly moral descriptions.

Wallace agrees that it is implausible to insist on a conceptual necessity tying moral judgment to motivation. Instead, he suggests that there is a *normative* connection. Someone who is deliberating correctly, Wallace claims, will be motivated by his reasons, insofar as he is practically rational; this Wallace calls the 'motivation requirement'. His formulation is significantly different from the more traditional thesis of 'internalism'. Moral reasons could fail to motivate someone who actually has them in two ways, consistent with the truth of the motivation requirement: first, the person might be suffering from weakness of will (and so practically irrational), and second the deliberation might be incorrect. The second case, as Wallace envisions it, would involve the person making incorrect judgments about what reasons she has, so that although she believes that a certain act is morally required, she decides that this fact has no normative significance for her. Of course, it is a non-trivial substantive normative assumption that moral requirements really *do* provide people with reasons, and if the assumption is false then so is Wallace's motivation requirement, since in that case someone really could deliberate correctly without granting moral considerations any normative significance. But that's how Wallace intends his version: the motivational significance of moral judgment is, he thinks, a substantive normative thesis and not a conceptual truth that stands independent of views about what reasons we really have.

Svavarsdóttir notes that her account is consistent with Wallace's normative claims. And she adds that the explanation for why it strikes us as *irrational* for a person to acknowledge the normative significance of a consideration without letting that consideration play any motivational role is that it is a function of the role and point of *deliberation* in our mental lives. The issues that remain between Wallace and Svavarsdóttir, and the philosophical considerations that could resolve their differences, are complex and subtle; my simplified account in this introduction has not done their debate full justice.

Moral Facts

In recent years, questions about *explanation* have loomed large in metaethics. In this volume we find three related explanation questions, all of them broadly metaethical. One, addressed by Nicholas Sturgeon and Nick Zangwill, is the question of whether moral facts and properties play any important role in the explanation of natural phenomena, and especially of our moral judgments. Another, much more recent in origin, is the question of whether and how general moral principles explain particular moral facts. But first up is a relatively new role for the question of explanation to play, having to do with the very basic question of whether and in what way it is correct to think of morality as having as its subject matter a domain of moral facts. Traditionally this question has been thought to be relatively straightforward, even if it is somewhat exotic and distinctively philosophical. So-called *anti-realists* deny that there are any moral facts, taking our moral talk and thought to be some sort of projection of affect, emotion, or practical attitude. So, rather than a discovery or investigation into an independently existing realm of moral facts, our moral thinking and discussion should be thought of as bringing to light the moral attitudes that structure our evaluations and intentions, our plans of action, our preferences and desires, according to the anti-realist view. Realists, by contrast, think the phenomenology of moral thought is that of "fact-finding," that our moral judgments at least purport to be (and sometimes really are) about the moral facts themselves, that the truth of the matter transcends the attitudes we bring to the table, that there is such a thing as getting it right or wrong. But recent work in metaethics and in other areas of philosophy have cast doubt on this straightforward way of posing the old issue. What is there to the idea of a 'moral fact', philosophers have asked, aside from the reaffirmation of the ordinary, first-order moral judgments that we all make when we are actually engaged in ethical deliberation? Besides the judgment we all want to make to the effect that slavery is morally wrong, what is there to the idea that 'it is a fact that slavery is morally wrong'?

Peter Railton and the team of Terry Horgan and Mark Timmons share the view that a plausible 'deflationism' about truth and its allied notions have thrown the traditional distinction into question. Still, they believe, there is a real question to be tackled about 'factualism', and they fall out on different sides of this question. Part of what divides them, we shall see, is a question of explanation: what account of moral concepts and meanings explains the most salient and distinctive phenomena?

Peter Railton lists a cluster of features of moral thought and language which might together be considered constitutive of the idea of morality. The features include the supervenience of the moral on the descriptive, the generality of moral judgment (distinguishing it from other forms of normative judgment), the practicality or prescriptive dimension of moral thought. Railton concedes that the motivational element of moral thought suggests non-factualism, but notes that, on the face of it, some logical features of the way moral language is used, especially in reasoning, can't be explained by non-factualist theories. After all, we call all sorts of moral judgments 'true' and 'false', and we employ them in arguments and other contexts in which we'd ordinarily think that only the true and the false are at home.

Now, Railton recognizes an important move in the debate between moral factualists and non-factualists, a move employed by Timmons and Horgan. Truth, according to a popular and powerful contemporary conception, is no big deal. Asserting something carries metaphysical commitment. Calling it true carries no more metaphysical commitment than that. To call something true carries no more metaphysical commitment than just asserting that thing carries. So, insofar as a non-factualist is herself happy to *make* moral judgments, she should be happy too to say that they are true (and just as happy to call them false as to deny some particular ones, by the same token). This is the 'minimalist' or 'deflationary' move. It allows truth back on the non-factualist stage. Horgan and Timmons doubt that there is any serious problem for non-factualists accounting for the apparent truth-aptness of moral judgments: after all, moral judgments *are* apt for truth, only truth itself is deflated and metaphysically uninteresting.

But the deflation of truth carries with it the deflation of *fact*. After all, it is just as much a tautology to say that snow is white if and only if it is a fact that snow is white, as it is to say that snow is white if and only if it is true that snow is white.[1] What is at stake between self-styled factualists and non-factualists can then become puzzling. Railton plausibly suggests that what is at issue is the question of how best to account for the 'character of moral judgment', that is, for the distinctive cluster of features that together constitute a judgment's being a moral one. One element of that cluster is the motivational feature of moral judgment, which is, we can see, why the debate between Wallace and Svavarsdóttir is so important to metaethics. One account might have it that the conditions of rational agency as such already require a certain type of motivational structure, one that is poised to endorse typically moral principles (so the debate between Blackburn and Kerstein is again critical). In that case, the motivational efficacy of moral judgment could be traced to something outside of moral concepts themselves, so the account would fall into the factualist category. Railton himself leans toward an 'externalist' account of the moral/motive connection, something in the same family as Svavarsdóttir's view. By contrast, Horgan and Timmons think that the motivational efficacy of moral judgment is due to the essential nature of the judgments themselves. Moral judgments, according to Horgan and Timmons, are not descriptive but prescriptive. The state of mind expressed by a moral assertion is a conation, not a representation. So Horgan and Timmons don't think of moral discourse and thought as factual. Their view is in the tradition of emotivism, but with some striking differences.

Horgan and Timmons subscribe to a kind of "*non-factualism* which denies that there are any moral properties possessed by actions or other objects of evaluation and so this view denies that there are in-the-world moral facts." They reject *realist* factualism on the grounds that there is no reasonable semantic story about how moral expressions could come to pick out one particular (natural) property determinately, *relativist* factualism on the grounds that it misconstrues (or fails to make out) some ordinary moral disagreement, and *constructivist* factualism on the grounds that it cannot avoid "slipping into relativism."

Even so, Horgan and Timmons do say that moral judgment is a kind of belief, that moral utterances are assertions, that moral sentences can be true or false. They agree with almost all of what traditional metaethical realists say. So they agree with Railton that the real dispute between factualists and non-factualists is not over the trappings of truth (as Fine 2001 puts it). The question of what exactly *is* at issue is a difficult one, not fully resolved by the present debaters.

Moral Explanation

We next turn to the older problem of moral explanation, framed by Gilbert Harman (1977). Harman asked us to focus on the difference between scientific observation and the observation of moral properties and facts. His point was not that there isn't any moral observation. To take his infamous example, we can imagine some boys torturing a cat, and an observer who judges that what the boys are doing is bad. Now the 'observation' of the badness, clearly, requires that the observer already have a certain moral sensibility, which we could think of as a kind of (possibly latent) background moral theory. But the need for this background does not distinguish moral observation from scientific observation. Compare a physicist observing a cloud chamber and remarking, "There goes a proton." The 'observation' of a proton requires a great deal of assumed background theory. Observation is in general, we might say, theory-laden.

Harman's point was rather that the *explanation* for the scientific observation, the best explanation we have, requires that we posit the presence of a proton. The proton itself enters into the best explanation of the observation. This explanatory role, according to Harman, is what gives us reason to believe that there are protons. And now we see the real contrast: our best explanation of the moral observation does not involve the badness of the act itself. Instead, it appeals to the psychology of the boys, the sentience of the cat, and other descriptive (rather than evaluative) properties. If explanations of observations never appeal to the moral properties themselves (as opposed to the moral sensibilities of human beings), then why should we believe in them?

Sturgeon raises several questions about Harman's argument. First, he wonders whether even if Harman is right that the moral properties, and facts themselves do not enter into our best explanation of moral judgments, they might not still enter into the explanations of other phenomena. For example, doesn't Hitler's moral depravity at least partly explain Hitler's actions? One might say that Hitler's character described non-morally does all the explaining necessary – his traits of character neutrally described, that is to say. But if we conclude that appeal to moral traits of character are thus unnecessary, won't we be stuck saying similarly that all sorts of ordinary facts are also explanatorily vacuous? Do we really have no reason to believe in, say, trains, because anything that locomotive facts can explain can be explained just as well by a more basic level of facts, the facts about steel and wheels and electricity, that do not explicitly mention trains? Maybe the point is to identify what properties occur in the *best* explanations of the phenomena. But Sturgeon notes that which explanations are "best" is highly context-sensitive and interest-relative. Sometimes we want "safe" explanations, explanations with the least chance of being mistaken; in that case, appeals to moral properties will be worse, but then so will explanations that commit us to protons (rather than simply mentioning vapor trails in cloud chambers). If we want explanations that will generalize, and generalize in the right way, it is not obvious that we can do better than citing someone's depravity, or injustice, or cruelty.

Nick Zangwill defends the unusual thesis that moral judgments are especially isolated from explanation by moral facts. All sorts of moral properties may explain all sorts of things, Zangwill argues, but they will never explain our beliefs about them. His argument depends on what he calls the "Because Constraint," namely, the thesis that whenever we think that something has a moral property, we must think so *because* it has some non-moral property. For instance, when we think that Billy is bad, we must think he is bad because of some non-moral fact about him. This seems clear enough. Zangwill says that because of the Because Constraint, we have no independent access to moral properties. The only access we have is via the natural properties that underlie the moral ones (like Billy's hard-heartedness, or his narcissism) plus some principles that take us from natural to moral. This No Independent Access thesis in turn shows that the non-moral properties themselves are always fully responsible for our moral beliefs; the moral properties can play no role. On that score, Zangwill argues, Harman was right. Though Zangwill's argument may not turn on it, the claim that we infer moral conclusions from non-moral facts plus moral *principles* is an important one.

Particularism

Generalism is the view that there are important, quite general, moral principles that ground particular moral judgments; particularism is the view that the order of explanation is the other way around. That is vaguely put, in part because it has not been altogether clear in the contemporary dispute over particularism just what is at stake. It certainly has something to do with the existence or role of universal, exceptionless moral rules. But, for example, there is the metaphysical question of whether there are any such rules, and if there are, whether they determine the particular moral facts or instead are determined by them; and then there is the epistemological question of whether our justification for particular moral judgments comes via general rules or whether instead we think of moral rules as hypotheses, speculative summaries of the particular moral judgments we have made and will make.

It may be helpful to think of particularism as a view about moral reasons, as Mark Lance and Margaret Little do. One model of reasons is the model of vectors. Reasons contribute to what we all-things-considered ought to do as individual component forces (the lift, thrust, drag, gravity on an airplane) contribute to the overall acceleration of the object on which the forces act. The acceleration can be decomposed into components, and the component forces are stable contributors from one context to another, always adding the same thing to the overall acceleration. Particularists doubt that reasons work that way. There are *no* considerations, they think, that always contribute the same "vector" to what we ought to do. Lance and Little add that we need not suppose that reasons get their "force" from any moral law lurking in the background (as gravity might be supposed to get its pull from a law of nature). And indeed, they argue that every conceivable consideration (where considerations must be framed in non-normative language) that counts in favor of an act could in principle count *against* an act, if the context were suitably changed. This possibility of "valence-switching" is a hallmark of particularism.

Robert Audi, though sympathetic to some of the milder planks of the particularist platform, explains also why some generalist claims have also to be paid proper respects. He begins by asking what sort of generality we should expect moral principles to exhibit. Audi wants to defend a kind of Rossian view, according to which there are some general moral principles that always provide us with reasons to follow them, although there is no formula that can tell us how to factor all conflicting reasons into a resultant final obligation. "Some moral principles are both wide in scope and useful in day-to-day moral thinking," Audi says.

Audi helpfully distinguishes between the *deliberative* relevance of a consideration and its *normative* relevance. There are many cases in which a smallish consideration, one that really does make a normative difference to the case at hand, should obviously be ignored since it is so plain that very much larger considerations are going to decide the issue; and Audi notes that the oddness that we feel in saying that, for example, the annoyance of a librarian at my outcry does count against my loudly alerting browsers to the fact that the stacks have caught fire might be explained by its deliberative irrelevance rather than by what a stronger particularist would say is its normative irrelevance.

Audi also points out that particular judgments might be thought to have a *normative* priority, an *epistemic* priority, a *methodological* priority, a *conceptual* priority, or a *genetic* priority, and that although these are related they are also quite distinct.

Lance and Little take their main opposition to be the idea that exceptions to general principles stand in the way of explanation. They think it is a mistake to insist that explanations must always involve subsumption of a case under an exceptionless law. This is a crucial point, because particularists deny that there are such exceptionless moral laws, but do think there can be moral explanations of moral facts. (Note that moral explanations of *moral* facts are not the subject of the debate between Sturgeon and Zangwill, who are talking about explanations of *non*-moral facts.) The worry is that if there are no descriptions of a case that together entail (via some graspable moral rule) that it is bad, or just, or wrong, then it will be left utterly mysterious how we could ever come to such a judgment.

A central claim of Lance and Little's is that moral reasons and prima facie principles do have a kind of standing; they are not just like the specks of color on a painting, which contribute literally nothing on their own to the painting's aesthetic value but only in relation to other specks. Reasons, like the fact that a certain act would be a lie, do have a kind of explanatory power that derives from their function in special, default contexts. In this respect they are like the events that we single out as causes, as opposed to the background conditions necessary for the causes to do their work. The striking of a match can be the cause of the flame, though the flame would not have come into being in other, oxygen-deprived circumstances, even if the match had there been struck too. That's because the situation in which there is oxygen (and the candle's wick is not wet, and the ambient temperature is not so low as to extinguish combustion immediately . . .) is the normal backdrop. Similarly, Lance and Little argue, that the act would be a lie is a reason not to do it, even though there are situations in which a lie is called for. Though lying isn't always wrong, nor always wrong-tending, it is always *defeasibly wrong-making*, in that it is always the sort of thing that in normal circumstances would be wrong, and this status is itself always significant in the explanatory role that lying plays in moral thought.

I hope these essays will give the reader new to the issues some background and insight and the reader already steeped in them something new to think about.

Notes

1 Oddly enough, it seems to be only the *philosopher's* usage of 'fact' that can be deflated in this way. There is an ordinary, non-jargony usage according to which something counts as a fact only if it is known, or confirmed in a publicly available, uncontroversial way. That is not the sense meant here, or by Railton, or anywhere in this volume.

References

Broome, J. (1999). "Goodness is reducible to betterness: the evil of death is the value of life." In Broome, *Ethics out of Economics*. Cambridge: Cambridge University Press.

Fine, K. (2001). "The question of realism." *Philosophers' Imprint*, 1(1) <http://www.philosophersimprint.org/001001/>

Harman, G. (1977). *The Nature of Morality*. New York: Oxford University Press.

Murphy, L. (1997). "A relatively plausible principle of beneficence: reply to Mulgan." *Philosophy & Public Affairs*, 26: 80–6.

Pettit, P. (1989). "Consequentialism and respect for persons." *Ethics*, 100: 116–26.

Rawls, J. (1971). *A Theory of Justice*. Cambridge, Mass.: Harvard University Press.

PART I

NORMATIVE THEORY

Is the Rightness of Action Determined by the Value of Consequences?

The Consequentialist Perspective

William Shaw

Philosophers use the term *consequentialism* to identify a general way of thinking about right and wrong and thereby provide a convenient label for a whole family of theories or possible theories in normative ethics. *Consequentialist* ethical theories maintain that right and wrong are a function of the consequences of our actions – more precisely, that our actions are right or wrong because, and only because, of their consequences. The *only because* is important because almost all ethical theories take consequences into account when assessing actions, and almost all philosophers believe that the consequences of our actions at least sometimes affect their rightness or wrongness. What distinguishes consequentialist from non-consequentialist ethical theories is the insistence that when it comes to rightness or wrongness, nothing matters but the results of our actions.

When consequentialists affirm that the results or consequences of an action determine whether it is right or wrong, they have in mind, more specifically, the value of those results. That is, it is the goodness or badness of an action's consequences that determines its rightness or wrongness. Different consequentialist theories spell out this relationship in different ways. In other words, if right and wrong are a function of the goodness and badness of the results of our actions, then different functions are possible, different ways of connecting consequences to rightness and wrongness. What I shall call *standard consequentialism* advances some further theses that distinguish it from other possible types of consequentialism.

Standard consequentialism asserts that the morally right action for an agent to perform is the action, of those actions that the agent could perform at the time, that has the best consequences or results in the most good. Standard consequentialism is a maximizing doctrine. By instructing us to bring about as much good as we can, standard consequentialism distinguishes itself from the thesis that an action is right if and only if it has good consequences (or consequences that are sufficiently good or that are good enough). Standard consequentialism holds, furthermore, that we are not merely permitted or encouraged to act so as to maximize good; we are required to do so. Accordingly, standard consequentialism rejects the idea that there can be degrees of rightness so that an agent might have several options open to him, all of which are right but some of which are more right than others. On the other hand, of the actions open to the agent, several might have equally optimal results. Thus, there may be no single best action and, hence, no uniquely right action. Put more precisely, then, standard consequentialism holds that an action is morally right if and only if there is no other action, among those available to the agent, that has better consequences; otherwise, the action is wrong. Thus, several actions might be equally right, and what morality requires is that the agent do one of them. Finally, an action might have bad consequences and yet be right. This will be the case if all alternative actions have worse results.

Further Features of Standard Consequentialism

In this section, I describe some further features of standard consequentialism. I call it standard consequentialism because it is the most familiar and widely discussed form of consequentialism; it is what I usually have in mind when discussing the subject. I am also inclined to think it is the most plausible form of consequentialism. But even if I am wrong on both counts, for purposes of discussion it will be helpful to focus on one reasonably specific version of consequentialism.

Outcome includes the value of the action itself

When consequentialists refer to the results or consequences of an action, they have in mind the entire upshot of the action, that is, its overall outcome. They are concerned with whether, and to what extent, the world is better or worse because the agent has elected a given course of conduct. Thus, consequentialists take into account whatever value, if any, the action has in itself, not merely the value of its subsequent effects.

This might sound odd, because when speaking of the 'results' or 'consequences' of an action, we frequently have in mind effects that are distinct from, subsequent to, and caused by the action. Consequentialists, however, don't limit results to effects in a narrow or causal sense, because they are interested in the consequences not only of one's acting in various positive ways, but also of one's refraining from acting. For example, it would seem odd to say that, by ignoring a panhandler's request for rent money, I "caused" his family to sleep outside tonight. Still, this may be one result of my not stopping to help him; if so, then consequentialists will take it into account in assessing my conduct.

Consequentialists, moreover, needn't assume that the line between an action and the effects that flow from it, between what we do and what results from what we do, is set in nature. Rather, this line is a function of how the situation is described. For example, what I did at the faculty seminar at 4.36 p.m. might be described as "opening my mouth wide and covering my ears with my hands," "feigning shock and horror," "expressing my disdain for the ontological argument," or "insulting my colleague."

"Feigning shock and horror" is a subsequent effect of my action when it is described as "opening my mouth wide and covering my ears," but not when it is described as "insulting my colleague." This fact buttresses the point that consequentialism is properly concerned with the entire upshot of our actions, with whether they make the world as a whole better or worse. We are to assess and compare the overall outcomes of the various actions we could perform, and these outcomes include the positive or negative value, if any, of each action viewed by itself as well as the positive or negative value of its subsequent effects.

The good is agent-neutral and independent of the right

Standard consequentialism assumes that we can sometimes makes objective, impartial, and agent-neutral judgments about the comparative goodness or badness of different states of affairs. At least sometimes it will be the case that one outcome is better than another outcome – not better merely from some particular perspective, but simply better, better *tout court*. Thus, for example, it is a better outcome (all other things being equal) when eight people have headaches and two people die than when two people have headaches and eight people die. Most people believe this, as do most philosophers, including many non-consequentialists. However, some non-consequentialists contend that this idea makes no sense (e.g., Thomson 2001: 12–19, 41). One state of affairs can be better for Fred or worse for Sarah than another state of affairs, they say, but it can't be said to be just plain better. There is no such thing as being just plain better, only better along some particular dimension or better for someone or better from some perspective. In line with this, some philosophers have proposed variants of consequentialism in which all or some judgments regarding the comparative value of states of affairs are agent-relative as opposed to agent-neutral. I shan't discuss these non-standard variants of consequentialism.

Standard consequentialism takes it for granted not only that the goodness or badness of an action's outcome is an agent-neutral matter, but also that this is something that can be identified prior to, and independently of, the normative assessment of the action. The point, after all, of consequentialism is to use the goodness or badness of an action to determine its rightness or wrongness. And circularity would threaten the theory if our notions of right and wrong were to infect our assessment of consequences as good or bad. Standard consequentialism thus assumes that we can identify states of affairs as good or bad, better or worse, without reference to normative principles of right and wrong. If we cannot do this, then the distinction between consequentialism and non-consequentialism begins to dissolve – leaving us, for example, unable to avoid labeling as consequentialist the deontological theorist who says that the right thing for an agent to do is to bring about the best state of affairs that he can, where the best state of affairs always consists in the agent's doing his duty, which in turn consists in his performing tokens of act types that are intrinsically right and refraining from performing tokens of act types that are intrinsically wrong.

Most non-consequentialists would agree with what I have just written. They grant that the good can be identified prior to, and independently of, the right, but they distinguish themselves from consequentialists by holding that the good doesn't, or doesn't always, determine the right. However, some self-described consequentialists would challenge the previous paragraph. They believe that it is theoretically acceptable for some normative notions to enter into our assessments of goodness and badness and that their doing so neither is viciously circular nor undermines the spirit of consequentialism. They might hold, for example, that one state of affairs may be better than another because it is just and the other unjust and that this fact may make bringing about the first state of affairs the right thing to do. Again, however, I'll be ignoring non-standard forms of consequentialism like this.

Expected consequences, not actual consequences, are what count

According to standard consequentialism, an action is right if and only if nothing the agent could do would have better results. However, we rarely know ahead of time and for certain what the consequences will be of each of the possible actions we could perform. Standard consequentialism therefore says that we should choose the action, the expected value of the outcome of which is at least as great as that of any other action open to us. The notion of expected value is mathematical in origin and conceptualized as follows. Every action that we might perform has a number of possible outcomes. The likelihood of those outcomes varies, but each can be assumed to have a certain probability of happening. In addition, each possible outcome of a given action has a certain value; that is, it is good or bad to some specified degree. Assume for the sake of discussion that we can assign numbers both to probabilities and to values. One would then calculate the expected value of hypothetical action A, with (let us suppose) three possible outcomes, by multiplying the probability of each outcome times its value and summing the three figures. Suppose that the first outcome has a probability of 0.7 and a value of 3, the second outcome has a probability of 0.2 and a value of -1, and the third outcome a probability of 0.1 and value of 2. The expected value of A is thus 2.1, which equals $(3 \times 0.7) + (-1 \times 0.2) + (2 - 0.1)$. A is the right action to perform if and only if no alternative has greater expected value.

In reality, of course, we never have more than rough, qualitative estimates of probabilities and values. Indeed, we are likely to be ignorant of some possible outcomes or misjudge their goodness or badness, and we may overlook altogether some possible courses of action. Nevertheless, the point being made is important. Standard consequentialism instructs the agent to do what is likely to have the best results as judged by what a reasonable and conscientious person in the agent's circumstances could be expected to know. It might turn out, however, that because of untoward circumstances, the action with the greatest expected value ends up producing poor results – worse results, in fact, than several other things the agent could have done instead. Assuming that the agent's original estimate of expected value was correct (or, at least, the most accurate estimate one could have arrived at in the circumstances), then this action remains the right thing to have done. Indeed, it is what the agent should do if he or she were faced with the same situation again. On the other hand, an agent might perform an action that has less expected value than several other actions the agent could have performed, and yet, through a fortuitous chain of circumstances, it turns out that the action has better results, brings more good into the world, than anything else the agent could have done. Nevertheless, standard consequentialism asserts that the agent acted wrongly.

Some consequentialists adopt the rival view that the right action is the one that actually brings about the best results (or would in fact have brought about the best results, had it been performed), regardless of its expected value. How can it be right, they ask, to do what in fact had suboptimal results? Or wrong to do the thing that had the best results? Because these consequentialists still want the agent to act in whatever way is likely to maximize value, they draw a distinction between objective rightness and the action it would have been reasonable (or subjectively right) for the agent to perform. Comparing the actual results of what we did with what the actual results would have been, had we done an alternative action, raises philosophical puzzles. But the main reason for orienting consequentialism toward probable results rather than actual results is that the theory, like other ethical theories, is supposed to be prospective and action-guiding. In acting so as to maximize expected value, the agent is doing what the theory wants him to do, and he is not to be blamed, nor is he necessarily to modify his future conduct, if this action does not, in fact, maximize value. Accordingly, standard consequentialism holds that this is not merely the reasonably, but also the morally right, way for the agent to act.

Further comments on the uncertainty of consequences

Critics of consequentialism perennially point to the inevitable uncertainty of our knowledge of future events, arguing that this uncertainty undermines the viability of consequentialism. Although, as was just discussed, we don't have to know what the outcome of an action will be in order to estimate its expected value, in fact we are unlikely to know all the possible outcomes an action might have, or to do more than guess at their comparative probabilities. And, depending on the particular theory of value the consequentialist adopts, he or she will have greater or lesser difficulty assigning values to those outcomes. These problems are compounded by the fact that the consequences of our actions continue indefinitely into the future, often in ways that are far from trivial even if they are unknowable.

Consequentialists can concede these points, yet affirm the viability of their theory. First, they can stress that, despite our ignorance, we already know quite a lot about the likely results of different actions. The human race wasn't born yesterday, and in reflecting on the possible consequences of an action, we do so with a wealth of experience behind us. Although by definition the specific situation in which one finds oneself is always unique, it is unlikely to be the first time human beings have pondered the results of performing actions of type A, B, or C in similar sorts of circumstances. Second, consequentialists can stress that the difficulties we face in identifying the best course of action do not undermine the goal of endeavoring to bring about as much good as we can. Whether we are consequentialists or not, we must act. And even though ignorance and uncertainty plague human action, they don't prevent us from striving to do as much good as we can. Third, and finally, consequentialists can point out that uncertainty about the future is a problem for other normative theories as well. Almost all normative theories take into account the likely consequences of the actions open to the agent and are thus to some extent infected by uncertainty about the future.

Utilitarianism

Consequentialism is not a complete ethical theory. (From now on by 'consequentialism' I mean 'standard consequentialism', unless otherwise indicated.) It tells us to act so as to bring about as much expected good as we can, but it doesn't say what the good is. Thus, depending on one's theory of value, there are different ways of filling out consequentialism and turning it into a complete ethical theory. Utilitarianism represents one way, and it is worth saying a little about it because utilitarianism is the most influential as well as the most widely discussed consequentialist ethical theory. In fact, only a couple of decades ago did philosophers begin to appreciate fully that an ethical theory could retain the consequentialist normative structure of utilitarianism while relinquishing its specific value commitments – that is, that an ethical theory could agree with utilitarianism that our actions should bring about as much good as possible and yet disagree with it about what the good is.

Utilitarianism takes happiness or, more broadly, well-being to be the only thing that is good in itself or valuable for its own sake. We don't need to explore what well-being involves to point out some important features of utilitarianism's value theory. First, the good, as utilitarians understand it, attaches only to particular individuals (that is, to human beings or other sentient creatures). Thus, a state of affairs is good or bad to some degree (and better or worse than some other state of affairs) only in virtue of the goodness or badness of the lives of particular individuals. There is no good or bad above and beyond that, no good or bad above and beyond the happiness or unhappiness of individuals. Second, utilitarians believe that the good is additive, that total or net happiness is just the sum of the happiness or unhappiness of each individual. More happiness here counterbalances less happiness there. Underlying this, of course, is the assumption that in principle we can compare people's levels of happiness or well-being. But one shouldn't interpret this assumption too rigorously. Utilitarians have always granted that interpersonal comparisons of happiness or well-being are difficult, and they can even concede that some issues of comparison and addition may be irresolvable in principle. Utilitarians need believe only that we can rank many states of affairs as better or worse. Finally, utilitarians believe that each person's well-being is equally valuable, and his happiness or unhappiness, her pleasure or pain, carries the same weight as that of any other person. As Bentham wrote, each person counts as one, and no one as more than one.

In sum, utilitarianism has a welfarist value theory, which holds that the happiness or well-being of persons is the only thing that is valuable for its own sake and that the well-being of any person is neither more nor less valuable than the well-being of any other. It holds that the good is additive and that we can – sometimes and to some extent – compare the relative gains and losses in the well-being of different persons. As a consequentialist theory, utilitarianism thus asserts that the standard of moral assessment is well-being and that the right course of action is the one that brings about the greatest expected net well-being.

Non-utilitarian variants of consequentialism drop this exclusive commitment to well-being, seeing things other than or in addition to it as having intrinsic non-moral value. A utilitarian believes that the things we normally take to be valuable – say, close personal bonds, knowledge, autonomy, or beauty – are valuable only because they typically lead, directly or indirectly, to enhanced well-being. Friendship, for instance, usually makes people happier, and human lives almost always go better with it than without it. By contrast, the non-utilitarian consequentialist holds that some things are valuable independently of their impact on well-being. Some of these things, like autonomy, say, may be things that are believed to be an intrinsically valuable component of any human life. They are thought to be good for an individual, regardless of whether they promote the individual's well-being. Some non-utilitarian consequentialists go further, however and cut the link between being good and being good for someone that is characteristic of utilitarianism. They hold that some states of affairs are intrinsically better than others even if they are not better for anyone. For example, a world with more equality or beauty or biological diversity might be thought intrinsically better than a world with less even if no one is aware of the increased equality, beauty, or diversity and it makes no individual's life more valuable.

In addition to, or instead of, challenging the unique value placed on well-being, a non-utilitarian consequentialist might deviate from utilitarianism by declining to count equally the well-being of each. For example, the non-utilitarian might believe that enhancing the well-being of those whose current level of well-being is below average is more valuable than enhancing by an equal amount the well-being of those whose current level of well-being is above average. Or the non-utilitarian consequentialist might give up the belief that the good is additive and that the net value of an outcome is a straightforward function of various individual goods and bads. G. E. Moore (1903), for example, famously urged that the value of a state of affairs bears no regular relation to the values of its constituent parts. Although the non-utilitarian consequentialist would, in these ways, be challenging the value theory of utilitarianism, he or she would remain committed to the proposition that one is always required to act so as to bring about as much good as possible.

Two common objections to utilitarianism

Many critics of utilitarianism object to its maximizing approach to right and wrong on the grounds that the theory sometimes condones immoral conduct and that it is indifferent to the distribution of well-being. Because utilitarianism entails that an action's rightness or wrongness depends on its expected consequences in the particular circumstances facing the agent, it follows that the theory might require an action that commonsense morality repudiates as evil because, in the given circumstances, the action would produce more well-being than any alternative would produce. Furthermore, utilitarianism places no intrinsic value on how well-being is distributed among individuals. It cares only about total well-being. As a result, critics charge that utilitarianism too easily permits one person's happiness to be sacrificed for the benefit of others and, more generally, that it subordinates considerations of justice, equality, and fairness to the principle of utility. Utilitarianism's critics have illustrated these two points with various imaginary but vivid examples, intended to embarrass the theory by showing that its implications are out of step with ordinary moral thinking.

Utilitarians, for their part, have a lot to say in their defense, and it is far from obvious that the above criticisms carry the day (see Shaw 1999: chs 4 and 5). Here, however, I wish only to note that these criticisms have less force against consequentialist theories that identify as intrinsically valuable various goods other than, or in addition to, well-being or that put greater priority on the well-being of those who are less well-off.

Consequentialism in Practice

According to consequentialism, an action is morally right if and only if, among the actions that the agent could perform, there is no other action, the outcome of which has greater expected value. To act in any other way is wrong. The consequentialist criterion of rightness is straightforward, but the theory's practical implications can be surprisingly subtle.

Praise and blame

For consequentialists, whether an agent acted wrongly is distinct from the question whether he or she should be blamed or criticized for so acting (and, if so, how severely). Consequentialists apply their normative standard to questions of blame or praise just as they do to other questions. In particular, they will ask whether it will maximize expected good to criticize someone for failing to maximize expected good. Blame, criticism, and rebuke, although hurtful, can have good results by encouraging both the agent and other people to do better in the future, whereas neglecting to reproach misconduct increases the likelihood that the agent (or others) will act in the same unsatisfactory way in the future. However, in some circumstances, to blame or criticize someone for acting wrongly would be pointless or even counterproductive – for example, if the person did so accidentally, was innocently misinformed, or was suffering from emotional distress. In such circumstances, chastising the person for not living up to the consequentialist standard might do more harm than good.

Suppose that a well intentioned agent acted in a beneficial way, but that she could have produced even more (expected) good had she acted in some other way. Should consequentialists criticize her? Depending on the circumstances, the answer may well be 'no'. Suppose she acted spontaneously but in a way that was unselfish or showed regard for others, or suppose that she could have produced more good only by violating a generally accepted rule, the following of which usually produces good results. Or imagine that pursuing the second course of conduct would have required a disregard for self-interest or for the interests of those who are near and dear to her that is more than we normally (or, perhaps, can reasonably) expect from human beings. In these cases, blame would seem to have little or no point. Indeed, if the agent behaved in a way that usually produces good, we may want to encourage others to follow her example (that is, to adhere to the same rule or act from the same motive) when they encounter similar situations. Praising an agent for an action that fails to live up to the consequentialist standard can sometimes be right. Consequentialists applaud instances of act-types they want to encourage, and they commend motivations, dispositions, and character traits they want to reinforce.

Motives, dispositions, and character traits

Consequentialists generally take an instrumental approach to motives. Good motives are those that tend to produce right conduct, whereas bad motives are those that tend to produce wrongful conduct. Consequentialists generally assess dispositions, behavioral patterns, and character traits in the same instrumental way: one determines which ones are good, and how good they are, by looking at the actions they lead to. According to some value theories, however, certain motives are intrinsically, not just instrumentally, good or bad; likewise, the exercise of certain dispositions or character traits might be judged intrinsically good or bad. If so, then the presence or absence of these factors will make a difference to the overall value of a state of affairs. This fact, in turn, will make more complex the consequentialist's analysis of how one ought to act.

Even if a consequentialist adopts an entirely instrumental approach to the assessment of motives, dispositions, and traits, it doesn't follow that the agent's only concern ought to be the impartial maximization of good. On the contrary, the consequentialist tradition has long urged that more good may come from people acting from other, more particular motivations, commitments, and dispositions than from their acting only and always from a desire to promote the general good. For one thing, a consequentialist should not try to compute the probabilities of all possible outcomes before each and every action. Even if this were humanly possible, it would be absurd and counterproductive. At least in trivial matters and routine situations, stopping and calculating will generally lead to poor results. One does better to act from habit or do what has proved right in similar situations or what seems intuitively or at a glance to be the best course of conduct. Thus, consequentialism implies that one should not always reason as a consequentialist or, at least, that one should not always reason in a fully and directly consequentialist way. Better results may come from people acting in accord with principles, procedures, or motives other than the basic consequentialist one.

This last statement may sound paradoxical, but the consequentialist standard itself determines in what circumstances we should employ that standard as our direct guide to acting. The proper criterion for assessing actions is one matter; in what ways we should deliberate, reason, or otherwise decide what to do (so as to meet that criterion as best we can) is another issue altogether. Consequentialists will naturally want to guide their lives, make decisions, and base their actions on principles, procedures, and motives, the following of which will produce the best results over the long run. Which principles, procedures, and motives produce the best results is a contingent matter, which depends in part on one's value theory. But a consequentialist will approve of people's acting out of a concern for things other than the general good or on the basis of values that his theory does not believe to be basic if the consequentialist believes that people's so acting is likely to bring about more good in the long run.

Following moral rules

Although consequentialism bases morality on one fundamental principle, it also stresses the importance in ordinary circumstances of following certain well-established rules or guidelines that can generally be relied upon to produce good results. Utilitarians, for example, believe that we should make it a practice to tell the truth and keep our promises, rather than try to calculate possible pleasures and pains in every routine case, because we know that in general telling the truth and keeping our promises result in more good than lying and breaking promises. Relying on secondary rules helps consequentialists deal with the no-time-to-calculate problem and the future-consequences-are-hard-to-foresee problem. It can also counteract the fact that even conscientious agents can err in estimating the likelihood of a particular result and thus the expected value of a given action. In particular, when our interests are engaged or when something we care about is at stake, bias can unconsciously skew our deliberations. For this reason, we are generally less likely to go wrong and more likely to promote good by cleaving to well-established secondary rules. Finally, when secondary rules are well known and generally followed, then people know what others are going to do in certain routine and easily recognizable situations, and they can rely on this knowledge. This improves social coordination and makes society more stable and secure.

An analogy with traffic laws and regulations illuminates these points. Society's goal, let's assume, is that the overall flow of automobile traffic maximize benefit by getting everyone to his or her destination as safely and promptly as possible. Now imagine a traffic system with just one law or rule: drive your car so as to maximize benefit. It's easy to see that such a one-rule traffic system would be far from ideal and that we do much better with a variety of more specific traffic regulations. Without secondary rules telling them, for example, to drive on the right side of the road and obey traffic signals, drivers would be left to do whatever they thought best at any given moment depending on their interpretation of the traffic situation and their calculation of the probable results of alternative actions. Some philosophers seem to think that if people were smart enough and well informed enough, and if time and effort were no consideration, then secondary rules would be unnecessary. But this is a delusion, as Brian Barry explains:

> The optimal course of action for me depends upon what I expect others to do, while the optimal course of action for others depends upon what they expect me to do.... Expectations can be coordinated only by a system of rules (such as that enjoining promise-keeping) which are adhered to without regard to consequences. Only within a matrix of stable expectations created in this way does it make sense for people to make judgments about the likely consequences of acting in one way or another. (1995: 220)

For the reasons just canvassed, consequentialists of all stripes agree that to promote the good effectively, we should, at least sometimes, rely and encourage others to rely on secondary rules, precepts, and guidelines. Moreover, it is widely agreed among consequentialists that the full benefit of secondary rules can only be reaped when they are treated as moral rules and not merely as rules of thumb or practical aids to decision-making. Having people strongly inclined to act in certain rule-designated ways, to feel guilty about failing to do so, and to use those rules to assess the conduct of others can have enormous utility. This is because it produces good results to have people strongly disposed to act in certain predictable ways, ways that generally (but perhaps not always) maximize expected benefit.

In practice, then, consequentialists approach issues of character and conduct from several distinct angles. First, about any action they can ask whether it was right in the sense of maximizing expected value. Second, they can ask whether it was an action the agent should have performed, knowing what she knew (or should have known) and feeling the obligation she should have felt to adhere to the rules that consequentialists would want people in her society to stick to. Third, if the action fell short in this respect, consequentialists can ask whether the agent should be criticized and, if so, how much. This will involve taking into account, among other things, how far the agent fell short, whether there were extenuating factors, what the alternatives were, and what could reasonably have been expected of someone in the agent's shoes, as well as the likely effects of criticizing the agent (and others like her) for the conduct in question. Finally, consequentialists can ask whether the agent's motivations are ones that should be reinforced and strengthened, or weakened and discouraged, and they can ask the same question about the broader character traits of which these motivations are an aspect. Looking at the matter from these various angles produces a nuanced, multi-dimensional assessment, but one that reflects the complicated reality of our moral lives.

The Appeal of Consequentialism

Although this essay abstains from metaethical questions, I incline toward the view that moral theories are "necessarily grounded in intuitions of truth or value that cannot be objectively demonstrated or disproved" (Hardin 1988: 179). At any rate, I know of no proof of consequentialism. G. E. Moore once thought otherwise. In his famous work *Principia Ethica* (1903), he argued that consequentialism is true by definition because 'morally right' simply means 'maximizes the good'. "The assertion 'I am morally bound to perform this action,'" he wrote, "is identical with the assertion 'This action will produce the greatest amount of good in the Universe'" (p. 82). A few years later, however, Moore admitted that he was mistaken, as indeed he was, to assert that these statements are identical in meaning. Nevertheless, Moore continued to maintain that the two propositions 'morally right' and 'produces the most good' are logically equivalent – that there is a "necessary and reciprocal connection" between them – even though they are not identical in meaning. Why? Moore's answer was simply that it is self-evident "that it must always be our duty to do what will produce the best effects *upon the whole*" (1912: 100; 1952: 562–3).

Too many reflective thinkers have rejected consequentialism for a Moore-like assertion of self-evidence to carry the day. But if this is so and if, as I suspect, ethical theories cannot be proved, then the question is whether one finds the ethical ideas, values, or assumptions that inspire consequentialism more attractive and convincing than those that guide non-consequentialist approaches to ethics and whether one believes that consequentialism provides the most coherent, systematic, and plausible orientation to ethics that one is likely to find.

As we have seen, consequentialists share the intuition that the morality of our actions must be a function of the goodness or badness of their outcomes and, more specifically, that an action is right if and only if it brings about the best outcome the agent could have brought about. Consequentialists find it difficult to see what the point of morality could be if it is not about acting in ways that directly or indirectly bring about as much good as possible. True, consequentialism may tell us not to guide ourselves directly by the consequential standard of right in our day-to-day actions, but the correctness of that basic standard has struck most thinkers in the consequentialist tradition as obvious. How, they ask, could the foundational principle of morality deem actions as morally right that fail to maximize expected benefit? Acting so as to maximize benefit strikes consequentialists as the essence of rationality. As John Stuart Mill writes:

> Whether happiness be or be not the end to which morality should be referred – that it be referred to an *end* of some sort, and not left in the dominion of vague feeling or inexplicable internal conviction, that it be made a matter of reason and calculation, and not merely of sentiment, is essential to the very idea of moral philosophy; is, in fact, what renders argument or discussion on moral questions possible. That the morality of actions depends on the consequences which they tend to produce, is the doctrine of rational persons of all schools; that the good or evil of those consequences is measured solely by pleasure and pain, is all of the doctrine of the school of utility, which is peculiar to it. (1838: 83)

Consequentialism's goal-oriented, maximizing approach to ethics coheres with what we implicitly believe to be rational conduct in other contexts, in particular, when it comes to assessing prudential behavior. When seeking to advance our personal interests, we take for granted that practical rationality requires us to weigh, balance, and make tradeoffs among the things we seek in order to maximize the net amount of good we obtain. Only a consequentialist approach tallies with that.

The conviction that moral assessment turns on consequences and that the promotion of what ultimately matters ought to be the guiding principle of ethics lies at the heart of consequentialism. Rival normative theories, of course, rely on other moral assumptions and appeal to different considered moral judgments. Compared to most non-consequentialist approaches, however, consequentialism requires a very small number of ethical assumptions, and these yield, or so consequentialists believe, a powerful but structurally simple normative theory, capable of unifying our understanding of a diverse range of ethical phenomena. By contrast, non-consequentialist approaches to ethics (such as the popular reflective equilibrium method of Rawls [1971] or the common-sense pluralism of Ross [1930]) typically have recourse to intuition at an array of different points. In practice, the result can be a hodgepodge of rules, principles, and injunctions of varying degrees of generality. Moreover, the ethical assumptions on which consequentialists rely are not only few in number, but also very general in character, whereas non-consequentialist theorists typically have recourse to various more specific lower-level intuitions, concerning the legitimacy of particular rules or the moral necessity of particular deontological permissions and restrictions. Intuitions about the rightness or wrongness of specific types of conduct seem more likely to be distorted by the authority of cultural tradition and the influence of customary practice than are the more abstract, high-level intuitions upon which consequentialism relies.

Objections to Consequentialism

Non-consequentialists believe either that it is sometimes wrong to act so as to maximize expected benefit, or that failing to so act is sometimes permissible, or both. That is, they distinguish themselves from consequentialists by affirming certain deontological restrictions or embracing certain deontological permissions.

Deontological restrictions

As mentioned earlier, the likelihood that a consequentialist theory will require conduct that conflicts with the injunctions of ordinary commonsense morality will depend on the particular value theory one adopts. However, even if consequentialists concede that unusual circumstances could, in theory, make it right to perform an action that people normally consider immoral, our earlier discussion should have made it clear that in practice the priority consequentialists give to promoting rules, motives, and dispositions that typically produce good results implies that they will endorse most of the deontological restrictions of everyday morality because doing so maximizes expected benefit.

Even if a consequentialist theory entailed that in the abstract it could be right, if the circumstances were bizarre enough, to do something that would normally be judged morally despicable, like, say, torturing an innocent child, in practice it will make for a much better world if people's characters are such that they would never even entertain the idea of torturing a child, regardless of the circumstances. True, if placed in the imaginary world where torturing the child maximizes good, such people will do the wrong thing (as judged by the consequentialist standard) by refraining from torturing the child. But the real world in which we live is certainly better the more widespread the inhibition on harming children is and the more deeply entrenched it is in people's psychology. Consequentialists prefer people to have the moral motivations that bring the best results in the everyday world, even if these motivations might lead them to behave suboptimally in fanciful situations. To this, non-consequentialists often reply that the consequentialist gets the right answer but for the wrong reason. Consequentialists, it is alleged, overlook the intrinsic wrongness of torturing. But consequentialists can explain perfectly well why torture is evil. And unless the non-consequentialist is an absolutist, he cannot say that torturing an innocent child is always wrong. What if doing so was the only way to stop a war of aggression? So, the non-consequentialist is reduced to saying that the consequentialist takes the possibility of torturing the child too lightly or is too ready to do it. But these allegations seem specious.

In fact, non-consequentialism's commitment to deontological restrictions is vulnerable to consequentialist counterattack. The non-consequentialist sees it as an important fact about our moral lives that an action can sometimes be wrong even though its outcome would be better than that of all alternative actions. Now suppose that somehow your violating a certain deontological restriction (call it R) would result in there being fewer violations of R overall. According to the deontologist, it would still be wrong for you to violate R. This is puzzling, and it is natural to ask: "If non-violation of R is so important, shouldn't that be the goal? How can a concern for the non-violation of R lead to the refusal to violate R when this would prevent more extensive violations of R?" (Nozick 1974: 30 [slightly modified]). Admittedly, these are abstract questions, but one can imagine circumstances in which only by telling a lie (breaking a promise, killing an innocent person) can one prevent several other people from telling lies (breaking promises, killing innocent people). Faced with such situations, deontological theories will, at least sometimes, forbid an action of a certain type even when performing it would result in fewer actions of the forbidden type. This point does not presuppose that the deontologist is an absolutist. Even a moderate non-consequentialist endorses restrictions that it would be wrong for one to violate, at least in some circumstances, even though one's doing so would minimize violations of the very same restriction. This fact leads consequentialists to argue that deontological restrictions are paradoxical or even irrational. For how can a normative theory plausibly say that it is wrong to act so as to decrease immoral conduct (that is, conduct that the theory itself identifies as immoral)? It seems illogical for a theory to forbid the performance of a morally objectionable act when doing so would reduce the total number of such actions and would have no other relevant consequences.

In practice consequentialists are likely to endorse many of the restrictions that deontologists insist upon. But these restrictions will be part of the moral code that consequentialists uphold in order to promote the good in the most effective way they can. However strongly agents are encouraged to adhere to these rules and to internalize a commitment to them, these restrictions are not, for the consequentialist, foundational, but derive from a more basic principle of morality.

Deontological permissions

Critics of consequentialism claim that it sets too high a standard and demands too much of us. Their argument goes like this. At many points in our day, when we are innocently relaxing, talking with friends, or simply at work doing our jobs, we could probably be doing something else instead that would create more good. Instead of watching television tonight, we could visit a nursing home to chat and play cards with its elderly residents. Instead of going to the beach with friends, we could work with the homeless. Instead of buying a new car, we could make do with our old one and give the rest of the money to charity. And so on: our lives are rarely so productive of good that it would be impossible for us to do more. In principle, or so the critics contend, consequentialism could require us to sacrifice our most basic interests in the name of the general good.

Because I have discussed this matter elsewhere (Shaw 1999: 129–32, 261–87) and because Alastair Norcross takes it up in his contribution to this volume (see chapter 3), I will be brief. How much sacrifice consequentialism demands of us will, again, depend on the values the consequentialist wants to see maximized. We must bear in mind the good that (on almost any plausible value theory) is likely to come from permitting people to pursue, as much as possible, their own goals and plans, as well as the possibility that it may bring better results "for a man to aim rather at goods affecting himself and those in whom he has a strong personal interest, than to attempt a more extended beneficence" (Moore 1903: 166–7). Suppose, however, that when conjoined with our most plausible theory of good, consequentialism entails that morality demands much, much more of us than people ordinarily think. It doesn't follow from this that consequentialism is mistaken. Intuitions about these matters, in particular, intuitions about how much effort, time, or money morality obliges us to give to assist those who need our assistance, are an unreliable foundation for normative theorizing because those intuitions reflect social expectations and customary practice in a socioeconomic system, the norms of which are themselves open to assessment.

There are, however, compelling reasons for believing that consequentialists will not advocate a norm requiring (for example) that people give away most of what they have to help those in other parts of the world who need it more. Instead, they will uphold the less demanding norm that we should aid strangers when the benefit to them is great and the cost to ourselves comparatively minor. Trying to instill the more demanding norm would be difficult, and the psychological and other costs of doing so (that is, of getting people to feel guilty about not giving away most of what they have) would be high. It is doubtful whether we could ever succeed in motivating people to comply with such a norm – at least not over the long run. In addressing problems like hunger and disease in the Third World, consequentialists will arguably do more good by upholding a less demanding norm and by supporting the institutions necessary to take over the task and reduce the burden on individual beneficence.

Conclusion

This essay has explained the consequentialist approach to ethics, sketched the rich normative resources at its disposal, given reasons for finding the theory appealing, and defended it against some common criticisms. In this way, I hope to have shown that consequentialism provides an account of right and wrong that is morally attractive, philosophically respectable, and viable in practice. However, a full explication and defense of consequentialism would require further discussion of many matters. Among other things, it would require us to say more about the good and to assess in more detail rival normative approaches.

Acknowledgment

I thank Peter Vallentyne for his helpful comments.

References

Barry, B. (1995). *Justice as Impartiality*. Oxford: Oxford University Press.

Hardin, R. (1988). *Morality Within the Limits of Reason*. Chicago: University of Chicago Press.

Mill, J. S. (1838 [2003]). "Bentham." In J. S. Mill, *Utilitarianism* and *On liberty*, ed M. Warnock. 2nd edn. Oxford: Blackwell.

Moore, G. E. (1903 [1968]). *Principia Ethica*. Cambridge: Cambridge University Press.

Moore, G. E. (1912 [1965]). *Ethics*. New York: Oxford University Press.

Moore, G. E. (1952). "A reply to my critics." In P. A. Schilpp (ed.), *The Philosophy of G. E. Moore*. 2nd edn. New York: Tudor.

Nozick, R. (1974). *Anarchy, State, and Utopia*. New York: Basic Books.

Rawls, J. (1971). *A Theory of Justice*. Cambridge, Mass.: Harvard University Press.

Ross, W. E. (1930). *The Right and the Good*. Oxford: Oxford University Press.

Shaw, W. H. (1999). *Contemporary Ethics: Taking Account of Utilitarianism*. Oxford: Blackwell.

Thomson, J. J. (2001). *Goodness and Advice*. Princeton, NJ: Princeton University Press.

Further Reading

Bennett, J. (1995). *The Act Itself*. Oxford: Oxford University Press.

Darwall, S. (ed.) (2003). *Consequentialism*. Oxford: Blackwell.

Dreier, J. (1993). "Structures of normative theories." *Monist*, 76: 22–40.

Feldman, F. (1997). *Utilitarianism, Hedonism, and Desert: Essays in Moral Philosophy*. Cambridge: Cambridge University Press.

Hare, R. M. (1981). *Moral Thinking: Its Levels, Methods, and Point*. Oxford: Oxford University Press.

Hooker, B. (2000). *Ideal Code, Real World*. Oxford: Oxford University Press.

Kagan, S. (1989). *The Limits of Morality*. Oxford: Oxford University Press.

Norcross, A. (1997). "Comparing harms: headaches and human lives." *Philosophy and Public Affairs*, 26: 135–67.

Parfit, D. (1986). *Reasons and Persons*. Oxford: Oxford University Press.

Pettit, P. (1991). "Consequentialism." In P. Singer (ed.), *A Companion to Ethics*. Oxford: Blackwell.

Scheffler, S. (ed.) (1988). *Consequentialism and its Critics*. Oxford: Oxford University Press.

Scheffler, S. (1994). *The Rejection of Consequentialism*. Rev. edn. Oxford: Oxford University Press.

Shaw, W. H. (1995). *Moore on Right and Wrong: The Normative Ethics of G. E. Moore*. Dordrecht: Kluwer.

Sosa, D. (1993). "Consequences of consequentialism." *Mind*, 102: 101–21.

Vallentyne, P. (1987). "Utilitarianism and the outcome of actions." *Pacific Philosophical Quarterly*, 68: 57–70.

Against Maximizing Act Consequentialism

Peter Vallentyne

Introduction

Maximizing act consequentialism holds that actions are morally permissible if and only if they maximize the value of consequences – if and only if, that is, no alternative action in the given choice situation has more valuable consequences.[1] It is subject to two main objections. One is that it fails to recognize that morality imposes certain constraints on how we may promote value. Maximizing act consequentialism fails to recognize, I shall argue, that the ends do not always justify the means. Actions with maximally valuable consequences are not always permissible. The second main objection to maximizing act consequentialism is that it mistakenly holds that morality requires us to *maximize* value. Morality, I shall argue, only requires that we satisfice (promote sufficiently) value, and thus leaves us a greater range of options than maximizing act consequentialism recognizes.

The issues discussed are, of course, highly complex, and space limitations prevent me from addressing them fully. Thus, the argument presented should be understood merely as the outline of an argument.

What is Consequentialism?

Act utilitarianism is the paradigm *act-consequentialist* theory. It holds that an action is permissible if and only if the aggregate (e.g., total or average) well-being that it produces is no less than that produced by any alternative feasible action. Rule utilitarianism is the paradigm *rule-consequentialist* theory. It holds, roughly, that an action is permissible if and only if it conforms to rules that, if generally followed (internalized, upheld, etc.), would produce aggregate well-being that is no less than that produced by any feasible alternative set of rules. Rule utilitarianism does not assess actions on the basis of the value of their consequences. Instead, it assesses them on the basis of their compliance with selected rules, and it selects rules on the basis of the value of the consequences of their being generally followed (etc.). In what follows, we shall restrict our attention to act consequentialism, and 'consequentialism' and its variants should be so understood. It is beyond the scope of this chapter to assess rule consequentialism.[2]

Consequentialism has been defined in several distinct ways, but all agree that it involves at least the following two claims:

Supervenience (of Permissibility on the Value of Outcomes): The permissibility of actions in a given choice situation supervenes on (is fully determined by) the value of their consequences.

Value promotion: If, in a given choice situation, one action is permissible, and a second is more valuable, then the second action is also permissible.

Supervenience claims that the moral permissibility of actions in choice situations is fully determined by the value of their consequences. In a given choice situation, two actions that have equally valuable consequences also have the same permissibility status (either both are permissible or neither is). Moreover, if two choice situations (of two different agents or of one agent on different occasions) are *value-isomorphic* – that is, have the same number of feasible actions and are such that their actions can be paired so that the value of the consequences of a given action in one choice situation is the same as its counterpart in the other choice situation – then the choice situations are *permissibility-isomorphic* – that is, an action is permissible if and only if its counterpart also is. This leaves open how permissibility is determined by the value of consequences. For example, a theory that holds that an action is permissible if and only if it *minimizes* the value of consequences satisfies supervenience. Value promotion adds that the supervenience must take the form of value promotion: if, in a given choice situation, one action is permissible, then so is any action with equal or greater value. Value maximization is one way of satisfying this condition, but satisfaction (i.e., promotion to some non-maximal adequate level) does so as well.[3]

Call a theory that satisfies supervenience and value promotion 'core consequentialist'. Such theories can involve any account of the relevant value (or values) that is (are) to be promoted. The value might, for example, be (agent-relative) prudential value (roughly: quality of life or well-being) for the agent only (e.g., as with ethical egoism), prudential value from some agent-neutral perspective (taking everyone's prudential value into account; e.g., utilitarianism), moral value from some agent-neutral perspective (e.g., the extent to which prudential benefits match desert), or (agent-relative) moral value from the perspective of the agent (e.g., that, from the perspective of the agent, views it morally worse for her to kill someone than for someone else to kill that person).[4] (Many authors call a theory 'consequentialist' only if it has an agent-neutral theory of value, so it's worth keeping in mind that I use the term more broadly.) It also leaves open what the correct conceptions are of the relevant kinds of value. It leaves open, for example, (1) whether prudential value is based on happiness, preference-satisfaction, or some perfectionist notion of flourishing, and (2) whether moral value is based on prudential value and, if so, how (total, average, leximin, degree of equality, extent to which it matches desert, etc.).

Core consequentialism can be understood broadly to cover theories that recognize several relevant values (e.g., the prudential value for each agent) rather than simply one overriding value. For simplicity, however, I shall restrict my attention to core consequentialism in the narrow sense, which requires that permissibility supervene on a single value. 'Consequentialism' should thus be understood as 'single value consequentialism'.

I shall object to both (1) maximizing consequentialism's failure to recognize that morality typically leaves us a significant array of *moral options* (morally permissible choices in given choice situation), and (2) core consequentialism's failure to recognize that there are *constraints* that limit how value may be permissibly promoted. The first objection applies only to maximizing consequentialist theories. The second applies to all core consequentialist theories.

These objections are not new. I shall simply be developing well-known points. Furthermore, these objections rest on the correctness of certain views of common-sense morality, which defenders of act consequentialism have questioned (roughly by arguing that moral options and moral constraints are irrational).[5] Although I shall answer some these challenges in passing, I shall not give a full rebuttal. Thus, the objections here raised to act consequentialism are merely presumptive at best.

Against Maximizing Consequentialism

Standard utilitarianism is a paradigm example of maximizing consequentialism. It holds that an action is permissible if and only if the agent-neutral value of its consequences is no less than that of any feasible alternative. One of the main objections to it – and, we shall see, all core consequentialist theories – is that it fails to recognize any (deontological) constraints on the promotion of value. *Constraints* (also called 'restrictions') – such as a constraint against killing innocent persons – rule actions impermissible independently of the value of their consequences. I shall develop this objection in the next section. For the purposes of this section, however, we shall set this issue aside. Our topic here is whether morality requires that, perhaps subject to some constraints, we maximize value. I shall argue that it does not.

The main argument for the impermissibility of actions that do not maximize value is the following (see, for example, Kagan 1989):

P1: An action is morally permissible only if it is best supported by moral reasons for action.
P2: The value of consequences is always a moral reason for action.
P3: The value of consequences is the *only* moral reason for action – except perhaps for certain prior constraints.
C: Thus, an action is morally permissible only if, perhaps subject to certain prior constraints, it maximizes the value of consequences.

To adequately assess this argument, we need to distinguish between insistent and non-insistent moral reasons for action. *Insistent* moral reasons for action (in a particular choice situation) are considerations that count for, or against, the moral *permissibility* of actions, whereas *non-insistent* moral reasons are considerations that *merely* count for, or against, the relative moral *desirability* of actions (but not for their morally permissibility). Thus, for example, according to common sense, although, under normal conditions, there is a non-insistent reason for me carefully to wrap my wife's birthday present (since it makes her happier), that reason is not an insistent reason. It is morally desirable for me to wrap it carefully, but that consideration is not relevant for the determination of whether it is permissible for me to do so (or not do so).

If P1 is to be plausible, moral reasons must be understood as insistent reasons. By definition, non-insistent reasons (in a given choice situation) are irrelevant to moral permissibility (in that situation). In what follows, then, we shall understand the argument as invoking insistent moral reasons only and not moral reasons generally.

Consider first P3, which claims that the value of consequences is the *only* moral reason for action – except perhaps for certain prior constraints. Given that it allows that there may be constraints on the promotion of value, it is, I believe, highly plausible. Some might wish to challenge it on the grounds, for example, that the intentions of agents provide insistent moral reasons for actions (in addition to, or instead of) the consequences of their actions. I, however, am happy to accept P3.

Consider now P2. We can grant that the value of consequences is always a reason for action. P2, as we are now interpreting it, however, claims something much stronger. It claims that the value of consequences is always an *insistent* moral reason for action. Some radical deontologists might deny it is *ever* such a reason, but almost everyone else accepts that it often is. The more controversial part is the claim that the value of consequences *always* is an insistent moral reason for action. Many would argue that, above some (perhaps context-specific) non-maximal but adequate level, the value of consequences ceases to be an insistent moral reason. Consequences must be good enough, but, beyond that, their value is not relevant to determining the permissibility of actions.[6] This, then, is one objection to the argument.

Consider finally P1. It claims that an action is morally permissible only if it is best supported by insistent moral reasons. It is not obvious, however, this is so. It may be that permissibility only requires *adequate* (as opposed to best) support. To this, it may be objected that this makes morality irrational. Rationality, it may be claimed, requires that only the best-supported actions be judged permissible. In reply to this objection, we can note, first, that it is not a conceptual truth that moral permissibility is sensitive to moral reasons in the same way that prudence is sensitive to prudential reasons. Thus, even if best support is required by prudential reason, it may not be required by moral reason. Furthermore, it's not even obvious that reason in general, or prudential rationality in particular, requires best support (by insistent reasons). The satisficing model of rationality has been defended by many, and it only requires adequate support for rational permissibility.[7]

Obviously, the issue is complex. My claim is that the above argument for (perhaps constrained) maximization of consequentialist value is not valid as a conceptual matter (given the concepts of moral permissibility, reasons for actions, etc.). This leaves open, of course, that (constrained or unconstrained) maximizing consequentialism may nonetheless be true. In the remainder of this section, I shall identify three substantive problems that maximizing consequentialist theories confront. If my analysis is correct, then we have good reason to reject maximizing consequentialism.

Standard utilitarianism is subject to the following three closely related objections: (1) it often requires agents to sacrifice excessively their well-being, (2) it leaves agents inadequate moral freedom (judges too few actions morally permissible), and (3) it leaves no room for permissible actions that are morally better than other permitted actions. I shall explain each below and show how, with certain qualifications, these objections apply to maximizing consequentialist theories generally.

One problem with utilitarianism is that it requires agents to make significant sacrifices in their own well-being in the name of value maximization. Only those actions that maximize value are judged permissible, and these often require agents to make significant sacrifices in their own well-being. The objection here is *not* that utilitarianism *sometimes* requires agents to make significant sacrifices; all plausible moral theories have this feature. Any plausible theory, for example, will typically judge it impermissible to steal a million dollars, even though one can get away with it and would greatly benefit from the result. The objection here is that utilitarianism *frequently* requires significant sacrifices from agents. It holds that typically it is wrong to spend money (e.g., for restaurants, clothes, or CDs) or time (e.g., watching TV, talking with friends) for one's own enjoyment, since usually this money or time would provide a greater benefit to disadvantaged persons. Of course, such activities are not always wrong, since the most effective way of helping others typically involves occasionally pampering oneself. Most of the time, however, utilitarianism judges it impermissible to devote more than minimal time or resources to oneself.

One way of countering, or at least weakening, this objection is to insist that, when assessing the sacrifices demanded by morality, one must factor in the *passive benefits* that morality provides by requiring *others* to make sacrifices for one's benefit. One must not, that is, only look at the cost when morality requires one to sacrifice one's well-being for the benefit of others; one most also look at the benefit when morality requires others to sacrifices their well-being for one's benefit.[8] This is an important issue that I cannot here address adequately. The main point on which I would insist is that there are significant limits on the extent to which morality requires one actively to sacrifice one's well-being. Active and passive benefits are not interchangeable. The mere fact, for example, that the level of required sacrifice is less than the passive benefits that morality provides (so that one comes out ahead even with the sacrifice) is not sufficient to establish that morality requires such sacrifice. The issue, however, is complex, and in what follows I shall simply assume, without adequate argument, that this is so.

The problem of excessive required sacrifice is, I believe, a powerful objection to utiltarianism. It is not, however, applicable to all maximizing consequentialist theories. Ethical egoism – which judges an action permissible if and only if it maximizes the agent's well-being – does not require excessive sacrifice. Nor do theories that give great weight to the agent's well-being as compared with others: for example, a theory that gives 50 percent of the total weight to the agent's well-being (and the other 50 percent spread equally among the well-being of others). Thus, if the value that is to be maximized is agent-relative and sufficiently *agent-favoring*, this objection does not apply to maximizing consequentialist theories.[9]

Even if the maximized value is *agent-neutral* (i.e., gives no special role to the agent), certain kinds of maximizing consequentialist theories are immune to the problem of excessive required sacrifice. It depends on whether the theory of value is relatively fine-grained and complete. A theory of value is *relatively fine-grained* just in case it makes enough distinctions in value so that ties are relatively unlikely. A theory of value is *relatively complete* just in case incomparability of value (neither of two outcomes being at least as good as the other) is relatively unlikely. Utilitarianism, at least its standard versions, has a fully fine-grained and complete theory of value. Thus, few feasible actions maximize agent-neutral value, and thus few are judged permissible. Given that value is agent-neutral, this means that agents will often be required to make significant sacrifices. If, however, value is relatively coarse-grained or incomplete, there may be many actions that maximize value. Suppose, for example, that value is coarse-grained in that outcomes have only three possible values – good for outcomes that are significantly better than the status quo, bad for outcomes that are significantly worse than the status quo, and neutral for all others. Typically, there will be many actions that maximize value. Likewise, if there is a lot of incomparability in value (e.g., incomparable whenever it is better for some people and worse for others), then there will be many actions that are judged permissible (since many actions will be such that no alternative action has more value). As long as the theory of value is not agent-disfavoring (i.e., is agent-neutral or agent-favoring), typically at least one of the permissible actions will not involve significant sacrifice.[10] Thus, if value (even if agent-neutral) is relatively coarse-grained or incomplete, the problem of excessive required sacrifice need not arise.

My first objection is thus that maximizing consequentialist theories based on value that is agent-neutral (or agent-disfavoring) and relatively fine-grained and complete require excessive sacrifices of agents. This objection does not apply to theories for which the value is (agent-relative and) sufficiently agent-favoring, nor to theories that have relatively coarse-grained or incomplete values.

A second objection to standard utilitarianism is that it leaves agents too little moral freedom. *Moral freedom* is the extent to which morality leaves agents free to choose among their feasible actions. Of course, morality does not leave agents perfectly free. It judges many actions impermissible (such as killing or assaulting innocents under normal conditions). The issue here concerns how much morality limits our freedom to choose. Utilitarianism effectively eliminates this freedom (except for the case of the occasional tie for best consequences), whereas common sense, which I claim is correct on this topic, holds that morality leaves us free to choose among a fairly significant range of choices (and thus leaves agents lots of room to decide how to live their lives).

The problem of limited moral freedom is distinct from that of excessive required sacrifice. Ethical egoism is not subject to the problem of excessive required sacrifices, but, if it has a relatively fined-grained and complete theory of value, it leaves agents little moral freedom. Only maximally good options are judged permissible, and almost no option is maximally good. Thus, the problem of insufficient moral freedom can arise when there is no problem of excessive required sacrifice. Furthermore, the problem of excessive required sacrifice can arise when there is no problem of insufficient moral freedom. Consider the bizarre and wildly implausible theory of 'satisficing anti-egoism', which holds that an action is permissible if and only if it is among the worst 30 percent for the agent. This leaves the agent a fair amount of moral freedom, but still requires excessive sacrifice from the agent.

The problem of limited moral freedom applies to all maximizing consequentialist theories with relatively fine-grained and complete theories of value – even if they are not agent-neutral. My claim is that morality recognizes a significant range of *moral options* (or *prerogatives*), which are morally optional actions (that is, actions that are permissible but not morally required). If, in a given choice situation, only one action is permissible, then there are no moral options; the one action is obligatory. If, however, more than one action is permissible, then each permissible action is optional. The greater the number of actions that are permissible, in a given choice situation, the greater the extent to which morality recognizes moral options (and hence moral freedom).[11]

So far, then, we have two independent (but related) objections to maximizing consequentialist theories with relatively fine-grained and complete theories of value: (1) when based on agent-neutral value, they require excessive sacrifices from agents, and (2) they leave agents little moral freedom. The first objection is concerned with the impact on the agent's well-being, whereas the second is concerned with the moral freedom left to the agent's will.[12]

A third problem with utilitarianism is that it holds that no actions are supererogatory. *Supererogatory actions* are actions that are morally optional (permissible but not obligatory), are significantly more valuable than other permissible alternatives, and involve significant sacrifice by the agent. Thus, for example, according to common sense, devoting all one's income and time to help others is supererogatory. Utilitarianism does not recognize supererogatory actions because it holds that no permissible action is more valuable than any other permissible action (since only maximally valuable actions are permissible). Common sense, which I claim is correct in this respect, however, holds that some permissible actions are better than others. It may be better for me to help a poor fatherless child, but I am permitted to watch television instead. Such help is supererogatory, not obligatory.

The problem of insufficient supererogation is closely related to, but distinct from, the problem of the lack of moral freedom identified above. It is closely related in that if moral freedom is severely limited, then so is the range of supererogatory actions (since an action is supererogatory only if it is optional). The problem is distinct, however, since abundant moral freedom does not entail any supererogation. A maximizing theory with a relatively coarse-grained or incomplete theory of value will leave a significant amount of moral freedom, but it does not recognize that some permissible actions are better than others (they are all either equally good or incomparable).

The problem of insufficient supererogation is also distinct from the problem of excessive required sacrifice. Satisficing anti-egoism (e.g., an action is permissible if and only if its outcome is among the worst 30 percent for the agent) recognizes sufficient supererogation but imposes excessive required sacrifice. Furthermore, ethical egoism fails to recognize supererogation but involves no excessive required sacrifice.

With one qualification, the problem of insufficient supererogation applies to all value-maximizing theories. It applies even to theories for which value is relatively coarse-grained or incomplete, since even such theories judge an action permissible only if no action has better consequences. The qualification is that the value that is used to assess betterness for supererogation must be the same value that is used to assess betterness for permissibility. If these are different values (e.g., the value of consequences is used for permissibility and the value of the agent's intentions is used to assess betterness for supererogation), then, of course, not all permissible actions – those that maximize one value – need be equally valuable according to the second value. Such a detachment of the value for permissibility from that for supererogation is, however, highly implausible, and I shall ignore this possibility.[13]

The three problems raised have, as I have indicated, different scopes. The problem of insufficient supererogation applies (with the above qualification) to all maximizing consequentialist theories. The problem of insufficient freedom applies to all such theories with relatively fine-grained and complete theories of value. The problem of excessive required sacrifice applies to all such theories with agent-neutral theories of value (or more generally: insufficiently agent-favoring theories of value).[14]

It's worth noting that these three objections arise independently of whether the value of an action is determined by the value of its consequences. They arise for any maximizing theory, no matter what the basis is for evaluating actions, as long as value is relatively fine-grained and complete, and, for the problem of excessive sacrifice, agent-neutral. Suppose, for example, that the value of actions has these features, is determined by the underlying intentions, and morality requires that agents maximize the value of actions. Such a theory requires agents to sacrifice excessively their well-being, leaves them inadequate moral freedom, and does not recognize any supererogatory actions.

If, as I believe, a plausible theory must avoid these three problems, then agent-neutral consequentialist theories must be satisficing rather than maximizing. There are many forms that satisfaction can take depending on how the satisfactory level of value is determined: for example, some percentage (e.g., 80 percent) of the maximum feasible value, some percentile value (e.g., the option that is at least as valuable as 80 percent of the feasible options), or the value produced if one maximizes a weighted function that gives extra weight to the agent's well-being (roughly the view defended by Scheffler 1982). There are, of course, many other possibilities, and I shall not here attempt to specific any particular version.[15]

Against Core Consequentialism

Core consequentialism holds that the permissibility of actions supervenes on (is fully determined by), and is positively sensitive to, the value of their consequences. This does not require value maximization; it only requires value promotion, where the relevant value is that of the consequences. I shall argue that core consequentialism, at least in its standard forms, is mistaken. The ends do not always justify the means.

If core consequentialism is true, then any action with maximally good consequences (in a given choice situation) is permissible. The main argument in favor of this claim is the following:

P1: An action is morally permissible if it is best supported by insistent moral reasons for action.
P2: The value of consequences is always an insistent moral reason for action.
P3: The value of consequences is the *only* insistent moral reason for action.
C: Thus, an action is morally permissible if it maximizes the value of consequences.

This is the same argument given in the previous section for the impermissibility of actions that do *not* have maximally good consequences, except that (1) the appeal to *insistent reasons* has been made explicit, (2) the necessary conditions of the original P1 and C have been converted to sufficient conditions, and (3) the qualification in P3 that allowed the possibility of some prior constraints has been dropped.

P1 is highly plausible. An action that is best supported by insistent moral reasons is surely permissible. P2 can be challenged, as I did earlier, on the ground that beyond some point the value of consequences ceases to be an insistent moral reason (once consequences are good enough, their value may only be a non-insistent reason). For the present purposes, however, we can grant this claim. The crucial claim is P3. It is implausible, because there are insistent moral reasons other than the value of consequences. There are also deontological insistent reasons, and these, or at least some of these, are lexical prior to the value of consequences. In particular, individuals have certain rights that may not be infringed simply because the consequences are better. Unlike prudential rationality, morality involves many distinct centers of will (choice) or interests, and these cannot simply be lumped together and traded off against each other.[16]

The basic problem with standard versions of core consequentialism is that they fail to recognize adequately the *normative separateness of persons*. Psychological autonomous beings (as well, perhaps, as other beings with moral standing) are not merely means for the promotion of value. They must be *respected* and *honored*, and this means that at least sometimes certain things may not be done to them, even though this promotes value overall. An innocent person may not be killed against her will, for example, in order to make a million happy people slightly happier. This would be sacrificing her for the benefit of others.

The claim here is that there are some constraints on how value may be promoted. The ends do not always justify the means. Moreover, these constraints, as I shall explain below, are grounded in the normative separateness of persons.[17]

Constraints may be personal or impersonal. An *impersonal constraint* against killing, for example, prohibits killing, independently of whether this is in the killed person's *interests* and independently of whether she has *consented to it* (i.e., is in conformance with her will). It would rule out, for example, well-informed suicide, voluntary euthanasia, and non-voluntary euthanasia where an incompetent individual is terminally ill and likely to be in great pain for the remainder of her life. Although impersonal constraints do reflect a normative separateness of individuals, they do not do so, I believe, in the relevant manner. They fail to capture the *respect due to persons*.

Persons (beings that are protected by morality for their own sake) have interests and often autonomous wills. Any constraint against treating a person in a specified way that applies even when the holder validly consents to such treatment and such treatment is in the holder's interest fails to reflect the respect due to that person. Impersonal constraints fail to reflect this respect, and I agree with core consequentialism's rejection of such constraints.

Constraints can, however, be *personal*. A personal constraint empowers the protected individual, and makes the prohibition conditional on it thwarting her interests or, alternatively, not being in conformance with her will. Personal constraints are waivable rights, and are waived (and hence not violated) when the breach of the constraint is – for *interest-protecting rights* – in the person's interests, or – for *choice-protecting rights* – when the person has given valid (e.g., free and informed) consent.[18] Thus, for example, well-informed suicide and voluntary euthanasia do not violate the choice-protecting right against being killed, and non-voluntary euthanasia for a person with a life not worth living does not violate her interest-protecting right against being killed.

Personal constraints – both choice-protecting and interest-protecting rights – reflect the normative separateness of persons in an appropriate manner. Like impersonal constraints, they require that the holder not be used merely as a means for promoting value. Unlike impersonal constraints, by giving a special role to the interests or will of the rights-holder, they further require that the holder be treated with respect.[19]

There are, of course, many important questions that need to be answered. One concerns the content of the rights. For the present purposes, we don't need to answer this question. All that matters is that there are some rights. I believe, for example, that one of our core rights is that of bodily security (e.g., against being killed, struck, or restrained). A second issue concerns whether the rights are choice-protecting or interest-protecting. The issue concerns the nature of the requisite respect that rights require. I'm inclined to think that psychologically autonomous agents have (mainly) choice-protecting rights and non-autonomous but sentient beings (such as young children and certain animals) have interest-protecting rights, but we need not resolve this issue here. All we need is the existence of some kind of right.

A third issue concerns whether the rights are absolute or conditional in certain ways. Rights with thresholds, for example, have no force when the value that would be foregone is above some threshold (e.g., a right against being killed might not apply where infringement is the only way of avoiding social catastrophe).[20] If there are thresholds, then at some point the normative separateness of persons yields to the promotion of value. For the present purposes, we can leave this open. As long as the rights at least sometimes have some force, the normative separateness of persons will be at least partially recognized in a way incompatible with core consequentialism.

The objection to core consequentialism is that it does not recognize that the ends do not always justify the means, and more specifically that the normative separateness of persons (as reflected in rights) make it impermissible to treat people in certain ways even if it promotes value.

All standard forms of core consequentialism are subject to this objection, but it's worth noting that certain non-standards forms are immune to it. If the value that agents are required to promote is sensitive in a certain way to the violation of the relevant constraints, the objection does not apply. For simplicity, I shall assume that the relevant constraints are absolute (have no thresholds), but the same point can be made (more cumbersomely) without this assumption. Suppose, first, that violation of the relevant constraint is a source of disvalue, and that such disvalue is *lexically prior* in importance to any other sources of value. Thus, an outcome in which a constraint is violated is always worse (agent-neutrally) than an outcome in which the constraint is not violated – even if large numbers of people are much better off when the constraint is violated. A theory like this might hold that it is better to have one violation now rather than five later (this is sometimes called 'utilitarianism [more strictly: consequentialism] of rights'). To block this, suppose further that the theory of value holds that there is a lexical priority of importance to *earlier times* with respect to constraint violation. Thus, an outcome in which the earliest time at which a constraint is violated is t is always worse than one in which the earliest constraint violation is later than t. With this condition built in, where it is possible to perform an action that does not violate a constraint, a maximizing consequentialist theory with this theory of value will judge it wrong to violate a constraint.[21]

Such a theory is not, however, totally immune to the objection. Where it is impossible to perform an action that does not violate a constraint, there is a difference between such a theory and a standard kind of constraint theory. A maximizing theory will always judge some constraint-violating action permissible, since there is always some action the consequences of which are no worse than those of any alternative action. It would hold it permissible, and perhaps obligatory, to infringe now one person's rights where the only alternative is to infringe now the same rights of two others. A constraint theory, however, will judge all feasible actions impermissible, if its constraints apply even in the case where it is impossible to avoid violating a constraint. (Some constraint theories, of course, may hold that the constraints do not apply in such cases.) There is thus an important sense in which such a maximizing consequentialist theory might still fail to recognize the normative separateness of persons. For the present purposes, however, we shall ignore this relatively small difference. A maximizing consequentialist theory based on the above constraint-violation theory of value will be at least roughly equivalent – with respect to permissible constraint violation – as a theory that imposes genuine constraints.

My objection against core consequentialism, then, does not apply to maximizing consequentialist theories with the above theory of value (and related theories). In what follows, I limit my criticism to standard kinds of consequentialism.

It's worth noting that the objection *does* apply to a certain kind of theory that has sometimes been thought to be immune to the objection. Suppose that value is *agent-relative*, and that constraint violation by the agent (as opposed to others) is lexically prior to other considerations of value – *but with no temporal lexical priority* concerning constraint violation.[22] Thus, from the agent's perspective, her violation of any constraint is always worse than any outcome in which she does not violate any constraints (even if others violate many constraints). This agent-relative concern for the agent's own violations is not sufficient to avoid the problem of failing to respect the normative separateness of persons. Such a theory would judge it permissible, indeed, obligatory, to violate a constraint now, where the only alternative is not violating any rights now, but then violating several later. Such a theory is concerned with "keeping the agent's hands as clean as possible" in a consequentialist way, but it does not adequately respect the normative separateness of persons. It judges it permissible for Jones to kill Smith in order to prevent Jones from later killing four other people.[23] This fails to respect the normative separateness of Smith from the others.

Before concluding, we need to consider the main objection to constraints. They are, it is claimed, irrational. There are several different versions of this claim. One is that it is simply irrational to deem the action with the best consequence impermissible merely because it infringes a constraint. This is indeed irrational, if the only insistent moral reasons are the values of consequences. We have seen, however, that there is good reason to deny this claim (since there are also deontological reasons protecting the normative separateness of persons). A second version of the irrationality claim is that, if constraint infringement is a source of disvalue, then surely, all else being equal, it should be permissible to infringe a given constraint when this is necessary and sufficient to minimize the infringements of that constraint. Surely, it is permissible to murder one innocent person when this is the only way to prevent four innocent persons from being murdered. This would indeed be permissible if constraint infringement were simply a source of disvalue. We have seen, however, that constraints do much more than this: they recognize the normative separateness of persons. Thus, the infringement of a constraint protecting one person cannot be simply traded off against infringements of that constraint (or other ones) protecting others. What matters is the respect of persons – not the respect of the constraints.

A third version of the irrationality claim has more force. It acknowledges the normative separateness of persons, but claims that it is irrational to judge it impermissible to infringe a constraint protecting a person when this minimizes the violations of constraints *protecting that very same person*. There are different versions of this objection, but at the core is the relatively weak claim that it is irrational to judge it impermissible for a given agent to infringe a given constraint protecting a given person when this minimizes the number of infringements by the *same agent* of the *same constraint* protecting the *same person*. It is irrational, for example, to judge it impermissible for Smith to steal $100 from Jones now when this minimizes the number of times that Smith steals $100 from Jones. This weak form of the objection is silent when different constraints or different agents are involved, but the objection still has a significant amount of force when different constraints and different agents are involved. The crucial point here is that, in this kind of case, the tradeoffs in constraint infringement are all *intra*personal – all involve the same protected person – and not interpersonal.

These are important points, and they may well show that it is irrational, or otherwise implausible, to prohibit constraint infringement when it minimizes constraint infringements in these victim-focused ways.[24] The central issue to be resolved is, I believe, what kind of respect is owed to persons and whether infringement-minimizing infringements are compatible with such respect. I shall not, however, here attempt to resolve this issue.[25] The important point is that, even if infringement-minimizing infringements are permissible, this does not show that there are no constraints on the promotion of the value. It would only show that the constraints are conditional and do not prohibit the specified actions when those actions have the requisite constraint-infringement minimizing feature. There would still be applicable constraints on the specified actions that do not minimize constraint violation in the requisite manner.

Conclusion

The moral permissibility of actions, I have granted, is based in part on how valuable their consequences are. Having maximally good consequences, however, is, assuming a "standard" theory of value, neither necessary nor sufficient for being permissible. It is not necessary, because only satisfaction is required. It is not sufficient, because some actions with maximally good consequences are impermissible because they do not adequately respect the normative separateness of persons.

Certain consequentialist theories with "non-standard" theories of value can avoid some of the problems that I have raised. First, the problems stemming from the requirement to maximize can be largely overcome, if the theory of value is relatively coarse-grained or incomplete. This avoids the problem of insufficient moral freedom. If value is not agent-disfavoring, then such theories also avoid the problem of excessive required sacrifice. Such theories still fail to recognize adequate supererogation, but this is the least powerful objection to maximizing theories. Second, the problems stemming from the absence of any constraints protecting the normative separateness of persons can also be largely overcome, if the theory of value focuses on rights infringement and gives lexical priority to earlier infringements. The important issue of whether *victim-focused* infringement-minimizing infringements are permissible was briefly addressed, but not resolved. Even if such infringements are permissible, non-minimizing infringements are still impermissible.

In short, the value of consequences is at least sometimes an insistent moral reason for action. Best support by insistent moral reasons, however, is not required for permissibility, and the value of consequences is not the only insistent moral reason. Maximizing consequentialism, at least in its standard forms, should therefore be rejected.[26]

Notes

1 Note that I formulate the maximization requirement as "no alternative action has more valuable consequences" rather than as "its consequences are at least as valuable as those of any alternative." The former is more general in that it covers cases where some consequences are incomparable in value (neither at least as valuable as the other).

2 For criticism of rule consequentialism, see Smart's essay in Smart and Williams (1973). For a state of the art defense of rule consequentialism, see Hooker (2000).

3 A full discussion of the definition of consequentialism would need to address several other issues. For example, are consequences understood as world prospects (roughly: probability distributions over possible world histories), full world histories (including the past), only world futures, or only the avoidable part of world futures? For further discussion of this and other related issues, see Vallentyne (1987a; 1987b; 1988a; 1988b).

4 For discussion of (the slightly unusual notion of) agent-relative moral value, see Portmore (2003) and Sen (1982).

5 The most influential work defending act consequentialism on the topics of options and constraints is Kagan (1989). Scheffler (1982) is the most influential defense of options (but he rejects constraints). See also Kagan (1998) and Scheffler (1988; 1992).

6 See, for example, Kamm (1996: ch. 8).

7 See, for example, Slote (1989).

8 For further discussion, see Murphy (2000), Lippert-Rasmussen (1996; 1999) and Kamm (1996: ch. 8).

9 *Agent-relativity* exists when permissibility is sensitive (involves an essential reference) to features of the agent (her beliefs, values, relationships, etc.) other than the specification of which choices are feasible (and certain related matters). It holds that at least sometimes the identification of who the agent is in a given choice situation is relevant for determining permissibility. *Agent-neutrality* denies this. Agent-relativity is compatible with the sensitivity being agent-favoring (as in ethical egoism), agent-*disfavoring* (as in pure ethical altruism), or *agent-indifferent* (as in a theory that favors the agent's relatives, but gives no special preference to the agent's well-being). For a superb discussion of these notions, see McNaughton and Rawling (1993).

10 Note that for highly agent-disfavoring theories of value, such as anti-egoism, the problem of excessive required sacrifice can arise even when value is relatively coarse or incomplete.

11 I here use 'option' in its broad sense. Many authors use it more narrowly to mean 'morally permitted action that does not (perhaps relative to applicable constraints) maximize the value of consequences'. (Options in this sense are sometimes called 'prerogatives'.) In my sense, but not this more restrictive sense, when two actions both maximize value, they are each options. A maximizing theory with a relatively coarse-grained or incomplete value recognizes many options in my sense but none in the narrow sense. I address the issue of options in the narrower sense below when I discuss the problem of insufficient supererogation.

12 Roughly speaking, both Kamm (2000) and Brock (1991) defend options on the basis of the need to leave adequate moral freedom (personal sovereignty, autonomy). Kamm further argues that (roughly) avoidance of excessive required sacrifice does not justify options on the grounds that (1) we are not permitted to control someone else's life (e.g., who they kiss) even if we care deeply about what they do, and (2) we are not permitted to mistreat people (e.g., kill, assault, or steal from) simply because we would get an enormous benefit from doing so. I fully agree that morality sometimes requires great sacrifice and that options are not justified solely by the need to avoid excessive sacrifice. This does not show, however, that avoidance of frequent excessive required sacrifice is not relevant to the justifications for options. An adequate theory must both leave agents adequate moral freedom and not require excessive sacrifice.

13 Not so implausible is the view that certain values are lexically posterior (relevant only for breaking ties) to others and that only the latter are relevant for determining permissibility. Such a view, however, is not really a maximizing theory.

14 Portmore (2003) argues that maximizing consequentialist theories can accommodate options and supererogation. His defense of this claim, however, involves invoking two values: moral value and all-things considered value, the latter of which is based on both moral value and prudential value for the agent. He defends a theory that holds that an action is permissible if and only if no other feasible action has consequences that are better *both* in terms of moral value and in terms of all things considered value. Such a theory, however, is equivalent to one based on a relatively incomplete theory of single value: one outcome is better than a second if and only if it is better with respect to both moral and

all-things-considered value. Thus, Portmore's approach is equivalent to adopting a certain relatively incomplete theory of value.

15 Satisficing consequentialism is, of course, highly controversial. One objection is that, if it is unconstrained, it permits the mistreatment of others for one's benefit much more frequently than the corresponding maximizing version. In the next section, however, I argue that consequentialism (whether satisficing or maximizing) needs to be constrained by certain rights. For a more general criticism of satisficing consequentialism, see Mulgan (2001).

16 Nozick (1974: 28), for example, emphasizes that a moral concern need not be a moral goal.

17 Another way of grounding constraints, which I shall not explore, is to hold that there is a constraint against using force against a person to impose a loss of well-being that that person is not required to impose on herself or to submit to. For insightful discussion of this strategy, see Myers (1999).

18 Throughout, I assume that interest-protecting rights are *direct* in the sense that a given right protects the holder's interests on *each* occasion, and not *indirect* in the sense of protecting the holder's interests overall (but not necessarily on each occasion). In this direct sense, an interest-protecting right is *waived* whenever infraction does not thwart the holder's interest, even if she has not consented. (Admittedly, this is a non-standard notion of waiving, since no person does the waiving. It is useful, however, since it preserves the parallel with choice-protecting rights in making a feature of the right-holder's person (interests or will) determinative of whether a boundary-crossing is an infringement.)

19 Victim-focused (personal rights-based) defenses of constraints are given by Kamm (1996: ch. 8; 2000), and Mack (1993; 1998).

20 For insightful discussion of rights with thresholds, see Brennan (1995).

21 Things are more complex, Kasper Lippert-Rasmussen pointed out to me, if an action can become a rights violation *after* it has been performed: If Evil fires a gun at Victim1, but this does not violate her rights until the bullet strikes her, then the maximizing theory of the text would judge it permissible, indeed obligatory, to throw Victim 2 in front of the bullet, since that rights violation would occur later than the retroactive rights violation of Victim 1 if the bullet strikes her. For simplicity, I ignore this complication.

22 Sen (1982) explores such a possibility.

23 Kamm (1992; 1996: chs. 8 & 9; 2000) and Mack (1993; 1998) both argue against the common (and mistaken) supposition that agent-relativity is the ground of constraints on the promotion of the good. They both argue, as have I, that it is rather a kind of agent-neutral concern for victims.

24 It may also be that the normative separateness of persons also allows the killing of Smith where (1) this saves at least one other person from being killed, and (2) Smith would be killed by someone else if one did not kill him. In such cases, Smith is arguably not being sacrificed for the benefit of others.

25 See Kamm (1996: ch. 8) and McNaughton and Rawling (1993) for insightful discussions.

26 For valuable comments, I thank Jamie Dreier, Brad Hooker, Paul Hurley, Kasper Lippert-Rasmussen, Piers Rawling, and Bill Shaw.

References

Brennan, S. (1995). "Thresholds for rights." *Southern Journal of Philosophy*, 33: 143–68.
Brock, D. (1991). "Defending options." *Philosophy and Phenomenological Research*, 51: 909–13.

Hooker, B. (2000). *Ideal Code, Real World.* Oxford: Oxford University Press.

Kagan, S. (1989). *The Limits of Morality.* New York: Oxford University Press.

Kagan, S. (1998). *Normative Ethics.* Boulder, Colo.: Westview Press.

Kamm, F. (1992). "Non-consequentialism, the person as end-in-itself, and the significance of status." *Philosophy and Public Affairs,* 21: 354–89.

Kamm, F. (1996). *Morality, Mortality II.* New York: Oxford University Press.

Kamm, F. (2000). "Non-Consequentialism." In H. LaFollete (ed.), *The Blackwell Guide to Ethical Theory* (pp. 205–26). Oxford: Blackwell Publishers.

Lippert-Rasmussen, K. (1996). "Moral status and the impermissibility of minimizing violations." *Philosophy and Public Affairs,* 25: 333–50.

Lippert-Rasmussen, K. (1999). "In what way are constraints paradoxical?" *Utilitas,* 11: 49–70.

Mack, E. (1993). "Agent-relativity of value, deontic restraints, and self-ownership." In R. G. Frey and C. Morris (eds.), *Value, Welfare, and Morality* (pp. 209–32). Cambridge, Mass.: Cambridge University Press.

Mack, E. (1998). "Deontic restraints are not agent-relative restrictions." *Social Philosophy and Policy,* 15: 61–83.

McNaughton, D. and Rawling, P. (1993). "Deontology and agency." *Monist,* 76: 81–100.

Mulgan, T. (2001). *The Demands of Consequentialism.* Oxford: Oxford University Press.

Murphy, L. (2000). *Moral Demands in Non-Ideal Theory.* Oxford: Oxford University Press.

Myers, R. (1999). *Self-Governance and Cooperation.* Oxford: Oxford University Press.

Nozick, R. (1974). *Anarchy, State and Utopia.* New York: Harper.

Portmore, D. W. (2003). "Position-relative consequentialism, agent-centered options, and supererogation." *Ethics,* 113: 303–32.

Scheffler, S. (1982). *The Rejection of Consequentialism.* Oxford: Clarendon Press.

Scheffler, S. (ed.) (1988). *Consequentialism and its Critics.* Oxford: Oxford University Press.

Scheffler, S. (1992). *Human Morality.* Oxford: Oxford University Press.

Sen, A. (1982). "Rights and Agency." *Philosophy and Public Affairs,* 11: 3–37.

Slote, M. (1989). *Beyond Optimizing.* Cambridge, Mass.,: Harvard University Press.

Smart, J. J. C. and Williams, B., *Utilitarianism: For and Against.* Cambridge: Cambridge University Press, 1973.

Vallentyne, P. (1987a). "The teleological/deontological distinction." *Journal of Value Inquiry,* 21: 21–32

Vallentyne P. (1987b). "Utilitarianism and the outcomes of actions." *The Pacific Philosophical Quarterly,* 68: 57–70.

Vallentyne P. (1988a). "Teleology, consequentialism, and the past." *Journal of Value Inquiry,* 22: 89–101.

Vallentyne P. (1988b). "Gimmicky representation of moral theories." *Metaphilosophy,* 19: 253–63.

Further Reading

Applbaum, A. (1998). "Are violations of rights ever right?" *Ethics,* 108: 340–66.

Bennett, J. (1995). *The Act Itself.* Oxford: Oxford University Press.

Brook, R. (1991). "Agency and morality." *Journal of Philosophy,* 88: 190–212.

Cummiskey, D. (1996). *Kantian Consequentialism.* Oxford: Oxford University Press.

Hurley, P. (1997). "Agent-centered restrictions: clearing the air of paradox." *Ethics,* 108:120–46.

Kagan, S. (1984). "Does consequentialism demand too much? Recent work on the limits of obligation." *Philosophy and Public Affairs,* 13: 239–54.

Kumar, R. (2000). "Defending the moral moderate: contractualism and common sense." *Philosophy and Public Affairs*, 28: 275–309.

McCarthy, D. (2000). "Harming and allowing harm." *Ethics*, 110: 749–79.

McMahon, C. (1991). "The paradox of deontology." *Philosophy and Public Affairs*, 20: 350–77.

Nagel, T. (1979). "The limits of objectivity." In S. McMurrin (ed.), *Tanner Lectures on Human Values* (pp. 75–139). Cambridge: Cambridge University Press.

Nagel, T. (1991). *Equality and Partiality*. New York: Oxford University Press.

Otsuka, M. (1997). "Kamm on the Morality of Killing." *Ethics*, 108: 197–207.

Parfit, D. (1984). *Reasons and Persons*. Oxford: Oxford University Press.

Pettit, P. (1988). "The consequentialist can recognize rights." *Philosophical Quarterly*, 38: 42–55.

Pettit, P. (ed.) (1993). *Consequentialism*. Brookfield: Dartmouth Publishing Company.

Ridge, M. (2001). "Saving Scanlon: contractualism and agent-relativity." *Journal of Political Philosophy*, 9: 472–81.

Scanlon, T. M. (1998). *What We Owe to Each Other*. Cambridge, Mass.: Belknap Press of Harvard University Press.

Scanlon, T. M. (2000). "Intention and permissibility." *Proceedings of the Aristotelian Society, Supplemental Volume*, 74: 301–17.

Sen, A. and Williams, B. (eds.) (1982). *Utilitarianism and Beyond*. Cambridge: Cambridge University Press.

Reasons Without Demands:
Rethinking Rightness

Alastair Norcross

Introduction

My concern in this paper is to argue that consequentialist theories such as utilitarianism are best understood purely as theories of the comparative value of alternative actions, not as theories of right and wrong that demand, forbid, or permit the performance of certain actions. Consequentialist morality, I will argue, provides reasons for actions, without issuing demands (or permissions). Such an approach can answer the three related criticisms of consequentialism that it requires too much sacrifice of agents, leaves inadequate room for moral freedom, and does not allow for supererogation.[1] These criticisms focus on the maximizing feature of the most common forms of consequentialism, pointing out that maximization leaves little room for options. I will also argue that these criticisms have very little force against more traditional versions of consequentialism, on any reasonable understanding of what rightness amounts to. The rejection of rightness, though, does not address a different type of criticism of consequentialism. According to some, consequentialist theories are unacceptable, because they fail to account for constraints on permissible behavior. I will briefly discuss Peter Vallentyne's version of this criticism, which claims that such constraints are required to recognize what he (and others) calls the "normative separateness of persons." I will argue that, despite the undoubted rhetorical appeal of this phrase, it does not provide the basis for a convincing criticism of consequentialism. Either 'the normative separateness of persons' signifies a feature fully accounted for by consequentialism (and probably not by rival theories), or it refers simply to the claims that (a) persons have certain rights, and (b) usually (or even always) rights not to be harmed are more stringent than rights to be aided. I shall conduct most of my discussion in terms of utilitarianism, since this is the most popular form of consequentialism. None of my points, however, will rely on the utilitarian value theory.[2] I will also not devote much time to explaining the basic structure of utilitarianism, since both William Shaw and Peter Vallentyne do an excellent job in that regard.

The Demands of Utilitarianism

The three criticisms of utilitarianism, that it requires too much sacrifice of agents, leaves inadequate room for moral freedom, and does not allow for supererogation, can be seen as applications of the more general criticism that utilitarianism is *too demanding*. But how, exactly, are we to take this criticism? Utilitarianism is too demanding *for what*? If I take up a hobby, say mountain climbing, I may well decide that it is too demanding *for me*. By that, I mean that I am simply not willing to accept the demands of this hobby. I may, therefore, decide to adopt the less demanding hobby of reading about mountain climbing instead. However, unless we adopt a radically subjectivist view of the nature of morality, according to which I am free simply to pick whichever moral theory pleases me, this approach will not work for the claim that utilitarianism is too demanding. When critics object to what they see as utilitarianism's demands, they are not simply declaring themselves unwilling to accept these demands, but are claiming that morality doesn't, in fact, make such demands. We are not, they claim, actually required to sacrifice our own interests for the good of others, at least not as much as utilitarianism tells us. Furthermore, we really do have a (fairly) wide range of moral freedom, and there really are times when we can go above and beyond the call of duty. Since utilitarianism seems to deny these claims, it must be rejected.

How should a utilitarian respond to this line of criticism? One perfectly respectable response is simply to deny the claims at the heart of it. We might insist that morality really is very demanding, in precisely the way utilitarianism says it is. But doesn't this fly in the face of common sense? Well, perhaps it does, but so what? Until relatively recently, moral "common sense" viewed women as having an inferior moral status to men, and some races as having an inferior status to others. These judgments were not restricted to the philosophically unsophisticated. Such illustrious philosophers as Aristotle and Hume accepted positions of this nature. Many utilitarians (myself included) believe that the interests of sentient non-human animals should be given equal consideration in moral decisions with the interests of humans. This claim certainly conflicts with the "common sense" of many (probably most) humans, and many (perhaps most) philosophers. It should not, on that account alone, be rejected. Indeed, very few philosophers base their rejection of a principle of equal consideration for non-human animals merely on its conflict with "common sense." Furthermore, it is worth noting that the main contemporary alternative to a (roughly) consequentialist approach to morality is often referred to as 'common-sense morality'.[3] Those who employ this phrase do not intend the label itself to constitute an argument against consequentialism.

As I said, a perfectly respectable utilitarian response to the criticism that utilitarianism is too demanding is simply to insist that morality really is very demanding. However, there are powerful reasons to take a different approach altogether. Instead of either maintaining the demands of maximizing utilitarianism or altering the theory to modify its demands, we should reject the notion that morality issues demands at all. In order to see why this might be an attractive option, I will briefly examine the alleged category of supererogatory actions, and an attempted modification of utilitarianism to accommodate it.

Maximizing utilitarianism, since it classifies as wrong all acts that fail to maximize, leaves no room for supererogation. A supererogatory act is generally characterized as an act which is not required, but which is in some way better than the alternatives. For example, a doctor, who hears of an epidemic in another town may choose to go to the assistance of the people who are suffering there, although in doing so he will be putting himself at great risk.[4] Such an action is not morally required of the doctor, but it produces more utility than the morally permissible alternative of remaining in his home town. The category of the supererogatory embodies two connected intuitions that are at odds with maximizing utilitarianism. First, it seems that people sometimes go beyond the call of duty. Maximizing utilitarianism would not allow that. To do your duty is to do the best thing you can possibly do. And second, people who fail to make certain extreme sacrifices for the greater good are usually not wrong. It seems harsh to demand or expect that the doctor sacrifice his life for the villagers.

The utilitarian can avoid these consequences by retreating to a form of satisficing utilitarianism.[5] For example, one can allow that the boundary between right and wrong can in some cases be located on the scale at some point short of the best. This would allow that an agent can do her duty without performing the best action available to her, and it would make it possible for her to go beyond the call of duty. The position of the boundary between right and wrong may be affected by such factors as how much self-sacrifice is required of the agent by the various options, and how much utility or disutility they will produce. For example, it may be perfectly permissible for the doctor to stay at home, even though the best option would have been to go and help with the epidemic. On the other hand, if all the doctor could do and needed to do to save the villagers were to send a box of tablets or a textbook on diseases, then he would be required to do all he could to save them.

Satisficing versions of utilitarianism, no less than the traditional ones, assume that the rightness of an action is an all-or-nothing property. If an action does not produce at least the required amount of good, then it is wrong; otherwise it is right. On a maximizing theory the required amount is the most good available. On a non-maximizing theory what is required may be less than the best. Both forms of utilitarianism share the view that a moral miss is as good as a mile. If you don't produce as much good as is required, then you do something wrong, and that's all there is to it.

Utilitarianism has traditionally been viewed as a theory of right action. Utilitarians have employed theories of value, theories that tell us what things are good and bad, in functions that tell us what actions are right and wrong. The most common function from the good to the right is the maximizing one: an act is right if and only if it produces at least as much good as any alternative available to the agent; otherwise it is wrong. According to this maximizing function, rightness and wrongness are not matters of degree. Utilitarians are not alone on this score. Deontologists concur that rightness and wrongness are not matters of degree. There is an important difference, though. In typical deontological theories, properties that make an action right

Reasons Without Demands: Rethinking Rightness

and wrong – e.g., being a keeping of a binding promise, a killing of an innocent person, or a telling of a lie – are *not* naturally thought of as matters of degree. So one wouldn't expect the rightness or wrongness of an act to be a matter of degree for deontology.[6] But this is not the case with utilitarianism. Goodness and badness are clearly matters of degree. So the property of an act that makes it right or wrong – how much good it produces relative to available alternatives – *is* naturally thought of as a matter of degree. Why, then, is rightness and wrongness not a matter of degree?

Scalar Utilitarianism

Here's an argument for the view that rightness and wrongness isn't an all-or-nothing affair.[7] Suppose that we have some obligations of beneficence, e.g. the wealthy are required to give up a minimal proportion of their incomes for the support of the poor and hungry. (Most people, including deontologists such as Kant and Ross, would accept this.) Suppose Jones is obligated to give 10 percent of his income to charity. The difference between giving 8 percent and 9 percent is the same, in some obvious physical sense, as the difference between giving 9 percent and 10 percent, or between giving 11 percent and 12 percent. Such similarities should be reflected in moral similarities. A moral theory which says that there is a *really significant* moral difference between giving 9 percent and 10 percent, but *not* between giving 11 percent and 12 percent, looks misguided. At least, no utilitarian should accept this. She will be equally concerned about the difference between giving 11 percent and 12 percent as the difference between giving 9 percent and 10 percent. To see this, suppose that Jones were torn between giving 11 percent and 12 percent and that Smith were torn between giving 9 percent and 10 percent. The utilitarian will tell you to spend the same amount of time persuading each to give the larger sum, assuming that other things are equal. This is because she is concerned with certain sorts of consequences, in this case, with getting money to people who need it. An extra $5,000 from Jones (who has already given 11 percent) would satisfy this goal as well as an extra $5,000 from Smith (who has given 9 percent). It does not matter whether the $5,000 comes from one who has already given 11 percent or from one who has given a mere 9 percent.

An all-or-nothing theory of right and wrong would have to say that there was a *threshold*, e.g., at 10 percent, such that if one chose to give 9 percent one would be wrong, whereas if one chose to give 10 percent one would be right. If this distinction is to be interesting, it must say that there is a *big* difference between right and wrong, between giving 9 percent and giving 10 percent, and a small difference between pairs of right actions, or pairs of wrong actions. The difference between giving 9 percent and 8 percent is just the difference between a wrong action and a slightly worse one; and the difference between giving 11 percent and 12 percent is just the difference between one supererogatory act and a slightly better one. Given the argument I just rehearsed, the utilitarian should not accept this.[8]

A related reason to reject an all-or-nothing line between right and wrong is that the choice of any point on the scale of possible options as a threshold for rightness will be *arbitrary*. Even maximization is subject to this criticism. One might think that the difference between the best and the next best option constitutes a really significant moral difference, quite apart from the difference in goodness between the options. We do, after all, attach great significance to the difference between winning a race and coming second, even if the two runners are separated by only a fraction of a second. We certainly don't attach anything like the same significance to the difference between finishing, say, seventh and eighth, even when a much larger interval separates the runners. True enough, but I don't think that it shows that there really is a greater significance in the difference between first and second than in any other difference. We do, after all, also attach great significance to finishing in the top three. We give medals to the top three and to no others. We could just as easily honor the top three equally and not distinguish between them. When we draw these lines – between the first and the rest, or between the top three and the rest, or between the final four and the others – we seem be laying down arbitrary conventions. And saying that giving 10 percent is right and giving only 9 percent is wrong seems analogously conventional and arbitrary.

By contrast, good and bad are scalar concepts, but as with many other scalar concepts, such as rich and tall, we speak of a state of affairs as good or bad (*simpliciter*). This distinction is not arbitrary or conventional. The utilitarian can give a fairly natural account of the distinction between good and bad states of affairs. For example: consider each morally significant being included in the state of affairs. Determine whether her conscious experience is better than no experience. Assign it a positive number if it is, and a negative one if it isn't. Then add together the numbers of all morally significant beings in the state of affairs. If the sum if positive, the state of affairs is good. If it is negative, the state of affairs is bad.

Note that although this gives an account of a real distinction between good and bad, it doesn't give us reason to attach much significance to the distinction. It doesn't make the difference between a minimally good state of affairs and a minimally bad state of affairs more significant than the difference between pairs of good states of affairs or between bad states of affairs. To see this, imagine that you are consulted by two highly powerful amoral gods, Bart and Lisa. Bart is trying to decide whether to create a world that is ever so slightly good overall or one that is ever so slightly bad overall. Lisa is trying to decide whether to create a world that is clearly, but not spectacularly, good, or one that is clearly spectacularly good. They each intend to flip a coin, unless you convince them one way or the other in the next five minutes. You can only talk to one of them at a time. It is clearly more important to convince Lisa to opt for the better of her two choices than to convince Bart to opt for the better of his two choices.

However, if utilitarianism only gives an account of goodness, how do we go about determining our moral obligations and duties? It's all very well to know how good my different options are, but this doesn't tell me what morality requires of me. Traditional maximizing versions of utilitarianism, though harsh, are perfectly clear on the question of moral obligation. My obligation is to do the best I can. Even a satisficing version can be clear about how much good it is my duty to produce. How could a utilitarian, or other consequentialist, theory count as a moral theory, if it didn't give an account of duty and obligation? After all, isn't the central task of a moral theory to give an account of moral duty and obligation?

Utilitarians, and consequentialists in general, seem to have agreed with deontologists that their central task was to give an account of moral obligation. They have disagreed, of course, sometimes vehemently, over what actually is morally required. Armed with an account of the good, utilitarians have proceeded to give an account of the right by means of a simple algorithm from the good to the right. In addition to telling us what is good and bad, they have told us that morality requires us to produce a certain amount of good, usually as much as possible, that we have a moral obligation to produce a certain amount of good, that any act that produces that much good is right, and any act that produces less good is wrong. And in doing so they have played into the hands of their deontological opponents.

A deontologist, as I said earlier, is typically concerned with such properties of an action as whether it is a killing of an innocent person, or a telling of a lie, or a keeping of a promise. Such properties do not usually come in degrees. (A notable exception is raised by the so-called duty of beneficence.) It is hard, therefore, to construct an argument against particular deontological duties along the lines of my argument against particular utility thresholds. If a utilitarian claims that one has an obligation to produce x amount of utility, it is hard to see how there can be a significant utilitarian distinction between an act that produces x utility and one that produces slightly less. If a deontologist claims that one has an obligation to keep one's promises, a similar problem does not arise. Between an act of promise-keeping and an alternative act that does not involve promise-keeping, there is clearly a significant deontological distinction, no matter how similar in other respects the latter act may be to the former. A utilitarian may, of course, claim that he is concerned not simply with utility, but with maximal utility. Whether an act produces at least as much utility as any alternative is not a matter of degree. But why should a utilitarian be concerned with maximal utility, or any other specific amount?

To be sure, a utilitarian cannot produce an account of duty and obligation to rival the deontologist's, unless he claims that there are morally significant utility thresholds. But why does he want to give a rival account of duty and obligation at all? Why not instead regard utilitarianism as a far more radical alternative to deontology, and simply reject the claim that duties or obligations constitute any part of fundamental morality, let alone the central part? My suggestion is that utilitarianism should be treated simply as a theory of the goodness of states of affairs and of the comparative value of actions, which rates alternative possible actions in comparison with each other. This system of evaluation yields information about which alternatives are better than which and by how much. In the example of the doctor, this account will say that the best thing to do is to go and help with the epidemic, but it will say neither that he is required to do so, nor that he is completely unstained morally if he fails to do so.

If a utilitarian has an account of goodness and badness, according to which they are scalar phenomena, why not say something similar about right and wrong: that they are scalar phenomena but that there is a point (perhaps a fuzzy point) at which wrong shades into right? Well, what would that point be? I said earlier that differences in goodness should be reflected by differences in rightness. Perhaps the dividing line between right and wrong is just the dividing line between good and bad. There are two reasons to reject this suggestion. The first is that it seems to collapse the concepts of right and wrong into those of good and bad respectively, and, hence, to make the former pair redundant. The second is that, on the account of good and bad states of affairs I offered the utilitarian, it is not clear that there is any satisfactory account of the difference between good and bad *actions* (as opposed to *states of affairs*) with which to equate the difference between right and wrong actions. I do not here have the space to defend this claim, though I have done so extensively elsewhere.[9]

If utilitarianism is interpreted as a scalar theory, that doesn't issue any demands at all, it clearly can't be criticized for being too demanding. Does this mean that the scalar utilitarian must agree with the critic who claims (i) we are not frequently required to sacrifice our own interests for the good of others, (ii) we really do have a (fairly) wide range of moral freedom, and (iii) there really are times when we can go above and beyond the call of duty? Strictly speaking, the answers are 'yes' to (i), 'no' to (iii), and 'it depends' to (ii). (i) It may frequently be better to sacrifice our interests for the good of others than to perform any action that preserves our interests. Sometimes it may be much better to do so. However, these facts don't entail any further facts to the effect that we are *required* to do so. (ii) If the claim that we have a wide range of moral freedom is simply the claim that morality doesn't demand only one course of action in most situations, then scalar utilitarians can agree with this. If, on the other hand, moral freedom is supposed to entail not only that morality doesn't narrow down our options with demands, but that we are frequently faced with a wide array of equally choiceworthy alternatives, scalar utilitarians will quite rightly deny this. (iii) As for supererogation, the scalar utilitarian will deny the existence of duty as a fundamental moral category, and so will deny the possibility of actions that go "beyond" our duty, in the sense of being better than whatever duty demands. The intuition that drives the belief in supererogation can, however, be explained in terms of actions that are considerably better than what would be expected of a reasonably decent person in the circumstances.

At this point, someone might object that I have thrown out the baby with the bath water. To be sure, scalar utilitarianism isn't too demanding: it's not nearly demanding enough! How can a theory that makes no demands fulfill the central function of morality, which is to guide our actions? I turn to this question in the next section.

Rightness and Goodness as Guides to Action

Utilitarianism should not be seen as giving an account of right action, in the sense of an action *demanded* by morality, but only as giving an account of what states of affairs are good and which actions are better than which other possible alternatives and by how much. The fundamental moral fact about an action is how good it is relative to other available alternatives. Once a range of options has been evaluated in terms of goodness, all the morally relevant facts about those options have been discovered. There is no further fact of the form '*x* is right', '*x* is to-be-done', or '*x* is demanded by morality'.

This is not to say that it is a bad thing for people to use the phrases such as 'right', 'wrong', 'ought to be done', or 'demanded by morality', in their moral decision-making, and even to set up systems of punishment and blame which assume that there is a clear and significant line between right and wrong. It may well be that societies that believe in such a line are happier than societies that don't. It might still be useful to employ the notions of rightness and wrongness for the purposes of everyday decision-making. If it is practically desirable that people should think that rightness is an all-or-nothing property, my proposed treatment of utilitarianism suggests an approach to the question of what function to employ to move from the good to the right. In different societies the results of employing different functions may well be different. These different results will themselves be comparable in terms of goodness. And so different functions can be assessed as better or worse depending on the results of employing them.

It is clear that the notions of right and wrong play a central role in the moral thinking of many. It will be instructive to see why this so. There are two main reasons for the concentration on rightness as an all-or-nothing property of actions: (i) a diet of examples which present a choice between options which differ greatly in goodness; (ii) the imperatival model of morality. Let's consider (i). When faced with a choice between helping a little old lady across the road, and mugging her, it is usually much better to help her across the road. If these are the only two options presented, it is easy to classify helping the old lady as the 'right' thing to do, and mugging her as 'wrong'. Even when there are other bad options, such as kidnapping her or killing and eating her, the gap between the best of these and helping her across the road is so great that there is no question as to what to do. When we move from considering choices such as these to considering choices between options which are much closer in value, such as helping the old lady or giving blood, it is easy to assume that one choice must be wrong and the other right.

Let us move now to (ii). Morality is commonly thought of as some sort of guide to life. People look to morality to tell them what to do in various circumstances, and so they see it as issuing commands. When they obey these, they do the right thing, and when they disobey, they do a wrong thing. This is the form of some simple versions of divine command ethics and some other forms of deontology. Part of the motivation for accepting such a theory is that it seems to give one a simple, easily applicable practical guide. Problems arise, of course, when someone finds herself in a situation in which she is subject to two different commands, either of which can be obeyed, but not both. In these cases we could say that there is a higher-order command for one rather than the other to be done, or that the agent cannot help doing wrong. The effect of allowing higher-order commands is to complicate the basic commands, so "Do not kill" becomes "Do not kill, unless . . . ." The effect of allowing that there could be situations in which an agent cannot help doing wrong is to admit that morality may not always help to make difficult choices. In either case, one of the motivations for accepting an imperatival model of morality – simplicity, and thus ease of application – is undermined.

Unless one does espouse a simple form of divine command theory, according to which the deity's commands should be obeyed just because they are the deity's commands, it seems that the main justification for the imperatival model of morality is pragmatic. After all, if we don't have the justification that the commands issue from a deity, it is always legitimate to ask what grounds them. That certain states of affairs are good or bad, and therefore should or should not be brought about, seems like a far more plausible candidate to be a fundamental moral fact than that someone should act in a certain way. However, it is generally easier to make choices if one sees oneself as following instructions. It may well be, then, that the imperatival model of morality, with the attendant prominence of the notions of right and wrong, has a part to play at the level of application. It may in fact be highly desirable that most people's moral thinking is conducted in terms of right and wrong. On the other hand, it may be desirable that everyone abandon the notions of right and wrong. I do not wish to argue for either option here, since the issue could probably only be settled by extensive empirical research.

The approach of the last few paragraphs might seem merely to relocate a problem to a different level. I have been claiming that, although morality doesn't actually tell us what we ought to do, there may be pragmatic benefits in adopting moral practices that include demands. Societies that adopt such practices may be better (happier, more flourishing, etc.) than those that don't. But surely this doesn't solve anything. We want to know whether we *ought* to adopt such practices. Scalar utilitarianism seems to be silent on that question. Since scalar utilitarianism doesn't tell us what we ought to do, it can't guide our actions (including our choices of what moral practices to adopt and/or encourage in society). But any adequate moral theory must guide our actions. Therefore the theory should be rejected. This argument has three premises:

1 If a theory doesn't guide our action, it is no good.
2 If a theory doesn't tell us what we ought to do, it doesn't guide our action.
3 Utilitarianism, as I have described it, does not tell us what we ought to do.

To assess this argument, we need to disambiguate its first premise. The expression 'guide our action' can mean several things. If it means 'tell us what we ought to do' then premise (1) is question-begging. I shall construe it to mean something more like, 'provide us with reasons for acting'. On that reading, I shall concede (1), and shall argue that (2) is false. Here is Sidgwick in defense of something like (2):

> Further, when I speak of the cognition or judgement that 'X ought to be done' – in the stricter ethical sense of the term ought – as a 'dictate' or 'precept' of reason to the persons to whom it relates, I imply that in rational beings as such this cognition gives an impulse or motive to action: though in human beings, of course, this is only one motive among others which are liable to conflict with it, and is not always – perhaps not usually – a predominant motive. (1981: 34)

As Sidgwick acknowledges, this reason can be overridden by other reasons, but when it is, it still exerts its pull in the form of guilt or uneasiness.

Sidgwick's point rests on internalism, the view that moral beliefs are essentially motivating. Internalism is controversial. Instead of coming down on one side or the other of this controversy, I shall argue that, whether one accepts internalism or externalism, the fact that a state of affairs is bad gives reason to avoid producing it as much as would the fact that producing it is wrong.

Suppose internalism is correct. In that case the belief that an act is wrong gives one a reason not to do it. Furthermore, such a reason is necessarily a motivating reason.[10] It seems that the utilitarian internalist should take the position that the belief that a state of affairs is *bad* is also a motivating reason to avoid producing it, and the belief that one state of affairs is *better than the other* may well give the believer a stronger reason to produce the first than the second. If the fact that an act is wrong gives us reason to avoid it, then the fact that it involves the production of a bad state of affairs, by itself, gives us reason to avoid it.

Now let's suppose externalism is true. In that case the fact that an act is wrong gives one a motivating reason to avoid doing it *if one cares about avoiding wrongdoing*. If this is what wrongness amounts to, then it seems no defect in a theory that it lacks a concept of wrongness. For it may be true that one cannot consistently want to avoid doing wrong, believe that an act is wrong, and do the act without feeling guilt. But this doesn't provide a distinctive account of wrongness, because we can replace each occurrence of the word 'wrong' and its cognates in the above sentence with other moral terms such as 'an action which produces less than the best possible consequences' or 'much worse than readily available alternatives' and the principle remains true. If the agent cares about doing the best he can, then he will be motivated to do so, feel guilt if he doesn't, and so on. It is true that few of us care about doing the best we can. But then, many of us do not care about doing what we ought either.[11]

Whether internalism is correct or not, it looks as if premise (2) in the above argument is false. Abolishing the notion of 'ought' will not seriously undermine the action-guiding nature of morality. The fact that one action is better than another gives us a moral reason to prefer the first to the second. Morality thus guides action in a scalar fashion. This should come as no surprise. Other action-guiding reasons also come in degrees. Prudential reasons certainly seem to function in this way. My judgment that pizza is better for me than cauliflower will guide my action differently depending on how much better I judge pizza to be than cauliflower. Whether moral facts are reasons for all who recognize them (the debate over internalism) is an issue beyond the scope of this paper, but whether they are or not, the significance each of us gives to such moral reasons relative to other reasons, such as prudential and aesthetic reasons, is not something which can be settled by a moral theory.

There are two other reasons I have encountered for requiring utilitarianism to provide an account of the right. The first might be expressed like this: "If utilitarianism is not a theory of the right, it must only be a theory of the good. Likewise, different consequentialist theories will be different theories of the good. But then how do we explain the difference between consequentialist and non-consequentialist theories in general? Since there are no restrictions on the kind of good that any particular version of consequentialism may be a theory of, we are left with nothing that is distinctive about consequentialism."[12]

This is not correct. I can still claim this distinctive feature for consequentialism: it includes the view that the relative value of an action depends entirely on the goodness of its consequences. Of the acts available to the agent, the best action will be the one that produces the best consequences, the next best will be the one that produces the next best consequences, and so on. I can also claim that the better the action, the stronger the moral reason to perform it. This is not to concede the point to my opponents. The fact that there is a moral reason to perform some action, even that there is more moral reason to perform it than any other action, doesn't mean that one ought to perform it. (Most of us would acknowledge that one has more moral reason to behave in a supererogatory fashion than simply to do one's duty.) This distinguishes consequentialism from deontology, which allows that one may have a stronger moral reason to perform an action which produces worse consequences. For example, if faced with a choice between killing one and letting five die, the deontologist may acknowledge that five deaths are worse than one, but insist that the better behavior is to allow the five to die. According to that view, morality provides stronger reasons for allowing five deaths than for killing one.[13] One advantage of the suggestion I offer here over, say, the view that it is of the essence of consequentialism to insist that the agent ought always to do whatever will produce the best consequences, is that it allows satisficing consequentialists and scalar consequentialists to count as consequentialists.

I have also encountered the following reason for requiring utilitarianism to provide an account of the right as well as the good: The utilitarian will have to provide a function from the good to the right in order to compare her theory with various deontological alternatives. Our chief method for comparing moral theories, according to this suggestion, consists in comparing their judgments about which acts are right or wrong. It is true that contemporary discussions of the relative merits of utilitarianism and deontology have often focused on particular examples, asking of the different theories what options are right or wrong. However, to assume that a moral theory must provide an account of the right in order to be subjected to critical scrutiny begs the question against my proposed treatment of utilitarianism. That utilitarians have felt the need to provide accounts of rightness is testimony to the pervasion of deontological approaches to ethics. Part of what makes utilitarianism such a radical alternative to deontology, in my view, is its claim that right and wrong are not fundamental ethical concepts.

Rightness as an Ideal

In this paper, I have argued that utilitarianism is best conceived as a theory of the good, that judges actions to be better or worse than possible alternatives, and thus provides reasons for actions. I have argued that the traditional utilitarian account of rightness as an all-or-nothing property, whether the maximizing or satisficing version, should be abandoned. However, there may be an alternative account of rightness that is particularly congenial to a utilitarian approach. If, instead of conceiving of rightness as a standard that *must* be met (perhaps to avoid censure), we conceive of it as an ideal to which we aspire, we may be able to accommodate it within a scalar framework. The suggestion is that the ideally right action is the maximizing action, and alternatives are more or less right, depending on how close they come to maximizing. Although the ideal itself is often difficult to attain, the theory cannot be charged with being too demanding, since it doesn't include the demand that one attain the ideal. Nonetheless, the ideal functions as a guide. This would be similar to the approach taken by many Christians, who view Christ as a moral exemplar. A common articulation of this view is the question "What would Jesus do?" – often abbreviated on bracelets, bumper stickers, handguns, and the like as "WWJD." Inasmuch as the extant accounts of Christ's life provide a basis for answering this question, the answer is clearly supposed to function as an ideal towards which we are supposed to aspire, and not as a demand that must be met in order to avoid wrongdoing. The closer we come to emulating the life or the actions of Christ, the better our lives or our actions are.

The utilitarian version (WWJSMD?) might be easier to apply, both epistemically and practically. There are, of course, well-known epistemic problems with even a subjective expected-utility version of utilitarianism, but these pale into insignificance compared with the difficulty of figuring out what Jesus would do, whether the (presumably) actual historical figure, or the literary composite portrayed in the biblical (and other) sources. As for the practical problems with viewing Christ as an exemplar, it may turn out that the ideal is not simply difficult to attain, but in some cases impossible. On the assumption that Christ had divine powers, an assumption that is undoubtedly accepted by most adherents of the Christ-as-exemplar moral theory, we may sometimes be literally unable to do what Jesus would have done. For example, suppose I am attending a wedding in Lubbock (TX), and the wine runs out. Amid the wailing and the gnashing of teeth I glance at the "WWJD" engraved on my cowboy boots. Well, it's clear what Jesus would do in this case (John: 2, 1–10), but I simply can't turn water into wine. However, the utilitarian ideal is, by definition, possible. In this case it might involve driving outside the city limits (Lubbock is dry in more than one sense) to one of the drive-through liquor stores, loading up on the surprisingly good local wines, and returning to spread cheer and much-needed intoxication to the wedding festivities. Or perhaps, more plausibly, it might involve sending the money to famine relief.

Prohibitions and the "Separateness of Persons"

For those who are inclined to think that traditional maximizing utilitarianism is seriously threatened by the objection that it is too demanding, the suggestion that we interpret the theory in scalar fashion, either abandoning the notion of rightness altogether or interpreting it as an ideal, may be particularly attractive. There are also, as I have argued, independent reasons for adopting a scalar version of utilitarianism.[14] However, adopting a scalar version of utilitarianism does not, as far as I can see, have any bearing on Peter Vallentyne's second line of criticism of consequentialist theories, that they don't include constraints required to recognize the "normative separateness of persons." I will, therefore, close with a brief discussion of why I don't think a utilitarian (any version) should be worried by this line of attack on the theory.

The criticism that utilitarianism does not recognize or account for the "separateness of persons" has become commonplace since Rawls (1971), but what exactly does it mean? Peter Vallentyne's explanation is fairly representative:

[I]ndividuals have certain rights that may not be infringed simply because the consequences are better. Unlike prudential rationality, morality involves many distinct centers of will (choice) or interests, and these cannot simply be lumped together and traded off against each other.

The basic problem with standard versions of core consequentialism is that they fail to recognize adequately the *normative separateness of persons*. Psychological autonomous beings (as well, perhaps, as other beings with moral standing) are not merely means for the promotion of value. They must be *respected* and *honored*, and this means that at least sometimes certain things may not be done to them, even though this promotes value overall. An innocent person may not be killed against her will, for example, in order to make a million happy people significantly happier. This would be sacrificing her for the benefit of others.

There seem to be several distinct ideas here. (1) Individuals have rights, that at least sometimes trump utility calculations. (2) Individuals' interests can't simply be traded off against each other. (3) Individuals must be *respected* or *honored*. Consider these claims in reverse order. A utilitarian may claim, with some justification, that the demand for equal consideration of interests embodied in her theory (and other consequentialist theories) is precisely what it means to respect or honor individuals. It is only when I weigh your interests equally with the interests of all others whom I can affect that I adequately respect or honor you. Deontological constraints function to disallow the consideration of certain interests in certain circumstances. Thus they, at least sometimes, prevent us from respecting or honoring certain individuals.

At this point, the critic of utilitarianism will no doubt claim that I have (perhaps willfully) misunderstood (3). In fact, he might claim that (1) and (2) explain *what it means* to honor or respect individuals. (2) denies the aggregative feature of utilitarianism. The problem with the denial of tradeoffs or aggregation is that even committed anti-consequentialists accept them in many circumstances. For example, suppose that Homer is faced with the painful choice between saving Barney from a burning building, or saving both Moe and Apu from the building. Clearly it is better for Homer to save the larger number, *precisely because it is a larger number*. The proponent of (ii) might try to accommodate this intuition by limiting the scope of tradeoffs. For example, perhaps we are allowed to trade lives for lives (or similarly serious harms), but we are not allowed to trade lives for convenience.[15] Homer can save the lives of Moe and Apu rather than Barney, but he can't leave Barney to die in order to provide all the inhabitants of Springfield with a few minutes extra free time every day.[16] However, any such attempt to limit the scope for tradeoffs faces at least two serious problems. First, such a move almost certainly entails denying the transitivity of 'all-things-considered better than'. Second, we commonly accept tradeoffs between lives and much lesser values, such as convenience. For example, we allow public projects such as building a bridge in order to make travel between two places more convenient, even when we know that several people will die in the course of the construction. Likewise, even most anti-consequentialists don't demand that highway speed limits be lowered to the optimal point for saving lives, even though the advantages of higher speed limits are increased convenience for many.[17]

We are left with (1), the claim that individuals have rights that sometimes trump utilities. Utilitarianism is criticized for failing to distinguish between the following pair of cases (adapted from Foot 1984): (a) Homer must choose whether to save Barney, who is trapped on one side of Springfield, or both Moe and Apu, who are trapped on the other side. He can't save all three, and no one else can save any of them. (b) Homer, and no one else, can save both Moe and Apu, who are trapped on the edge of Springfield Gorge. However, in order to reach them in time to save them, he must run over and kill Barney, who is trapped on a narrow segment of the only road leading to the gorge. We are supposed to agree that Homer may choose to save Moe and Apu in (a), but not in (b). If he saves Moe and Apu in (b), he will violate Barney's right not to be killed. But don't Moe and Apu have the right to be saved? Perhaps, but, if so, it is not as important (strict, stringent, etc.) as Barney's right not to be killed. In general, if the rights view is to present a genuine alternative to consequentialism, negative rights not to be harmed in some way must be stronger than the corresponding positive rights, if any, to be aided in avoiding such harm. More specifically, the duty not to harm in a certain way must be stricter than the corresponding duty to prevent such harm. Claims that negative rights and duties are (at least usually) stronger than positive rights and duties will have to be grounded in an account of the alleged moral significance of the general distinction between doing and allowing, of which the distinction between killing and letting die is a specific example. This topic is the subject of much debate, which I don't have the space here to recapitulate.[18] It is, however, no surprise that consequentialists deny the moral significance of the doing/allowing distinction.[19] If, as I have only briefly suggested here, the criticism that consequentialism does not recognize the "normative separateness of persons" really amounts to the claim that consequentialism does not endow the doing/allowing distinction with intrinsic moral significance, no consequentialist should be troubled by it.

Notes

1 Given certain ways of stating the second and third objections, my theory doesn't answer them. Peter Vallentyne's statements of these criticisms of utilitarianism are "(2) it leaves agents inadequate moral freedom (judges too few actions morally permissible), and (3) it leaves no room for permissible actions that are morally better than other permitted actions." On my approach, *no* actions are permissible. However, since no actions are impermissible either, the spirit of the criticisms clearly doesn't apply.
2 I am concerned only with theories which are agent-neutral, and whose value theories are relatively fine-grained.
3 My apologies to the proponents of virtue ethics, the third-party candidate of ethical theories.
4 See, for example, Feinberg (1961).
5 Slote (1985: ch. 3) discusses this suggestion.
6 Though the approach of W. D. Ross might plausibly be interpreted in a scalar fashion.
7 I take the term 'scalar' from Slote (1985), who discusses scalar morality in his chapter 5.
8 It might be objected that maximizing utilitarianism does in fact give a scalar account of wrongness, if not of rightness. Some actions are closer to being right than are others, and

so are less wrong. However, the claim that an action is closer to the best action than is another is quite consistent with the claim that it is no less wrong than the latter.

9 Norcross (1997a).

10 There can be reasons that are not necessarily motivating, e.g. prudential reasons. You may have a prudential reason to act in a certain way, be aware of the reason, and yet be not in the least motivated so to act. I am not here thinking of cases in which other motivations – moral, aesthetic, self-indulgent, and the like – simply overwhelm prudential motivations. In such cases you would still be motivated to act prudentially, but more motivated to act in other ways. If you simply didn't care about your own well-being, prudential reasons would not be in the least motivating. But someone who didn't care about her own well-being could still have, and even be aware of, prudential reasons. Similarly, if you are asked what is the sum of five and seven, you have a reason to reply 'twelve', but you may be not in the least motivated to do so, for you may not care about arithmetic truth, or any other truth. There may be reasons other than moral reasons that are necessarily motivating. For example, the belief that a particular action is the best way to satisfy one of your desires may provide a necessarily motivating reason to perform that action. The motivation may be outweighed by other motivations.

11 Slote (1985) points this out.

12 I have heard this objection from Daniel Howard-Snyder and Shelly Kagan.

13 The full story about what distinguishes consequentialism from deontology will have to be more complicated than this. It may, for example, incorporate the claim that the consequentialist ranking of states of affairs is not agent-centered. See Scheffler (1982) for a discussion of this notion. On the other hand, we may wish to maintain (as Peter Vallentyne does in his contribution to this volume) that an agent-relative value theory may be incorporated into a consequentialist structure to give a form of consequentialism. Whether we classify, for example, ethical egoism as a form of consequentialism or as an entirely different form of moral theory (or not as a moral theory at all) seems to me to be of very little interest.

14 For more discussion of these and other reasons see, for example, Howard-Snyder and Norcross (1993), Norcross (1997a; 2004).

15 Scanlon (1998) tries such a move. I critique it in Norcross (2002).

16 I leave the reader to fill in the details of this and other examples involving the endlessly fascinating inhabitants of Springfield.

17 For detailed discussion of both these points, see Norcross (1997b).

18 See, for example, Bennett (1995), Norcross (2003), Steinbock and Norcross (1994).

19 It may be possible to construct a consequentialist theory that is sensitive to this distinction (see Norcross 1995), but I know of no one who embraces such a theory.

References

Bennett, J. (1995). *The Act Itself.* Oxford: Oxford University Press.

Feinberg, J. (1961). "Supererogation and rules." *Ethics*, 71: 276–88.

Foot, P. (1984). "Killing and letting die." Repr. in Steinbock and Norcross (eds.), 280–9.

Howard-Snyder, F. and Norcross, A. (1993). "A consequentialist case for rejecting the right." *The Journal of Philosophical Research*, 18: 109–25.

Norcross, A. (1995). "Should utilitarianism accommodate moral dilemmas?" *Philosophical Studies*, 79(1): 59–85.

Norcross, A. (1997a). "Good and bad actions." *The Philosophical Review*, 106(1): 1–34.

Norcross, A. (1997b). "Comparing harms: headaches and human lives." *Philosophy and Public Affairs*, 26(2): 135–67.

Norcross, A. (2002). "Contractualism and aggregation." *Social Theory and Practice*, 28(2): 303–14.

Norcross, A. (2003). "Killing and letting die." In R. G. Frey and C. H. Wellman (eds.), *The Blackwell Companion to Applied Ethics*. Oxford: Blackwell.

Norcross, A. (2004). "Scalar act-utilitarianism." In H. West (ed.), *Blackwell Guide to Mill's Utilitarianism*. Oxford: Blackwell.

Rawls, J. (1971). *A Theory of Justice*. Cambridge, Mass.: Belknap Press of Harvard University Press.

Scanlon, T. M. (1998). *What We Owe to Each Other*. Cambridge, Mass.: Belknap Press of Harvard University Press.

Scheffler, S. (1982). *The Rejection of Consequentialism*. Oxford: Clarendon Press.

Sidgwick, H. (1981). *The Methods of Ethics*. 7th edn. Indianapolis, Ind.: Hackett.

Slote, M. (1985). *Common-sense Morality and Consequentialism*. Boston: Routledge and Kegan Paul.

Steinbock, B. and Norcross, A. (eds.) (1994). *Killing and Letting Die*. 2nd edn. New York: Fordham University Press.

Further Reading

Howard-Snyder, F. (1994). "The heart of consequentialism." *Philosophical Studies*, 76(1): 107–29.

Kagan, S. (1989). *The Limits of Morality*. New York: Oxford.

Kagan, S. (1998). *Normative Ethics*. Boulder, Colo.: Westview Press.

Parfit, D. (1984). *Reasons and Persons*. Oxford: Oxford University Press.

Scheffler, S. (ed.) (1988). *Consequentialism and its Critics*. Oxford: Oxford University Press.

Smart, J. J. C. and Williams, B. (1973) *Utilitarianism: For and Against*. Cambridge: Cambridge University Press.

Unger, P. (1996) *Living High and Letting Die: Our Illusion of Innocence*. Oxford: Oxford University Press.

Can Contract Theory
Ground Morality?

Moral Contractarianism as a Foundation for Interpersonal Morality

Samuel Freeman

Foundationalism in Interest-based and Right-based Contract Views

Contractarianism's intuitive appeal lies in the idea that since moral norms impose demands and constraints on conduct, they ought to be freely acceptable to people and for their mutual benefit. Characteristic of contract views is the idea that justice and morality are the principles that *could* or *would* be freely agreed to among equals under appropriately defined conditions, where each is motivated partly by reasons or interests not shared by everyone else. Contract views differ in how the hypothetical "contract" or agreement is specified: What is the object of agreement (a constitution, principles of justice, morality generally)? Who are the parties and how are they situated (status quo, state of nature, or strict equality)? What are the intentions and interests of contracting parties, and what rights and powers do they have? What are the parties' motivations (purely self-concern, or other-regarding and/or moral motives too)? What sort of knowledge do they have (particular as well as general knowledge about themselves and society)? Since these and other features may differ, there are a variety of contract views.

One type is already found in ancient philosophy. In *The Republic* Plato discusses and rejects the Sophists' position (later espoused by Epicurus) that justice or the ground rules of society result from a pact among rational egoists. Hobbes revived this doctrine in *Leviathan* to explain the conditions of society and justify absolute political authority. Contemporary thinkers, drawing on the theory of rational choice, have developed highly sophisticated versions of self-interest contract doctrine.[1] A defining feature of these views is that persons are primarily motivated to promote some state of themselves (their own pleasure, power, reputation, etc.), and that a person's good is definable in such self-focused terms. A primary aim of self-interest contract doctrines is to explain why, given self-interest, we should care about and comply with morality's demands. In this and other regards these accounts are *reductionist*; they seek to "reduce" morality to other terms, by eliminating all reference to moral notions and showing that what is right and reasonable can be explicated purely in terms of (self-focused) desires and principles of rational choice.[2] For example, assuming that impartiality and treating like cases alike are features of justice, self-interest doctrine attempts to justify these norms by showing that such conduct effectively promotes a person's interests within society. So Hobbes argued that acknowledging others as equals and dealing with them impartially are conditions of peace and that it benefits each person to comply with these norms.[3] Presumably if these empirical claims were proven false, then we would not have sufficient reason to treat others impartially or as equals and the reduction of justice to rational interest would fail.

Significantly, people's interests do not need to be defined egotistically or in purely self-focused terms in order to provide a reductionist contract account. (Hobbes himself saw "conjugall affection" as the second most compelling motive people have after self-preservation.)[4] It is enough that people's interests and objects desired be definable in terms of natural states of the world and non-moral terms – without reference to concepts of right, impartiality, duty, justice, and so on. The important point is to show that morality's norms are definable as instrumental to achieving people's non-moral purposes and interests, whatever these might be.

The reduction of justice and morality to (non-moral) interests and principles of rational choice is one way to argue for the contractarian *foundations* of morality. I call such reductionist accounts 'interest-based contract views'.[5] The driving aims of such accounts are to show that (a) morality's demands promote each person's desires and interests in some way, and (b) each person has sufficient reason, based in her particular desires and interests, to accept and abide by morality's requirements.

A different kind of contract doctrine is found in Locke, Rousseau, and Kant. The leading idea of their natural rights theory of the social contract is that justice consists of norms that could or would be agreed to by free moral agents from an idealized position of equal right. This tradition and its modern followers assume that people are not moved purely by interests in themselves, but that they have concerns for others' good; moreover people are capable of wanting to do what is right and just for its own sake, and this moral motivation is not itself irrational or unreasonable. Recognition of an independent moral motivation (to be reasonable) implies that 'right-based' accounts (as I call them)[6] are non-reductionist: They do not attempt to explain or justify justice and morality purely in terms of (non-moral) interests and principles of rational choice. Right-based contract accounts deny that any reduction can be achieved. Morality is "autonomous" or (partly) independent of purely rational choice and the instrumental means to achieving non-moral ends. Even if empirical facts could be marshaled to show that it is in each person's interest to comply with moral demands, this would not explain or justify morality. It might be a happy coincidence which provides agents with added incentives to do their duty, but it would not account for the content or demandingness of morality or for moral motivation. Arguments of the form, 'You ought to treat people honestly and fairly and respect them if you want to have a good reputation and be successful', do not strike us as moral justifications but as counsels of prudence. For right-based theorists morality cannot be explained or justified simply in terms of prudential norms and contingencies. This is the wrong kind of explanation or justification of morality since it tells us only why, given pre-existing preferences, we should be moved to abide by morality's demands. It does not tell us whether our pre-existing preferences are reasonable or unreasonable, nor say why moral demands and the purposes they serve are worth taking seriously independent of what peoples' preferences might happen to be.

Right-based contract views are 'foundational' in a different sense from that of interest-based views. Rather than trying to reduce morality to a rational bargain among people with conflicting interests, they aim to *elucidate* morality in terms of a reasonable agreement (or a rational agreement among reasonable morally motivated persons). On the assumption that morality concerns the quality of interpersonal relationships, right-based views aim to account for the content and demandingness of moral principles by appealing to a (hypothetical) agreement among free persons who regard one another as equals. If it can be shown that core moral judgments reasonable people take as especially important can be justified by principles that are agreeable to free agents equally positioned, and that these principles themselves stand up to our critical reflection when compared with other principles, then we have an adequate foundation for morality.[7]

A third way a contract doctrine may be 'foundational' is in its account of the subject matter of morality. *Philosophical contractualism* contends that the subject matter of morality is reasonable agreement among equals – that is to say, morality consists of those norms that could not be reasonably rejected by morally motivated individuals in a process of uncoerced and general agreement. Underlying this account is the notion that morality basically involves mutual recognition and respect among persons. This contrasts with 'philosophical utilitarianism' (as Scanlon calls it) – often called 'welfarism' – which says that the "point" of morality and what morality is "about" is the promotion of human interests or well-being.[8] Both views are "metaethical" positions regarding the source and nature of moral reasons, and do not necessarily commit one to a particular normative view. Many philosophical utilitarians (or welfarists) adopt normative utilitarianism too, but others (such as Gauthier) are interest-based contractarians. Most who advocate philosophical contractualism also accept a right-based normative contract view. Still some (normative) utilitarians claim their view is compatible with philosophical contractualism. Finally, a complete philosophical contractualism should provide a way to address other metaethical questions regarding the nature of moral motivation, moral truth and objectivity, and the conditions and possibility of moral knowledge.

I have suggested three ways contract doctrine might seek to provide a "foundation" for morality:

1   In response to the question 'What moral principles are true?' a contract account can seek to "reduce" morality to rational interests. Hobbes, Gauthier, and other interest-based views are foundational in this reductionist sense.
2   An alternative contract account denies this reduction and insists on the (partial) independence of moral reasoning from prudential reasoning. There are moral reasons independent of considerations about what promotes individuals' preferences or particular interests. The task of a moral theory is to *elucidate* what moral reasons imply by reference to a "reasonable" agreement among free

rational persons who are morally motivated and equally situated. Rawls and Scanlon are the major contemporary advocates of such a conception.

3   In response to the metaethical question regarding the "subject matter" of morality and the possibilities of moral knowledge, objectivity, and moral truth, a philosophical account might depict morality as the principles that could be justified and agreed to among reasonable persons as a basis for uncoerced, general agreement. This is Scanlon's contractualism.[9]

I will discuss and offer support for the idea that contract doctrine is 'foundational' for morality in the second and third ways mentioned. Right-based contract doctrines that affirm both (2) and (3) will be referred to as 'moral contractarianism'. I hope my use of the terms 'foundations for morality' is clear enough. There are different senses of foundationalism in philosophy, and none is without problems. No doubt the senses in which I will use the term, especially the second, will seem too thin for those with more robust philosophical sensibilities. Still, if a case can be made that (interpersonal) morality can be explicated in terms of a general agreement in the ways suggested, then perhaps some progress can be made in discussing these controversial issues.

Finally, two points bear emphasis before proceeding. First, the social contract tradition in moral philosophy always has relied on an idea of *hypothetical* agreement among equals under artificial conditions (a state of nature, an original position, etc.). The different idea of an *actual tacit* social contract among real persons has been used by social scientists to explain the existing morality and mores of particular historical communities. This idea is suggested by Hume in his account of the convention of justice, and is found in contemporary accounts of morality as a convention.[10] This is a naturalistic (as opposed to a normative) use of the idea of a social contract. While it may help to explain the behavioral patterns of members of a particular society, it does not have the moral force for humankind generally which is assumed by the social contract traditions discussed above.

Second, the fact that moral contractarians contend that morality is based in a hypothetical agreement among artificial moral agents does not imply that the moral norms they would agree to apply only in the unrealistic circumstances where norms are hypothetically accepted. Such an account of morality would be of little use in our real-world circumstances where many people do not regularly exhibit the moral characteristics of hypothetical contracting parties. But the idea of hypothetical agreement among equal moral agents can be used to justify moral principles for all kinds of circumstances. Hypothetical contracting parties can just as well deliberate about the moral principles that are to apply under non-ideal circumstances as they can about the moral principles that are to apply to conscientious moral agents like themselves who can be counted on consistently to observe these principles. (For example, they can agree to the appropriate principles of punishment for people who commit felonious crimes, or the appropriate moral sanctions for people who breach a promise or a trust, or the political rights of people who do not respect or cannot comply with democratic norms.) The fact that agreement to moral principles takes place among idealized moral agents under hypothetical conditions does not mean that the range of principles agreed to also can apply only under similar conditions. Ideal moral agents can agree to principles that apply to all sorts of situations, non-ideal as well as ideal.

Moral Contractarianism, Interpersonal Morality, and the Publicity of Moral Principles

Assume then that morality is not "reducible" to non-moral principles but that morality and its demands have a kind of independence that is to be elucidated largely in its own (moral) terms, according to independent moral reasons. The question then is: 'What are the moral reasons and terms that best account for what morality is about, or what morality's "foundations" are?' Begin by considering the main concepts of moral reasoning, 'the good' and 'the right'. As John Rawls says, what distinguishes moral conceptions is how they interrelate these key notions.[11] Consequentialists are distinctive in that they see the concept of the good as primary and explain right actions and just institutions as instrumentally promoting (maximizing, or perhaps "satisficing") good states of affairs. Utilitarianism and perfectionism of certain forms are primary examples of consequentialist conceptions.[12]

Consequentialists regard it as a truism that people ought to do what they can to promote the good and avoid (or even minimize) evil, and generally make the world as good a place as possible.[13] For them it is hard to see how morality could permit people to act in ways that result in more rather than less evil, or a lesser rather than a greater good. These are among the abstract intuitions that lead consequentialists to affirm that right acts are those that best promote good states of affairs. Add to this the idea that if morality is to have any point at all then it must be the promotion of (people's or sentient beings') happiness or well-being as experienced by them and we have the main ingredients of utilitarianism.

One peculiarity of a consequentialist conception is that it conceives of morality *impersonally* rather than *interpersonally*. To say morality is *interpersonal* means that it is fundamentally concerned with the norms that regulate individual agents' interpersonal relations, which norms agents themselves appeal to in order to guide their actions, justify their conduct to each other, and make possible cooperation and social life generally. Consequentialism, by contrast, does not conceive of morality, in the first instance, from the point of view of individual moral agents who have specific concerns, aims, and commitments that they act to further.[14] In saying that consequentialism conceives of morality *impersonally*, I mean, first, consequentialism abstracts from the points of view of individual agents, including the reasons, purposes, and relationships to which agents themselves appeal and which give life meaning for them. Consequentialism is geared toward the promotion of ends that no one (except perhaps the most sincere and conscientious consequentialists) pursues or endorses, or which they even recognize as ends that they ought to further (e.g., maximum aggregate utility). Whatever people's personal aims and plans, consequentialism sees them as worthy of pursuit only to the degree that they advance aggregate goodness. Second, consequentialism (in its more robust forms at least) is impersonal insofar as the truth value of moral judgments is made to depend on the aggregate goodness of states of affairs that are to be promoted. What is ultimately important is maximum good (maximum overall utility, for example, or maximum achievements of culture, or minimizing rights-violations). Such judgments generally ignore boundaries between persons, focusing instead only on the sum total of impersonal goodness to be accomplished by moral action, with no regard for how it is to be distributed to individuals. That there may be distinct persons, each with separate purposes and lives to live, is not all that relevant to the truth of consequentialist judgment. A third way consequentialism is impersonal is in its account of practical reasoning. To characterize the highest level of deciding what is right to do, consequentialists (utilitarians especially) often appeal to the impersonal standpoint of a detached disinterested observer with full knowledge of relevant information (about people's desires, etc.), who gives equal weight to everyone's interests, and whose primary concern is the overall amount of goodness to be promoted in the world.[15] Sidgwick called this moral standpoint "the point of view of the universe." It is the perspective that a supremely benevolent Being, concerned only with total goodness, might have occupied when it created the universe. It is not the point of view of any person who is situated in the world and actively engaged in social relations within it.

Moral contractarianism, by contrast, conceives of morality "phenomenologically," so to speak, in the way that agents themselves regard it.[16] Morality should not be confused with a religious "ethics of creation" providing instructions for promoting the maximal sum of impersonal good in the universe. Instead, morality's role is to regulate the interpersonal and cooperative activities of agents engaged in the world as they pursue their primary and often conflicting purposes. As such, morality consists of the interpersonal norms and constraints that we agents should use to guide our conduct and to which we are to appeal to justify our actions to one another as we pursue the distinct aims that give our lives meaning. When contractarians invoke idealizations from which hypothetical persons deliberate about morality, these idealizations do not involve the kind of detached disinterested agency characteristic of consequentialist ideal observers. Rather, contractarians model the deliberations of moral agents actively engaged in social interaction who have their own ends and commitments, and who seek to establish the norms that everyone is expected to observe in their pursuits and activities.

Now given its interpersonal form, why should we conceive of morality as grounded in some sort of hypothetical agreement among moral agents or their representatives? One reason is that it blocks the tendency to aggregate interests, by focusing attention from the outset upon distinct individuals with different purposes rather than upon the sum total of goodness of states of affairs. Unless they are perfect altruists, individual agents with their own plans, purposes, and relationships have little reason to care about sacrificing their own ends for the sake of maximizing the total goodness of impersonal states of affairs. Instead they are concerned with discovering rules everyone can voluntarily accept and observe which enable them to accomplish their purposes and commitments. This is one regard in which moral contractarianism exhibits respect for persons as such, as opposed to impersonal states of affairs.

It is often said that morality is fundamentally a matter of equal respect for others as persons and that this is what underlies the contractarian emphasis on agreement. While equal respect for persons is important, this idea by itself does not tell us enough to distinguish contractarianism from other moral conceptions. Kant's categorical imperative is a non-contractarian account that also embodies respect for persons and their individual claims. Even utilitarians claim their doctrine respects others as persons, for in utilitarian calculations equal respect is given when everyone's preferences or interests are taken into account.[17] I believe this claim is based on a confusion. For it is not really persons that are given equal consideration in aggregative utilitarian procedures, but rather preferences or interests in proportion to their intensity (or other measure of significance). That persons exist as carriers of interests is only incidental to utilitarian calculations (accentuated by the fact that most utilitarians consider the interests of all sentient beings). To take all interests into account is simply an initial step necessary to maximize aggregate utility and has nothing to do with respecting persons. How else can aggregate happiness be maximized except by considering all preferences or interests? As J. S. Mill says, equal consideration is not a moral presupposition of an equal right to happiness but simply an arithmetical truth implicit in the principle of utility.[18]

We need an account of the distinct way in which contractarian morality exhibits recognition and respect for others as persons. Return to the idea of the interpersonal nature of morality. One way to understand morality's interpersonal nature is in terms of the *publicity* of moral norms. A primary feature of moral contractarianism is that it sees morality in the first instance as a public system of rules that individuals themselves apply not only to guide their deliberations and actions, but also to justify or criticize their own and others' conduct. In this regard, morality is not simply a group of rules that individuals follow which make social life possible; it is also a system of public rules which people generally accept and appeal to in order to justify their conduct and critically assess others' actions. Contractarians seek to model this aspect of interpersonal morality.

Now consequentialists would recognize that to be effective (most) moral norms must be public; otherwise agents would not know what is required of them, and the good that consequentialist morality promotes would not be promoted. Moreover moral rules and principles must play an important role for any consequentialist in moral education and in the normal practices of moral argument when dilemmas and conflicts arise. Still, there is no practical need that those to whom moral rules and principles apply be aware of the final consequences that ordinary moral rules are supposed to promote. It might even be counterproductive, for if they knew these consequences then even the most conscientious might devise periodic exceptions to the rules, reasoning that the ultimate good is better promoted if one acts differently on this occasion. More importantly, those who do not endorse the ends of consequentialist morality (perhaps because of the exceptional burdens it puts on them) might especially be inclined to make exceptions to the rules if they were aware that their aims and well-being were being compromised for the sake of greater overall good. So Sidgwick says that utilitarianism might be better served if it remains an "esoteric morality," hidden from most people's view, and knowledge of which is "confine[d] to an enlightened few."[19] Ordinary people then would be subject to a public "morality of common sense" which, unbeknownst to them, optimally promotes aggregate utility. To provide people with incentives to abide by common-sense moral rules, they should be made to believe that it has some other foundation than aggregate utility (the will of God, for example).

The "esoteric" nature of utilitarianism that is required to make it effective emphasizes the degree to which it is impersonal. One reason for depicting morality as contractual is that the idea of a general agreement on moral norms makes especially prominent the public nature of moral reasons and principles, even at the highest levels of reasoning about what we ought to do. When made public, moral principles are among the reasons that are available to us to employ in practical reasoning. This means that the most basic principles that structure and regulate moral relations (including social and political relations) are also capable of serving agents as principles of practical deliberation, justification and criticism.[20] Here it is worth emphasizing the contrast with utilitarianism and other consequentialist principles which do not, indeed cannot, play the same role in practical reasoning as is countenanced for them by a contractarian view.

There are several reasons for the publicity of moral principles and the reasons supporting moral requirements. First, we want to know whether we are mistaken, or whether we are being deceived or misled, about moral rules and what they accomplish. If I knew that the main argument for respecting property and existing distributions, as defined by law, is that they are designed to benefit the wealthy at the expense of the poor, then I might have different attitudes towards ownership and existing distributions of property.

Second, it seems to be a condition of treating people as equals that they have available the reasons behind the moral regulations and restrictions all are expected to comply with. The problem with seeing basic moral principles as "esoteric" and "confined to an enlightened few" is that it implies a fundamental inequality among people. People are divided into a class of followers (or "proles," as R. M. Hare says) and a minority of governing elites. There may be circumstances where it is not feasible to treat people as equals in this way (in backward societies marked by illiteracy and corruption, for example, where knowledge of basic principles lessens the likelihood of compliance with ordinary moral rules.) But to see a morality as esoteric seems to acknowledge that there are no feasible circumstances under which people can be brought to understand, accept, and have true beliefs about the moral bases of their relations. It suggests that people are simply not constitutionally capable of understanding and dealing with the bases of morality, even when social impediments to understanding (illiteracy, poverty, corruption, etc.) are removed. The idea of an esoteric morality implies that ordinary people are not by nature up to morality's demands. Only experts and those especially intelligent and virtuous can live with the truth of what morality is about. This suggests that many people do not warrant respect as equals at some level (either because they are not smart enough or because people's good is always to be subordinated to the impersonal and dominant ends of morality).[21]

A third reason for the publicity of moral principles and other reasons for moral demands is that it is important that people be in a position to justify their conduct to one another. No one likes to think that his or her conduct is unjustified, and people go to great lengths to convince others that their actions do not violate moral requirements and rules of human decency. Indeed, it is rare to find people who care nothing about how others judge the morality of their actions; most of us would think such people to be sociopaths. It seems then that we value a great deal being able to morally justify our actions to others.[22] But for us to do so requires that we have publicly available the moral reasons and principles that underlie moral requirements.

Finally, it is important to people that they not be under illusions about their relations with others. Even if we are confident that moral norms and beliefs are reliable or true, we want to know the reasons for them in so far as we aim to be free and responsible agents. One feature of free responsible agents is that they are capable of deliberating rationally and critically about worthwhile ends. Deciding whether a desired object is worth pursuing is part of what is involved in being self-governing. Without that capacity one is governed by passions or unreflective (if not "brute") desires. Free agency in this sense involves a kind of practical self-knowledge: knowing the reasons why one's desires are as they are and why one's purposes are (believed) worthwhile. Now moral and legal norms are the most stringent constraints on what we do. They deeply affect our desires and the ends we pursue as well as our characters and the kinds of persons we are. Knowing the reasons why our actions are regulated and constrained as they are by moral and legal norms is part of the self-knowledge of free agency. To know and to be able to endorse the most basic reasons and principles that underlie and justify (if they do) the norms that regulate and constrain our conduct is an essential part of free agency and the ideal of a free person.

There are two levels at which contractarianism embodies the publicity of moral principles. First, the publicity of moral principles is implicit in the act of hypothetical agreement itself. Moral principles are made public to artificial moral agents simply by virtue of the fact that they could be justified and agreed to by all of them. A utilitarian can reply here that this does little to distinguish contractarianism from utilitarianism; for just as sincere and conscientious moral agents with different ends and a desire to justify their conduct would all publicly agree to contractarian moral principles, sincere and conscientious moral agents who all recognize that well-being is the sole ultimate good would publicly accept and agree to the principle of utility. At the level of choice by hypothetical moral agents, utilitarianism can satisfy a publicity condition too. True, but notice that in order to achieve general agreement on the principle of utility, moral agents have to be impracticably described as endorsing the same ultimate good, namely aggregate well-being. Moral contractarianism, by contrast, represents moral agents more realistically, as having different aims and commitments, and a shared aim of justifying their conduct to one another *given* their different perspectives. The publicity condition on moral principles is not the empty requirement that a moral principle should be publicly acceptable to a society of hypothetical agents, each of whom already accepts that principle entirely for reasons extraneous to their agreement. The requirement rather is that moral principles should be publicly justifiable and acceptable to moral agents, each of whom (in having different ends and commitments) acts for different reasons, and who aim to justify their conduct to one another *precisely because* they recognize different such different reasons.

The second level at which publicity applies in a contract conception is under conditions of a feasible social world. Hypothetical contracting agents are envisioned as deliberating about the moral principles that are to apply, not to artificial people like themselves with full knowledge and who make no mistakes in reasoning (impossible people in effect), but to real-world moral agents like you and me, who are conscientious and morally motivated to do what is right, but with our limited knowledge and other shortcomings. This is the level at which Sidgwick says the principle of utility has to be "esoteric." He recognized that, because people, even morally conscientious people, will not all accept that pleasure or well-being is the sole ultimate good, there is no realistic social world in which conscientious moral agents can generally accept the principle of utility as a basis for moral justification. For example, people denied life's basic necessities for the sake of promoting greater happiness of those significantly better off will not willingly concede the worthlessness (from the perspective of aggregate utility) of their lives, aims, and ambitions. People are not normally self-sacrificing in this way, and this is a fact about human nature. (Some would say evolution did not select for complete self-effacement or impartial benevolence.) Here, contractarianism is in a much better position to serve as a public basis for morality. For it takes into account the fact that people do have different primary purposes and commitments, and that very few people could ever accept an impersonal end like aggregate well-being as the final end of all their endeavors. Utilitarians and other consequentialists might respond that the degree to which a moral conception is publicly acceptable in any feasible social world is irrelevant to the justification of a moral conception. But if the freedom of individuals and the condition 'ought implies can' are important, then a moral conception's capability of public acknowledgment among conscientious moral agents in the real world is entirely appropriate.

Moral Justification, Moral Agency and a Person's Good

It is sometimes said that the reason for depicting morality contractually is that moral norms are "social" in a number of important ways (interpersonal norms make social cooperation possible; they apply to everyone's conduct unlike other norms; for reasons of coordination many moral norms, to be effective, have to be accepted and observed by most people, and so on). But the fact that moral norms are social in various ways does not imply they must be based in any sort of contract or agreement. They could be natural laws or some sort of peculiar facts about the world, for example. Now the same might be said to hold true of the publicity of moral reasons and principles and the idea that they should be capable of a role in the practical reasoning of conscientious moral agents. Fundamental moral reasons and principles may be publicly acknowledgeable by conscientious moral agents because they are knowable by a rational intuition (as Locke held of the "fundamental law of nature"). Or they may be part of the structure of pure practical reason (as Kant held of the categorical imperative). Their publicity in these regards does not mean they have a basis in any kind of contract or agreement. So it seems that however much the social and public nature of moral norms and reasons lead people to use the contract idiom, additional considerations are needed to warrant the idea of a contractarian framework for morality. In what follows I discuss two of these. First, a view about moral justification, namely, that it is social and public in that it is addressed *to* others and is not simply a matter of formal demonstration or showing-to-be-true. Second, an idealization of moral agency where free persons are conceived as autonomous, responsible not only for their actions and ends but also for the very rules and principles by which they regulate their actions and pursue their ends.[23]

There are different ways to think about justification. On one account, to justify a principle is to show-it-as-true. The model here is justification as a kind of proof. But a full justification ultimately must go beyond proof, for proof assumes a justification of its premises.[24] Moreover, justification in one domain of reasoning may not be subject to the same requirements as those of another. Justifications within moral reasoning might depart in some significant way from justifications in math, the sciences, or other theoretical domains. Morality differs from theoretical inquiries in that it involves rules that appeal to the practical reason of agents, which rules demand actions and constrains agents in pursuit of their particular interests. Since morality is geared toward actions mediated by reason, it is reasonable to suppose that the rules that fix moral requirements be endorsable by agents in some capacity. For without the acceptance and willing compliance of agents, morality's demands are ineffective if not utopian. Unlike law, morality loses not only its effectiveness but its point if its demands have to be coercively enforced among wide groups of people. Then it no longer governs cooperative efforts of free self-directing agents, but becomes rules enforced by an outsider for the efficient coordination of behavior to achieve some purpose they do not endorse (like prisoners on a work gang).

It is because of the special nature of moral norms, their regulative role in cooperative and other interactions, that moral contractarians see moral justification as a special kind of case, not on a par with justifications in other domains where showing-the-truth might be appropriate. Moral justification is not simply about demonstrating the truth, but is argument addressed *to* others. This means that it involves searching for reasons and principles that they can accept. Here one has to be careful, of course, since taking people as they are, the fact that they can accept something does not mean it is any sort of justification. Mere conventional acceptance of some principle by a group of misguided, egotistical, or evil persons is not justification. Moral contractarians say that what makes for justification in ethics is not simply acceptance by people, but *reasonable* acceptance by people described in a certain way.[25] Since morality applies to everyone's actions, a moral justification addresses them in a specific capacity or status that they all share with others, namely, in their capacity *as* rational self-governing moral agents.

Of course people share other statuses as well; all are members of the human species, or more broadly, all are conscious beings capable of pleasurable experiences. Why should not some other universal status of persons be the relevant focal point for justifications to others? What is so special about the human capacities for rational self-directed moral agency? Perhaps it is enough to say here (though clearly more needs be said at some point) that what warrants focusing on our status as rational self-governing moral agents (as the ideal of the person to whom moral justifications are to be addressed) is that this conception of the person includes the capacities that both enable us to understand, apply, and conform to moral norms, and also to give justifications for our actions. For moral contractarians, those who can give justifications should receive them, in the sense that moral justification is to be addressed to people with the capacities for moral reasoning and justification as well as capacities for reasoning about their good, and an interest in exercising these capacities. On this account, moral justification is not to be addressed to "the world at large"[26] or to a munificent Being, or a detached ideal observer.

This is one approach to the idea that to justify moral principles is to show that they are acceptable to a person *as* a free self-governing moral agent (who is motivated to justify himself to like moral agents on terms they can accept). Since moral principles apply to everyone, they should be acceptable to everyone in a capacity they share with others, and which is directly relevant to compliance with moral requirements.

There is then a claim about the nature of moral justification that underlies moral contractarianism. It is argument addressed *to* others and it involves searching for reasons and principles that they can all reasonably accept. Reasonable acceptability is best understood in terms of an ideal of persons, as moral agents who have an interest in exercising their capacities for moral agency, and a willingness to comply with principles agreeable to other moral agents who are likewise morally motivated.

To reach the claim that morality has its basis in a kind of reasonable agreement among moral agents, the following objection needs to be addressed:

Grant for argument's sake that (reasonable and rational) moral agents who are properly informed would all accept and agree to the same moral principles. Still, this does not show that morality has any kind of basis in their agreement. For (a) what moral agents with an interest in exercising their capacities for moral agency would all accept, if they had all the relevant information and could see matters clearly, is that basic moral principles are the commands of a Superior Being, which are promulgated so that moral agents might experience Its divinity. Or alternatively, (b) reasonable moral agents, each with an undistorted view of the nature of value, would all agree that happiness is the ultimate good, and that the most reasonable moral principle is the principle of utility.

Either alternative poses serious if not fatal problems for moral contractarianism, for if true they verify the criticism (first made by Hume) of contractarian doctrines, namely that appeals to general agreements are unnecessary and mask the true basis for morality (God's commands according to the first objection, and the maximal promotion of human happiness according to the second). To respond to these objections and show that the idea of general agreement is doing any real work, moral contractarians must assume and argue then that these sorts of arguments are mistaken (so that, if there is a God, then God is not the origin of morality.) Moreover contractarians must assume that people do not simply have different and conflicting ends (which is obvious) but that they have different and conflicting goods, at least to some degree. If there is only one ultimate good that is rational for all persons to pursue, and it is univocal (the Vision of God, say, or the sum of pleasurable experiences), then it is much more difficult to see why there should be a need (or place) for a contractarian justification for morality. Central to contractarianism (of any form) then is the idea of *a person's good*. A person's good might be distinctive to him or her but it need not be entirely. This does not commit contractarians to a subjective conception of value, wherein a person's good is ultimately to be resolved into an account of what he or she (rationally) desires. Moral contractarians can and do claim that there are objective goods, but also, importantly, they is a plurality of goods. Moreover, which of these goods it is rational for a person to pursue depends on facts peculiar to that person, such as her circumstances, capacities, skills, rational desires, and so on. A second assumption for (most if not all) contractarians is: whatever a person's rational good may be and however much it may differ from others', it is part of everyone's good that he or she have the *freedom* to decide their good and construct their own scheme of activities and purposes. Individuals' freedom in this sense of rational autonomy is a fundamental assumption of contractarianism.[27]

These two claims (the plurality of goods and individuals' fundamental interest in having the freedom to determine what is good for themselves) are needed, I believe, to generate the essential contractarian claim that people have not simply different and conflicting conceptions of their good, but that they have different and conflicting goods.[28] A *person's good* is (roughly) the scheme of activities and ends that he or she, given adequate information, would freely and rationally choose from among the set of objective goods (if there are any) that best fit with his or her circumstances and capacities and so on, and which would be enjoyed by that person.[29] Being in love is an objective good for most, if not all, persons, but perhaps not under all circumstances or at all periods in their lives, so love would not then be part of many persons' good during those periods. Ballet and creative dance are also objective goods, since they involve the complex development and sophisticated exercise of physical capacities; but they are not part of *my* good nor is it good for me to engage in these activities, since I do not have the capacities to either do them well or enjoy them. One can make sense of the idea of a person's good without resorting to a purely subjective (desire-based) conception of value.

People then have conflicting goods depending in part on what scheme of values it is rational for them to freely affirm and choose, on the bases of their wants and abilities, to pursue. Now if we take justification to be addressed *to* persons, then the questions becomes: How are we to justify to people who have conflicting goods the regulations and constraints on the pursuit of their aims that are necessary for social cooperation and harmonious interaction? Since there is no single ultimate good that is rational or in each person's interest to pursue which might be appealed to in order to justify norms that resolve their potential conflicts and make social life possible, we have to find some other basis for morality. Assuming (1) that the aim of justification addressed to others with conflicting purposes is their *reasonable agreement*, and (2) given that moral norms apply to everyone's conduct and all will be held responsible to comply, it is natural to try out the idea that morality has its basis in some kind of agreement or "social contract" among persons who freely pursue different and conflicting goods. After all, what other generally acceptable source could be given for morality that would elicit agreement and acceptance of moral norms among free and reasonable persons with different and conflicting rational goods?

To summarize the discussion: Interpersonal moral norms, at all levels of generality, are (a) social and (b) public; moreover, (c) they are backed by (or justified by) principles and reasons that are public and shareable too among reasonable agents (without untoward consequences–such as instability of moral norms). (d) There is a plurality of goods worthy of pursuit, (e) but whatever conception of the good is appropriate for a person, it must be one that is rational and freely chosen by that person, given her circumstances, abilities, etc. So we might say, persons have a *fundamental interest* in maintaining their freedom (including the capacities for free agency.) Given (d) and (e), the public principles (c) that are needed to justify moral norms should be acceptable *to* people in their capacity as rational moral agents; moreover, principles should be *generally* acceptable, and thus have their basis in general agreement. For, to give another (free person) reasons that are public is to present considerations that · are shareable, and which are acceptable to him as relevant and in favor of a principle or some proposition. These are some (if not all) of the considerations that underlie the idea that interpersonal morality has its basis in a general agreement among equals.

Some Objections

Turn again to the criticism that the idea of a social contract is an unnecessary shuffle which masks the true reasons supporting moral norms. Hume makes this criticism of Locke, and Joseph Raz, Philip Pettit, and others have made similar criticisms against contemporary contract doctrines. If people agree or would agree because of certain reasons and interests they have, then why don't we just appeal directly to these reasons as the basis for morality or principles of justice?[30] The idea that free people could or would agree to them does not add any more support to the argument for moral principles than is already present in the reasons for their agreement.

To respond, the appropriate question to ask here is: In what way are we to take into account and realize the reasons contractarians appeal to and which underlie contractarian agreement to principles? Even supposing that contractarians and their opponents recognize only the same reasons as relevant to argument for moral principles (normally they do not), the way that contractarians take these reasons into account and assign them significance differs from these other forms of argument. My suspicion is that the Humean argument often (if not always[31]) contains an implicit consequentialist assumption, that morality and justice involve promoting certain values or interests so as to achieve maximal good. But this just ignores the contractarian assumption that there are different persons with their own perspectives and their own good, and that they warrant respect for their free pursuit of their legitimate purposes. The primary point of appealing to an agreement among moral agents is to avoid the idea that the relationship between morality and people's good is one of promoting aggregate goodness or the best consequences overall. If this is so, the appropriate contractarian reply to the Humean criticism is that, because interpersonal morality is not a matter of promoting the best consequences, but instead is about justification to people who exercise their capacities for agency pursuing a plurality of valuable and often conflicting ends, the only way ultimately to justify moral norms is by supposing a hypothetical agreement among free rational agents with different conceptions of the good. To appeal directly to the reasons for their agreement (to maintain their free agency, for example) and contend that we ought to do whatever best promotes (maximizes the achievement of) that reason, does not exhibit the proper attitude toward the reasons that underlie contractarian agreement.[32] We do not recognize and respect persons as equal self-governing moral agents by maximizing the (exercise of) capacities for free agency, whatever that might mean. Rather, we exhibit respect by treating them according to principles they freely would agree to from an appropriately defined position of equality. So regarded, we might say (using Kantian terms) that moral principles *express* the freedom of equal moral persons; moreover, actions consistently motivated by principles expressing their freedom enables people to *realize* the capacities for rational and moral agency.

So the proper response to the Humean claim that a social contract is unnecessary and misleading, and we should appeal directly to the reasons and values that underlie a purported agreement, is this: The process of discovery and justification of the moral principles that moral reasons require must be indirect.[33] Reasoning from what would or could be agreed to among free persons situated in ideal circumstances is the only reliable way to discover and justify what the (moral) reasons and interests are that morality is supposed to realize and achieve. To try to directly achieve those reasons or values by taking the most effective means to maximally promote them misunderstands what morality is about. Morality is not about promoting maximally good states of affairs, but concerns the rules that regulate interpersonal and cooperative relationships among responsible moral agents as they freely pursue their good.

Here it is surely relevant that those who object that a social contract is unnecessary almost always affirm different moral principles from contractarians. Consequentialists do not affirm the moral principles Rawls argues for from the original position. Also, Hume was more conservative than Locke, and was not disturbed by a benevolent despot; as a conservative utilitarian he would not have supported the liberal revolution that Locke justified by a social contract. But even if he would have, then surely there must be other kinds of government that are supportable by social contract doctrine which are not justified by utilitarianism and other non-contractarian views, and vice versa. For the charge to stand that the social contract is unnecessary, it must be shown that the same principles argued for by contractarians can be justified by some other form of argument, and that this other form of argument is (on all relevant dimensions) a better account of justice and morality than that offered by contractarians.

Finally, I've said moral contractarianism conceives of morality in the way that agents themselves regard it: as involving interpersonal norms and constraints that are used to guide our conduct, and to which we appeal in order to justify our actions to one another. I've also mentioned (without further discussion) that the way a contractarian justification of the content of moral norms must proceed is by relying on our considered moral convictions (seeking to achieve a reflective equilibrium). Here it might be objected that, to rely on people's sense of what morality is about and their "intuitions" about the content and correctness of moral norms is like relying on the judgments of religious people to depict the subject matter of religion and the truth of its claims. If scientific method has taught us anything it is that we cannot rely on people's beliefs or intuitions, no matter how well considered, to learn the truth of much of anything.

The problem with this objection is that morality and considered moral "intuitions" are not like the data or considered claims used within either the sciences or religion, both of which make claims (factual and metaphysical) about the world. The problem with "considered religious intuitions" is that they involve physical and psychological claims that contravene the claims of the sciences. For this reason we have reason to suspect they are false. But morality as moral contractarians conceive of it makes no such suspicious or controversial metaphysical, epistemological, or empirical assumptions. For our considered moral judgments to be reliable, there is no need that they correspond to, or be causally related to, moral properties or other "moral facts" that exist independent of the way we reason about morality. The kind of objectivity appropriate to morality is different from the kind needed to support judgments about the way the world is. For moral convictions to be objective is for them to be supported by a preponderant order of reasons. For moral contractarians, this order of reasons is finally ascertained by agreement in the judgments of ideal reasonable and rational agents who are conscientious, intelligent, and adequately informed of relevant factual information, and who survey sufficiently all pertinent grounds under conditions favorable to due reflection.[34]

Moreover, appeals to what is often called (misleadingly) "moral intuitions" are not peculiar to moral contractarianism. All moral conceptions – utilitarianism, Kantianism perfectionism, Hobbesian contract doctrine, and so on – rely on considered moral convictions at some level of generality. (Sidgwick's "principle of benevolence" – that we ought to promote the good impartially construed – is, he says, a "philosophical intuition" essential to utilitarianism.) The normative theory of rational choice, which is effectively used in the social sciences, has been applied in illuminating ways by moral philosophers (Kantians and utilitarians, as well as Hobbists). But none pretends that rational choice theory alone can be used in moral philosophy without supplement from independent moral assumptions.

It might be argued that in moral philosophy we should rely as much as we can on the natural and human sciences and their methods, minimizing appeals to moral judgments and intuitions. (As if appealing to one moral intuition is always better than invoking two or three.) One problem here is that the human sciences are largely in dispute. There is very little of significance to moral philosophy in economics, psychology, and other human sciences that is not contested, not only by non-practitioners, but among economists or psychologists themselves. More seriously, the fewer secure moral convictions a philosopher appeals to, the more likely the theory is controversial. (Hence, for many, Sidgwick's purportedly self-evident principle of impartial benevolence appears false. Why should we maximize any good – pleasure, happiness, knowledge, the vision of God, or what have you – without regard to how it gets distributed or its deleterious effects on the pursuit of other values, not to mention its effects on those who are worse off?) Considered moral convictions at any level of generality do not exist isolated *in situ*, but are part of a complicated web of moral judgments, each of which receives its sense and significance from others that are part of the network. If so, then there is something misguided about attempts to minimize appeals to considered moral judgments while appealing to the methods and mechanisms of the human and biological sciences. Of course some of our considered moral convictions may be false, but this is more likely to be discovered via a moral theory which takes them all into consideration and seeks to combine them into a coherent view – as opposed to a moral theory which privileges only a few moral intuitions and ignores all the others, perhaps in the hope that scientific methods will

Moral Contractarianism as a Foundation for Interpersonal Morality

salvage something resembling morality by somehow enabling us to decide which of our remaining convictions are more reliable.

Two final points. First, it is worth noting that, in depicting morality "phenomenologically" or in terms that moral agents themselves conceive of it, moral contractarianism occupies a middle position between the two extremes of prevailing moral conceptions. Morality is not seen in purely self-focused and strategic terms and as a matter of enlightened self-interest as Hobbesians hold; nor is morality viewed wholly impersonally as consequentialists would have it, as the promotion of states of affairs in the world that no particular person is concerned with. Instead morality is depicted as the interpersonal norms that regulate the interactions and cooperative endeavors of responsible moral agents who are motivated to do what is right and just as they freely pursue the different kinds of values that make life worth living for them.

The second point. Earlier I said that we needed to work out the particular sense in which moral contractarians see morality as involving respect for persons. To respect another as a person is to give a justification for actions and institutions that she can accept in her capacity as a moral agent. It is to address oneself to those capacities of persons by virtue of which they are responsible moral agents with conceptions of the good that are worthy of pursuit. It is in this regard that moral contractarianism seeks to depict morality as involving mutual recognition and respect for persons.[35]

Notes

1 See for example Gauthier 1986.
2 By 'principles of rational choice' I mean such norms as taking effective means to one's ends, minimizing costs in achieving ends, making one's ends consistent, and so on. For an account, see Rawls (1971: sects. 63–4).
3 These are the 9th and 11th "Laws of Nature." See Hobbes (1651/1991: ch. 15).
4 See ibid. ch. 30.
5 I borrow the term from John Rawls, who credits it to Joshua Cohen.
6 I call them 'right-based' since they rely in part on moral reasons and principles of right, not because they all assume an account of moral or "natural" rights. A rights-based account such as that found in Locke would be right-based in my sense, but so too would Rawls's and Scanlon's accounts, which are not grounded in an account of individuals' moral rights.
7 I believe the best way to understand how this "foundation" is arrived at is by way of Rawls's idea of reflective equilibrium, but there may be some other mode of justification. The advantage of reflective equilibrium is that it allows us to dispense with appeals to self-evidence and other controversial metaphysical and epistemological notions.
8 Some welfarist accounts are reductionist and others are not. Interest-based contract views are welfarist since they regard morality mainly in terms of the promotion of individual human interests. Other welfarist views, such as (normative) utilitarianism, are non-reductionist – they do not see morality as reducible to individual interests per se. Instead, morality involves the promotion of individual interest impartially (or impersonally) construed. The utilitarian emphasis on impartiality, or equal consideration of interests, is not given a reductionist explanation. Instead, utilitarians, like right-based contractarians, see the concept of impartiality as part of what morality consists in. (For example, Sidgwick [1981] sees a "principle of equity" and a "principle of [impartial] benevolence" as self-evident "philosophical intuitions" that are implicit in practical reason.)

9 Rawls (1993: 49–50n) indicates that his normative contractarian account of justice assumes a version of Scanlon's earlier contractualist account of moral motivation.

10 See Hume (1978: Bk. III, sect.2, pp. 491, 498); Harman (1977).

11 Rawls says the concept of 'moral worth' of persons is a third concept that is subsidiary since it is to be accounted for in terms of the concepts of rightness and goodness (1971: sects. 5–6). Some may argue that the concept of 'moral virtue' is also a primary concept of ethics which fits into none of the three moral concepts in Rawls's (Kantian) framework.

12 Roughly, utilitarianism sees happiness as the good state of affairs to be promoted by morality, while perfectionism sees the good to be promoted in terms of excellences of character and perfections of culture.

13 See Scheffler (1988: 1).

14 In saying that consequentialists depict morality "impersonally," I do not mean to deny that they aim to promote states of affairs that are personal in some sense. For example, utilitarianism promotes pleasurable states of consciousness experienced by persons (though not exclusively), and perfectionism in most forms aims to promote the achievement of excellence and states of character of persons.

15 See Scheffler (1988: 1).

16 T. M. Scanlon speaks of the "phenomenological" accuracy of contractualism's depiction of morality (1998: 155).

17 See for example, Hare (1981: 154) on equal concern and respect, and ibid. (4–5) on the close relationship between Kant's categorical imperative and Bentham's principle of equal consideration. Of course the claim that utilitarianism exhibits equal respect for persons does not apply to those versions which see the good as the aggregate pleasures or interests of all sentient beings.

18 J. S. Mill, *Utilitarianism*, ch. 5, n.1, in Gray (1991: 199n). For a discussion of this point, see my "Utilitarianism, deontology, and the priority of right" (Freeman 1994).

19 Sidgwick (1981: 490).

20 R. Jay Wallace suggested to me the connection between the publicity of moral principles and their role as principles of practical reasoning. See also Christine Korsgaard, who sees the public nature of reasons as implying they are "conversational" too (2003: 55).

21 Perhaps consequentialist morality requires that *no one* has knowledge of its foundations or basic principles, a position that might solve the problem of unequal respect. But it raises further questions about the status of a conception whose basic justification everyone must be ignorant of. Is it a moral conception at all if its basic principles have no role in practical reasoning and are not appealed to in order to resolve moral issues?

22 T. M. Scanlon has said that one reason he calls his account 'contractualist' is that it calls attention to the idea of justifiability to others, and holds "that this is something we have reason to value in itself and that is presupposed by relations with others that we have reason to value" (2003: 73).

23 It may be that either of these considerations is sufficient to warrant pursuing the idea of a contractual basis for interpersonal morality. Some contractarians think so (for example, Scanlon accepts the first consideration but seemingly not the second.) I will discuss both approaches to moral contractarianism, and will not regard either as sufficient by itself.

24 See Rawls (1971: sect. 87) on this.

25 See here Rawls's account of reasonable judgment, as judgments that are "supported by the preponderance of reasons specified by the principles of right and justice issuing from a procedure that correctly formulates the principles of practical reason in union with appropriate conceptions of society and person" (1993: 111).

26 Thomas Nagel (1979: 67–8) distinguishes interpersonal justification to a person from justification to the world at large.

27 Here perhaps Scanlon does not see this second assumption as necessary to his contractualism.

28 Consequentialists such as G. E. Moore (1982: 97–105) and modern followers (e.g. Donald Regan) have doubted that the idea of 'a person's good' makes sense. Contrast Sidgwick, who held that a principle of individual prudence is a "philosophical intuition" of practical reason.

29 See here, Rawls (1971: ch. 7), on 'goodness as rationality' and the accounts of deliberative rationality and the Aristotelian principle that underlie this sketch of a person's good.

30 In "Of the Original Contract" Hume says, responding to Locke's "Whig view," that there is no point in appealing to a contractual agreement to support political obligations of allegiance to government. For it can always be asked, why should we keep our promise or agreement to respect law and political authority? The only sensible way to explain both duties of allegiance and of fidelity to promises, Hume says, is public utility. Joseph Raz (1994: 355–69) makes a similar argument (without appealing to utility). See also Pettit (1993: 297–307), discussed in note 32.

31 Since Joseph Raz's account (as I understand it) is not consequentialist in the sense used here the reply in this paragraph does not respond to his version of the Humean criticism, though my remarks in the next two paragraphs may be still be relevant.

32 Philip Pettit puts the objection this way: "How can we treat the hypothetical property (of agreement) as the criterion of rightness when that property is grounded, as it were, in the categorical property? How can we avoid the conclusion that the real, right-making property is the categorical one and that what the contractual connection does is draw attention to the appeal of that property? . . . Suppose that the contractors argue for a basic structure on the grounds that it best promotes liberty. In that case, so this argument goes, the real right-making property is the categorical one of maximizing the expectation of liberty" (1993: 297–307).

A problem with this suggestion is that for contractarians the "right-making property" is not "maximizing the expectation of liberty" (whether aggregate or equal liberty), or any other state of affairs. Contractarians presume that each contracting party agrees to principles in part to secure an interest in his or her *own* liberty (as opposed to an interest in the sum of liberty). But this is not the right-making property, for what makes a principle right or just is not that it advances only your or my interests in liberty. Nor is the right-making property even simply that a principle advances each person's interest in liberty. Rather, what makes principles just is that they *secure each person's liberty in a way that is reasonable or fair to everyone*. This is the right making property (if anything is) with respect to principles of justice. It is a reason (or property) that is not discernible from the point of view of the parties, but only from the point of view of you and me when we deliberate on the principles that could be agreed to by hypothetical agents from a position of equality. The ultimate point of appealing to unanimous consent to decide principles of justice is that it provides an indispensable procedure for deliberating and deciding on the basic principles needed to secure each person's interests in her liberty in a way that is fair to others. In so far as principles could be justified and agreed to among hypothetically situated individuals, then they secure each person's liberty in a way that is fair to everyone, and therefore are just. Reference to general agreement is necessary in this definition and explication of justice. (Cf. Rawls: "Explication is elimination," in his 1971: 95.)

33 See here Scanlon's claim (1998: 160) that morality involves very general requirements governing the reasons we can accept, and concerns as much *how* we should take these reasons into account as it concerns the reasons themselves.

34 Cf. Rawls (1993: 119).

35 See Rawls (1971: 58); Scanlon (1998: 106). My thoughts on moral contractarianism have been shaped by Rawls's and Scanlon's works. I have also learned from Rahul Kumar's papers on contractualism, and benefited from very detailed comments by R. Jay Wallace. I am also grateful for suggestions by James Dreier, and comments by audiences at Northwestern, University of Illinois, Bowling Green State University, US Naval Academy, and a conference on Contractarianism and Law at the University of Pennsylvania Law School.

References

Freeman, S. (1994). "Utilitarianism, deontology, and the priority of right." *Philosophy and Public Affairs*, 23 (Fall): 313–49.

Gauthier, D. (1986). *Morals by Agreement*. Oxford: Oxford University Press.

Gray, J. (ed.) (1991). *On Liberty and Other Essays*. Oxford: Oxford University Press.

Hare, R. M. (1981). *Moral Thinking*. Oxford: Oxford University Press.

Harman, G. (1977). *The Nature of Morality*. Oxford: Oxford University Press.

Hobbes, T. (1651/1991). *Leviathan*, ed. R. Tuck. Cambridge: Cambridge University Press.

Hume, D. (1978). *A Treatise of Human Nature*. Oxford: Oxford University Press.

Korsgaard, C. (2003). "Internalism and the Sources of Normativity: An Interview with Christine M. Korsgaard." In Herlinde Pauer-Studer (ed.), *Constructions of Practical Reason: Interviews on Moral and Political Philosophy*. Stanford, Calif.: Stanford University Press.

Moore, G. E. (1982[1903]). *Principia Ethica*. Cambridge: Cambridge University Press.

Nagel, T. (1979). "War and massacre." In Nagel, *Mortal Questions*. Cambridge: Cambridge University Press.

Pettit, P. (1993). *The Common Mind: An Essay on Psychology, Society and Politics*. New York: Oxford University Press.

Rawls, J. (1971). *A Theory of Justice*. Oxford: Oxford University Press.

Rawls, J. (1993). *Political Liberalism*. New York: Columbia University Press.

Raz, J. (1994). "Government by consent." In Raz, *Ethics in the Public Domain*. Oxford: Oxford University Press.

Scanlon, T. M. (1998). *What We Owe To Each Other*. Cambridge, Mass.: Harvard University Press.

Scanlon, T. M. (2003). "Thomas M. Scanlon: contractualism and what we owe to each other." In Herlinde Pauer-Studer (ed.), *Constructions of Practical Reason: Interviews on Moral and Political Philosophy*. Stanford, Calif.: Stanford University Press.

Scheffler, S. (1988). "Introduction." In Scheffler (ed.), *Consequentialism and its Critics*. Oxford: Oxford University Press.

Sidgwick, H. (1981). *The Methods of Ethics*. 7th edn. Indianapolis: Hackett.

CHAPTER FIVE

Can Contract Theory Ground Morality?

Philip Pettit

Introduction

The contractualist theory of morality that has recently been developed by T. M. Scanlon (1982, 1998), building on the work of John Rawls (1971, 1993), represents a new departure in ethical thought, and an advance on pre-existing ways of thinking. True, it has some structural affinity with the mutual-advantage theory of morality developed by David Gauthier (1986), and some substantive resemblance to the discourse ethics associated with Jürgen Habermas (1990). But it is not clear how deep these go. In any case I shall concentrate on Scanlon's version of contractualism in this chapter.

Although it is original and imaginative, I do not think that contractualism succeeds, at least not in its own terms. More particularly, I do not think that it succeeds in displacing consequentialism as a grounding theory of moral rightness. The goal of displacing consequentialism in that role goes back to Scanlon's (1982) first statement of the doctrine, and it is a centerpiece of the Rawlsian theory of justice on which he builds. I am a consequentialist myself, and it may not be surprising that I take issue with contractualism at this point (Pettit 1991, 1997). But though I take issue there, I still think that the doctrine is of immense interest and I hope that this will come through in what follows.

This chapter is in three sections. In the first I offer a characterization of contractualism, explaining along the way that under this representation it is proof against two more or less obvious consequentialist objections. In the second section I argue that even when characterized in this manner, however, there remains an attractive and plausible way of taking contractualism that would make it consistent with consequentialism; this would cast it as a theory of the relatively right – the right relative to a practice – rather than the absolutely right. And then in the third section I show that even if this relativized way of taking it is rejected, as Scanlon himself would certainly reject it, there is a second way in which contractualism can in principle be rendered consistent with consequentialism; it may be cast as a partial rather than a complete theory of the absolutely right. Under neither of these ways of taking the doctrine would contractualism ground morality – not at least in every relevant sense – but under each it would retain a significant place in moral theory.

The Characterization of Contractualism

The main points in contractualist doctrine are the following (Pettit 2000b):

1   The central sense of 'right' and 'wrong' derives from what we owe to others, and it is this interpersonal sense that is explicated in contractualism. It contrasts with the intrapersonal sense associated with talk of what I owe to myself and the impersonal sense associated with talk of how to improve the world or society (Scanlon 1998: 6).

2   'Wrong' is the primary moral predicate; 'right' is defined simply as 'not wrong'. That an option is right will mean that it is permitted, not that it is mandatory, though of course a right option will be mandatory in the special event that it is the only option permitted – the only option that is not wrong.

3   An action is wrong in the central, interpersonal sense just in case it is disallowed by principles for the regulation of conduct that no one could reasonably reject as part of an informed, unforced agreement with others (Scanlon 1998: 153, 202); it is wrong, intuitively, just so far as it is unjustifiable from the point of view of others – just so far as it is exposed to reasonable complaint on the part of others (ibid. 229).

4   This is a contractualist account of wrongness and rightness, because a principle will be compelling under Scanlon's approach, and will serve to justify actions, if and only if no one could reasonably reject it as a general principle of cooperation: if and only if it is, in that sense, contractually irresistible (ibid. 197).

5   There is no simple algorithm for deciding which principles could not be reasonably rejected. The matter can only be determined by reflection on the sorts of personal reasons – reasons are taken to form a more or less autonomous, cognitively accessible domain (ibid. ch. 1) – to which we would give relevance and weight in thinking about what cooperative life with others requires (ibid. 225, 246).

6   An action that is wrong and unjustifiable to someone will always be unjustifiable for a reason – because he or she finds it unfair, or unkind, or insensitive, or whatever. But the wrongness is not to be equated with any such lower-order basis of unjustifiability; it is just the higher-order property of being, on whatever basis, unjustifiable (ibid. 5, 155–6).

7   The wrongness of an action, understood in this way, explains why wrong actions have an aspect under which they are inherently unattractive. We shrink from acting in a way that is unjustifiable in the light of others' claims quite independently of shrinking – as we do also shrink – from doing something that

has an unjustifiablity-producing feature: doing something that is unfair or insensitive or whatever (ibid. 11).

8 This is the primary reason, so it is said, why the contractualist theory of rightness and wrongness is persuasive. As Scanlon puts it: "I myself accept contractualism largely because the account it offers of moral motivation is phenomenologically more accurate than any other I know of" (ibid. 187; cf. 153, 163).

9 A second reason that allegedly supports such contractualism, however, is that avoiding the unjustifiable in Scanlon's sense necessarily involves "respecting the value of human (rational) life" (ibid. 106). If people avoid the unjustifiable in this sense then they will treat one another in a way that acknowledges their individual capacities for assessing and acting on reasons. By doing right, then, they will also do good: they will give rise to a palpably desirable form of community.

The notion at the centre of this theory is that of unjustifiability to others. The theory identifies the central property of wrongness – the "normative kind" (ibid. 12) that such wrongness constitutes – with the property of being unjustifiable in that sense. Unjustifiability to others means unjustifiability-to-any-other-individual, not unjustifiability-to-others-generally. That is why the doctrine can be said to equate what is wrong with what is open to reasonable complaint on the part of any other. As Scanlon himself says: "The Complaint Model calls attention to a central feature of contractualism that I would not want to give up: its insistence that the justifiability of a moral principle depends only on various *individuals'* reasons for objecting to that principle and alternatives to it" (ibid. 229).

The striking novelty in the contractualist approach, so understood, is that it switches the traditionally recognized priority of rightness and justifiability, or indeed wrongness and unjustifiability (Scanlon 2003: 183–7). Everyone will agree that in some sense of 'justifiable' any right action will be justifiable so far as it is right or because it is right. But contractualists hold that there is an interpersonal sense of justification to others such that the reverse can also be true. An action can be right because it is justifiable to others; it is right because it is allowed under the principles for regulating behaviour that no one could reasonably reject – because it is not exposed to any reasonable complaint on the part of others.

There are two important ambiguities to resolve, however, in the formulation offered of contractualism. It is important to resolve these, because otherwise the approach will seem to be vulnerable to two fairly straightforward consequentialist objections.

First objection, first ambiguity

The first objection that may be made to the doctrine is premised on the assumption that the reasons that are supposed to move contractors in rejecting or not rejecting a principle are impersonal values such as justice or kindness or happiness or whatever. The objection is that if contractors find a principle unrejectable – and therefore the actions it disallows wrong – because of such values, then what ultimately makes the principle unrejectable is that it satisfies those values. This means, in a consequentialist version of what satisfaction of values requires, that the principle has its unrejectable status because it maximizes expected neutral value.

Suppose, for example, that contractors were moved only by considerations to do with what was for the maximization of happiness overall; suppose they were consequentialists of a utilitarian stamp. In that case, so the objection goes, the right would be determined for them by reference to the utilitarian criterion. But if, by their lights, the right just was whatever maximized happiness overall, then why should contractualism suggest that it was determined rather by reference to what they, the utilitarian contractors, found reasonably unrejectable? The utilitarian criterion of right would surely be basic, the contractualist derived.

A number of authors, myself included, took contractualism under earlier formulations to collapse in this manner into an independent – most plausibly, a consequentialist – theory of rightness (Pettit 1993: 302; 1997). But though not everyone agrees (Blackburn 1999; McGinn 1999; see too Stratton-Lake 2003), I think that Scanlon's 1998 book *What We Owe To Each Other* makes it clear that his doctrine can avoid that quick collapse.

Scanlon is explicit in that book that the reasons that are to count with people in identifying unrejectable principles are "personal" reasons (1998: 219) or "agent-relative" reasons (Ridge 2001); reasons, in a phrase he takes from Allan Gibbard, that you have "on your own behalf" (Scanlon 2003: 185). As he explicitly says, "impersonal values do not provide, in themselves, reason for rejecting principles of right and wrong" (1998: 222).

Under this construal of contractualism, you or I might reasonably reject a principle for the personal reason that it would serve our interests or projects or friends badly. And while you or I may not reasonably reject a principle for an impersonal reason, we might do so on a personal basis that is tied indirectly to the impersonal reasons that weigh with us. Seeing the principle as offending against a certain strongly held impersonal value – seeing it, say, as licensing cruelty to animals – I might reasonably reject it because of the personal affront or difficulty associated with having to live with the flouting of that value: having to live as if animal pain did not concern me. "If the pain of an animal is something we have strong reason to prevent, then we have good reason to reject a principle that would prevent us from acting on this reason, by requiring us to give animal suffering no more weight than personal inconvenience as a factor affecting our obligations" (Scanlon 1998: 222).

Contractualist principles are selected for not activating any personal reasons for complaint, by this account, not for promoting the expected realization of impersonal values, or any condition of that kind. They will have to pass the hurdle of my reasonable complaint, the hurdle of your reasonable complaint, the hurdle of yet another person's, and so on. But they may do this without having any profile in the space of impersonal values. There need be nothing that characterizes them in our ways of actively representing them over and beyond the fact of that they surmount those personal-level tests.

This feature of contractualism explains why there is no room for the utilitarian possibility considered earlier. Were contractors to be moved only by considerations of happiness then, plausibly, the complaints they made would all bear on the failure of certain principles to take account of the relatively low level of happiness accruing to them or theirs. The complaints would have a personal character, with each speaking from his or her own point of view; they would not be complaints about the failure of the principles to guarantee a utilitarian optimum.

What makes an action wrong in the sense that Scanlon targets, then, is the fact that it flouts a principle for regulating behavior that no one finds good personal reason to reject – that no one finds a good reason to complain about. What makes it wrong, in other words, is that someone is bound to have a reason to complain about it, given that it flouts such a principle. Being personal in character, the reasonable complaints that show an action to be wrong in this way may be various, being backed here on this basis, there on that. What matters to the action's being wrong – what makes the action wrong (Stratton-Lake 2003) – is not the diverse bases behind the complaints but just the simple fact that the complaints can be reasonably made. Being wrong involves being such as to occasion reasonable complaint from one or another person, on one or another personal basis. Being right involves being immune to that sort of complaint: being justifiable in that sense to others.

Second objection, second ambiguity

In the presentation of contractualism above, it is said that an action is wrong in the central, interpersonal sense just in case it is disallowed by principles for the regulation of conduct that no one could reasonably reject as part of an informed, unforced agreement with others. A very natural way of taking that claim allows of the following explication:

An action is wrong in a situation R (for Real-world) just in case it is disallowed by principles for the regulation of conduct that no one could reasonably reject in a situation I (for Ideal-world) of informed, unforced agreement with others about how to behave in I.

This is a natural way of taking contractualism, since many of Scanlon's own formulations suggest something on these lines, and none of them rules it out. He says, for example: "An act is wrong if its performance under the circumstances would be disallowed by any set of principles for the general regulation of behavior that no one could reasonably reject as a basis for informed, unforced general agreement" (1998: 153).

To speak of the principles that no one could reasonably reject as a basis for informed, unforced general agreement is very strongly to suggest that the ideal conditions of informed, unforced agreement are relevant, not just when people are given the chance to reject a principle, but also when they implement them in their own behavior. The suggestion is that the circumstances for which the principles are to be designed, as well as the circumstances in which they are examined and selected, are ones where informed, unforced agreement – for short, cooperation – rules.

Scanlon is not alone in offering a formulation which suggests that contractualism be understood in this ideal-world way. Samuel Freeman writes in explication of Scanlon's approach, for example:

Imagine a community of free and informed agents, each of whom is conscientious, sincere and motivated by a desire to justify their actions, ends and expectations to everyone else similarly motivated. Morality is the set of public norms which such idealized persons would jointly affirm and commit to. (1998: 664)

If contractualism is taken in this way, then it is construed in a manner that makes it akin to rule-consequentialism and, on some interpretations, Kantianism. Those doctrines hold that we need to identify certain privileged rules or maxims before we can tell whether an action is right or wrong. We identify in the one case the rules such that it would be for the best overall if people were generally to internalize them or act on them or whatever (Hooker 2000); in the other the maxims such that everyone can treat them – treat them simultaneously – as general laws: the maxims satisfied by everyone in the kingdom of ends. We then say that an action is wrong – wrong in the actual, non-ideal world – if it flouts one of those ideal rules, or one of those ideal maxims, right if it does not do so.

But there is a long-standing tradition, at least within consequentialist circles, of criticizing approaches of this kind to the characterization of right and wrong action. The criticism is that while acting on a certain rule or maxim may be for the best in a world of total compliance with those principles – a world like the kingdom of ends – it need not be for the best in a world where not everyone complies: a world of merely partial compliance. It may amount in that world to a waste of effort, or it may be downright counterproductive. Let no one else do anything for the environment, for example, and it is not clear that I achieve anything other than wasted effort by making my lone attempts to be ecologically sound. Let some other people be willing to impose violence on their fellows and my eschewal of violence, admirable though it would be in the kingdom of ends, may be actively counterproductive, ensuring that there is more violence overall, not less.

The point here is quite general. The theory of the second best, as developed by economists, tells us roughly that if the fulfillment of a certain number of conditions is for the (first) best, and one or more of those conditions fails, there is no reason to think that it will be for the (second) best to have as many as possible of the other conditions fulfilled (Brennan 1993: 128; Goodin 1995). The theory implies that if everyone's complying with certain principles is for the (first) best, and one or more people fail to comply, then there is no reason to think that it will be for the (second) best that as many as possible – let alone one person on their own – should comply.

Let contractualism be understood in the idealized way characterized, and it will be open to a similar line of criticism, as indeed I have argued elsewhere (Pettit 2000a). But while I think that the idealized mode of interpretation is natural in some respects, I am now persuaded that it is not the construal intended by Scanlon. What he has in mind, I think, is better rendered in a formula that exchanges the second reference to situation I for a reference – a second reference – to situation R (Scanlon 1982: 111).

An action is wrong in a situation R just in case it is disallowed by principles for the regulation of conduct that no one could reasonably reject in a situation I of informed, unforced agreement with others about how to behave in R.

The shift here is very small but it is of great significance (cf. Smith 1994). The real-world situation may vary greatly. At one highly unlikely extreme it may involve circumstances where others display informed, unforced cooperation and comply with the principles suited to ideal circumstances. But it is much more likely to involve some others defecting, whether out of ignorance, weakness, or malice, and of course it is much more likely to be a situation where cooperation is going to require a degree of force or coercion. This being the case, the people in situation I will have to agree, not just about principles that are to rule in situations of ideal cooperation, but also about the principles that are to apply in situations where some or even all others fail to comply fully with ideal principles.

Why do I say that Scanlon adopts this real-world reading of contractualism, rather than the ideal-world version? Basically, because his comments on cases of partial compliance, if not his formulations of abstract claims (but see Scanlon 1982: 111), make clear that this is the right interpretation.

Consider what he says about the punishment of the non-compliant, for example. He suggests that the possibility of defection will be something that well-intentioned cooperators may be able to foresee, recognizing that none of them is immune to temptation and may later fall away. And so he argues that the principles that none of them is in a position to reject with reason – not from the *ex ante* point of view of intending to agree with others on principles for the regulation of behavior (Scanlon 2003: 182) – may include principles governing how they should be punished for various *ex post* failures to stick with those principles. When punished for an offence, he says, "such a person has no legitimate complaint against having this penalty inflicted" (1998: 265). The reason, presumably, is that that person would be unable to complain reasonably about such treatment: no unrejectable principle would disallow it.

Or consider again what he says in an exchange where I had asked how the principle of mutual aid would apply in a case where only one donor appears from among the ranks of the rich; I did this, because of taking him to endorse the ideal-world interpretation (Pettit 2000a). Scanlon argues that provided the burden on that person is not too great, he or she should contribute in a measure that makes up for the shortfall in the contributions of other, equally rich people:

Perhaps the most equitable principle would require these burdens to be shared in some way by all of those who are in a position to contribute. But even if this is so, it does not follow that a person who is in a position to alleviate someone's suffering is released from any obligation to do so if others refuse to share this burden. It might be reasonable to reject a principle requiring one to provide assistance when doing so would be a great burden, but this does not seem to be the case in Pettit's example. (2000: 237)

Consider, finally, a comment that Scanlon makes on a somewhat different case of non-compliance with ideal principles, where the focus is not on when cooperators may be entitled to punish defectors, nor on when they may be obliged to make up for the failure of defectors to do good, but on when they may equally be obliged to do ill – or what would otherwise be ill – in order to compensate for the evil done by defectors. He argues that it may be right to kill the innocent in order to reduce the number of overall deaths in prospect, and presumably to do this even when certain defectors would otherwise be responsible for the deaths that occur. It may be right to extend in this way, he says, a principle that would support saving a larger rather than a smaller number of people (1998: 234).

> This extension is necessary not only to handle cases involving the potential death of millions, but also to deal with more modest cases, such as the famous trolley problem, in which it is permissible to switch the trolley, thus killing one instead of letting five die. (Scanlon 2000: 238)

These comments make it plain that Scanlon intends his contractualist theory of the right to be a theory that is liable to pick out a different action as right, depending on the circumstances prevailing in the real world; or at least he intends it to do this within intuitive limits on how fine-tuned to circumstances principles may be (1998: 205). He does not envisage it as an ideal-world theory according to which the right action in any circumstance is the action that is identified as right in ideal circumstances of cooperation. And so he is not open to the consequentialist objection that where that action might have been for the best in the ideal world, it is likely to occasion very undesirable consequences in real-world situations: in particular, consequences so undesirable as to make the theory counterintuitive.

A Theory of the Absolutely Right or the Relatively Right?

Two readings of contractualism

I mentioned earlier that Scanlon draws a distinction between different senses of 'right' and 'wrong', in particular between the sense of those words that applies in certain interpersonal contexts and the senses that apply when we are considering what someone should do for himself or herself, or what they should do in promoting impersonal causes. Let us put aside the other senses of 'right' and 'wrong' and concentrate on the sense that he targets.

If we do this, we can still find a further distinction between two ways in which 'right' and 'wrong' may be used. One is the absolute sense, as I call it, the other the relative sense: specifically, a sense of the terms that is relativized to one or another practice. The absolute sense of the terms is that which we invoke in deeming something right or wrong, without qualification; right or wrong, period. We employ a relative sense of 'right' and 'wrong', by contrast, when we speak of what is legally right or wrong, or what is right and wrong according to etiquette. In each case we take a certain practice as given – the law or etiquette – and we use 'right' to designate what accords with the rules of the practice, 'wrong' to denote anything that is in breach of them. What is right in this sense will be obligatory if the alternatives are all wrong and it will be permissible but not obligatory if some alternatives are right too.

Taking 'right' and 'wrong' in the way projected in the contractualist formula, the next question that arises is whether they can be understood in either of these ways. There is little doubt but that Scanlon means them to be understood in the absolute manner, for he never suggests – putting aside the other senses of the terms – that what is right according to the contractualist formula might not be right, period. He invariably takes the contractually right and wrong to represent the bottom line, as it were, in determining what is right and wrong overall.

But it remains possible, nonetheless, to read contractualism in a more modest way, as identifying a certain practice and then as presenting a formula for determining what is practice-dependently right and wrong, not what is right and wrong, period. Scanlon himself takes the interpersonal sense of 'right' and 'wrong' to be associated with "a system of co-deliberation" and he says that the moral criticism that such terms may mediate is always addressed to another "as a fellow participant in a system of co-deliberation" (1998: 268). The moral reasoning that may underlie such criticism, as he describes it, looks like an attempt to work out the rules implicit in the practice of co-deliberation and to identify what is right and what is wrong, according to those rules. He writes: "moral reasoning is an attempt to work out principles that each of us could be asked to employ as a basis for deliberation and accept as a basis of criticism."

In further support of this practice-relative reading of contractualism, it may also be worth mentioning that in another context Scanlon suggests that as the contractualist formula seeks to explicate what is right-in-interpersonal-practice, as we might put it, there is also a case for seeking out what is right-in-intrapersonal-practice: that is, what is right according to the system of prudential deliberation with myself across time. He writes:

> The decisions we make at earlier stages of life have obvious consequences for the options we will have later. So the question arises of "what we owe" to ourselves at other times. . . . I trust it is clear how this might lead to a structure quite similar to the one I have defended in the case of interpersonal morality. (2003: 188–9)

How should we think of the associated interpersonal practice, if we construe contractualism as a more or less modest attempt to identify what is right and wrong according to the practice? One way might be as the practice of deliberative exchange in which we engage when we seek to influence one another but only so far as we can present reasons that others should endorse, by their own lights, and do in fact come to endorse; in particular, only so far as we can do this without reducing the options that others face – without resorting, for example, to threat and coercion.

I have argued elsewhere for the centrality of deliberative exchange in social life. Michael Smith and I sum up the characterization of that practice as follows (Pettit and Smith 2004; see also Pettit 2001a: ch. 4). Deliberative exchange occurs just so far as:

- the parties sincerely communicate their beliefs, openly seeking to get one another to recognize and share them;
- the communication is intended as an epistemic exploration of one another's reasons for believing or doing various things, individually, reciprocally, or collectively;
- there are no vitiators present, so that any avowals of attitude – any commitments – are inescapable under the rules of the practice: only a later change of circumstances can excuse non-compliance.

This sort of practice has associated rules of participation – rules that must be respected for the practice to occur – and rules of compliance: rules governing how people should behave in the light of their communication within deliberative exchange. Intuitively, for example, the rules of participation outlaw force, manipulation, deception, coercion, and intimidation in the practice of deliberation with others, and the rules of compliance outlaw failures to live up to commitments made within exchange with others, where circumstances are as envisaged at the time when the commitments were made.

Although Smith and I did not make this move, it is also reasonable to suppose that the practice of deliberative exchange dictates rules governing how we should respond to failures on the part of others to conform to what we take to be the relevant rules. Such regulative rules, as we may call them, would spell out the responses that are consistent with keeping the possibility of a return to deliberative exchange open. They might require that others are given a chance to explain themselves, for example, or the chance to apologize, before any punishment is imposed. And they might outlaw vengeful responses of punishment, but allow responses of a more measured kind.

Assuming that a practice of this kind is in operation among people, we might cast contractualism as an attempt to work out and systematize the relevant rules of deliberative participation, compliance, and regulation. We might think of it as a project of explicating, not what is right and wrong period, but what is deliberatively right and deliberatively wrong, where 'deliberatively' operates like 'legally' in talk of legally right and legally wrong. On this construal, the contractualist formula can be seen as a nice way of summing up the sorts of rules that bind us, by our own intuitions, so far as we are engaged in deliberative exchange with others.

As I said earlier, I do not think that Scanlon ever thinks of his contractualism in this relativized and modest fashion. He takes it, more radically, to offer us a theory of the absolutely rather than the relatively right – though the absolutely right only in the interpersonal sense of the term. He takes it, in answer to the title question of this chapter, to ground moral theory, not just to have the derivative place within it that the relativized account would offer. But I do believe that the relativized construal points us toward quite an interesting version of contractualist doctrine.

There are three reasons for thinking this. The first is that the relativized construal represents contractualism as the explication of a significant human practice, not just a practice of passing interest; the second that it represents it in a way that makes it consistent with consequentialism; and the third that it represents it in a way that compares well with Scanlon's own representation.

An explication of a significant practice

One reason for taking the relativized construal of contractualism to be interesting is that deliberative exchange lies at the centre of human life and interaction. This appears in the fact that, short of going straight to threat and intimidation, I can hardly open my mouth in addressing another without activating an assumption – and so without having to acquiesce in the assumption – that I am bent on deliberative exchange with my addressees. Just by making an innocuous remark or asking an ingenuous question I will activate the assumption that I am meaning to communicate sincerely, in a spirit of exploring reasons, and without relying on any inhibiting, intimidating or other vitiating effect (Pettit and Smith 2004).

Whatever my actual intentions, then – and these may be to deceive or manipulate or whatever – I can hardly address others without having to accept that I am subject to the jurisdiction of deliberative exchange. I will have to accept, for example, that should I deviate I will be judged according to the rules of deliberative practice and that I will not be able to declare those rules irrelevant when they are invoked in condemnation of my behavior. Any alleged breach of the rules in my mode of participation, in my compliance with commitments undertaken, or in the way I respond regulatively to breaches on the part of others, will be interrogated for whether it is in tune with deliberative practice and will be indicted if it is not. And I will not be able to claim indifference to the indictment, so far as I will have acquiesced earlier in the presumption of intending deliberative exchange.

An explication consistent with consequentialism

Another reason for thinking that the relativized construal of contractualism is interesting is that it leaves open the possibility of a particularly plausible consequentialist accommodation (Pettit 2000a). Consequentialism is a theory of rightness according to which the right option in any choice – any choice of action or principle or motive or a mix of these (Pettit and Smith 2000) – is that which promotes impersonal value in whatever is taken to be the relevant sense: in a common version, that which maximizes expected impersonal value. The consequentialist accommodation that I have in mind would argue that the practice of deliberative exchange promotes impersonal value in a high degree and for that reason people should routinely immerse themselves within it.

Why might it be important, from a consequentialist perspective, that the practice of deliberative exchange prevail in human life? Because the world is a much better place, and we are a much more fulfilled species, for the fact that deliberation reigns amongst us, where indeed it does reign. That is to say, because people's generally conforming to the practice of deliberative exchange – like their generally conforming to the institution of friendship – has extremely beneficial consequences. This connects with the sort of consideration mentioned by Scanlon when he says that a reason for sticking to choices that resist reasonable complaint on the part of any other is that this necessarily involves "respecting the value of human (rational) life" (1998: 106). If people behave in deliberative or deliberation-friendly ways, so his thought goes, they will treat one another in a manner that acknowledges their individual capacities for assessing and acting on reasons. By doing right, as he construes what is right, they will also do good: they will give rise to a desirable form of community.

But once we construct Scanlon's insight in this way, then it appears that we can easily find a way toward a consequentialist accommodation. It is a long-established consequentialist observation that the best prospect of making choices which maximize expected impersonal value is associated with following decision-making procedures that are localized and restrictive (Railton 1984; Pettit and Brennan 1986). Since being a friend is inconsistent with calculating about each and every response that you make to a friend's overture, for example, and since friendship is a highly beneficial practice, the consequentialist is likely to think that in most circumstances people should simply conform without any further thought to the demands of friendship; in such circumstances, they should put themselves under the control of the institution of friendship – ultimately under their friends' control – confident in the belief that that is almost certainly for the best. Such people will not live and behave like friends because that is for the best: like everyone else, they will be moved by the natural inclinations that sustain friendships. Their recognition that behaving like a friend is for the best will explain, not their acting out of friendship, but rather their not seeking to eliminate or restrain their friendship-related inclinations. They act out of friendship with a clear, consequentialist conscience. But while that conscience monitors their behavior, it does not motor it (but see Scanlon 2000).

The model on which consequentialists are likely to think of friendship gives us a model on which they can also think of the practice of deliberative exchange. If Scanlon is right, then just as we have a natural inclination to favor friends, so we have a natural inclination to put ourselves in the right with others: to able to justify what we do in a way that should silence reasonable complaint. Just as consequentialists can argue, then, that the normal practice for people should be to give way to their inclinations of friendship, so their normal practice should be to allow their desire for such justifiability to others – such deliberative coexistence – to shape the ways in which they behave toward others in general. As consequentialists would want people to put themselves under the pilot of friendship in most relevant circumstances, so they would equally want them generally to put themselves under the pilot of deliberative exchange. Indeed, they are likely to think that the practice of deliberative exchange is much more important than friendship in this way, since it would be intuitively for the bad to allow the demands of one's friends to justify breaches of deliberative practice in one's dealing with others.

An explication that compares well with Scanlon's

The consequentialist accommodation suggested would leave intact a single sense of 'right' and 'wrong' – that is, absolute right and wrong – identifying this with the idea of maximizing expected impersonal value. It would argue that it may usually be right to do whatever turns out to be required under deliberative practice, as it would argue that it may usually be right to do whatever is required under the practice of friendship. It would argue indeed, as we just saw, that conformity to such practices should normally be quite automatic. But still consequentialism is going to allow that practice-relative requirements should indeed be flouted when, as it appears, abiding by them is not for the best overall. And so it would require that agents who engage in these practices should give themselves the right to review their behavior occasionally just to make sure that it is for the best; and that they should certainly review it in any instance where the red lights go on: where there are signs that by acting in a deliberatively proper way toward some, they may bring about bad consequences overall.

None of this seems outlandish, however, for it is entirely plausible that there are cases where the demands of deliberative exchange may have to be breached, however reluctantly, as there are cases where the demands of friendship will have to be breached. It is said that a friend will help you move an apartment, a good friend help you move a body; but this is a joke precisely because there are intuitive moral bounds on what can be asked in the name of friendship (Cocking and Kennett 2000). What is true of friendship is going to be true, though perhaps not so often, of deliberative exchange. Someone who absolutizes the demands of the practice – as we can take Scanlon's contractualism to do – will have to think that those demands carry even in some cases where this is not for the best overall, since otherwise the doctrine will collapse into consequentialism. And it is surely plausible in such cases to demur, as consequentialists will demur, and argue that no, this is where the demands of deliberative exchange run out.

The consequentialist picture compares favorably, I think, with Scanlon's own picture. It keeps a single sense of 'right' and 'wrong' in place and argues that the demands of practices such as friendship and deliberative exchange, like the demands of intrapersonal prudence and impersonal benevolence, are all important, but none definitive, in determining what is right and what is wrong. Acknowledging that there are clearly some cases where we judge of what is right without reference to interpersonal, deliberative demands, Scanlon asserts that there is no single sense of 'right' and 'wrong' and that we have to live with "the fragmentation of the moral" (1998: 171). We have to think of 'interpersonally right', 'intrapersonally right' and 'impersonally right' as terms that direct us to quite different properties, and properties that do not add up or balance in any further argument as to what we ought to do, period.

This fragmentation is justified by Scanlon on the grounds that the different senses of 'right' pick out a 'diverse set of values'. But he acknowledges that in determining what is interpersonally right, we often have to balance very different claims by different people, and presumably he would acknowledge that there is a similar diversity of claims or values relevant to determining what is intrapersonally or impersonally right in a given context (Wallace 2002). So why is the diversity in the one case allowed to argue for fragmentation, but in the other case not? Why in particular is this so, given the moral indeterminacy to which we become committed once we allow the word and concept 'right' to multiply into unadjudicably different terms?

It would make much more sense to allow, as consequentialism allows, that in making up our minds as to what we ought to do, 'right' refers to the option that we take to be what we ought to do: what we ought to do overall, abstracting from the variety of considerations we may have had to take into account in our reasoning. If we were to take this line, then we could think of the interpersonal considerations to which Scanlon draws attention as having a particular importance in determining what is right overall – this, because of the importance of deliberative exchange in human life – but we would not have to insulate them behind a proprietary sense of the word 'right', protecting them from comparison with the other considerations that will often also be relevant in determining what we ought to do.

To sum up, then, the difference between the two explications of contractualism rehearsed here turns on how it is to make room for the fact that considerations that are not of an interpersonal kind often move us in judging about what we ought to do: what, as we say, is right. The modest version that I like would put a single sense of 'right' in play – in my own view, it ought to do this with a consequentialist sense of 'right' – and argue that different sorts of considerations, interpersonal and otherwise, may be relevant to the judgment as to what is right in that overall sense. The radical version that Scanlon prefers would say that one sense of 'right' answers to the interpersonal considerations, other senses to other considerations, and that there is no further base from which we can adjudicate between the demands of these different senses of 'right': these different properties. But it is unclear why he feels obliged to go that way, since the diversity he invokes in explanation is not confined to this area. And given the moral indeterminacy that plural senses of 'right' occasion, it is unclear why he is willing to pay the high price of taking such a path.

A Complete or Partial Theory of the Right?

Let us suppose, however, that we go along with Scanlon and adopt his more radical reading of contractualism as a theory of what is absolutely right – right in the interpersonal sense of the term – not just right according to a practice. Does this mean that there is no room left for the possibility that it is consistent with consequentialism? I argue in this section that it does not. Were contractualism in this sense sound, it would still have to be construed so as to leave open the possibility that there is truth in consequentialism; it would call on a second front for a modest rather than a radical reading. The modest reading would construe it as a partial theory of the right and the wrong, the radical as a complete theory (cf. Pettit 2000b).

As we use the terms 'right' and 'wrong' in ordinary language, we load them with a variety of connotations. Plausibly, for example, we expect any option that deserves to be called 'right':

- to be an option that we desire or would desire in the absence of failures of will;
- to be an option that we would be prepared to prescribe for any agent, not just ourselves, in the situation on hand;
- to be an option that has rightness-making properties of a familiar kind, such as fairness or kindness or just being for the best;
- to be an option that virtuous agents might choose;
- and of course to be an option that we could justify to others, being able to answer any objections they might make.

Any philosophical theory as to what rightness is will seek to marshall such connotations (Jackson and Pettit 1995; Pettit 2001b). It must select out the allegedly crucial candidate or candidates and try to show that they on their own capture the essential character of rightness: they explain the "observed normative features," as Scanlon (1998: 12) puts it, of the property. Thus an 'impartial-spectator' theory will say that the right option in any choice is that which we, were we ideally situated, would want ourselves to perform in the situation in question. A theory like R. M. Hare's (1981) 'prescriptivism' will maintain that it is the option that we would be prepared to prescribe universally, recommending it for any arbitrary agent; the fact that Hare is a non-cognitivist about judgments of right makes for a complication that I shall ignore here. A consequentialist theory will hold that it is the option that best promotes neutral goods or values: say, fairness and kindness and happiness and so on (Pettit 1997). And a 'virtue-ethical' theory might declare that it is the option that would prove eligible for the virtuous agent. Each of these theories orders the ordinary connotations of the word 'right' in different ways: it gives axiomatic status to one or more connotations and – assuming it is not a revisionary doctrine – derives other plausible connotations as theorems.

The theories mentioned are all familiar stories about the nature of rightness and under the interpretation of contractualism as a theory of what is absolutely right, it constitutes a further story in this vein: a rival axiomatization of rightness and, more fundamentally, wrongness. Among the connotations of rightness, it privileges the linkage with justifiability – specifically, with justifiability to others in the sense characterized in the first section – and argues that all we know and need to know is that in the relevant interpersonal sense of the term, rightness is justifiability, justifiability rightness.

The fact that contractualism is a theory of rightness in this sense, however, is quite consistent with its not being a complete theory of rightness and, more specifically, with consequentialism supplying the complementary component required for a full theory. The point is best appreciated by considering the approach taken by Hare, with its particular connection to consequentialism.

Hare (1981) argues that we should think of the right as that which proves to be universally prescribable. I see an option as right just so far as I am willing to prescribe it for anyone in that situation; and this, no matter how I am positioned in the situation, and no matter how the action will impact on me. He axiomatizes the connotations of rightness, in other words, so that the second connotation on the little list given becomes the most prominent one. But though Hare embraces this prescriptivist approach as a theory of what rightness is, he goes on to argue that at another level it gives support to a preference-based utilitarianism – that is, a species of consequentialism.

He argues that if we think about whether a given action is universally prescribable, we must take account of the preferences of everyone affected; we have to be willing to prescribe that an arbitrary agent perform the action, after all, no matter what position we occupy. And he insists that if we do this, we are bound to find only those actions prescribable that maximize the expected preference-satisfaction of those involved (for a critique, see Pettit 1987). His idea is that the test of universal prescribability is a filter that will only let certain types of action through and that we can see, as a matter of a priori argument, that the only types that are going to pass through the filter are those that maximize expected preference-satisfaction. His prescriptivism is an upstream theory, as it were, and it gives support in this way to a downstream consequentialism: specifically, a downstream utilitarianism.

As it is with Hare, so it may be, for all we have seen, with the contractualist theory as to what constitutes rightness, or at least rightness in the interpersonal sense. Take the contractualist test of looking at the options that would survive reasonable complaint on anyone's part: the option that would not be disallowed under any principle for regulating behavior that no one could reasonably reject. Why can't we treat that test, on the model of how Hare treats his test, as a filter that we may expect to sift out options with a certain independent character: a character that makes them fit to survive reasonable complaint? And why then shouldn't we be open to the thought that as we survey the actions likely to survive reasonable complaint, we may find reason to think that they will have a certain consequentialist character?

The suggestion is not, notice, that there is a quick argument to this conclusion, as there might be under the first objection considered in the opening section. That objection was that the potential complainants we envisage will always base their complaints on considerations of impersonal value and that anything that survives those complaints, therefore, will do so by serving the cause of impersonal value: say, in the consequentialist formula, by maximizing the expected realization of such value. The response to that objection was that people are only allowed to complain about actions and principles on the basis of personal reasons – reasons that they hold on their own behalf.

But consistently with complainants only being allowed to invoke personal reasons in rejecting a principle for the general regulation of behavior, it may still be the case that the principles and actions that are going to be proof against reasonable complaints must have an independent character; that character would explain why precisely they are proof against complaint. And it may still be that the independent character that they have is of a consequentialist cast. In other words, it may be that from contractualism as an upstream theory we may hope to be able to derive a downstream consequentialism.

There is good reason to think that those actions that receive a contractualist blessing must indeed have an independent character, though no ready argument for why that character must be consequentialist. Consider the contrast between the contractualist formula and the majoritarian formula – as it happens, an objectionable one – according to which an action is right if and only if it has majority support among those in the society where it occurs. It is clearly possible for just about any type of action to pass the majoritarian test, given the assumption that there's naught so queer as folk, in the old Yorkshire saying, and that there's no saying in advance where the folk may go. Thus it may be that the only commonality to be found in the various actions that satisfy the majoritarian formula will be that, well, they satisfy the formula. Their each being endorsed by the majority may be the only property that they possess in common. There may be no character that they have, independent of that property.

Might something similar be true of the options that pass the contractualist test? Surely not. What is required of those options is not just that they should happen to escape complaint as a matter of fact, but that they should be proof against complaint, in particular reasonable complaint. But how could they be proof against reasonable complaint without their being complaint-proof in virtue of their inherent nature? After all, there must be something about the options, some independent character, in virtue of which no one can raise a reasonable complaint against them.

Won't that independent character, then, be the ultimate ground or explanation of their being right options to choose? Won't it be a property that unites right options at a more basic level than that at which they display contractual, counterfactual unity: the unity associated with the fact that no one could reasonably object to them? The word 'right' may be used of those option-types because of their contractual unity – it may be, for all we have said, that this is what guides ordinary speakers in the use of the term – but it will still be the case that contractualism is not the whole story about rightness. A full understanding of this normative kind will force us beyond the limits of contractualist theory, as Hare would have argued that a full understanding of rightness forces us beyond the bounds of prescriptivist theory.

Just to illustrate the point, suppose that ordinary people were like the contractors we imagined in the first section, being disposed to treat as reasonable all and only complaints that this or that principle, this or that option-type, would reduce the complainant to a relatively low level of happiness. People would not think of the principles they were reasonably disposed to reject in any common, impersonal terms, as utilitarians might do; they would each make their complaints on a personal, particularistic basis. But still, the principles or options that prove immune to their diverse, personal complaints would prove immune in virtue of an independent character; it is that character that would explain why they and they only enjoy such immunity. Can we say anything about that character? We certainly can. On the supposition with which we are working, the complaint-proof principles and option-types would have in common the fact of ensuring a certain relative level of happiness for the worst off in the population: a level that would silence complaint even from those in that quarter. Did people in that society not recognize this feature of the options regarded as right amongst them – were they sensitive only to the contractualist truth that obtains in the scenario imagined – then there would be something important that they were missing in their understanding of rightness.

Does this line of reasoning establish definitively, then, that contractualism is at best a partial theory of rightness? Does it demonstrate that contractualism calls or at least allows for supplementation by a theory – perhaps a downstream consequentialism, perhaps a downstream non-consequentialism – that identifies the independent character of rightness? Not quite.

Contractualists might say in response that while there is always going to be an explanation as to why any particular category of option, A, is complaint-proof – it will consist in the character of the A-option in question – there need not be any general explanation as to why options in categories A, B, C . . . are complaint-proof. There may be no independent pattern in the different categories of option, and the associated principles, that pass the contractualist filter. The A option-type may prove complaint-proof because of having an independent a-character, the B-type because of having an independent b-character, and so on. Yet there need be nothing in common to those characters: nothing binding them into a pattern (cf. Jackson et al. 1999).

This response cannot be right, however. Presumably it is by thinking about the possible realization of this or that option-type, independently characterized, that you or I or a third party is put in a position to determine, however fallibly, that no one could reasonably object to it: the type is such that we can envisage no objection that would count as reasonable. But this means that in principle we should be capable of reviewing the various option-types relevant and of fixing on the character shared by those types to which we can imagine no reasonable objection. The character shared may be disjunctive, of course, if there really is nothing in common between the feature that makes one option-type right and the features that make others right. But that disjunctive character won't matter so long as there is only a finite number of suitably distinct option-types on offer, as will presumably always be the case. The disjunction that tells us that right option-types are of an a-character, a b-character . . . or an n-character, up to finite 'n', will still be informative. It will still represent a way of understanding the normative kind associated with the predicate 'right' that increases the understanding available from the contractualist formula alone – assuming, as we have been doing in this secton, that that formula is sound.

What sort of understanding will this independent, possibly disjunctive characterization of right option-types provide? It will give us an insight into the substantial "suchness" that we are directed to when we are told that an option-type is right if it is *such* that no one could reasonably object to anyone else's enacting it. There may be no substantial suchness shared by all the measures that are such as to attact or to have attracted majority support, given people vote in any old way. But there is bound to be a substantial suchness shared by those option-types that are such that no one could reasonably complain about them. It is going to be that suchness, that inherent character, that explains why they resist *reasonable* complaint. It is going to be that suchness that unites right option-types in themselves, explaining the unity that they have in relation to us: the unity which consists in the fact they resist reasonable complaint.

When asked about why a given type of option is right by contractualist lights, of course, we will not give a disjunctive characterization of right options in response; we will provide the characterization appropriate to the relevant disjunct, pointing to the a-character for the A option-type, the b-character for the B option-type, and so on. But that is not because the disjunctive character is irrelevant in the general characterization of rightness; it is only because, when a question is raised about any particular case, the better, more informative explanation will naturally take us to the disjunct that applies there.

Assuming that contractualism is intended as an absolute theory of rightness – rightness in the interpersonal sense of the term – and assuming that it serves well in this role, how damaging is the claim that it cannot be a complete theory: that it calls or allows for supplementation by an independent characterization of right option-types? The claim is consistent, as already mentioned, with conceding that what guides ordinary people in the use of the word 'right' – what provides the nominal essence of rightness, as it were (Pettit 2000b) – is a sense that the option-types to which it is applied satisfy the contractualist formula, being such as to resist reasonable complaint. And it is consistent with thinking that we do better in reflecting on practical questions of ethical judgment to concentrate mainly on where that formula leads; doing this may be heuristically more valuable than trying to extrapolate from the inherent character of option-types that we do regard as right or wrong. In these ways, then, the partiality of contractualist theory will not matter greatly.

Where it will matter, however, is in consideration of the question raised in the title of this chapter. It will mean that there is a sense in which the fact that an option-type is morally right is grounded, not merely in the subjunctive fact that it would resist reasonable objection, but in the categorical fact that it is of a certain independent type: the type that ensures it would resist reasonable objection. It is because right option-types have that categorical character that they would resist contractual complaint, even if it is the fact that they resist such complaint that prompts us to think of them as right.

There is an important sense, then, in which the normative kind associated with rightness will not, contrary to Scanlon's claims (1998: 12), be fully and properly characterized in contractualist terms. Contract theory identifies a role that right option-types will play, parallel to the role of being universally prescribable that Hare privileges; this is the role of proving immune to reasonable complaint. But it tends to ignore the issue, presumably amenable to philosophical, a priori specification, of what sort of property fills or realizes that role; it offers nothing akin to what Hare provides in his downstream utilitarian claims. Thus there is a sense in which contractualism does not take us to rock bottom. Under the absolute construal of the doctrine that Scanlon endorses, as under the relativized construal that I myself find attractive, contract theory fails to provide a complete grounding for morality.

References

Blackburn, S. (1999). "Am I right?" *New York Times*. New York.

Brennan, G. (1993). "Economics." In P. Pettit (ed.), *A Companion to Contemporary Political Philosophy*. Oxford: Blackwell.

Cocking, D. and Kennett, J. (2000). "Friendship and Moral Danger." *Journal of Philosophy*, 97: 278–96.

Freeman, S. (1998). "Contractarianism." In E. Craig (ed.), *The Routledge Encyclopedia of Philosophy*. Vol. 2. London: Routledge.

Gauthier, D. (1986). *Morals by Agreement*. Oxford: Oxford University Press.

Goodin, R. E. (1995). "Political ideals and political practice." *British Journal of Political Science*, 44: 635–46.

Habermas, J. (1990). *Moral Consciousness and Communicative Action*. Cambridge: Polity.

Hare, R. M. (1981). *Moral Thinking: Its Levels, Method and Point*. Oxford: Oxford University Press.

Hooker, B. (2000). *Ideal Code, Real World*. Oxford: Oxford University Press.

Jackson, F. and Pettit, P. (1995). "Moral functionalism and moral motivation." *Philosophical Quarterly*, 45: 20–40.

Jackson, F., Pettit, P., and Smith, M. (1999). "Ethical particularism and patterns." In B. Hooker and M. Little (eds.), *Moral Particularism*. Oxford: Clarendon Press.

McGinn, C. (1999). "Reasons and unreasons." *The New Republic*: 34–8.

Pettit, P. (1987). "Universalizability without utilitarianism." *Mind*, 96: 74–82.

Pettit, P. (1991). "Consequentialism." In P. Singer (ed.), *A Companion to Ethics*. Oxford: Blackwell.

Pettit, P. (1993). *The Common Mind: An Essay on Psychology, Society and Politics*. New York: Oxford University Press.

Pettit, P. (1997). "A consequentialist perspective on ethics." In Pettit, *Three Methods of Ethics: A Debate*. Oxford: Blackwell.

Pettit, P. (2000a). "A consequentialist perspective on contractualism." *Theoria*, 66: 228–36.

Pettit, P. (2000b). "Two construals of Scanlon's contractualism." *Journal of Philosophy*, 97: 148–64.

Pettit, P. (2001a). *A Theory of Freedom: From the Psychology to the Politics of Agency*. Cambridge and New York: Polity and Oxford University Press.

Pettit, P. (2001b). "Embracing objectivity in ethics." In B. Leiter (ed.), *Objectivity in Law and Morals*. Cambridge: Cambridge University Press.

Pettit, P. and Brennan, G. (1986). "Restrictive consequentialism." *Australasian Journal of Philosophy*, 64: 438–55.

Pettit, P. and Smith, M. (2000). "Global consequentialism." In D. E. Miller (ed.), *Morality, Rules and Consequences*. Edinburgh: Edinburgh University Press.

Pettit, P. and M. Smith (2004). "The truth in deontology." In M. Smith (ed.), *Reason and Value: Themes from the Moral Philosophy of Joseph Raz*. Oxford: Oxford University Press.

Railton, P. (1984). "Alienation, consequentialism and the demands of morality." *Philosophy and Public Affairs*, 13: 134–71.

Rawls, J. (1971). *A Theory of Justice*. Oxford: Oxford University Press.

Rawls, J. (1993). *Political Liberalism*. New York: Columbia University Press.

Ridge, M. (2001). "Saving Scanlon: contractualism and agent-relativity." *Journal of Political Philosophy*, 9: 472–81.

Ridge, M. (2003). "Contractualism and the new and improved redundancy objection." *Analysis*: 337–42.

Scanlon, T. M. (1982). "Contractualism and utilitarianism." In B. Williams (ed.), *Utilitarianism and Beyond*. Cambridge: Cambridge University Press.

Scanlon, T. M. (1998). *What We Owe To Each Other*. Cambridge, Mass.: Harvard University Press.

Scanlon, T. M. (2000). "A contractualist reply." *Theoria*, 66: 237–45.

Scanlon, T. M. (2003). "Reply to Gauthier and Gibbard." *Philosophy and Phenomenological Research*, 66: 176–89.

Smith, M. (1994). *The Moral Problem*. Oxford: Blackwell.

Stratton-Lake, P. (2003). "Scanlon's contractualism and the redundancy objection." *Analysis*, 63: 70–5.

Wallace, J. (2002). "Scanlon's contractualism." *Ethics*, 112: 429–70.

Acknowledgment

My thanks to Jamie Dreier, Nic Southwood, Michael Ridge, Tim Scanlon, Michael Smith, and Jay Wallace for very useful comments on an earlier draft of this piece.

Are the Virtues the Proper Starting Point for Ethical Theory?

Are Virtues the Proper Starting Point For Morality?

Rosalind Hursthouse

An instructive way to trace the rise of modern virtue ethics is through the successive editions of Beauchamp and Childress's *Principles of Biomedical Ethics*. The first edition (1979) perfectly reflects the contemporary state of play – biomedical issues have been under discussion for some time and although many of the utilitarians and deontologists who have been writing about them remain implacably opposed, some have benefited from reading each other and begun to think that they have enough common ground regarding rules and principles to make progress together. The book is mostly about these rules and principles and how they are to be applied to issues in biomedical ethics. Virtue ethics is not mentioned and "virtues" (not "virtue") has just four entries in the index, all of which refer to a very brief section in Chapter 8 on "Virtues and character."

The second edition (1983) is not very different but the third (1989) is strikingly so. Now "virtue" is in the index, and only a couple of its fifteen entries refer to the greatly expanded section on "Virtues and character." In the fourth (1994), the real sea change occurs. Much of that expanded section now appears, not in the "Here are some other important bits and pieces," Chapter 8, but in the major early chapter on "Types of ethical theory."

The fourth (and fifth) editions might well be said to reflect the state of play as it still is now – viewed that is, from the perspective of many consequentialists and deontologists. As moderately anti-virtue ethicists, they claim that "what we need" (for a complete ethical theory) is an ethics of virtue *and* an ethics of rules, since (a) the concept of virtue is "irreducible" (hence the need for an ethics of virtue), but (b) an ethics of virtue cannot provide action-guidance and hence must be supplemented by an ethics of rules such as consequentialists and deontologists provide. Less moderate opponents of virtue ethics, agreeing with (b), deny (a) and aim to give an account of the virtues in terms of their favored normative approach. This is now called 'virtue *theory*' as distinct from 'virtue *ethics*'.

Virtue ethicists, naturally, support (a) and deny (b). Their positions on the two are related, for many of the criticisms of virtue ethics as a normative approach are, virtue ethicists maintain, based on an inadequate account of what a virtue is. Most contemporary virtue ethicists acquire their concept of virtue from Aristotle and hang on to it. Many contemporary consequentialists and deontologists do not, and hence the virtue theories they produce are, from the virtue ethical point of view, quite inadequate. I think myself that this is, at least in part, because they are working within a reductivist framework which I want to dismantle before continuing.

Against the Rawlsian Framework

One explanation of why the first supporters of virtue ethics had such a hard time getting their audience to hear their claim that virtue ethics really did offer a third type of normative approach is the exceptionally pervasive – and deleterious – influence of Rawls's *A Theory of Justice* (1971).

According to Rawls, as is well known, there are just two types of ethical theory: deontology is an example of one, utilitarianism of the other. The reason why there are just two types is that there are just two "main concepts" or "basic notions" in ethics, the 'right' and the 'good', and the differentiating structures of the two types are (largely) determined by how they define and connect these two. Might one not have expected to read that *virtue* was a third (albeit recently neglected) main concept in ethics? Well, the word 'virtue' does not even appear in Rawls's index, but a sentence sweeps the thought away – the concept of a "morally worthy person," Rawls believes, is derived from the other two.

If only Rawls had said nothing about Aristotle, the first supporters of virtue ethics might have had an easier time. After all, a lot of people in their audience had not read Aristotle and might have been receptive to the unsurprising idea that three great moral philosophers of the Western tradition, namely Aristotle, Kant, and Mill could each inspire a distinctive type of normative ethical approach that was worth considering, giving us three rather than two. But alas, Rawls did say a bit about Aristotle, suggesting that he is, not a utilitarian, but in the same camp – a 'teleologist' (or, as we would now say, a 'consequentialist') committed to a maximizing principle. This was simply an unfortunate howler, but to this day one hears consequentialists saying to virtue ethicists: "Surely the virtuous agent must aim at maximizing virtue (or virtuous action or *eudaimonia*) because that is what your theory maintains is the good."

Rawls himself asserts the attractively simple slogan that 'teleological' theories define the right in terms of the good but did not commit himself to a parallel one for deontological theories. However, his many followers quickly supplied one, and several other pairs as well. And so we get such claims as: "Utilitarianism defines the right in terms of the good and deontology defines the good in terms of the right;" "Utilitarianism begins with the good and derives the right, whereas deontology begins with the right and derives the good;" "The basic/most important concept in utilitarianism is that of the good, whereas in deontology it is that of the right." Belief in the truth of such slogans made it well nigh impossible to recognize that virtue ethics could be a third, distinctive approach. For surely it would have to opt for the good or the right and hence align itself with one of the two established approaches? After all, its only alternative is to derive both the good and the right from the concept of virtue, and that is obviously an impossible task.

But the slogans should be dismissed as nonsense, not merely because they block getting virtue ethics off the ground, but because, as I have argued elsewhere (Hursthouse 1999), they seriously distort deontology and utilitarianism too. It would, for instance, be a travesty of Kant to describe him as "taking the good as his basic concept" on the grounds that he attaches such importance to the good will. But any such crudity would be a travesty of any great moral philosopher. The important thing to do with them is not to look for their "basic" concept (especially not if it is settled in advance that this must be one of the good, the right, or virtue), but to understand what they say about a whole host of concepts relevant to moral philosophy, including what they say about how those concepts connect and knit together.

It is noteworthy that the new wave of Kantian interpretation places much more emphasis on *connecting* what Kant has to say about virtue with what he has to say about the good will and the kingdom of ends than on trying to define virtue in "more basic" terms. Unfortunately, other deontologists, and most consequentialists, are still working within the confines of the Rawlsian reductivist slogans, aiming for derivations rather than connections – and demanding that virtue ethics do the same. But no virtue ethicist remotely inspired by Aristotle aims for the reduction of significant moral concepts to others. On the contrary, we seek acknowledgment of a much larger number than is common – not only *good* in contexts other than those pertaining to consequences, but also *evil* and *harm*, the *worthwhile*, the *advantageous*, the *pleasant*, the *important*, the *necessary*. We are not even, as I shall argue later, out to reduce or derive the concept of the right.

The Aristotelian Concept of Virtue

What of those who are still seeking to derive the concept of virtue? Well, there are, I suppose, stricter and looser derivations, but the concept of virtue we acquire from Aristotle is rich, far too rich one suspects, to emerge in all its required complexity from anything that could be described as a derivation from one or two abstract concepts. As Julia Annas has argued (2004), what we tend to get in the non-virtue ethical virtue theories are "reduced" accounts of virtue which simply leave out important features of the classical account.

The full Aristotelian concept of virtue is the concept of a complex character trait, that is, a disposition that is well entrenched in its possessor and, as we say, "goes all the way down." The disposition, far from being a single-track disposition to do, say, honest actions, or even honest actions for certain reasons, is multi-track, involving many other actions as well: desires, emotions and emotional reactions, perceptions, attitudes, interests, and expectations. This is because your virtues (and your vices) are a matter of what sort of adult you are, and involve, most particularly, your values – what you regard as worth pursuing or preserving or doing and what you regard as not so. Christine Swanton encapsulates this complexity by describing a virtue as a disposition "to respond to, or acknowledge, items within its field" (2003: 19) and emphasizing the plurality of "kinds of responsiveness."

Anti-virtue ethicists typically pay lip service to the idea that virtues (and vices) are complex character traits, but it is often the case that, when they are arguing against virtue ethics, they forget this fact. Brad Hooker (2002) thinks my "naturalism" will have the distasteful consequence that homosexuality is a vice; my response, in brief, is that homosexuality, like heterosexuality, is *not* a character trait, and hence not the sort of thing that even gets into the running for being assessed as a virtue or a vice. I appeal to the following fact: that if all I know about a man is that he is heterosexual, I know *nothing* about his character – about what he typically does, for what reasons, about whether he loves women or hates them, is disgusted by heterosexual intercourse or revels in it, about his values or what he counts as worth pursuing or preserving – at all. He might be licentious or temperate, violent or gentle, cruel or compassionate, wise or foolish, and so on. And, to the unprejudiced, the same (*mutatis mutandis*) is obviously true if all I know about him is that he is homosexual.

By the same token, I take it as obvious that water phobia is not a character flaw, whereas Julia Driver takes it as obvious that it is. As before, it seems to me that, if all I know about a man is that he has a water phobia, I know nothing about his character, for well or ill, at all. He might be kind or cruel, just or unjust, honest or dishonest, courageous or cowardly, wise or foolish. All I know about him, *ex hypothesi*, is that if he gets into water, he freezes and is likely to drown, which isn't even a disposition to action.

Given that the virtuous disposition is multi-track, no virtue ethicist would dream of making "the fundamental attribution error" and ascribing honesty or charity to someone on the basis of a single honest or charitable action or even a series of them. Quite aside from anything else, well-brought-up adolescents will behave thus, and in some sense, for the right sorts of reasons, but we do not attribute the Aristotelian concept of virtue until we have some grounds for supposing that the agent has made the reasons she has been taught her own.

When we bear in mind that an agent with a particular virtue (or vice), V, reasons to action in a characteristic way, we recognize that the result may well not be what we would call a V action. For example, recognizing a proposed end as worthless, the courageous agent may well avoid danger as carefully as the coward, while the reckless plunge ahead. Another common mistake is to think only in terms of a thin disposition to V acts.

Driver (2001) has made much of the "virtues of ignorance," but it seems to me that she has slipped into regarding the 'virtues' in question as no more than such thin dispositions. If we think seriously about the way her V agents reason, her virtues of ignorance turn out not be virtues even by her own lights (i.e. more conducive than not to the good).

According to Driver, the "modest" agent underestimates her own worth and is thereby disposed to "modest" actions such as not bragging and giving up her share of scarce goods to those she believes are more deserving than her, both of which are conducive to the good. But is that all that someone who underestimates herself typically does? Aristotle's diagnostic of the "small-souled" man, who "thinks himself worthy of lesser things than he is worthy of" is no less accurate than Driver's – "these people abstain from noble actions and projects" as well as from external goods, "because they feel unworthy of them." In praising modesty as both charming and conducive to the good, Driver must surely have overlooked the fact that her modest person is the one who will never volunteer to do the difficult and responsible jobs and who resists taking them on even when her turn is well overdue, saying: "I can't, I'm no good at that sort of thing, I'll only make a mess of it." She speaks with perfect sincerity, but, *ex hypothesi*, what she says is not true and everyone resents her resistance, especially if it is successful and the job has to fall on the shoulders of someone who doesn't do it as well as she could have, none of which conduces to the good at all.

This is not to deny the common-sense view that modesty is a virtue. It is, rather, to insist on the Aristotelian view (supported incidentally by the *Oxford English Dictionary*) that modesty involves correctly estimating oneself as moderately worthy.

Driver similarly overlooks, in my view, the obvious ways in which the "blind charity" possessed by Jane Bennett in *Pride and Prejudice* will fail to conduce to the good. Jane is indeed an exceptionally sweet-natured young woman, and her sister Elizabeth needs to emulate her "wish not be hasty in censuring anyone," which the sharp-eyed, sharp-tongued Elizabeth still actually enjoys. But it is significant that she is *young*, with older people to care for her and no one yet in her care. If she is not to become a disastrously irresponsible parent, she had better acquire some of Elizabeth's eye for what is bad in people.

Driver wants to reject a feature of the Aristotelian concept of virtue that I have not yet made explicit, namely the point that the virtuous (excellent) person's practical reasoning is itself excellent; she gets things right. What makes someone excellent in practical reasoning is the excellence (virtue) of *phronesis* or practical wisdom, which is inseparable from the full version of any of the other virtues. The introduction of *phronesis* is sometimes thought to bring with it not only the idea that virtue is rare, but further that it is guaranteed to be limited to the intellectually sophisticated. It is true that, when talking about moral knowledge (and *phronesis* is a form of moral knowledge), most philosophers find it hard to avoid talking as though they believed that it could only be acquired by studying academic philosophy; it's an occupational hazard we tend to share whatever our favored theory. But practical wisdom is certainly not supposed to be something that only the intellectually sophisticated can acquire. You cannot possess the virtue of courage without a correct grasp of which goals or ends are worth pursuing or preserving and in what circumstances, and accordingly reasoning with a view to such ends. (Risking your life for a worthless and trivial end is not courageous, but reckless.) But recognizing that risking your life by donating a kidney may well be worthwhile, whereas risking it to have your body sculpted into a sexier shape is not, seems to be the sort of thing that any ordinary grown up is capable of.

As I said above, an agent with a particular virtue, V, reasons to action in a characteristic way. The requirement of *phronesis* as part of virtue embodies the idea that an agent who does not do such reasoning tolerably well cannot be said to have the virtue in question.

We appeal to the norm of practical wisdom when we say such things as "She should have known, realized, recognized, appreciated that . . . ," and we don't say that about the recondite. It comes up, for instance, in relation to the cases where we recognize good intentions but deplore their outcome. We don't usually criticize small children when, trying to help without being asked for the first time, they smash some of the best china. They don't know some china is better than others and they don't know they are clumsy, and we don't expect them to. But we do expect clumsy adults to have noticed that they are clumsy and that this is something that they must take into account in their practical reasoning if they are to avoid distressing other people. When, without asking or telling you, they do the washing up "because you looked so tired," and, inevitably, smash the irreplaceable teapot lid and thereby ruin the whole teaset, you can reasonably complain that they should have recognized they were quite likely to break something you cherished and should have appreciated that it would be considerate to ask you so that you had a chance to say, "Oh yes, the dirty saucepans please, but not the teapot because it's part of the set I had from my mother."

So to give up on *phronesis* as requisite for virtue is to give up the notion of culpable ignorance, leaving us with nothing to say in criticism of the mature Jane when, unwilling to censure, she leaves her daughter in the hands of her uncle despite her knowledge that he is a twice-convicted child molester, or entrusts her health to a notoriously incompetent doctor. And we lose more than the notion of culpable ignorance.

We noted above that the Aristotelian concept of virtue is the concept of a character trait that involves actions *and* feelings, and any account of virtue that does not depart too far from Aristotle preserves his distinction between *enkrateia*, continence or strength of will, and virtue. "Virtuous conduct gives pleasure to the lover of virtue" (*Nichomachean Ethics* 1099a12) because reason and inclination/desire are in harmony in such a person; they characteristically do what is virtuous desiring to do it. (Characteristically, but not invariably; see Hursthouse 1999: 92–8.)

We should be clear about why, within the Aristotelian tradition, the distinction is important. It is not just that the enkratic might be less reliable in action, or that the world would be a cheerier place if it contained agents' good feelings about their right actions as well as the actions, but that the enkratic are still imperfect in practical rationality. The Aristotelian view of human nature is that, *qua* rational, it can be perfected by getting our inclinations into harmony with our reason. If my inclinations are not in harmony with my reason, and *if* getting them into harmony is something that human rationality can achieve, then the people whose inclinations are in harmony are, *ceteris paribus*, better human beings, closer to excellence (virtue), than I am.

Given that we are, by nature, rational animals, I do not see how one can maintain that someone who has a failing in human rationality that pertains to their character may still possess full virtue, without abandoning the idea that virtue is *excellence*. As I understand her, this is something that Driver is not only willing but eager to do. But abandoning this idea is very serious indeed, because it is to abandon the idea of virtue as an ideal – something for us to strive to attain in our own lives, and hope to see more closely attained by our children and in better societies than our own. That full justice and charity – justice and charity that bring the emotions into complete harmony with reason – are probably well nigh impossible to achieve if one has been brought up in a racist society is a reason (amongst others) for lamenting the state of society at the time, not a reason for allowing or encouraging those who have done their best within it to congratulate themselves with the thought that no one could be better than they are.

We need not deny that 'virtue', in modern parlance, is a threshold concept (Swanton 2003: 24). (Perhaps even 'excellence' is. After all, we say A− [or perhaps A] to A+ on our students' essays means 'Excellent'.) If someone gets over the threshold then they certainly are not vicious. But grammatically, 'virtue', and the terms for the individual virtues, accept a whole range of qualifications – "quite V, admirably V, for his age/for her time/in his society/given her disadvantages" – where the qualifications enable us both to give credit where credit is due but also to register the point that the ideal standard has not yet been met. Giving due credit to people such as Huck Finn or the supportive husbands of the Victorian suffragettes (who, like their wives, remained blindly indifferent to their exploitation of working-class women) is one thing; giving up on the idea that human beings can be better is another thing entirely.

The mention of excellence in practical reasoning brings us not to the full doctrine of the unity of the virtues (according to which you cannot possess one virtue without possessing them all), but to some limited version of it. This is the idea that at least the major or "core" virtues are not isolable dispositions, but are interconnected by the characteristic reasoning each involves. One's own life is usually worth preserving, the good of others is usually worth pursuing and preserving, and the latter is, sometimes, truly worth risking or even sacrificing the former for. So someone who is courageous cannot be callous but must be at least well on the way to being benevolent or charitable – how can she not be, if she is prepared to lay down her life for others? Charity or benevolence requires a correct conception of what is beneficial (and harmful) to human beings. What is truly beneficial to them is, quite often, hearing the truth, or the truth's being told. So if someone is benevolent or charitable he must be at least on the way to being honest – at the very least, he cannot be someone who just tells lies or conceals the truth to suit himself. How could he be if he is prepared to go out of his way in truthfulness for the sake of others? And if someone is honest, they cannot lack courage in every way. They may be honest and a physical coward, but they cannot be honest without having "the courage of their convictions," as we say, and someone quite incapable of defending others in physical ways may still boldly tell the truth in their defense in full knowledge of the fact that doing so is a death warrant.

This limited unity, governed by the norm of *phronesis* as necessary for full virtue, makes it much harder than Driver supposes to say, without careful qualification, that virtuous people may act wrongly precisely because of their virtue. If I can't bring myself to kill the bird my cat has mauled and am thereby forced to leave it to perish miserably, I should be berating myself for my squeamishness, not congratulating myself on my compassion. It may well be that the perfect harmony Aristotle envisages is not in fact possible for human nature, that those who are capable of "tough love" are inevitably thereby less capable of tender sympathy and vice versa. That is still not a reason for lowering the standard and giving up on the idea that if I could – as perhaps I can – make myself just a bit tougher or a bit more tender I would be better, and so should try.

Right Action

How then is this Aristotelian concept of virtue related to the concept of right action?

During the 1980s, virtue ethics seemed vulnerable to "the application problem" – the objection that it can't provide action guidance or be applied and is hence unable to do what a normative ethical theory is pre-eminently supposed to do. The objection was based on the premise that the only guidance virtue ethics could come up with was that you should do what the virtuous agent would do in the circumstances, and it is true that the earlier virtue ethics literature offered little more. The stress on "in the circumstances" went hand in hand with the same literature's professed scorn for the very idea of ethical choices or conduct as rule-guided or rule-governed. And this made it not at all implausible to believe that virtue ethics simply could not get off the ground as a normative theory. When, anxious to make the right moral decision, I turn to it, what does it tell me to do? Apparently, to find a virtuous person and ask them what they would do in my circumstances. But suppose I can't, or not soon enough? Then it seems I am left with nothing. Or suppose I think I can, and they say "I would do so and so." It would surely be reasonable for me to ask "Why?" and, unfortunately, much of the available virtue ethics literature suggested that the only answer I would receive would be, "My *phronesis* (practical wisdom) enables me to perceive that so and so would be the virtuous thing to do in the circumstances." At which point it might occur to me that anyone sufficiently confident, whether virtuous or corrupt but self-righteous, could give me that answer, and hence that if virtue ethics could not tell me how to identify a virtuous person, its telling me to find and ask one was no guidance at all. ("How do I get to Amarillo?" "Find the right road and follow it.")

I realized that there was an obvious way to elaborate on "The right action is what a virtuous person would do (in the circumstances)" which completely blocked this form of the application problem. By and large, we do not need to find a virtuous agent, because in one way, we know what she does and would do. She does, and would do, what is virtuous, not vicious; that is, she does what is courageous, just, honest, charitable, loyal, kind, generous – and does not do what is cowardly or reckless, unjust, dishonest, uncharitable, malevolent, disloyal, unkind, stingy. So each virtue generates a prescription – "Do what is courageous, just, etc." – and every vice a prohibition – "Do not do what is cowardly or reckless, unjust, etc." – and in order to do what the virtuous agent would do in the circumstances, one acts in accordance with these, which I have called 'v-rules'. And so I committed myself to the view that "An action is right iff it is what a virtuous agent would, characteristically, (i.e. acting in character) do in the circumstances," and triumphantly pointed out that, contrary to the premise that virtue ethics did not offer any action-guiding rules or principles, it thereby came up with an impressively long and helpful list: the v-rules.

It seems to me that, in the specific context of the application problem, the most interesting aspect of this view is not the biconditional itself but the discovery of the v-rules. The existence of these, expressed in the vocabulary of the virtues and vices, refutes (literally) the premise on which the objection was based.

Naturally, the v-rules have been criticized, but the standard criticisms fall foul of obvious *tu quoque* responses. Of course, the requirements of the different virtues may, at least apparently, conflict. Honesty points to telling the hurtful truth, kindness or compassion to remaining silent or even lying. But so too do the related deontologists' and rule-consequentialists' rules, rightly reflecting the fact (ignored by the old act utilitarians) that life does present us with dilemmas whose resolution, even if correct, should leave us with a remainder of regret. Like the other two approaches, virtue ethics seeks resolutions of such conflicts in a more refined or nuanced understanding or application of the rules involved; and as with the other approaches, its proponents may disagree about the correct resolution,

Perhaps over-impressed by MacIntyre's early work (1981; but see his 1999 for a very different account), critics of virtue ethics have commonly asserted that the v-rules are inherently culturally specific and conservative because they are developed within existing traditions and societies. Virtue ethicists may take heart from the empirical fact of the Virtues Project (go to <www.virtuesproject.com>), an international educational program based on 52(!) virtues found to be common to seven of the world's cultural traditions, which has been translated into numerous languages and successfully used in schools all over the world. At a more theoretical level, virtue ethicists are amused by the implicit assumption that what their opponents find "reasonable" or "rationally acceptable" is not shaped by modern Western culture and (predominantly) American society, and ask their rivals to join them in admitting that none of us has reason to suppose that our lists of rules are complete or beyond revision. And we all share "the justification problem," that is, the problem of finding ways to validate whatever list we have come up with so far.

However, virtue ethicists do point out that their list of rules is remarkably long in comparison with any that their rivals have produced, and grows naturally (albeit within our own culture) as people's experience of modern life contributes new terms. This is perhaps particularly noticeable with respect to rules couched in terms that connote, if not strictly, vices, at least ways of falling seriously short of virtue. And they appeal to their list to rebut the charge that the guidance they offer is less specific than that provided by others. "Tell the truth," even if filled out to provide plausible answers to "All of it? Always? To anyone?" is still much less specific than what is yielded by "Do what is honest," "Do not do what is disingenuous, rude, insensitive, spiteful, hypocritical, untrustworthy, treacherous, phoney, sneaky, manipulative . . ."

The claim is that these provide better action-guidance than the sorts of rules that deontologists and rule-consequentialists come up with (because there are so many more and they are so much more specific and subtly nuanced), and better action-guidance than straight act utilitarianism, which notoriously prescribes far too many hair-raisingly wrong actions. It is this claim, rather than the biconditional itself, which is the denial of (b) above, namely that we need an 'ethics of rules' (by which is meant rules that are *not* expressed in virtue and vice terms). To establish (b), you have to argue against the claimed adequacy of the v-rules in general, which, as far as I know, no one has attempted to do, not just find fault with the biconditional itself. (Merely pointing to the inadequacy (which I admit) of "Do what is just/do not do what is unjust" will not suffice, for it too is open to the *tu quoque* response.)

But what of the biconditional? Well, what is the point of any simple biconditional with 'An action is right iff . . .' on the left-hand side? It is only within the reductive Rawlsian framework that it is taken to offer a definition or derivation of 'the right' in relation to just one other concept which appears on the right-hand side. As I noted above, though this may, perhaps, be a plausible way of taking the biconditional that captures the crudest form of act utilitarianism, it will not do justice to one that captures deontology. I originally described all of them as "forging a link" between the concept of right action and the concept that appeared on the right-hand side and that still seems to me much better. For what we should all recognize, regardless of our allegiance to one normative approach or another, is that we employ the concept of right action in a variety of ways; it is essentially linked to a number of concepts and those to others. What will distinguish our approaches most clearly is which concept – if indeed any one – we take as our entry point and focus, and how, starting where we do, we treat the others. Virtue ethics starts with the concept of the virtuous agent; let us look at some of the other concepts right action is (somehow) linked to.

One is the concept of right decision. (Morally) right decisions are what normative ethical theories are supposed to help or enable us to come up with; that is what action-guidance is all about. They do so by giving some account or specification of right action, for, platitudinously, right action is that at which good decision-making is aimed. When the decision is correct, and moreover comes off – when the agent succeeds in doing what she intended to do – we get right action.

Or rather, that is what we characteristically get. Resolvable dilemmas which present us with a forced choice between morally unpalatable alternatives show that the concept of right action has another link which may pull against right decision in such cases. *Right* as opposed to *wrong* action is the proper object of approval, the kind that merits praise rather than blame, and "the satisfactory review of one's own conduct" rather than shame or regret on the part of the agent. But the right decision that correctly resolves an unpalatable dilemma results, if it comes off, in an action that apparently calls for justification and regret rather than meriting praise or pride.

What are we to say about this? My biconditional, rather felicitously I thought, directed us to say that, in some cases, the action, though the outcome of a right decision, was not right, not what a virtuous agent would have done in the circumstances. All the cases have the feature that a virtuous agent would never have landed herself in those circumstances in the first place. If it is your own wrongdoing that has brought you to this pass, then resolving the dilemma correctly does not free you from blame and shame; the link between right action and right decision does not hold here.

However, I did not want to deny that agents, including the virtuous, could be faced with unpalatable dilemmas through no fault of their own, and thinking about how it would be when the virtuous resolved them correctly made me realize that there are two ways to read my biconditional which correspond to two ways in which we talk about right action. (If this makes the biconditional "indeterminate," as Driver claims, the indeterminacy is a point in its favor, for it captures the corresponding indeterminacy of "right action.")

We often confidently say that an action was right regardless of the reasons why it was done (say Kant's shopkeeper). We have, after all, a strong interest in people doing what is honest, just, generous, charitable, or benevolent, etc.; to a large extent that's what keeps society ticking over and enables us to live together fairly pleasantly, and that – or those – purposes are served tolerably well even when a lot of people are doing what is right for the wrong reasons – out of fear of disapproval or the law, or because it suits them better than doing otherwise, or to curry favor or whatever. So a lot of the time we don't raise questions about the reasons for the action, just approve it as right and accept it as a truism that you do not have to be virtuous to do what is right.

But we may also think of what is right and merits approval in contexts relating to moral improvement – of ourselves, of our children, of the way too many doctors behave – and then we up the standard. In these contexts, assessing the actions by the standard of the virtuous agent – with her full panoply of not only right reasons but also right emotions – we frequently assess them not as wrong, but certainly not as deserving unqualified approval. Thinking of the virtuous agent as the one who sets the standard to which we should all aspire, we get a richer notion of "what is done." What you *do* does not count as right unless it is what the virtuous agent would *do*, say, "tell the truth, after much painful thought, for the right reasons, feeling deep regret, having put in place all that can be done to support the person on the receiving end afterwards." Only if you get all of that right are you entitled to the satisfactory review of your own conduct, and we want the children, and the insensitive arrogant doctors, and ourselves to grant that simply making the right decision, and telling the truth just wasn't good enough to merit approval.

In fact, in these and other contexts in which we are looking for, or hoping for, manifestations of virtue, we sometimes do reassess the actions as just plain wrong when the wrong reasons and/or the accompanying emotions turn out to be strikingly contrary to virtue. There I was, confident in assessing the plain-speaking of a colleague in a meeting as right, because honest – just the kind of straightforwardness we need in order to come to mutual decisions effectively and enable the department to run. And then I discover that the truth-teller is in fact usually evasive, manipulative, and plain mendacious in such meetings, and that his truth-telling on this occasion was motivated purely by spite, and I reassess it. "The ratbag!" I say. "What a rotten thing to do, to say that just to upset so and so." And if you press me on whether his action wasn't, all the same, right in *some* way, because honest, I shall say (a) that it would have been right, because honest, coming from, for example, John, but (b) that it wasn't honest coming from him and he would have done better to hold his tongue.

So my biconditional works so far. But right action, insofar as it is the proper object of approval, cannot be terrible and horrible, and tragic dilemmas, which present the agent with a forced choice between terrible actions, sever the link between right action and the virtuous agent.

Driver (2002) suggested that one might insist that such actions *are* right, in this unusual context, and explain that "there are good instrumental reasons to balk at calling the action 'right' since that seems an honorific." I am not sure whether her idea was that a virtue ethicist might do this, or that it would be the obvious consequentialist strategy, but either way, I think the suggestion is incoherent. The semantic fact is that 'right' *is* an honorific; I can't even *think* that such actions are right because they are so terrible. Some people thought I should have preserved my biconditional (for what purpose?) by claiming that, in the context of a tragic dilemma, the virtuous agent acts uncharacteristically. But that seemed to me manifestly false. It may be utterly characteristic of a virtuous agent that she resolves a tragic dilemma the way she does (if resolvable) or recognizes it as irresolvable if that's what it is, for such resolving, or recognition, may call on all her virtue and moral wisdom. It would also be utterly characteristic of her to recognize that what she has done *is* terrible and that her life can never be the same again now she has been forced to do this terrible thing.

The fact that the link is severed by tragic dilemmas, far from inclining me to give up the focus on the virtuous agent, seemed to me to harmonize perfectly with certain aspects of the classical Aristotelian account of virtue and its relation to *eudaimonia* (true happiness, or flourishing). What the virtuous agent is forced to do in a tragic dilemma is not an instance of that *acting well* or *good action* which makes up the *eudaimon* life, the sort of thing that allows the agent to look back at the end of her life and say truly "that was a *good* human life." On the contrary, it is precisely the sort of action that, looking back, the virtuous agent rightly describes as having marred her life.

The action category of the terrible or "intolerable" is, as Louden (1984) rightly noted, an important one. He thinks such actions (i) can be identified in deontological rules that mark off "clear boundaries" and (ii) are limited to those which "produce harm of such magnitude that they destroy the bonds of community and render . . . the achievement of moral goods impossible," but in my view this is a mistake on both counts (insofar as I understand the second.). British, though not US, legal history, testifies to the fact that our attempts to capture in law precisely which cases of homicide – the really *wicked* ones – deserved capital punishment always foundered because they could not provide "clear boundaries;" that is part of the reason we gave them up. They always had to resort to attempts to lay down what the gratuitously *callous* or *cruel* taking of human life was, attempting to specify the killing as something that, in the particular circumstances, only someone markedly callous or cruel would have done, never, ever, the even minimally virtuous. But that is not a deontological "clear boundary." It is a v-rule, and although these can be, as I have stressed, very specific and readily applicable, in difficult cases they could serve the purposes of law only if we were able to select our jurors on the basis of their *phronesis*.

Moreover, even if a deontological rule could lay out precisely those conditions in which the taking of a human life was, in the circumstances, something that only a wicked person would do, all it would have captured is a type/kind of action that the virtuous would never, ever, do. I agree that the characteristic actions of the really wicked do in some sense strike at the foundations of our moral community. Perhaps, often, they produce striking amounts of unnecessary suffering too. But neither feature, I think, exhausts our concept of "the terrible" in action. The intentional bringing about of the death of the adult nearest and dearest to you, the companion with whom you have shared much of your life, whose good has been your good, even if it is the right, unavoidable, decision, is terrible, horrible, notwithstanding the fact no one wicked would ever be in a position to do such a thing. Only the (at least fairly) virtuous think that such relationships are worth pursuing and preserving; only they thus give hostages to fortune and run the risk of having their lives marred by, tragically, having to destroy the one they hold most dear.

This is a way to map the terrain of 'the terrible' and 'the tragic' – which any adequate account of act appraisals should do – when you start with the concept of the virtuous agent. Let me turn, finally to the virtue ethics account of the distinction between 'the obligatory' and 'the supererogatory'.

Driver claims to find a deplorable indeterminacy in the phrase "what the virtuous agent would do *in the circumstances.*" Have I not left it fatally unclear whether "real character flaws" are included in the circumstances? Well I haven't – as Driver herself works out, if you include *real* character flaws such as cowardice in the circumstances, the account becomes incoherent. In fact it is this very distinction – between the circumstances (which of course do not include character flaws) and the character flaws themselves – that Foot – and following her, I – rely on in giving an account of the supererogatory.

Foot (1978) discusses two apparently clashing intuitions we have: on the one hand, "the harder it is for a man to act virtuously the more virtue he shows if he acts well" (usually identified with Kant) and, on the other, "the harder it is for a man to act virtuously, the less virtue he shows if he acts well" (usually associated with Aristotle.) Foot brilliantly extracts this clash from the mire in which the Kantian/Aristotelian debate has obscured it and argues that the intuitions do not clash but simply pertain to different cases.

If what makes it hard (on a particular occasion) for an agent to act virtuously is the *circumstances*, then the more virtue he shows if he acts well – as the first intuition had it. But: if what makes it hard (on a particular occasion) for an agent to act virtuously is (not the circumstances but) a flaw or imperfection of his character, then the *less* virtue he shows if he acts well – as the second intuition had it. So if what makes it "hard for me" to restore the full purse I saw someone drop is that I am strongly tempted to pocket it and have to conquer the temptation, then what makes it hard for me is an imperfection in my honesty; I am less than thoroughly honest in character and morally inferior to someone who hastens to restore it with no thought of keeping what is not theirs. But there are at least two different sorts of *circumstances* in which the thoroughly honest agent hastens to return the purse with no thought of keeping it. One is that in which she is comfortably off, the other is that in which she is poor. In the former case, it is easy for her to return it; her honesty is not, as Foot puts it, "severely tested," and what she does, though good and right, is not, given the circumstances, strikingly admirable. However, in the latter case, it is hard for the agent to restore the purse – hard insofar as she is hardly circumstanced – and her honesty is severely tested. If it comes through, and she still restores it with no thought of doing otherwise, what she does is strikingly admirable.

And this distinction, between right action where virtue is not severely tested and right action where virtue *is* severely tested and comes through, is the virtue ethics account of the distinction between 'the obligatory' and 'the supererogatory', a distinction that no adequate account of 'the right' can ignore.

No doubt someone will protest, "But this isn't what your biconditional *says*. You are just adding things on." But no approach's simple biconditional can say anything about the distinction between the obligatory and the supererogatory while the left-hand side is simply 'An action is right', since both the obligatory and the supererogatory are right. That is why it would be stupid to regard any such biconditional as giving a complete definition when 'right action' has these two different uses. My biconditional is consistent with both and, taking the virtuous agent as the starting point as Foot does, leads us easily into an extremely plausible account of each as qualified versions of the original. And this isn't "just adding things on." It's a test of the original that it passes with flying colours.

There are other significant uses of 'right action' that my simple biconditional does not capture, which space does not permit me to discuss. Swanton's (2003) account, for instance, captures that use of 'right action' which disconnects it from praiseworthiness and Johnson (2003) identifies a very interesting use in the context of moral self-improvement. But none I have seen so far inclines me to give up the idea that, when we want to understand the concept of right action, the concept of the virtuous agent and thereby the virtues, should be our entry point and focus.

References

Annas, J. (2004). "Virtue ethics." In D. Copp (ed.), *The Oxford Companion to Ethical Theory*. Oxford: Oxford University Press.

Beauchamp, T. L. and Childress, J. F. (1979, 1983, 1989, 1994, 2001). *Principles of Biomedical Ethics*. New York: Oxford University Press.

Driver, J. (2001). *Uneasy Virtue*. Cambridge: Cambridge University Press.

Driver, J. (2002). "On virtue ethics. (Book review)." *Philosophical Review*, 111: 122–6.

Foot, P. (1978). "Virtues and vices." In Foot, *Virtues and Vices*. Oxford: Basil Blackwell.

Hooker, B. (2002). "The collapse of virtue ethics." *Utilitas*, 14: 22–40.

Hursthouse, R. (1999). *On Virtue Ethics*. Oxford: Oxford University Press.

Johnson, R. (2003). "Virtue and right." *Ethics*, 113: 810–34.

Louden, R. B. (1984). "On some vices of virtue ethics." *American Philosophical Quarterly*, 21: 227–36.

MacIntyre, A. (1981). *After Virtue*. Notre Dame: University of Notre Dame Press.

MacIntyre, A. (1999). *Dependent Rational Animals*. Chicago: Open Court.

Rawls, J. (1971). *A Theory of Justice*. Oxford: Oxford University Press.

Swanton, C. (2003). *Virtue Ethics: A Pluralistic View*. Oxford: Oxford University Press.

Further Reading

Anscombe, G. E. M. (1958). "Modern moral philosophy." Repr. in Crisp and Slote (1997).

Crisp, R. and Slote, M. (eds.), (1997). *Virtue Ethics*. Oxford: Oxford University Press.

Statman, D. (ed.) (1997). *Virtue Ethics*. Edinburgh: Edinburgh University Press.

Virtue Theory

Julia Driver

The interest in virtues expressed in the ethical theory literature has focused attention on (1) how the "standard" ethical theories, such as utilitarianism and Kantian ethics, account for virtue evaluation and (2) virtue-based alternatives of those standard theories. (1) and (2) help make up the field of virtue theory. (2) is virtue ethics. Since this paper is a debate between myself and a virtue ethicist, it will focus on (2) and the various shortcomings of this approach to ethical theory, concentrating particularly on the practical problem – how the theory can be applied in giving an assessment of courses of action as 'right' or 'wrong.'

Shortly after virtue ethics began to be explored as a serious option in normative ethical theory, a flurry of papers came out attacking the very idea. Many criticisms focused on the practical issue of actually trying to apply a virtue ethics. Virtue ethics was widely seen as advocating a rejection of rules for guiding action. This rejection led some writers, such as Robert Louden, to question whether virtue ethics could be applied at all. How, for example, can it be used to guide action if it provides no rules for agents to follow? If one is guided by virtue ethics, what decision procedure is used in trying to figure out what one ought to do? We also need rules to help set public policy, since these rules are publicly accessible standards which can be appealed to in the public justification of policies. Virtue ethics seems woefully inadequate in this regard, and thus, Louden charges, fails as a practical theory.[1]

For a long time, this problem – which I will term the 'application problem' for the duration of this essay – posed a serious threat to advocates of virtue ethics. This problem was compounded by the fact that virtue ethics was really only understood negatively – defined more by attacks on established theories than by any positive position. This made it even more difficult to discuss the application problem, since no concrete alternative had been suggested which could be tested. Other critics, such as Gary Watson, expressed skepticism that a genuine alternative to deontological and consequentialist theories could be worked out – and in the absence of a positive alternative, this challenge has also been difficult to rebut.

That has changed in recent years in large part due to the impressive efforts of writers such as Rosalind Hursthouse, Michael Slote, and Christine Swanton.[2] Hursthouse, in *On Virtue Ethics* (1999) as well as some earlier publications, has offered an account of right action which she considers virtue ethical, and which she claims can guide action better than (or at least as well as) decision procedures offered by other theories. Hursthouse rejects the eliminativist strand of virtue ethics, traceable to G. E. M. Anscombe's "Modern moral philosophy" (1958), which rejects 'right' and which seems to have been adopted by anti-theorists. Nevertheless, Hursthouse's theory is virtue ethical because it holds virtue evaluation to be the primary mode of evaluation.[3] Right action is defined in terms of virtue, not virtue in terms of right action. If one doesn't think the theory better than utilitarianism or Kantianism, she also argues that it at least holds its own. My claim here is that she is overly optimistic about this.

A Virtue Ethical Account of Right Action

Hursthouse (1999: 28) offers the following definition of right action:

> P1. An action is right iff it is what a virtuous agent would characteristically (i.e. acting in character) do in the circumstances.

On her view, this allows one to derive rules, what she terms 'v-rules' which will guide action, and it also provides a guide for making assessments of actions as 'right' or 'wrong'. She points out that her virtue ethical account of right action is supposed to both provide a decision procedure for determining what one ought to do, as well as a criterion of evaluation. She puts it this way:

> [I]s the virtue ethics account of right action only providing action guidance, yielding answers to the question, "What is the morally right decision for me to make here?", or is it also providing action assessment, yielding answers to the question, "What is the morally right thing for me to do here?" Well, given that "There isn't one" is an answer to the latter question, albeit not an answer we usually expect, I think we should say that it is dong both. (Ibid. 51)

V-rules embody virtues that are readily identifiable – "Be honest," "Be kind," and so on – so, one knows one ought to be honest. Hursthouse notes that most normal adults will know what honesty consists in. If one performs an action that the honest person would perform and as the honest person would perform it – one that is properly motivated, done for the right sorts of reasons, even if, overall, one happens not to be virtuous – the action is nevertheless the right action.[4] It is right, and one ought to do it, and it warrants a "tick of approval," in Hursthouse's words. So, for example, we might readily concede that a character like Oskar Schindler is not fully virtuous because of his personal flaws, yet hold that he acted rightly when he helped to save Jews from the Nazis. This characterization of right action is, however, crucially indeterminate in a variety of respects – an issue I plan to develop further in this paper.

But the simple formulation suffers from a problem that Hursthouse readily admits. It has a difficulty with certain moral dilemmas, the ones she labels "tragic." Tragic dilemmas are ones "from which the virtuous agent cannot emerge with her life unmarred" (ibid. 79). One example she discusses is Williams's notorious Jim and Pedro case, where Jim is given a choice of killing 1 villager to save 19 others, or allowing all 20 to be killed by Pedro (Williams 1973: 98–100). These are particularly problematic for Hursthouse's initial definition of 'right action' since, though there may be a truth to the matter as to what the virtuous person would do in those circumstances, yet any option is so awful we cannot actually approve of it.

Consider another example one frequently sees discussed in the literature on moral dilemmas. That is the *Sophie's Choice* example in which a mother is required to choose which child to send to immediate death.[5] Even supposing it is crystal clear to Sophie which child should be sacrificed, Hursthouse would probably argue that in making that decision Sophie has thereby destroyed her own life by doing something supremely horrible. It may have been the right thing to do in the purely action-guiding sense, but she argues that it does not warrant a "tick of approval" and thus is not right in the evaluative sense. One cannot approve of the sacrifice of one's child, and this is a situation from which a virtuous person – in this context, the kind, caring, and nurturing mother – cannot emerge with her life unmarred. So, the virtuous person would do something which does not warrant the tick of approval, and this seems to be a problem for Hursthouse's initial definition of right action. These sorts of cases motivate her to make the following modification to the definition:

> An action is right iff it is what a virtuous agent would, characteristically, do in the circumstances, except for tragic dilemmas, in which case a decision is right iff it is what such an agent would decide, but the action decided on may be too terrible to be called 'right' or 'good'. (And a tragic dilemma is one from which a virtuous agent cannot emerge with her life unmarred.) (1999: 79)

As I've claimed elsewhere, however, there are a variety of less ad hoc strategies she could pursue.[6] For example, one could hold that Sophie acted rightly, and approve of her action under those circumstances – circumstances which are truly horrific ones and thankfully do not reflect the sorts of lives most of us (who are reading this) face. A person can admit that she acted rightly and yet feel terrible about it. She feels terrible about having to make that sort of choice, of being placed in a situation inherently tragic.

There's another worry that Hursthouse bites the bullet on. That's the messiness worry. One might note that given the variety of responses in many situations open to the virtuous person, there will be an awful lot of right actions in a given context. Dilemma situations highlight this, and these are the ones she focuses on, but even more ordinary situations bring this out. For example, in trying to figure out what sort of present to buy for one's child there may be no determinate right answer, and wide range satisfies the requirement. So, in many situations there is no *the* right answer. Any theory which pretends to give you a decision procedure that will tell you *the* right answer is hopelessly flawed and misleading on her view. Real life is messy, and Hursthouse's theory may be messy, but it reflects real life. She embraces messiness. Indeed, this is presented as superior to the utilitarian who provides a false sense of precision, and it is entirely in harmony with the Aristotelian approach.

However, we should note a distinction between epistemic messiness and metaphysical messiness. Even the most hard-core objective consequentialist who thinks that for almost any choice there is one right answer can herself embrace epistemic messiness. Just because there is, objectively, a best outcome doesn't mean that ordinary agents are in a position to know what that outcome is. A huge variety of alternatives could be equally well supported by the available evidence. Noting this, I believe, goes a long way toward rehabilitating the utilitarian account, if one did feel the need to embrace messiness as a theoretical desideratum.

Application Problems for Hursthouse's Account

Now I'd like to consider what I believe to be the most serious problem Hursthouse's account has in dealing adequately with the application problem. It is too indeterminate. The right action is the action that the virtuous agent would perform in the circumstances – but how are we to understand "the action that the virtuous agent would perform in the circumstances"? 'Circumstances' covers a lot of ground. Is this to include the agent's motives or reasons for acting, or not? Is Kant's shopkeeper who pays his debts out of selfish concern for his own reputation acting rightly? I think that we have a powerful intuition in the affirmative – yes, he's doing the right thing, but for the wrong reasons.

But Hursthouse at least seems to disagree; for her, what the virtuous agent would do includes the reasons, and they must be the right reasons:

> This rules out helping, or facing danger, or telling the truth, or whatever for ulterior reasons or under compulsion. (It is common, but a little misleading, to describe such cases as "doing the right thing for the wrong reason(s)." What is misleading about this phrase is that it obscures the fact that, in one way, the agent is not "doing the right thing." What she is doing is, say, trying to impress the onlookers, or hurting someone's feelings, or avoiding punishment.) (Ibid. 125)

As indicated, Hursthouse's account of right action seems plausible when it comes to handling cases of bad people who nevertheless do good things, because they've been motivated properly in a given instance – maybe Oskar Schindler is like this: someone whose overall life might be morally problematic, yet who was stirred by compassion to save lives at considerable risk to himself. Hursthouse clearly holds the sensible view that one need not oneself be perfectly virtuous to perform right actions. But the action that one performs, for it to qualify as right, would have to be, loosely speaking, well motivated in that context.

To me, the gloss Hursthouse gives seems implausible because there are cases where we believe good people act wrongly sometimes precisely because they are good, and bad people act rightly precisely because they are bad. Her gloss doesn't seem to allow this split. Suppose that the only way to get rid of an evil dictator who has taken over one's country is to kill him and the only way to do this (let's suppose) is by strangling him with one's shoelace. It may well be that the kind, compassionate person would not be able to carry it through, whereas a ruthless person would be able to. It seems very natural to me to say that the ruthless person – the person who hated the dictator with an all-consuming passion and was able to carry it through on that hatred – did the right thing in killing the evil dictator, though he was only able to do it because he was ruthless. The compassionate person who could not carry it through acted wrongly. In these cases Hursthouse's theory seems to give the wrong answer.

However, a lot hinges on your view of what the virtuous agent would do. What the compassionate person would do, arguably, would be to let the dictator get away. For Hursthouse to deny this seems to involve making use of an implausible – to me, anyway – empirical claim that that's not how compassionate people really behave.[7] Along these lines one might hold that a truly compassionate person has inner resources of ruthlessness that only show themselves at the right times.

Or, the intuitions she wants to be reaching here could be due to the fact that we think that the compassionate person should kill the evil dictator; that's what he ought to do, because that's what anybody ought to do, and virtuous people – that is, people who are truly virtuous – are those who do what they ought to do. But then her definition wouldn't be giving an independent standard for determining what we ought to do. It becomes trivialized, simply making the claim that the right action is the one that the person who performs right actions would do under the circumstances.

Suppose that Hursthouse were instead to be arguing that the right action is one that the person who is well motivated would perform, but the agent actually performing the action need not be well motivated for the action to be right. Thus, the shopkeeper is acting rightly in handing out the correct change even though motivated purely out of contempt, let's say, for the people he interacts with. This, however, still leaves the account open to criticism due to other sorts of indeterminacy. For example, are we really to do what the virtuous person would do? But surely this is not right in many contexts. Consider first a case involving what is intuitively a non-moral virtue. Suppose that Al is walking along a river and happens to see some children struggling in the water – in danger and in need of assistance. Suppose also that it's clear to him that the assistance could be rendered at little risk to the normal person. The virtuous person – given an acceptable level of risk – would enter the river and try to help them (by pulling them to the river bank, for example). But suppose Al knows that – given his severe water phobia – he would simply enter the river and freeze, and thus risk drowning along with the others. Under these circumstances, it seems that that is not the right thing to do. Instead he should do something else, like call the police or a rescue squad. Of course, one could argue that the water phobia should be part of the circumstances, so the real issue is what a virtuous person who had a water phobia would do. But then, do we build real character flaws into the circumstances? Suppose that it isn't a water phobia, but just plain cowardice that keeps Al from entering the water. It seems incoherent to ask what a virtuous person – who was a coward, i.e. vicious – would do in that case. So, if flaws are not considered to be part of the circumstances, this account gives us the wrong answer. If flaws are counted, then it risks being incoherent. This seems to me to be a problem. It seems the account isn't easily applicable after all.

One alternative formulation, however, might be to define 'right action' as that action which the virtuous person would advise one to perform in the circumstances. In fact, this alternative seems in keeping with some of Hursthouse's comments on using the virtue ethical account of right action:

> [I]f I know that I am far from perfect, and am quite unclear what a virtuous agent would do in the circumstances in which I find myself, the obvious thing to do is to go and ask one, should this be possible . . . we do not always act as "autonomous," utterly self-determining agents, but quite often seek moral guidance from people we think are morally better than ourselves. . . . If you want to do what is right, and doing what is right is doing what the virtuous agent would do in the circumstances, then you should find out what she would do if you do not already know. (Ibid. 35)

However, what Hursthouse is discussing here is how one goes about, as a practical matter, identifying what the virtuous person would do. If in doubt, ask her! This is in response to the epistemological worry that the ordinary agent might have difficulty determining the right action because she would have difficulty determining what the virtuous agent would do. This is quite different from defining right action as that action the virtuous agent would advise one do in the circumstances. If we go this latter route (which Hursthouse is not actually doing – it's just one way to go on spelling out the account) in defining 'right action', then we've ended up with a modified ideal observer account of what a right action is. And this will, I believe, either lead the account to be obviously false, or put it at risk of circularity or vacuousness. This is because it seems natural to ask the further question, "Why would the virtuous agent advise me to do A?" If the answer is simply that what the virtuous agent advises determines right action, independent of any other reasons or considerations, then the account seems quite capricious; if, on the other hand, there are independent reasons, then aren't those the right-making features – and then isn't what the virtuous agent advises superfluous? The mistake would be something like thinking that clean water is the water that the EPA advises me is perfectly okay to drink. The water is not clean because of the EPA's advice. Rather, there are factors the EPA takes into consideration that warrant following its advice. It is those factors which determine whether or not the water is clean (one hopes, anyway).

It is also worth noting that this same sort of worry will afflict the initial definition of right action, since one will be curious about the features the virtuous agent is apparently picking up on and responding to. If one fixes on features of the motivational and emotional structure of the virtuous agent as crucial, then one winds up having to deal with the other difficulties I mention.

Now if Hursthouse were to adopt this modification, then this sort of worry might be met by her later development of the naturalistic aspects of her account. Thus, one defines right action in terms of the virtuous agent (what he would do, what he would advise be done, etc.) and then one understands the virtuous agent as embodying human excellences which are understood entirely naturalistically. So the right action is the one that the well-functioning human being would advise me to do because it embodies human excellence, or virtue, to the extent possible in the present circumstances. And to avoid circularity human excellence must be understood completely independently of the moral concept of 'right'. But, as writers like Gary Watson (1990) point out, this type of account runs the risk of making virtue a sort of health concept, lacking the right kind of normativity (moral normativity). Suppose, for example, that we understand 'well-functioning' as normal functioning, and then understand normal functioning in some kind of statistical way – then it could turn out that well-functioning human beings fail to risk themselves for the sake of others. While this surely does not seem a requirement of virtue, such risk is quite compatible with virtue, so an account that would render this behavior vicious seems problematic. Yet, one can't appeal to notions of moral goodness or rightness to explain why such behavior is virtuous.

There is the further issue of why we should even care. Suppose it was pointed out to me that normal human beings, or the typical human being, brushed his or her teeth at least once a day. Why would this make me care one way or the other about brushing my teeth?

The general problem is that 'well-functioning' can be understood as neutral, or even, possibly, bad – at least in principle. We seem to want intuitively some independent standard which would help us to understand the sort of 'well-functioning' that seems relevant to virtue. But then we begin the drift away from a view in which virtue terms themselves have moral primacy. Instead, we need to look at 'well-functioning' and define virtue in terms of it. In which case, right action can be better understood in terms of this concept. Indeed, this latter problem may turn out to be a problem for any neo-Aristotelian account which attempts to define 'right action' in terms of 'virtue'.[8]

The above critical points have focused on unpacking 'right action'. But in applying an ethical theory it is also useful to have a sense of one's obligations; the view that there is a wide range of actions which might qualify as 'right' seems akin to noting that there is a wide range of actions that qualify as permissible. But this doesn't tell us what we have an obligation to do. Hursthouse could respond by noting that her theory does provide some guidance along these lines: an action is wrong if it is what a vicious person, acting characteristically, would do in the circumstances. And one is obligated not to perform wrong actions. It is interesting to ask, however, where the category of the supererogatory would fall. Clearly, a supererogatory action would fall into the category of right, but how do we determine which actions are supererogatory and which are merely right or permissible? When confronted with the children in distress of the earlier example, some virtuous persons would seek assistance and some would go into the water themselves to save the children, so both of these qualify as 'right'. Yet, intuitively, we regard one as the minimally decent thing to do, and the other as heroic or supererogatory. One could go on to argue that obligation is set by the minimally demanding action that falls within the range of right actions. But judged against a virtue standard even this seems, in its own way, to be rather demanding. Consider actions which are suberogatory – that are bad, but not forbidden.[9] Performing suberogatory actions does not involve violating obligations, yet they do carry with them some degree of negative moral evaluation. An example: Alicia rudely refuses to tell Barbara the time of day. Well, virtuous persons are not rude. It would then seem to follow that not only is telling her the time the right thing to do, it is obligatory. This is a trivial sort of example, but suberogatory acts can involve, in principle, more serious harms to others – for example, a brother who refuses to donate a kidney to his ailing sibling, for example. Virtuous persons, plausibly, do more, typically, that live up to minimal obligations. This will be a problem for any fuller account of moral distinctions drawn along strictly virtue ethical lines.

Hursthouse is free to employ the *tu quoque* response again, and note that other theories also have problems drawing such distinctions. Utilitarianism, just as an example, while it can set a fairly clear, though perhaps onerous, standard of moral obligation, has difficulty with the supererogatory and the suberogatory as well.

One virtue ethicist who discusses this issue is Christine Swanton (2002). Swanton takes on a virtue ethical analysis of the demandingness problem. Usually this is presented as a problem for utilitarianism, a theory that maintains one ought to maximize or optimize the good. This can impose fairly extreme obligations – obligations to donate all one's wealth to famine relief, for example, to the point where one is living at a subsistence level, or just slightly above it. However, the same problem could be posed for a virtue ethicist – if, for example, one believed that one ought to do what the perfectly virtuous person would do, and if one thought that the perfectly virtuous person was someone like Mother Teresa, who did in fact dedicate her life to alleviating the suffering of others, then, again, the demandingness problem arises. Also, as we saw in the discussion of Hursthouse's account, there is no comfortable way to accommodate the supererogatory.

Swanton's account is a mix of different approaches to virtues. One such approach incorporates Nietzschean insights. Thus, she takes very seriously Nietzsche's instruction to "not be virtuous beyond our strength." This supports a "moderate" rather than an "extreme" view of the demands of morality – one that does not require utter self-sacrifice for the sake of virtue. However, Swanton also thinks the entire demandingness problem has been misframed, partly because it has been presented as a way of understanding ethical theories that are not virtue ethical. The key to her account is to argue that there is a variety of ways to approach value. Like the utilitarians, one may promote value (and this leads to the classic problem of demandingness as explained above), or one may honor value; but more centrally, value itself is not the be-all and end-all of morality. Swanton writes: "If we allow as fundamental bases of moral acknowledgment bonds and status as well as value, pursuing one's passion for art rather than saving extra lives may well lose its paradoxical air from a moral perspective" (2002: 200).

It is morally just fine for me to give preference to my own projects since I have a special bond of self-love with them, and to those of family and friends, even though I could otherwise save lives because I have a special bond with them and they have a special status relative to me. Balance and a moderately demanding morality is achieved by weighing different sorts of things against each other and giving due weight to projects one has a bond to as well as more humanitarian objectives. The story that Swanton ends up with is, of course, the story everyone wants to hear (except, perhaps, for the starving persons who happen not to have a special bond with any of us). But the very pluralism which allows her to make accommodation to ordinary moral practice gives her account a kind of messiness; what is the right way to weigh the various considerations? Leave aside the issue of whether or not one can actually do it; in principle, how would it be done even by the ideal agent?

Trying to retain 'right' as a category of evaluation, and giving an account of right action in terms of virtue – attempting to give priority to virtue – will inevitably lead to variations on some of the problems I discuss here. For example, Michael Slote (2001) has provided an account of a Humean virtue ethics, one that ties right action to the agent's motivation in performing the action. Slote's view is much more internalist than either Hursthouse's or Swanton's. He argues for an agent-based account in which right action is completely defined as an 'expression' of a person's good or virtuous motive. This is agent-based because it treats virtue as primary (and is thus a virtue ethics), but it also claims that it is internal features of the agent which are the only things that matter morally. Neither Hursthouse, who is a neo-Aristotelian and who thus ties virtue to actual human flourishing, nor Swanton, who views "effectiveness" as one important moral factor, adopts such an extreme internalism. One of Slote's major problems, of which he is well aware, is that his view seems to cut the agent off from the world. Given that the effects of one's actions and character matter not a whit to their value, a person can act rightly or be virtuous even if their behavior systematically leads to disaster. Slote tries to avoid this objection by noting that, though consequences per se matter not, caring about consequences does. The virtuous agent does care about what happens in the world. This problem of what Slote terms "moral autism" is, it seems to me, fairly serious. As I note elsewhere, it does mean that the moral quality of the person's actions is not contingent on what happens external to the agent, that is, for example, on factors such as consequences. However, there is a very serious circularity worry with this account – as with most virtue ethical accounts – of right action. Slote argues that the good action is an expression of good motive. How do we know what a good motive is without also appealing to some other factors? We have an intuitive grasp of this. But what explains the goodness of the motive irrespective of how we come to see it as good? It is tempting to explain the goodness of motives in terms of the good effects they generate, but this is certainly not open to Slote. Aside from this, he needs to give an account of what the "expression" of a motive is. It is distinct from mere causation. A good action is expressed by a good motive when the action is not only caused by the motive but also conforms to the content of the motive that renders the motive good. So, for example, eating an orange is not an expression of a good motive (even if, somehow, it were caused by the good motive). But does this mean that the morally good, or right action, is caused by the motive that enjoins one to perform morally good, or right, actions? If so, we have a kind of vacuous account. I think that there are ways for Slote to expand on this account, but the circularity worry clearly needs to be met.

Conclusion

Virtue ethics has clearly been developed as an alternative ethical theory, and really one with it's own set of problems and clarificatory issues. My own view, however, is that it certainly offers no advantages over consequentialism: views such as Hursthouse's and Swanton's are complicated by the fact that they want to have their cake and eat it too. They want theories that have a strong internalist component and yet don't cut the agent off from the world, so also have an external success or effectiveness condition. What this means is that the theories have numerous problems associated with both conditions: they have the problem of Slote's account in trying to give criteria for "good" internal states, and they also have many of the standard problems for consequentialism – how, for example, do we limit the scope of consequences that are "relevant" to determinations of virtue? Slote's account, on the other hand, has the moral autism problem and a real difficulty in knowing how in principle even to apply the theory. Good laws may come from bad motives, as might a just act or decision; and there's a good deal of intuitive plausibility to the claim, "she did the right thing, though her motives weren't so good."

None of what I've said should be taken to imply that virtue ethics has no value. What virtue ethicists have done is to generate a Renaissance for virtue theory – the study of virtues – within ethical theory. This is extremely significant, and has led to an enormous amount of interesting and fruitful research on the nature of virtues, or virtue evaluation, and character. My task in this essay has been to focus on and criticize a particular attempt to award virtue primacy – the attention that virtue ethicists have drawn to a neglected topic, however, is only to be applauded.[10]

Notes

1 Some writers, such as Edmund Pincoffs (1986), reject this criticism on the grounds that modern ethics is too concerned with dealing with "quandaries" and thus neglects most of what is morally significant in our everyday lives.

2 Other writers, such as Jorge Garcia (1990), would develop virtue ethical accounts of "right," though did not apply the account.

3 See Watson (1990: 449–69).

4 Note that this definition distinguishes her account from that offered as a possibility for virtue ethics by Gary Watson, who offers the following as a possibility for how one might try to develop a virtue ethical account of right action in terms of the explanatory primacy of virtue:

> Right and proper conduct is conduct that is contrary to no virtue (does not exemplify a vice). Good conduct is conduct that displays a virtue. Wrong or improper conduct is conduct that is contrary to some virtue (or exemplifies a vice). (1990: 455)

This is a weaker definition. On this view, buying a bagel for breakfast is the right thing to do. But then so is buying a muffin instead.

5 See William Styron's *Sophie's Choice*; extensively discussed in the literature. See, for example, Sinnott-Armstrong (1988).

6 For further critical discussion of this feature of Hursthouse's account see my review of *On Virtue Ethics* (Driver 2002).

7 David Estlund pointed out to me that, strictly speaking, Hursthouse's definition is too broad, and this presents another problem. Suppose that it turns out that virtuous persons characteristically (if that is understood as "typically") knock three times, or let the phone ring three times before answering, etc. It would follow that all of those are thereby "right,"

yet this seems absurd, since surely they are neutral. Knocking on a door four times would not be immoral. To avoid this, some more detailed understanding of 'characteristically' would have to be provided.

8   I believe that this is the worry Watson alludes to in "On the Primacy of Character."
9   I discuss this category of action in more detail in my article "The Suberogatory" (Driver 1992).
10 An earlier version of this essay was presented at the Pacific Division Meetings of the American Philosophical Association in March 2002, at an "Author meets critics" panel in honor of Rosalind Hursthouse's book. Some of this material also figured into a presentation on the application problem for virtue ethics delivered at CAPPE, Canberra, in August 2001. I thank the members of those audiences for their very helpful comments, particularly Dave Estlund, Michael Ridge, and Michael Smith.

References

Anscombe, G. E. M. (1958). "Modern moral philosophy." In R. Crisp and M. Slote (eds.), *Virtue Ethics*. Oxford: Oxford University Press, 1997.

Driver, J. (1992). "The suberogatory," *The Australasian Journal of Philosophy* (September).

Driver, J. (2002). Review of Hursthouse's *On Virtue Ethics*. *The Philosophical Review* (January): 122–7.

Garcia, J. (1990). "The primacy of the virtuous." *Philosophia*, 20: 69–91.

Hursthouse, R. (1999). *On Virtue Ethics*. Oxford: Oxford University Press.

Pincoffs, E. (1986). *Quandaries and Virtues*. Lawrence, KS: University Press of Kansas.

Sinnott-Armstrong, W. (1988). *Moral Dilemmas*. Oxford: Blackwell.

Slote, M. (2001). *Morals From Motives*. New York: Oxford University Press.

Swanton, C. (2002). *Virtue Ethics*. New York: Oxford University Press.

Watson, G. (1990). "On the primacy of character." In Owen Flanagan and Amelie Rorty (eds.), *Identity, Character, and Morality*. Cambridge, Mass.: MIT Press.

Williams, B. (1973). *Utilitarianism*. New York: Cambridge University Press.

REASON AND MOTIVATION

Are Moral Requirements Derived from Reason?

Reason, Sentiment, and Categorical Imperatives

Samuel J. Kerstein

Morality is based in reason. That slogan is (and ought to be) associated with Kant's ethics. But the slogan's simplicity should not obscure that it represents a number of distinct and complex claims. Among them is the following: According to common sense, morality contains categorical imperatives; and such imperatives can be grounded only in reason. Here I defend this claim against a sentimentalist opponent.

After summarizing a sentimentalist moral theory, I argue that it is incompatible with the notion that there are absolutely necessary and universal obligations, that is, categorical imperatives. Such imperatives cannot be grounded in feelings. I then contend that the account of obligation suggested by sentimentalism clashes with ordinary moral thinking in ways that a Kantian account does not. In particular, sentimentalism is unable to accommodate the widespread judgment that, in many circumstances, members of a group have an obligation not to manipulate, exploit, or coerce outsiders, even if the members believe that doing so will benefit their group. I resist the sentimentalist suggestion that we forfeit nothing significant if, unable to assert that the members of the group are obligated to treat outsiders decently, we simply designate the members' behavior as vicious or odious when they fail to treat them decently. Finally, I underscore the plausibility of believing in categorical imperatives. I suggest that it is no more odd to believe in them than it is to hold 'the hypothetical imperative' to be valid. It is even reasonable to think that sentimentalism (or at least the version of it I consider) is itself committed to there being a categorical imperative.

The main claim I defend is not transparent. It is not obvious what a categorical imperative is supposed to be, let alone what it would mean for one to be grounded in reason. But the meaning of the claim comes to light if we examine it in relation to several other claims underlying the Kantian slogan that morality is based in reason.

Reason and Morality According to Kant

To begin, Kant contends that philosophical argument rationally compels all of us to hold the Categorical Imperative to be valid. In one well-known version, the Formula of Humanity, the Categorical Imperative commands: "So act that you treat humanity, whether in your own person or in the person of any other, always at the same time as an end, never merely as a means" (Kant 1996b: 80; italics omitted). To hold this principle to be valid is to maintain that it is unconditionally binding on all rational agents; we always ought, all things considered, to act in accordance with it, no matter what we might desire to do. In the third section of the *Groundwork of the Metaphysics of Morals*, Kant unfurls a complex philosophical argument, which he calls a "deduction," in an attempt to demonstrate the Categorical Imperative's validity. If the attempt succeeds, then, in Kant's view, he establishes that this imperative is the supreme principle of morality.

But Kant soon abandons the attempt to construct a deduction of the Categorical Imperative. In the *Critique of Practical Reason*, published three years after the *Groundwork*, he asserts that "the objective reality" of the Categorical Imperative "cannot be proved by any deduction" (1996a: 177–8). For present purposes, let us call a philosophical argument one that rests (or purports to rest) on premises that it is demonstrably irrational to deny since, for example, it can be shown that denying them involves self-contradiction. Kant here seems to claim that no philosophical argument can establish the Categorical Imperative's validity. Nevertheless, he says, the Categorical Imperative (or the moral law) "is given, as it were, as a fact of pure reason of which we are a priori conscious and which is apodictically certain" (ibid. 177); the Categorical Imperative is "firmly established of itself" (ibid. 178). Precisely what Kant means here is debatable, but I think he implies at least the following. Since we have a certain capacity, namely reason, the Categorical Imperative is binding on us. Each rational agent's own reason demands that he abide by the Categorical Imperative. Moreover, each rational agent is able to realize that he is bound by this principle. So the Kantian slogan that morality is based in reason also contains the claim that it is partly constitutive of being a rational agent to be bound by the Categorical Imperative and to be able to realize that one is so bound.

In a third sense, the dictum that morality is based in reason amounts to the claim that for all agents all the time, it is irrational to act contrary to the Categorical Imperative. Immoral action is irrational action. Our own reason sets forth this imperative, so it is contrary to reason to disobey it. For Kant the irrationality of immoral conduct is a function of its clashing with a valid demand of reason. If the Categorical Imperative was not valid, then in Kant's view there would not necessarily be anything at all irrational in someone's pursuing his goal of getting rich by making a false promise or always refusing to help others in need.

A fourth Kantian claim that lies beneath the slogan that morality derives from reason takes shape against the background of a terminological distinction. Kant and Kantians use 'categorical imperative' in several different ways. I employ 'Categorical Imperative' (capitalized) to refer to the imperative that Kant takes to be the supreme principle of morality. I use the term 'categorical imperative' (lower case) in a more general sense, namely to refer to any principle that has two characteristics. The first is that of absolute necessity. A principle is absolutely necessary just in case all agents within its scope are, all things considered, obligated to do what it specifies, and, moreover, their obligation is unconditional in that it does not depend on the agents' having any particular desires or ends.[1] An absolutely necessary principle can be "overridden" neither by any other principle, nor by any inclination or need, no matter how pressing. A categorical imperative's second characteristic is universality, that is, a scope that extends to all rational agents. According to Kant, of course, the Categorical Imperative counts as a categorical imperative. (That's another way of saying that the Categorical Imperative is valid.) But we need to keep in mind that a categorical imperative is any principle, invoked by Kant or not, that has these characteristics. A fourth claim implicit in the slogan that morality is grounded in reason is the following. According to reflective common sense, morality contains categorical imperatives. But philosophical inquiry reveals that the only way there can be categorical imperatives is if they are demands placed on rational agents by the agents' own reason. Categorical imperatives cannot exist if morality is based entirely on God's will, custom, sentiment, and so forth. Kant defends this claim (at least implicitly) in section 2 of the *Groundwork of the Metaphysics of Morals*.

A fifth Kantian claim implicit in the slogan that morality is based in reason invokes Kant's concept of moral worth. Kant holds that an action has moral worth if and only if it is done from duty. On my interpretation, Kant maintains that an agent acts from duty just in case: her motive for acting stems from the notion that some categorical imperative requires the action; this notion itself provides sufficient motive for her acting; she acts against the background of conscientious reflection; and she does her best to realize her action's end (Kerstein 2002: 138). Actions done from duty involve reason in two main ways. First, a product of reasoning, namely the idea that some categorical imperative requires the action, not only motivates the action but itself provides a sufficient motive for it. When an agent does something from duty, the ultimate source of her motivation to do it can be simply the thought that doing it is required by some unconditionally and universally binding principle. In Kant's terminology, pure reason can be practical (1996a: 165). Actions done from duty invoke reason in a second way in that they involve (what I call) "conscientious reflection." Since, when someone acts from duty, he is interested in doing what is morally required, he must take (or have taken) an active interest in finding out just what that is. The person need not delve into casuistry before every action, but he needs to act against the background of reflection on the moral status of what he does. Such reflection involves reasoning – for example, determining whether a particular sort of action is forbidden by some principle. For Kant, morally worthy action necessarily involves the use of reason, both as a tool for discovering that the action is morally required and as a motive for doing it. This is the fifth claim.

These five claims do not exhaust the ways in which, according to Kant, morality is based in reason. But when someone defends the Kantian slogan, chances are she is championing at least one of them. Listed together, the claims are:

1 Philosophical argument rationally compels all of us to hold that the Categorical Imperative is valid.

2 It is partly constitutive of being a rational agent to be bound by the Categorical Imperative and to be able to realize that one is so bound.

3 It is always irrational for an agent to act contrary to the Categorical Imperative.

4 According to everyday moral thinking, there are categorical imperatives; moreover, categorical imperatives can only be demands placed on rational agents by the agents' own reason.

5 Morally worthy action necessarily involves the use of reason, both as a means taken to discover that the action is required and as a motive for doing it.

A few points regarding the relations between these claims warrant attention. The truth of the second claim does not seem to depend on that of the first. No philosophical argument, let us suppose, is so good that it would be irrational for anyone to deny that it demonstrated the Categorical Imperative to be valid. It might nevertheless be part of what it means to be a rational agent to be bound by this imperative and to be able to realize that one is. Second, for Kant the third claim derives any force it has from the first or the second. If it is true neither that philosophical argument rationally compels all of us to hold the Categorical Imperative to be valid, nor that it is constitutive of being a rational agent to be bound by this imperative, then from Kant's perspective there is no basis for claiming that it is always irrational for an agent to act contrary to the Categorical Imperative. So for him the third claim is derivative. A final point to notice about the relations among the five claims is that the last two might be true even if the first three are all false. Neither (4) nor (5) invokes the Categorical Imperative. To focus on (4), suppose that part of the content of morality is constituted by universal and unconditional imperatives placed on agents by their own reason. If we suppose this, it follows that among these imperatives agents are neither able to find, nor rationally compelled to find, the Categorical Imperative – nor, of course, does it follow that acting contrary to the Categorical Imperative is irrational. Some of Kant's claims regarding morality's being based in reason are independent of his advocacy of the specific principles that count as formulas of the Categorical Imperative, that is, principles such as the Formula of Humanity.

Defending Kant's Claims

Perhaps the most dramatic claim of the five, and the one that a Kantian would be most eager to defend, is the first, namely that philosophical argument rationally compels us to hold the Categorical Imperative to be valid. I would like to defend it. But the deduction of the Categorical Imperative that Kant undertakes in *Groundwork* III is notoriously difficult to interpret, and on no interpretation I am aware of does the argument succeed. For example, on one reading the argument unfolds (in very broad outline) as follows: "Since we take ourselves to be rational, we must assume that we are free, that is, capable of acting spontaneously. But spontaneous action must be governed by some law. And this law could only be the Categorical Imperative. Therefore, we must assume that we are bound by the Categorical Imperative."[2] Each step of this argument is controversial. But even if we accept the first and second steps, it remains unclear why we should embrace the third. What argument establishes that the Categorical Imperative is the only law capable of governing a free will? I simply do not know how to make Kant's deduction of the Categorical Imperative work. Of course, even if no one else at present does either, it does not follow that no one will make it work.

Some contemporary philosophers have defended claims that bear a family resemblance to (1). Christine Korsgaard, for example, tries to demonstrate that unless we take humanity to be valuable, we condemn ourselves to complete practical skepticism, that is, to the view that we have no reason to do anything at all (1996: 122). In other words, if we assume that we have reasons for our actions, then we must value all persons. If Korsgaard's project is successful, then a philosophical argument rationally compels those of us who hold that we have reasons for what we do (i.e., almost all of us) to embrace a morally significant conclusion. An argument that did this would perhaps not be as dramatic as one that rationally compelled us to hold the Categorical Imperative to be valid, but it would be striking nonetheless. Yet, as I explain elsewhere (Kerstein 2001), I do not believe that Korsgaard's argument succeeds. I am aware of no convincing contemporary effort to establish a claim akin to (1). Nevertheless, it is, I think, premature for us to give up hope that a proof will emerge.

But even if we do, we are not forced to give up the slogan that morality is based in reason. As is now evident, this slogan incorporates several claims that do not depend on (1). Elsewhere (Kerstein 2002) I have endorsed some aspects of (5). I think it is plausible to claim that all actions from duty involve reason, and that all such actions have moral worth. But my main aim here is to defend claim (4), namely that according to everyday moral thinking there are categorical imperatives, and that these imperatives can only be demands placed on rational agents by their own reason. In particular, I want to defend this claim against sentimentalism – a philosophical view that vehemently rejects the idea that morality is based in reason.

The claim at issue has two components. The first is relatively straightforward, namely that, according to reflective common sense, there is at least one principle of conduct that is absolutely necessary and universal binding. The second component is a bit more complex. What would it mean for categorical imperatives to be demands placed on rational agents by their own reason? To answer this question thoroughly from the perspective of Kant's ethics would require a long discussion of his theory of agency and his concept of autonomy. Since this is not the place for such a discussion, it makes sense to appeal to aspects of claims (1) and (2) above and to maintain the following. A demand is placed on rational agents by their own reason only if either we are all rationally compelled by philosophical argument to abide by it, or it is partly constitutive of being a rational agent to be bound by it. According to this latter possibility, any failure to honor the demand constitutes a form of irrationality, unless it is sanctioned by some overriding demand that is itself based in reason. The burden of defending the second component is to show that agents' own reason is the only viable candidate for the source of a categorical imperative. In other words, the only way that a principle can have the universality and absolute necessity distinctive of a categorical imperative is for it to be a demand of reason. It will not have it simply by virtue of being commanded by God, or being such that adherence to it will maximize the general welfare, and so forth.

This is a significant burden, and I do not assume it all here. But I do attempt to support the second component of (4). I try to show that a version of sentimentalism recently developed by Simon Blackburn, my opponent in this debate, is incompatible with the notion that there are categorical imperatives. I then argue that this incompatibility is not a mere philosophical curiosity, but brings sentimentalism into conflict with ordinary moral thinking. I thus offer some support for the first component of (4), namely the claim that in our everyday moral reflection we endorse the notion that there are categorical imperatives. Sentimentalism pays a high price for denying that morality is grounded in reason.

In what follows, I take Blackburn's sentimentalism, which is inspired by the theories of David Hume and Adam Smith, as representative of sentimentalism as a whole. For ease of expression, I will refer to his theory simply as 'sentimentalism'. Of course, there are many different versions of sentimentalism, and some might be less vulnerable to the Kantian criticisms presented here than Blackburn's. But I am skeptical of whether any sentimentalist account will be immune to them.

Sentimentalism and Obligation

Blackburn offers a succinct summary of sentimentalism's core:

> First we love one or another quality in people when we come across it, possibly because we have been educated to do so. Then we take up the common point of view which turns love to esteem, assessing a trait of character as admirable or the reverse. Third, we can become aware that this is a trait that we ourselves exhibit, or do not. And fourth, when we do so we are moved to a self-satisfaction and pride, or unease and shame, corresponding to our original assessment, and imagining this assessment made of us by others. This is a kind of internal vibration in sympathy with the imagined sentiments of others. (1998: 203)

Blackburn cites with apparent approval Hume's notion that we love character traits that render those who possess them useful or agreeable to themselves or to others. So suppose a person loves the character trait of being just to strangers. (Someone with this trait will have a disposition, for example, to refrain from cheating people he does not know.) The person then takes the "common point of view" and ends up esteeming this trait as admirable. The common point of view does not amount to the perspective of an impartial spectator, Blackburn suggests. To take this view is not to take into account the interests of all persons, but rather to abstract from one's own position and consider the impact that a trait of character has on "a fairly immediate circle," including the person who possesses it and, for example, his family and friends (ibid. 210). Moreover, to take the common point of view is to embrace a certain kind of civility to others. It is to refuse to "rest content with relations with outsiders that we cannot see ourselves justifying to them" (ibid. 210–11). So presumably in the process of discerning whether the character trait in question is admirable, the person would consider whether, in acting in accordance with it, he could see himself justifying his action to those outside of his circle. A person who had a disposition to be just to strangers would exhibit civility, it seems. Proceeding through Blackburn's account, the person then becomes aware of whether she has the character trait of being just to strangers. Let us suppose that she finds that she does not. Imagining others' disapproval at not having this trait, she experiences the displeasing sentiments of unease and shame.

Blackburn's summary leaves unclear how sentimentalist theory makes room for requirements to perform or refrain from performing certain actions. How do moral obligations stem from the process he describes? To my knowledge, Blackburn does not answer this question. But he would, I gather, embrace an answer suggested by Hume: "[W]hen any action or quality of the mind, pleases us after a certain manner, we say it is virtuous; and when the neglect, or non-performance of it, displeases us after a like manner, we say that we lie under an obligation to perform it" (Hume 1978: 517; italics omitted). So it is the person's displeasing sentiments, ones such as unease or shame, that form the basis of her obligation to acquire the character trait of being just to strangers, or at least to act in a way that a person with this trait would act.

This last point is crucial to the issue of whether sentimentalism coheres with the idea that there are categorical imperatives. On this account, the basis for an agent's obligation to do something is a displeasing sentiment she has when, after taking the "common point of view," she contemplates her not doing it or, perhaps, her not possessing the character of someone who would do it. (For the sake of simplicity, I omit mentioning this latter possibility below.) If an agent does not have this sentiment, then she has no obligation. Of course, if an agent has no obligation to perform a certain action, then a principle commanding that action does not count as a categorical imperative. For it belongs to the concept of a categorical imperative that everyone within its scope is obligated to do what it enjoins. So in order for sentimentalism to ground a particular categorical imperative, each and every person, after taking the common point of view and so forth, must have a displeasing sentiment toward not doing what the imperative commands.

Yet is it plausible to think that everyone would? Blackburn recognizes that there are people who "confine their concerns to their immediate tribe or group or class or gender," and for whom others "don't count as much or just don't count at all." These people might even gain in reputation and honor "by callous or fraudulent dealings" with others outside of their circle. Blackburn calls these people "foreign office knaves," evoking the image of a colonial administrator exploiting a native population (1998: 211).[3] This term is acceptable, as long as we keep in mind that the vast majority of foreign office knaves are found outside of any foreign office. It is naive to deny that they exist in virtually all walks of life, and in an extremely wide variety of cultures (both historical and extant). Limiting ourselves to a slice of the here and now, the Hutus and the Tutsis each have their share of foreign office knaves, and so do the Serbs and Croats, the Palestinians and Israelis, and so forth.

With foreign office knaves in view, take the following candidate for a categorical imperative: 'Do not treat strangers unjustly'. (Let us assume that unjust treatment includes fraud, exploitation, and so forth.) Obviously, the knaves might have no displeasing sentiment toward failing to treat strangers justly. On the sentimentalist account, such a sentiment would emerge from taking the common point of view. But a foreign office knave might not take this point of view. In particular, he might lack the impetus to think about whether he could see himself justifying his actions to outsiders. What the knave cares about is his own welfare and the welfare of his people. A foreign office knave who does not take the common point of view and who thus has no displeasing sentiment toward treating strangers outside of his group unjustly would, according to sentimentalism (at least sometimes), have no obligation to act in accordance with the principle 'Do not treat strangers unjustly'. Sentimentalism would therefore not allow this principle to stand as a categorical imperative.

Of course, that does not entail that it would allow no principle to stand as such. But it does cast serious doubt on the possibility. Take any action. At least one person would fail to have a displeasing sentiment at the prospect of not performing it, it seems reasonable to conclude; and such a person would not be obligated to perform the action. So an imperative prescribing the action's performance would not count as a categorical imperative.

As I mentioned, Blackburn does not explain how moral obligations stem from moral sentiments. So perhaps he would reject the account suggested here, according to which an agent is obligated to do P just in case, after he takes the common point of view, he has a displeasing sentiment toward not doing P. Might a different account of sentimentalist obligation support categorical imperatives? Perhaps, but I do not know what that account would be. Someone might try to render sentimentalist obligation less subjective and contingent by claiming that an agent is obligated to do P just in case, *if he took the common point of view, then he would have* a displeasing sentiment toward not doing P. On this account, obligation would stem not from an agent's actually having a certain sentiment after taking the common point of view, but rather from the fact that he would have this sentiment if he did take the common point of view. But I do not think this hypothetical account helps very much.

Consider again a foreign office knave. In taking the common point of view, he would be asking himself (roughly) whether an individual's exploiting foreigners would be beneficial to that individual's circle. And the answer to that question might, of course, be yes. The knave would also be asking himself whether, in accordance with a notion of civility, he (the knave) could see himself justifying his action to foreigners he was exploiting. Now this is a difficult question to answer, since Blackburn leaves the notion of civility very vague. But the knave might believe that he could fulfill it by saying something like this to those he exploited: "What I have done to you, I consider to be morally unobjectionable. But I would also consider it morally unobjectionable for you to do the same to me (though I would not be happy about it). It is morally permissible for each of us to pursue the good of our own circle." So even if he takes the common point of view, the knave might have a pleasing sentiment toward exploiting foreigners, and so not be obligated to refrain from doing so.

One might object that the knave has not here really taken the common point of view, since he has not really embraced the notion of civility. But is it clear that he has not? The knave does at least see himself to be offering a minimal justification; for he underscores that he is not making an exception of himself: the same standard applies to him as it does to those whom he exploits. (He is appealing to something like what I later call the principle of reasons universalism.) To dismiss the knave's effort as unacceptable, we would need a more thorough account of the distinction between appropriately and inappropriately seeing oneself as able to justify one's actions to outsiders. In any case this objection has little impact. For the sake of argument let us grant that if the knave properly took the common point of view, then he would find that in exploiting others, he would fall short of exhibiting civility. The problem is that for him this realization might not be accompanied by a disagreeable sentiment. Again, the foreign office knave just does not care about anyone outside of his circle. So why think that he would have such a sentiment? Why assume that taking the common point of view would work emotional magic? If, as seems plausible to assume, it would not, then he would not be obligated to refrain from exploiting foreigners. Once again, we find a version of sentimentalism unable to support the principle 'Do not treat strangers unjustly' as a categorical imperative.

These considerations do not prove that no form of sentimentalism could support any categorical imperative. But they do, I believe, cast significant doubt on the possibility of grounding universal, unconditional obligation in moral sentiments. Sentimentalism does not really threaten Kant's claim that categorical imperatives can only be demands placed on rational agents by the agents' own reason.

No Categorical Imperatives, No Problem?

At the tip of the sentimentalist's tongue might be the following rejoinder. So what if sentimentalism is incompatible with the notion that there are categorical imperatives? What does it matter? It matters, I think, because this incompatibility has implications unacceptable to reflective moral common sense. Showing that it does will lend some support to Kant's contention that in our moral thinking we are committed to there being categorical imperatives.

First, sentimentalism must deny that people have obligations when many of us are convinced they do. This point emerges clearly from reflection on a thought experiment suggested by Hume. He invokes the image of "a species of creatures intermingled with men, which, though rational, were possessed of such inferior strength, both of body and mind, that they were incapable of all resistance, and could never, upon the highest provocation, make us feel the effects of their resentment" (1975: 190). We, that is, the human beings intermingled with these creatures, would have no obligation to treat them justly, says Hume. For justice is grounded solely in public utility, which in this case is our utility, and the creatures' weakness renders it useless for us to treat them justly. Nevertheless, Hume suggests that we are "bound by the laws of humanity to give gentle usage to these creatures" (ibid.). Apparently, we are so bound ultimately because treating them well would give us pleasing sentiments (or abusing them would give us displeasing ones). Hume calls our "compassion and kindness the only check, by which [these weak rational creatures] curb our lawless will" (ibid. 190–1). But now suppose that these weak rational creatures were intermingled with a group of foreign office knaves. Devoid of displeasing sentiments toward exploiting these creatures, the knaves would, on Blackburn's (and presumably Hume's) sentimentalist account, have no obligation to treat them decently: to refrain from exploiting, enslaving, or even torturing them. To many of us, this conclusion seems shocking. But a belief that morality embodies categorical imperatives puts us in position to resist it. For it is open to us to maintain that the foreign office knaves are obligated to treat the weak rational creatures decently, since not to do so is to violate a universally and unconditionally binding principle – for example the Kantian imperative not to treat rational agents merely as means.

Second, holding that moral obligations are a matter of sentiment rather than categorical imperatives has implausible implications regarding temporal features of obligations. Imagine you have been raised to your late teens in an insular, protected, and somewhat clannish social group. Prevalent in it is an antipathy toward an ethnic minority whose members are repeatedly represented as lazy, untrustworthy, and vicious. Your concerns are limited almost exclusively to your own happiness and to that of your group. The prospect of exploiting members of this minority gives you no displeasing sentiment whatsoever. You do not ask yourself (and do not care) whether you could justify to them treating them in one way or another. You do not take the common point of view. On Blackburn's sentimentalist account, you have at this point no obligation to refrain from abusing the minority. (That is disconcerting, to say the least, but it is not the issue here.) Now suppose that, much to your chagrin, you and a member of the despised minority must cooperate in the workplace. At the beginning things are tense, but slowly you warm to him and your attitude toward his ethnic group becomes less hostile and dismissive. You do not mention your change of attitude in your own group until one of your friends hatches a plan to cheat a member of the minority out of her paycheck. Almost to your surprise, the prospect of carrying out the plan is very disagreeable to you. You tell your friends that you will not participate, and that it would be better if they left the woman alone. The sentimentalist might say that with your change in attitude, you have come to have an obligation not to exploit the minority. You did not have the obligation before, but you do now. But how would you think of the situation? Would you not believe rather that, before your work experience, you had an obligation not to mistreat the minority, but that you were, regrettably, unaware that you did? That the obligation itself suddenly appeared with the sentiment seems an unlikely thing for you to hold, though it would be quite natural for you to believe that the sentiment helped you become cognizant of the obligation.

If it is odd to think of a person's acquiring an obligation simply through coming to have a certain sentiment, it is perhaps even stranger to think of him as forfeiting it if his sentiments change. Suppose that members of your own group were so persistent and clever in promoting loyalty to them and condemning the minority that your sentiments underwent yet another turn. You found yourself once again unwilling to take the common point of view and devoid of displeasure at the prospect of mistreating the minority. Your obligation not to mistreat the minority would thereby dissolve, according to sentimentalism. But obligations do not seem to pop in and out of existence like that, or so many of us believe. A moral theory that can embrace categorical imperatives can respect this belief. For categorical imperatives would be unconditionally binding.

Is Obligation Overrated?

Here a sentimentalist might object that we have been making entirely too much of the notion of obligation. He might point out, for example, that though on his account we cannot say that the foreign office knaves have an obligation to treat weak rational creatures decently, we can (and undoubtedly would) call the knaves vile and odious. That we can condemn the knaves in these terms shows that sentimentalism is in accord with ordinary moral thinking (Blackburn 1998: 223). Nothing significant is lost. So contrary to the Kantian claim, we are not committed to there being any categorical imperatives.

This objection seems misguided. Some of what is lost can be isolated by considering how a knave might respond to a sentimentalist condemnation of him: "You call my exploitation of the weak vile and odious. But I do not believe that it is, and I am under no obligation to change my behavior." On Blackburn's account, all of what the knave says may well be true. But an advocate of categorical imperatives is able to hold that the last part of what he says is false. Contrary to what the knave contends, he is obligated to treat the weak decently. The sentimentalist gives up any hope of accusing the knave of uttering a falsehood, and thus clashes with ordinary moral thinking.

The sentimentalist seems to forfeit something else as well. The concept of obligation is closely linked to that of blame. A person would not morally blame another for failing to do something if he did not believe it to be morally obligatory to do it, it seems. For example, you would not blame me for taking a vacation if, in your view, I had no obligation to refrain from taking one. Of course, a person might be disappointed when another fails to do something, even if the person does not believe the other's doing it to be obligatory. For example, someone who rejects the idea that donating a third of one's income to charity is morally required might nevertheless regret that his very wealthy friend does not reach that level of giving: he might think she would be a better person if she did. But she would not be the object of his blame. A necessary condition for a person's morally blaming another for doing something seems to be that he believe that refraining from doing it is morally obligatory. If this is correct, then, unlike an advocate of categorical imperatives, the sentimentalist cannot ever blame a foreign office knave for abusing outsiders. The sentimentalist's evaluational capacities seem stunted. For in many circumstances, we do hold foreign office knaves morally blamable. Granted, the sentimentalist can use some of the words we often employ in our judgments of foreign office knaves. He can call a knave odious and vicious. But he can call him this only in a sense that does not imply moral blame. We employ this sense when we apply the terms to bacteria and fungi. In the sentimentalist's scheme, the moral notion of blame disappears along with that of obligation in cases like that of the knave. And many of us believe this to be a genuine loss. It thus appears not only that the sentimentalist's theory is incompatible with categorical imperatives, but also that its being incompatible with them has a significant cost.

A Case for Categorical Imperatives

Acknowledging these points would not doom the sentimentalist. For he can admit that his theory has some unfortunate implications, but maintain that it is the best we can do. It was understandable and even noble to try to show that morality incorporates categorical imperatives that are grounded ultimately in reason. But we can see now that it is a project doomed to failure (Blackburn 1998: 214–24).

I am unaware of any successful attempt to prove through philosophical argument that all of us are rationally compelled to embrace a particular principle as a categorical imperative. To my knowledge, no one has shown, for example, that self-contradiction is the price of denying Kant's Formula of Humanity to be valid. In my view, it is too early to give up on such attempts. But even if we do, we are not forced to abandon the position that morality is based in reason. We can hold that morality contains categorical imperatives, and that (along the lines of Kant's second claim above) it is partly constitutive of being a rational agent to be bound by them.

Let me now try to illustrate the plausibility of holding this. A principle of reason, let us say, is any principle to which all rational agents ought to conform, unless doing so would violate some other, overriding principle to which all rational agents ought to conform. A categorical imperative, then, is a principle of reason that can never be overridden. Now to many of us, Kant seems on target in suggesting that the following is a principle of reason: "If you will an end, then will the means to it that are necessary and in your power" (1996b: 70). An agent would act contrary to this principle, sometimes called 'the hypothetical imperative', and thus irrationally, by willing an end, say to lose weight, but failing to take the means he realizes to be necessary and in his power to attaining it, say significantly reducing his caloric intake. The dieter wills an end but, contrary to reason, fails to do what he understands he needs to do in order to attain it. (Kant, I think, rightly rejects the idea that in all cases such as this the agent does not really will the end.) I know of no successful philosophical argument, that is, no successful argument that rests on premises that purport to be demonstratively irrational to deny, that proves irrationality to be the price of rejecting the hypothetical imperative as a principle of reason. It seems wrong-headed and even bizarre to deny (as Hume sometimes appears to) that there is ever any irrationality in willing an end but failing to will the means to it that one realizes to be necessary and in one's power. Yet as far as I can tell it would be unwarranted at this point to embrace a conclusion as strong, say, as that anyone who denies this thereby falls into self-contradiction. Echoing Kant's remarks regarding the moral law, it seems nevertheless that the hypothetical imperative is "firmly established of itself." A principle might be a principle of reason even though, strictly speaking, no philosophical argument demonstrates that it is.

Someone might acknowledge this point, and perhaps even agree that the hypothetical imperative (or something like it) has a legitimate claim to be a principle of reason, but nevertheless express doubt as to whether there are any categorical imperatives. But consider (what I call) the 'principle of reasons universalism': "If you judge an action permissible for a rational agent in given circumstances, then you must also (are rationally compelled also to) judge it permissible for any other rational agent in relevantly similar circumstances." Despite being hypothetical in grammatical form, this principle is a candidate for a categorical imperative. The principle might make a non-overridable and unconditional claim on all of us. According to it, a person must not judge that an action is permissible for him but not for another solely on the grounds that he is he and the other is the other. If someone judges that an action is permissible for himself but not for another, then it must be on the grounds that their circumstances, perhaps including their personal qualities, somehow differ. It is very hard to envisage circumstances in which the principle would be trumped by any other principle of reason. How, for example, could it come into conflict with (and therefore be overridden by) an important, morally robust categorical imperative like one that says, 'Do not treat persons merely as means'? It seems plausible to hold the principle of reasons universalism to be a categorical imperative, albeit a very modest one. The principle would not prohibit much. As we have seen, it would not forbid a foreign office knave from judging that it is permissible for him to exploit foreigners, as long as he is willing to acknowledge that it is also permissible for foreigners to exploit him when they are in circumstances analogous to his own.

Why focus on such a modest principle? It seems to have just as much claim to being a principle of reason as the hypothetical imperative. But the principle of reasons universalism appears to be a categorical imperative. So it is not as odd as one might think to believe in categorical imperatives.

It is even legitimate to wonder whether sentimentalism itself implicitly relies on a categorical imperative. According to Blackburn: "It is at least as natural to us pretty much to confine our cares to the family or tribe or other local group, as it is to expand our view to include sympathetic practical concern with everyone" (1998: 213). This seems to be correct. Yet recall that for Blackburn the common point of view has two components. It involves asking oneself whether, if an individual performed an action like this, it would have a positive impact on the individual's family, tribe, or other local group. It also involves asking oneself whether one could see oneself justifying this action to persons outside one's circle. If we answer either question negatively, then we will (supposedly) have a disagreeable sentiment toward the action and will presumably be obligated not to perform it. But why is this second component part of the common point of view? If, as Blackburn implies, for many if not most of us it is not natural to have sympathetic practical concern for everyone, why would we care whether we could see ourselves as justifying a course of action to outsiders? It would be unconvincing for the sentimentalist to reply simply that we have a pleasing sentiment towards the idea of our being able to justify ourselves to outsiders. For if we had this pleasing sentiment, then why would so many of us lack sympathetic practical concern for outsiders?

The sentimentalist might say that this aspect of the common point of view has its origins in self-interest (or group interest). Blackburn suggests that this is Hume's response (ibid. 210). The idea seems to be that we cannot avoid interacting with outsiders, and to do well for our circle we need to see ourselves as able to justify our actions to them. This response is open to familiar objections. If we are devoid of sympathetic practical concern for a particular group of outsiders, and they (or their agents) are unable to do us significant harm, then the promotion of our self-interest depends not at all on our ability to justify (or see ourselves as able to justify) our actions to them. Indeed, Hume suggests this point when he argues that we would not be obligated to be just to weak, rational creatures intermingled with us. Moreover, suppose that a different group of outsiders can do us significant harm and that we also have no sympathetic, practical concern for them. In order to promote our own interests, we might need to get them to believe that our actions towards them are justified. But we might accomplish this through deceit and manipulation, all the while caring not a whit that, in our own view, we are unable to justify our actions to them.

Objections such as these might be overcome, but I doubt it. So why might we care whether we are able to see ourselves as justifying our actions to outsiders? It is tempting to reply that it is because a principle of reason commands it. The principle might be a categorical imperative, such as 'Treat rational agents only in ways that, in your view, you can justify to them'. To me this seems every bit as plausible as claiming that what prompts us to care is self-interest alone. Of course, depending on the notion of justification employed, the implications of the imperative might be very weak. As we have noted, an agent might see himself as justified in treating an outsider in any way, as long as he acknowledges that, in similar circumstances, the outsider would be justified in treating him (the agent) in that way. On this notion of justification, fraud or coercion would not necessarily be ruled out.

My own view is that it is reasonable to believe in more robust categorical imperatives. A principle I take to be a plausible candidate is implicit in Kant's Formula of Humanity. It is this: 'Never treat rational agents merely as means'. Very roughly, this imperative forbids any agent in his interaction with another from behaving in a way to which the other cannot consent and, at the same time, pursuing an end which the other cannot share. Elsewhere I hope to offer a detailed defense of this principle. Doing so will, of course, involve making a case for the view that it possesses each feature of a categorical imperative. For example, it might seem that there are instances in which the principle would be overridden. Cases come to mind in which treating one person merely as a means seems to be morally permissible, since doing so is necessary to save the lives of many others. Part of the burden of defending the principle would be to show either that, despite initial appearances, these are not cases that violate it, or that, upon reflection, we are not committed in these cases to the view that violating the principle is morally permissible. If successful, this type of defense will show that it is reasonable to hold a particular principle to be a categorical imperative. It will not prove that inconsistency is the penalty for failing to do so.

Notes

1 In another sense, however, an absolutely necessary principle might not be unconditional. That the imperative 'If you are a parent, you must promote the welfare of your child' contains a condition does not disqualify it from being absolutely necessary.
2 For a very different reading of *Groundwork* III, one that seems better grounded in Kant's texts, see Schönecker (2005).
3 He is, of course, also invoking Hume's "sensible knave," namely someone who "in particular incidents, may think that an act of iniquity or infidelity will make a considerable addition to his fortune, without causing any considerable breach in the social union and confederacy" (Hume 1975: 282).
4 Thanks to David Lefkowitz and Dieter Schönecker for help on this essay.

References

Blackburn, S. (1998). *Ruling Passions.* Oxford: Clarendon Press.

Hume, D. (1975). *Enquiries Concerning Human Understanding and Concerning the Principles of Morals.* Oxford: Clarendon Press. (Original work published 1777.)

Hume, D. (1978). *A Treatise of Human Nature.* Oxford: Clarendon Press. (Original work published 1739–40.)

Kant, I. (1996a). *Critique of Practical Reason.* In Kant, *Practical Philosophy*, trans. Mary Gregor. Cambridge: Cambridge University Press (Original work published 1788.)

Kant, I. (1996b). *Groundwork of the Metaphysics of Morals.* In Kant, *Practical Philosophy*, trans. Mary Gregor. Cambridge: Cambridge University Press (Original work published 1785.)

Kerstein, S. (2001) "Korsgaard's Kantian arguments for the value of humanity." *Canadian Journal of Philosophy*, 31: 23–52.

Kerstein, S. (2002). *Kant's Search for the Supreme Principle of Morality.* Cambridge: Cambridge University Press.

Korsgaard, C. (1996). *The Sources of Normativity.* Cambridge: Cambridge University Press.

Schönecker, D. (2005). "How is a categorical imperative possible? Kant's deduction of the moral law in *Groundwork* III." In Christoph Horn and Dieter Schönecker (eds.), *Kant's Groundwork for the Metaphysics of Morals: New Interpretations.* Berlin: de Gruyter.

Further Reading

Bittner, R. (1989). *What Reason Demands.* Cambridge: Cambridge University Press.

Darwall, S. (1995). *The British Moralists and the Internal 'Ought'.* Cambridge: Cambridge University Press.

Hill, T., Jr. (1992). "Kant's argument for the rationality of moral conduct." In Hill, *Dignity and Practical Reason.* Ithaca: Cornell University Press.

Hill, T, Jr. (2002) "Reasonable self-interest." In Hill, *Human Welfare and Moral Worth.* Oxford: Clarendon Press.

Wood, A. (1999). *Kant's Ethical Thought.* Cambridge: Cambridge University Press.

Must We Weep for Sentimentalism?

Simon Blackburn

A Misunderstanding

Hume said that the distinct boundaries and offices of reason and taste are easily ascertained, including under the heading of "taste" the moral sentiments (1998: Appx 1, p. 163). Alas, he proved over-optimistic. I doubt if any question in moral theory has proved more vexatious. The area is confounded by difficulties over the identification of attitudes and beliefs, over the distinction between senses of the word 'reason' that sentimentalists can admit from those they must deny, over the relation between properties and concepts, over the metaphysics of the categorical imperative, and over much else besides. In this brief essay I can therefore not attempt a full-scale defense of sentimentalism. I shall simply defend the theory against various recent assaults, one of which is mounted in Samuel Kerstein's defense of rationalism in this debate (see this volume, ch. 8). My impression is that Kerstein does not stand alone, but is a spokesman for a whole phalanx of people, perhaps calling themselves 'Kantians', who would sympathize with his assault, or at least fail to understand how a sentimentalist could withstand it.

It is fortunate, then, that the misunderstanding that permeates Kerstein's treatment of sentimentalism is highly visible, and I shall concentrate on one particularly exposed passage. After giving an account of my own neo-Humean description of the emotions and attitudes that underlie our propensity to go in for ethics and morals, he considers the issue of justice to strangers or outsiders. He writes that, on my view, "it is the person's displeasing sentiments, ones such as unease or shame, that form the basis of her obligation to acquire the character trait of being just to strangers, or at least to act in a way that a person with this trait would act." He continues:

This last point is crucial to the issue of whether sentimentalism coheres with the idea that there are categorical imperatives. On this account, the basis for an agent's obligation to do something is a displeasing sentiment she has when, after taking the "common point of view," she contemplates her not doing it or, perhaps, her not possessing the character of someone who would do it. . . . If an agent does not have this sentiment, then she has no obligation. Of course, if an agent has no obligation to perform a certain action, then a principle commanding that action does not count as a categorical imperative. For it belongs to the concept of a categorical imperative that everyone within its scope is obligated to do what it enjoins. So in order for sentimentalism to ground a particular categorical imperative, each and every person, after taking the common point of view and so forth, must have a displeasing sentiment toward not doing what the imperative commands.

So, although Kerstein also chides me for failing to answer the question of how moral obligations "stem from" the processes I have described, he supposes that such an account, were it provided, would inevitably suppose that people without the sentiments are free of the obligation: the "basis" of her obligation is a sentiment, so that "if an agent does not have this sentiment, then she has no obligation." In a similar vein he imagines someone with no sympathy for members of some minority within his society, and says that "on Blackburn's sentimentalist account, you have at this point no obligation to refrain from abusing the minority."

And then, unsurprisingly, he can go on to point out that there are legions of unhappily bad Samaritans, and what I called foreign-office knaves, when I was stressing and lamenting the same sad fact about humanity. These people do not have the appropriate sentiments. Hence, Kerstein concludes, for the sentimentalist, there are people who lie under no obligation to universal justice. Hence, there are no categorical imperatives, for the categorical imperative embraces everyone.

Whatever else is to be said about it, we should notice that this argument is remarkable for its scope. It can be directed not only against sentimentalism, but against any theory that seeks to explain our moral capacities in terms of contingent and potentially variable facets of human nature: language, culture, upbringing, acquired "second nature," and so on. Even reason, insofar as it is empirically variable, or leaves its possessors liable to partial and self-serving policies, will not be enough. Only a universal birthright – and one strong enough to deliver commands to the will – could withstand it. It is a pity, then, that Kerstein himself is not confident of a Kantian story of this kind, since it seems to be the only hope for a theory of the requisite standing. Otherwise there seems to be a straightforward empirical problem. If there is an inner mechanism of reason strong enough to dragoon us all into the ranks of the caring and just, it seems odd that so few of us get affected by it.

Why does Kerstein make the extraordinary supposition that on a sentimentalist story, the knaves and villains not only fail to feel obligations, which they obviously do, but are for that very reason exempt from them? Do you escape a debt if you do not care about it? I should have thought no moral philosopher, except perhaps Gilbert Harman, and certainly not Hume or myself, could have been thought to suggest such a thing. In fact, it seems to me such a shocking thing to say that I am at a loss to understand how Kerstein could have read Hume, or me, and perhaps others such as Allan Gibbard, as saying anything that implies it. For the record, I explicitly say the reverse, fairly often (1998: 210, 230, 265 – and elsewhere).[1]

Must We Weep for Sentimentalism?

The only explanation I can offer for the misreading is that it comes from conflating two different projects. One, the project of the anatomist, in Hume's terms, is to give an accurate and complete account of the states of mind that gain expression in moral thinking. The other, a moralistic project appropriate to Hume's painter, is to give an account of the "sources" of our obligations. In my discussion of Christine Korsgaard's account of 'the normative question' I voice some doubts about how to conduct this second project. Like other pluralists, I think obligations arise for different reasons, and I am not myself wedded to the idea that any one, clear, univocal concept, such as 'utility' or 'self-legislation' might have been thought to be, plays the same explanatory role when we try to describe why we lie under one or another obligation. But it is the anatomist's project that occupies the bulk of my work, and that justifies calling me a 'sentimentalist'.

If you confuse these two projects, you might end up saying that moral obligations "stem from" or "are based in" psychological states, and thence infer that in the absence of the psychological states, the obligations disappear as well. The anatomical view is then supposed to lead to bad morals or bad painting. But it is not I who say that. I would say, for instance, that your obligations as a parent stem from the dependency of your children, their needs, and the absence of other social resources provide a substitute if you fail to meet those needs. If you don't care about your child, you are in breach of the obligation that the child's need places on you.[2] The obligation does not come and go according to your affections, any more than your debt comes and goes depending on whether you care about it. And I think it shocking to suppose otherwise. The obligations you lie under, like the debts you owe, don't decrease or disappear when you stop caring about them.

I think, then, that parents of young children lie under a complex obligation, O. According to the sentimentalist, I say this by way of expressing a complex of attitudes and feelings toward the relationship between parents and their young children – what I shall call 'these sentiments'. Now let us say that someone who ignores or negligently or deliberately falls short in fulfilling an obligation fails O. Finally, suppose we say that people who have no sentiments corresponding to feeling the weight of an obligation laugh-off O. Then we must recognize the distinction between:

If I (we) had not had these sentiments, I (we) would not have been condemning parents who fail O or even those who laugh-off O.

If I (we) had not had these sentiments, I (we) would have failed O or laughed-off O.

If parents X do not have these sentiments, then they are likely to fail O or laugh-off O.

If parents X do not have these sentiments, then they are under no obligation O.

The first three of these are true and harmless. The last is false and absurdly so. But it is the last that is being foisted upon the sentimentalist in the passages I quoted.

I think the transition from the harmless to the absurd is lubricated by careless use of phrases like 'is based upon', or 'stems from'. If you ask me what moral thought itself stems from or is based upon, then, as an anatomist, I give the sentimentalist reply. If you ask me what a particular obligation or duty stems from or is based upon, then my painterly answer may vary, but will seldom cite the feelings of the agent. In this case it stems from the needs of the children, and the sociological structures that make the parent the person responsible for meeting those needs. In the case of a debt, it will have arisen from past contract. In the case of justice to outsiders, again it may stem from the needs of the outsiders, or our overall needs for accommodation with them, or perhaps it stems from fundamental rights to equal treatment. I am not sure: the relationship between justice and mutual advantage, and reciprocity, and equality, is obscure enough for me and many others to feel insecure about exactly how best to paint it. What I am sure about is that you cannot get rid of obligations by laughing them off.

Peacocke's Hi-Tech Version

A trivial misunderstanding becomes worrying when you find it shared by enough people. As I have said, I fear that Kerstein is not alone. Christopher Peacocke (2004) has suggested that sufficient attention to two-dimensional modal logic conjures up a dependency claim which the quasi-realist must accept, but which offends against some conviction that we hold. So, contrary to what I have repeatedly claimed, there is a mind-dependency claim which causes trouble for any sentiment-oriented theory of value. The technology in Peacocke's discussion will doubtless shock and awe enough readers for it to be worth some trouble to show that it is in fact a smokescreen. The issues can be put simply enough, and when they are, the objection disappears.

In a nutshell, the issue goes like this. Peacocke recognizes the general strategy I have repeatedly used. It is an integral part of our ethical lives that we can evaluate scenarios that are described to us, whether past, present, or merely possible or fictional. So if you bring me a story about people and their doings, I can train my thoughts on it, and, according to the attitudes it elicits, I will admire it or condemn it, or hold a whole variety of more or less nuanced responses. If you tell me a story in which people fail to meet their children's needs, I react badly, and I express the conviction that what they are doing is cruel and wrong. I hope we all do. If asked why I condemn their behavior, at least a prime part of my answer is about the needs that are not being met. Perhaps this simplifies a little, since the indifference of the perpetrators also matters, and that is a feature of the perpetrator rather than of the children. But for clarity, and as a harmless simplification, I shall say the verdict is appropriate because of the needs of the children: it is child-dependent. If you told me a story about people causing pain to animals such as dogs, my verdict would be dog-dependent.

So far so good. Now suppose your story is more complicated. You tell me a story in which people not only ignore their children's needs, but *also* in which they fail to condemn such behavior, or even admire it. Perhaps they congratulate and esteem especially harsh or negligent parents. Their moral sensibilities are here the opposite from ours. What am I to say about this? It looks equally bad or somewhat worse to me. In the first story we could imagine some guilt attaching to the behavior: perhaps it is mainly adolescents or criminals or failures who are bad with children, and their ordinary morality condemns it. But in the second story, there is no condemnation from the people who are described. They admire negligence or brutality. It is a horrible scenario, and I deplore it the more.

I have often stressed two further related points. The first is that someone *could* disagree with me about what I have just said. He could urge that the fact that they find it admirable makes all the difference, makes it admirable in fact. We have a moral disagreement, for I deny that. I hold that it is the sad life of a child that is so shocking, and in this imagined society, the parents' self-congratulation at what they are doing takes none of that away, but actually adds to it, making it even more shocking. The second addition is that there might be examples – call them etiquette examples – where the structure looks similar, but my opponent would be right. For there are cases where the bad we do would not be bad at all were it not for the community's unfavorable take on it. I can imagine communities (perhaps there are some) where it is very bad form indeed to give a gift in return for a gift received. In such a community it would be insulting and wrong to do something which amongst us would be a normal expression of gratitude or reciprocated friendship, and it would be right to do something – omitting to reciprocate – which amongst us would be a breach of manners, and even insulting and wrong. In such a case it is true that had we had these different attitudes, different actions would have been right or wrong.[3] Their value is due to the conventions of etiquette that people follow, and these might have been harmlessly different. In the child case, that is not so; as I said, it is due to the unmet needs of the child.

How does Peacocke hope to embarrass this analysis? He says some curious things about it. He says at the beginning of the discussion: "It is very hard to see how it can be denied that, under [my] approach, the conditions under which someone is correct in asserting a moral proposition have something to do with expressed mental states" (2004: 208). And the intention is to show that although, as he recognizes, I claim not to have a "mind-dependent" treatment of morality, in fact I do. Unfortunately these wordings, like Kerstein's above, are ambiguous. Obviously an expressivist treatment of ethics is "mind-dependent" in one sense – it starts from reflections on the kind of mental state that gets expressed when values are made public and exchanged. Obviously as well, "the conditions under which someone is correct in asserting a moral proposition have something to do with expressed mental states" in one sense, although the language is so imprecise that we have to struggle to find it. Still, were the expressed mental states different, the proposition would be different and would be correct under different circumstances. For example, if the sentence "kicking dogs is wrong" standardly expressed approval of kicking dogs, anyone voicing it would be correct only in quite different circumstances, such as ones in which dogs have no conscious states. But there is nothing worrying to the expressivist (or anyone else) in thoughts such as those. The conditions under which someone is correct in asserting *any* proposition has something to do with expressed mental states, in this sense. It has to do with which beliefs are being expressed. Of course, in another sense it has nothing to do with mental states: unless a proposition is explicitly about the mind, its truth condition will be world-dependent rather than mind-dependent. But similarly, the truth (for I say it is a truth) that you have an obligation to your children is child-dependent, and the truth that you should not kick friendly dogs for fun is dog-dependent.

Peacocke pursues his discussion via an indexing of propositions, corresponding to reference first to the "world" from which an evaluation is made, and secondly to the "world" that is being evaluated. To this end he introduces the double index $P(w_1, w_2)$, explained as:

Proposition P, when evaluated from the standpoint of psychological states in w_1, holds with respect to w_2. (Ibid. 210)

Here P is some moral proposition, such as 'it is wrong to kick dogs for fun' or 'the infliction of avoidable pain is wrong'. The overall proposition $P(w_1, w_2)$ is, however, not entirely clear, because of the curious and treacherous word "holds" (with its shades of Kerstein's "based on" and "stems from"). Suppose someone says that the proposition that the war in Iraq was justified holds from George Bush's point of view. I can hear that as a contorted way of saying that George Bush believes that the war in Iraq was justified, and it is probably true. What I should not do is hear it as some kind of insinuation that the war in Iraq was justified. It's a description of what George Bush thinks, not an endorsement of the way he thinks. Only a confused relativist of some sophomoric stamp would accept the transition from 'the war in Iraq is justified from George Bush's point of view' to 'the war in Iraq is justified'.

With that clear for the moment, we can turn to the 'w_2' variable. For that to do any work, there has to be some space between the proposition P and the variety of worlds to which it applies, or in which it is evaluated. And this may be granted. 'It is wrong to kick dogs for fun' can be tested against this world, or, if we are imaginative enough, against slightly different worlds, for instance in which there are still dogs and people, but only dogs that are unconscious, or in which there are only people who can survive by nutrition from the pain of other animals. And then it may turn out that the moral proposition is only true contingently on aspects of our world, and would get a different truth value were these other things different. Or of course, it may not. We may suppose that however worlds vary, it is always wrong to cause unnecessary pain, although even that may wobble if we bring in, for instance, apparently possible people who like pain.

With these explanations we can agree with Peacocke when he says that nobody can object to the employment of this doubly indexed proposition. Indeed, nobody can object to it, for $P(w_1, w_2)$ can be the form of good enough propositions, that can be regarded as true or as false in various cases, although they will often be indeterminate, when we have not given definite enough interpretations of the variables. Given what I have said, the evaluation of such propositions goes like this. First we introduce a moral proposition P. Second, we introduce some possible people with attitudes. And third, we present a possible scenario, and we imagine the people we just introduced evaluating what goes on in the scenario, in accordance with the attitudes we gave them. If the people introduced evaluate the introduced scenario in the way that would properly gain expression by P, then $P(w_1, w_2)$ should be accorded T, otherwise not. It corresponds to: "The people we have introduced evaluate the scenario we imagined them to be contemplating, in a way that could be expressed by saying that P."

More concisely, we can say that the people we have introduced evaluate the scenario we imagine them to be contemplating in the P-way.

Not surprisingly, we can vary the people or psychological states introduced, and we can vary the scenarios we conjure for them to be contemplating. So $P(w_i, w_j)$ can vary in two dimensions: there are two variables to be given interpretations before we turn it into a definite claim. And filling in one does not determine how we fill in the other. Or, of course we could quantify. $(\forall w_i)P(w_i, x)$ would mean that everyone from any possible story evaluates some given scenario x in the P-way, and $(\forall w_j)P(z, w_j)$ would mean that the introduced persons with the psychological states z evaluate every possible scenario in the P-way. $(\forall w_i)(\forall w_j)P(w_i, w_j)$ would mean that everyone, whatever their other differences, evaluates everything in the P-way.

This is the machinery in all its gleaming splendor, so what happens when it is set in motion? Alas, nothing at all. We get a variety of rather cumbersome descriptions of what different people think about different scenarios, and whether they would express themselves as agreeing with some moral or ethical proposition. We get things like: "We, as we are, think that in the world, as it is, kicking dogs is wrong" (true, I hope). Or: "We, as we would be were we to become coarse and callous, would think that in the world as it is, kicking dogs is wrong" (false, no doubt). We can keep the people constant ('us') giving what Peacocke calls the "vertical" reading, or we can vary people and scenarios together, giving what he calls a "diagonal" reading, such as the true "We, as we would be were we to become coarse and callous, would think that in a possible world in which dogs feel pain slightly less than they do, kicking dogs is OK."

Peacocke claims that since there is this diagonal reading, there is a "mind dependency" claim that the quasi-realist has not acknowledged. But that is not true. Propositions such as this last one amount to *descriptions* of how people of some particular attitude (which we may or may not share) react to different scenarios. And there is nothing in general in these descriptions to offend the quasi-realist (or anyone else). It does not amount to giving our own verdict on those same scenarios, although if we make ourselves the topic, and describe ourselves rightly, there will be the coincidence that what we say about ourselves will be true just if we do assent to the verdict P.

The locutions that Peacocke uses clearly reveal him to be in the same swamp as Kerstein:

> On the quasi-realist's theory the acceptability of basic moral principles depends on some psychological attitudes. However this dependence is formulated, it must be possible in thought to consider which propositions are correct when we vary the standpoint of evaluation; that is, when we vary the first parameter. (Ibid. 214)

The first sentence is again ambiguous. On the quasi-realist's theory the question of which basic moral principles are accepted by people indeed depends upon (is the same thing as) their psychological attitudes. Whether they are right to accept those principles is a different thing altogether, and we will only settle it by ourselves finding a verdict on their approvals and disapprovals. If people in outer modal space, or for that matter people in benighted corners of the earth, accept the principle that it is OK to cause unnecessary pain to sentient creatures for fun, then they are cruel and callous and it would be good if they would change. The second of Peacocke's quoted sentences is therefore technically correct but highly misleading, for it implies that in general changing the first parameter (that is, considering different evaluative standpoints) changes the *correctness* of a verdict. But it doesn't! It only changes whether it is *supposed* to be correct, by whichever evaluators are introduced. Except in the cases that I called those of etiquette, it merely brings the evaluators into the embrace of our verdict, perhaps to their discredit, as in this case.

Peacocke continues:

> Take a specific moral principle identified by its content, say 'Prima facie, the infliction of avoidable pain is wrong' (w,w). It seems to me that the quasi-realist, like other mind-dependent theorists, must say this is false. It is false at those entries in the diagonal for worlds in which we have different attitudes to the infliction of avoidable pain. (Ibid.)

This is hard to follow, because in accordance with his own explanation of the notation, propositions of the form $P(w_1, w_2)$ are not moral principles at all. First, they describe whether the evaluation from w_1, of the scenario of w_2, could gain expression by P: they are descriptions, not evaluations. And second, they are not even that until the variables are bound or replaced by actual values, so neither the quasi-realist nor anyone else has any business saying that $P(w, w)$ is true, or false. It is an open sentence, not a closed one.

Perhaps Peacocke is thinking of the double universal quantification: "Everyone, from whatever evaluative standpoint, and considering any scenario whatever, would agree that inflicting avoidable pain is wrong." I do indeed doubt whether this is true, but that doubt has nothing to do with quasi-realism. It has more to do with pessimism about varieties of the wicked human heart, and if we are in outer modal space, the even more wicked Martian heart. And after all, Peacocke shares the doubt, for he allows worlds in which inhabitants have different attitudes to the infliction of pain. That's the point on the diagonal that he is brandishing. Or perhaps it is not a double quantification but an anaphoric reference back to the world of the people with the evaluative standpoint: "Everyone, from whatever evaluative standpoint, and considering the world they inhabit, would agree that inflicting avoidable pain is wrong." Alas, the same pessimism is appropriate.

Peacocke's ambition is clearly to get the quasi-realist *both* to treat some proposition of the form $P(w_1, w_2)$ as a genuine moral principle, *and* to evaluate it as false when we think of worlds in which the wicked hearts rule. But the noisy machinery takes him not one inch nearer to that goal. Worlds in which the wicked hearts rule are still worlds in which, prima facie, the infliction of avoidable pain is wrong. The wicked hearts may not agree with this, but then that is just what's wrong with them.

I said that the word 'holds', as it occurs in the clarification of his notation, is treacherous, and by now we are compelled to think that Peacocke has actually been betrayed by it. It seems he really does want to index the question of whether a moral principle is true to the various worlds whose inhabitants either agree or disagree with it. I think that is preposterous. It would be like saying that the proposition that the Iraq war was a good thing holds – really holds – in Republican circles in America, and really does not hold in most of the UK. And if that is what it means, the quasi-realist simply refuses to adopt the notation. It differs from the legitimate meaning we have so far allowed it, aiming at something more like this: "The people we have introduced evaluate the scenario we imagined them to be contemplating, in a way that could be expressed by saying that P *and as a result P is true*." But the quasi-realist has no use for this dog's breakfast of an assertion (it will be false except in etiquette cases). The Iraq war was a bad thing whatever other people think about it. It is not true-in-London but false-in-Texas. Nor is it a matter of etiquette, so that enough thinking it a good thing might make it one. That way lies sophomoric relativism, not sentimentalism. The criminality of the Iraq war is dead-innocent-Iraqi-dependent, not Republican-sentiment-dependent.

Far from taking him into the sunny uplands of rationalism, then, Peacocke's machinery grinds to a halt in the swamp of a relativism of his own devising. But he finishes the discussion by considering the neighboring case of color, and the possibility that creatures with different perceptual systems might see physically different things and surfaces as red, and the case is interesting enough to deserve a visit.

Peacocke says that it is widely agreed that things would not stop being red if humans lost their color vision and saw only in shades of grey. That may be so, although it ought also to be widely agreed that there is much more indeterminacy here than in the case of values. Jonathan Bennett's example of phenol-thio-urea, which tastes bitter to some people and bland to others, led many people to think that if the former group breeds into a huge majority, the world becomes one in which the stuff is bitter, while if the latter group does, the world becomes one in which it is bland. In other words, the 'response-dependency' of secondary properties is a much better candidate for providing a genuine truth condition for ascriptions of them than any similar attempt to provide a 'truth-condition' for ascriptions of value.

However, Peacocke is also correct that two-dimensionalism allows different formulations of the idea that colors are mind-dependent. Where Q is some underlying physical power, such as a disposition to reflect light of a certain wavelength more than other light, and we imagine varying perceptual systems, we could say that:

For any world, whatever perceptual systems its inhabitants have, Q objects are red, as they would be judged by us, as we actually are.

We would also want to say:

In some worlds, Q objects are not red, as judged by the inhabitants of those worlds.

And given Bennett's case, we might remain ambivalent about whether

For any world, whatever perceptual systems its inhabitants have, Q objects are red

since we would be ambivalent about, as it were, sticking with our own judgments, or entering into the world-view of the people with the other perceptual system.

The reason this ambivalence is harmless is that once we bring other perceptual systems into view, then provided they are equally discriminatory, we lose any very robust attachment to the idea that ours is *right* and theirs is *wrong*. Similarly we do

Must We Weep for Sentimentalism?

not maintain skeptical fears that perhaps our sense of smell, or sense of color, may in general be letting us down, so that perhaps things really smell differently from the way we smell them, or have different hues from those we see them as having. People who taste phenol-thio-urea the other way are not wrong, just different. But there is no reason to suppose that this ambivalence extends similarly to the case of value.[4] People who are coarse and brutal are not "just" different. They are also depraved, and as a result they are rotten judges of value. If we are invited to "see the world as they see it," we can, perhaps, manage it, but we ourselves can attach no weight to the verdicts we would imagine giving as we do so.

Before leaving this part of the discussion, it may be useful to reflect upon a difference between sentimentalism, as a theory of the origin of the moral sentiments, and a partly parallel exercise of quasi-realism, attempting to see our verdicts of modal necessity as the upshot of various features of the shape of our minds that determine what we can or cannot imagine (see Blackburn 1993). Here there is a legitimate pressure to see a contingent source of imaginative limitation as an undermining or debunking account of logical or metaphysical necessity. If 'We cannot think otherwise' is sourced in contingent facts about us, an inference to 'Things could not be otherwise' is compromised rather than explained.

Someone might be tempted to use the modal case as a Trojan horse, bringing the same worry into the theory of morals. But if so, they would be wrong. The asymmetry lies in what we say about the states of mind in question and how it relates to the kinds of verdict we are making. In the modal case, if we find that the modes of thought, or the absence of alternatives, are only contingent, their source as an explanation of real necessity is compromised. But in the moral case, it would be not finding that they are *metaphysically* contingent that would give them a parallel debunking power. The parallel would be finding that they are *morally* indifferent. If it were morally alright to have the other sentiments – say, approving of cruelty to dogs or neglect of children – then it would be hard to believe that the ones we actually have could source a robust confidence in an obligation to refrain from cruelty and neglect. At least in general, if it is OK to think that some action is OK, then the action is OK.

But the sentimentalist is not saying that it is OK to have the contrary sentiments. As I have already said, the sentiments of those who would think otherwise fall within the scope of proper disapproval. We do not just disapprove of neglect of children, but perhaps even more so, and certainly just as much, we disapprove of those who approve of it or even tolerate it.

And rationalists had better not find the metaphysical contingency of modes of moral thought unsettling. If rationalist moral conviction is to falter whenever it comes upon people who do not share it or do not feel its force, then it is a fragile thing indeed. For knavery exists. Indeed, it often rules, and this is why a robust conviction of its baseness is so important.

Justice and Gentle Usage

Kerstein is not the first to worry about the scope of justice on Hume's theory. According to Manfred Kuehn's biography (2001), Kant himself was led to reject Hutcheson's sentimentalism for a very similar reason. Reading Rousseau apparently convinced Kant that while the sentimentalist allows that we have duties of charity to the dispossessed of the world, this is not enough. The poor or excluded have a right to more than charity. It is not charity they want or need, but justice. If sentimentalism cannot deliver that, then it delivers an inadequate account of the actual nature of our moral thought.

Hume makes himself a target for this kind of outraged reaction:

> Were there a species of creatures intermingled with men, which, though rational, were possessed of such inferior strength, both of body and mind, that they were incapable of all resistance, and could never, upon the highest provocation, make us feel the effects of their resentment; the necessary consequence, I think, is that we should be bound by the laws of humanity to give gentle usage to these creatures, but should not, properly speaking, lie under any restraint of justice with regard to them, nor could they possess any right or property, exclusive of such arbitrary lords. Our intercourse with them could not be called society, which supposes a degree of equality; but absolute command on the one side, and servile obedience on the other. Whatever we covet, they must instantly resign: Our permission is the only tenure, by which they hold their possessions: Our compassion and kindness the only check, by which they curb our lawless will: And as no inconvenience ever results from the exercise of power, so firmly established in nature, the restraints of justice and property, being totally *useless*, would never have place in so unequal a confederacy. (1998: 190–1)

There are many things to say about this passage, and quite how Hume thought it related to the human cases he goes on to discuss, which are, first, European relationships to indigenous American people and, second, men's relationships with women. The clear implication is that the model applies in neither case, but only at best to our relationship with animals, or perhaps imagined animals.

Nevertheless we might want to modify the account to make justice clearly applicable, even in the circumstances of the thought experiment. I shall consider how that might be done in a moment. Meanwhile, the important point is that it is not Hume's sentimentalism that leads him here, but his strict delineation of the circumstances of justice and its source in mutual advantage. Hume does not deny that we have *obligations* to the creatures he presents. He says that we are "bound by the laws of humanity" to give them gentle usage. The only issue is the way we are to understand this obligation. Remembering that for Hume the virtue of justice is both "cautious and jealous" and above all artificial, it may not be so bad for these creatures if the source of that obligation lies elsewhere. But it is important to see that if we insist on the word 'justice', the sentimentalist can give it to us.

Hume mentions the resentment these creatures have, but which, because of their inferior strength and power, they can do nothing to visit upon us. This opens up a new sentimentalist vista, much more thoroughly explored by Adam Smith.[5] As Raphael explains in his editor's introduction, for Smith the sympathy that lies at the bottom of our capacity for morals has a slightly different shape than it does in Hume (Smith 1976: 13). In Hume, we sympathize with the pleasure or pain that an action gives to a person. In Smith, we sympathize with different states of mind, including the motives of an agent, and more relevantly to the current case, with the gratitude or resentment of those affected by the action. Indeed our sense of justice, for Smith, is dependent on reactions of resentment or gratitude to actions, which need not vary as the actual quantity of harm or benefit they bring about.

The "sympathy" that is so prominent in each of Hume and Smith is translated, by the one into respect for the general point of view, and by the other into the voice of the impartial spectator, the "man within the breast" who represents the reactions of those without. There is, of course, much to be said about the ways in which each writer identifies and handles the mechanism, and the relation between them.[6] There is also much to be said about whether either mechanism implies some concession to rationalism, bringing in as they do some notion of "corrected" sentiments. I cannot rehearse all that needs saying about that here, but shall have to take it as given that neither writer betrays sentimentalism by their construction of the more complex sensitivity.[7] So suppose we bring in the lynchpin of Smith's sentimentalism, the "real, revered, and impartial spectator" whose function is to bring home to us the resentment of those affected by our delinquencies. When the voice of this spectator is heard as it should be, we may recoil from our own contemplated or actual conduct. In Hume's terms, we can no longer bear our own survey. Recognizing this resentment of our conduct, and feeling no defense against it, we admit the injustice.

Suppose, then, that we have been minded to take from one of Hume's creatures something which they evidently cherish. They cannot visit their resentment upon us, but somehow we know that they feel it, and we know that we would feel it in their shoes. The man within the breast voices this resentment on their behalf, and we find we cannot dismiss it (we cannot resent their resentment, as we sometimes can). This unpleasant impact is the same as guilty awareness of the injustice of our conduct. What more could the sternest moralist ask from us?

Smith's modification of Hume may still leave us falling short of full-blown Kantian rationalism. But it is at least telling that the most fervent contemporary Kantians find it hard to do better. Korsgaard, for instance gives us the crucial moment in the genesis of obligation to others like this:

> How does this obligation come about? Just the way that Nagel says that it does. I invite you to consider how you would like it if someone did that to you. You realize that you would not merely dislike it, you would resent it. You would think that the other has a reason to stop – more, an obligation to stop. And that obligation would spring from your own objection to what he does to you. (1996: 98)

Korsgaard goes on to employ a cognitive or rationalistic vocabulary, but it is hard not to feel that the central process is exactly the same as in Smith. The potential victim forces you to recognize his resentment, and to "put yourself in his shoes." His fundamental question is: "How would you *like* it if someone did that to you?" – and once you find that you would not, then, other things being equal, his not liking or resenting it translates into your own discomfort at your own behavior. Of course, as Smith sensibly recognizes, things are not always equal. We have an abundance of defense mechanisms against this incipient discomfort, including ignoring the impartial spectator, or more often convincing ourselves the he would be on our side or "of our faction."[8]

At this point the sentimentalist will certainly face another familiar challenge. The account finds the source of feelings of obligation and injustice in a certain emotional identification: in this case a contingent (of course) capacity to internalize the resentments of others. But might not this very notion of resentment itself import, and depend upon, an unacknowledged cognitivism? Resentment, as Korsgaard says, is more than mere dislike. Perhaps it is more like bitterness, but bitterness at the dispensation of some agent. Anyone suffering a third summer holiday in succession blighted by continuous rain might feel bitter, but only a theist can resent it. This quickly suggests that resentment is more like bitterness at the injustice of the behavior, in which case a perception of injustice cannot be explained in terms of resentment and sympathy with it, but must be identified in some pre-existent cognition. Similar objections may be made to sentimentalist uses of notions like guilt, or even anger: if anger is the attitude or emotion of those who perceive themselves to have been wronged, and guilt is the attitude or emotion of those who recognize themselves to have done wrong, then we cannot understand the judgments by citing the emotions.

There is a simple lacuna in this popular line of thought. The equations in question are things like 'Anger is perception of wrong' or 'Resentment is recognition of injustice to oneself'. The objection implicitly supposes that these equations need to be read from right to left, so that the apparent cognition explains the emotion. The sentimentalist tradition, by contrast, reads them from left to right, so that the emotion or attitude explains the thought of wrong or injustice in terms of which it gets expressed. This is not the place to rehearse all the moves in this debate. You just have to try out the different directions of explanation, and you have to ask which is psychologically or metaphysically the more economical. But at least a preliminary remark is that as they stand, of course, the equations are absurdly simple. Anger is not perception of wrong, nor is resentment recognition of injustice to oneself. Each is both more in one respect and less in another. More, because the pure cognition leaves out the upheaval and the motivational force, so that in fact perception of wrong may not lead to anger, and recognition of injustice to oneself may not lead to resentment. Less, because each has a primitive identity in which ethical thought is not yet present. We should not forget that Darwin called his great work *The Expression of Emotion in Man and Animals*. The guard dog does a fair job of being angry at the intruder or afraid of a snake, and the pet which throws its food around the house on being left behind does a fair job of resenting being neglected. Emotions and attitudes have a primitive aetiology, and are there to be socially harnessed and refined.[9]

A different strand in Smith is the idea that unlike obligations of benevolence, obligations of justice can be exacted from us. They bring in the potential force of the community or the civil power: "The person himself who meditates an injustice is sensible of this, and feels that force may, with the utmost propriety, be made use of both by the person whom he is about to injure, and by others, either to obstruct the execution of his crime, or to punish him when he has executed it" (Smith 1976: 79–80). Applied to Hume's example, this suggests that the question of whether there is an obligation of justice may hinge on whether we think a spectator, contemplating a breach of "gentle usage," could permissibly use pre-emptive or retaliatory force on the perpetrator. I am not sure whether we do think this in general. If we can take the case of animals as indicative, our actual animal welfare legislation suggests we think that if the breach is severe enough then the criminal law has a say, but at least in our jurisprudence, if not in our studies, we seem prepared to let a fair amount of not so gentle usage go on unprevented and unpunished.

However we solve this issue, if we stand back for a moment it should be obvious that this particular issue about justice is not a promising basis from which to attack sentimentalism. The structure of the case disqualifies it from that task. The idea is to arouse our sense of what is due to these creatures, and to encourage shock and outrage at the base behavior to which Hume's agents might be led, or to excite us to lament the outrages which they might get away with, and to wring our hands over the sad plight of the poor defenseless creatures. All this is excellent. It shows us sympathizing with the downtrodden and their resentment, perhaps desiring or wishing for a civil order in which the powerful would be punished, feeling that things are out of joint unless they are brought to account for their crimes, and so on. In other words, it shows that our sense of outrage and injustice is mobilized, not merely our benevolence. But it cannot show *more* than that. It cannot show that what is mobilized lies outside the sentiments altogether. Hume's example may make us hot under the collar about the indignities the powerful may visit on the weak, but it does not afford any evidence that getting hot under the collar is anything other than feeling an attitude and emotion, directed upon a particular social structure and the abuses it looks set to allow.

Where This Leaves Us

I have not, in this chapter, been exclusively defending expressivism. Other views which stress the place of sentiments, or imagination and culture, in the genesis of our ethical thought were equal possible targets of Kerstein's and Peacocke's attacks. Some of these others, perhaps a naive subjectivism less deft with the notion of 'mind-dependence', might even fall to such attacks, for instance by giving the moral judgment a truth-condition that is not child-dependent or dog-dependent, but genuinely mind-dependent. Others may avoid them only by inappropriate reliance on "actually" operators and other pieces of doubtful machinery. If so, I am glad to part company with them.

The popularity of rationalism, and the general feeling that there "must be something to" the kinds of argument I have been discussing, are very deep-rooted. Partly, they represent a noble dream. They answer a wish that the knaves of the world can be not only confined and confounded, but also refuted – refuted as well by standards that they have to acknowledge. Ideally, they will be shown to be in a state akin to self-contradiction. Kerstein acknowledges that Kant and neo-Kantians have not achieved anything like this result. But it is still tantalizingly there as a goal or ideal, the Holy Grail of moral philosophy, and many suppose that all right-thinking people must join the pilgrimage to find it.

We sentimentalists do not like our good behavior to be hostage to such a search. We don't altogether approve of Holy Grails. We do not see the need for them. We are not quite on all fours with those who do. And we do not quite see why, even if by some secret alchemy a philosopher managed to glimpse one, it should ameliorate his behavior, let alone that of other people. We think instead that human beings are ruled by passions, and the best we can do is to educate people so that the best passions are also the most forceful. We say of rationalistic moral philosophy what Hume says of abstract reasonings in general, that when we leave our closet, and engage in the common affairs of life, its conclusions seem to vanish, like the phantoms of the night on the appearance of the morning (1978: pt 1, sec. 1).

Notes

1 And why does Kerstein think I call the foreign-office knave a knave?
2 If you (wrongly) think that we cannot lie under an obligation to feel various ways, perhaps because "ought" implies "can," read it as "behaving as though you care for the child."
3 One could play with complexities introduced by the thought that in some sense "not giving a gift back" in the described community is performing the same action as "giving a gift back" in ours. They do not affect the point.
4 Margaret Wilson (1992) comments on a constant tendency in "the modern philosophy" to vacillate over whether colors are in the mind, are categorical or primary grounds in the atomic constitution of things and their surfaces, or are powers to excite human perceptual systems. The vacillation is more excusable if we reflect that in the case of color we never have to decide on "what to say" about the case when the same physical properties have different powers because of varying perceptual systems.
5 In the paragraphs that follow, on Smith, I am much indebted to work by Michael Ridge.
6 See, for instance, Cohon (1997), Korsgaard (1999), Radcliffe (1994), Sayre-McCord (1994).
7 In *Ruling Passions* I argue that the idea of the general point of view involves no such concession, but only introduces what I call a 'Hume-friendly' notion of reason (Blackburn 1998: chs. 7 and 8).
8 Smith: "The propriety of our moral sentiments is never so apt to be corrupted, as when the indulgent and partial spectator is at hand, while the indifferent and impartial one is at a great distance" (1976: 154).
9 For more on these themes, see Blackburn (2002).

References

Blackburn, S. (1993). "Morals and modals." In Blackburn, *Essays in Quasi-Realism*. New York: Oxford University Press.
Blackburn, S. (1998). *Ruling Passions*. Oxford: Oxford University Press.
Blackburn, S. (2002). "How emotional is the virtuous person?" In Peter Goldie (ed.), *Understanding Emotions: Mind and Morals*. Aldershot: Ashgate Publishing.
Cohon, R. (1997). "The common point of view in Hume's ethics." *Philosophy and Phenomenological Research*, 57: 827–50.
Hume, D. (1998). *An Enquiry Concerning the Principles of Morals*, ed. Tom Beauchamp. Oxford: Oxford University Press.
Hume, D. (1978). *A Treatise of Human Nature*, Book III, ed. Selby-Bigge. Oxford: Clarendon Press.
Korsgaard, C. (1999). "The general point of view: love and moral approval in Hume's ethics." *Hume Studies*, 25: 3–42.
Kuehn, M. (2001). *Kant*. Cambridge: Cambridge University Press.

Peacocke, C. (2004). *The Realm of Reason*. Oxford: Oxford University Press.

Radcliffe, E. (1994). "Hume on motivating sentiments, the general point of view, and the inculcation of morality." *Hume Studies*, 20: 37–58.

Sayre-McCord, G. (1994). "On why Hume's 'general point of view' isn't ideal – and shouldn't be." *Social Philosophy and Policy*, 11: 202–28.

Smith, A. (1976). *The Theory of Moral Sentiments*, ed. D. D. Raphael and A. M. Macfie. Oxford: Oxford University Press.

Wilson, M. (1992). "History of philosophy in philosophy today: and the case of the sensible qualities." *Philosophical Review*, 101: 191–226.

Is Motivation Internal to Moral Judgment?

How Do Moral Judgments Motivate?

Sigrún Svavarsdóttir

Motivational Internalism vs Externalism

A prevalent view in moral philosophy is that motivation is internal to moral judgment. The first question to ask is: What is meant? What is it for motivation to be internal, rather than external, to moral judgment? To answer this question, let's start by considering the notion of moral judgment and, then, examine what sort of claim is being made about moral judgments when it is said that motivation is internal to them. 'Judgment' is standardly used to designate a mental event (a cognitive act) closely related to the cognitive state of believing something: the belief that such and such is a state that grounds the disposition to judge such and such. When judging such and such, an agent is affirming, in thought or language, that such and such is the case. Given this, moral judgment should trivially be the affirmation that something has a moral characteristic. But this is in fact a controversial claim within the metaethical literature. 'Moral judgment' has become a term of art. It is used to refer to the mental and speech acts central to moral evaluation and expressed in moral terms. A controversy rages over the nature of these mental and speech acts. Some philosophers claim that they are judgments in the standard sense of 'judgment', i.e., they affirm that something has such and such characteristics, while others claim that their nature is much more akin to expressions of emotions or preferences. It has become standard to refer to proponents of the former view as moral cognitivists and to advocates of the latter view as moral non-cognitivists or expressivists. So, the claim that motivation is internal to moral judgment is a claim about the kind of mental and speech act that is standardly expressed by sentences like 'This is the morally right course of action', 'You have a moral obligation to help', 'This policy is wrong', 'Kindness is a moral virtue'. The question now is what exactly is being claimed.

What is sometimes being claimed is that with such a mental act comes motivation to act that is not rooted in any accompanying conative state of mind. The motivation is directed at doing what is deemed good or right and shunning what is deemed bad or wrong. The act of making a moral judgment motivates on its own, and the judgment is not correctly ascribed to an agent unless he has the relevant motivation. Let's refer to this thesis as *strong motivational internalism* and reserve *weak motivational internalism* for the view that a moral judgment is not correctly ascribed to an agent unless he has the relevant motivation. This view does not take a stand on the mechanics of moral motivation – whether moral judgment motivates on its own or only in collaboration with some other mental states – but agrees with strong motivational internalism that an agent has not made a genuine moral judgment unless he has the relevant motivation. Notice that neither view implies that we always act on our moral judgments. They only imply that we are always *motivated*, at least a tiny bit, to act on our moral judgments; other motivations may nevertheless override the moral motivation and lead us astray.

Michael Stocker (1979) has famously observed that under conditions of deep depression, weakness of will, and other maladies of the spirit, the connection between moral judgment and motivation may be severed, even in people who are usually motivated by their moral judgments. Still, many moral philosophers believe that motivational internalism, either in its stronger or weaker form, is right in spirit, even if the connection between moral judgment and motivation is defeasible. In another place (Svavarsdóttir 1999: 163–5), I have suggested that the most uncontroversial way for a motivational internalist to avoid Stocker's counterexamples is to make an exception for agents suffering from motivational disorders that affect them more generally. In its weaker form, motivational internalism then comes down to the thesis that a moral judgment is not ascribable to an agent unless either he is suffering from a motivational disorder that affects him more generally or he is motivated to pursue (or promote) what is judged favorably and to shun (or prevent) what is judged unfavorably. Strong motivational internalists add that the motivation stems from the judgment alone. Motivational externalists contest both claims.

The significance of this disagreement for the dispute between moral cognitivists and moral non-cognitivists should be apparent. Non-cognitivism would not be plausible unless motivational internalism were true. If moral judgments are akin to expressions of emotions or preferences, they should have some motivational import. Also, it is much harder to defend moral cognitivism on the assumption that motivational internalism is true, even if some cognitivists are motivational internalists. Generally, judgments in the standard sense are not necessarily tied to motivation. If moral judgments are judgments in the standard sense but are necessarily tied to motivation, we need some explanation of why they have this unique motivational status. This has not proved easy to explain. Thus, the outcome of the debate between motivational internalists and externalists is of importance for metaethics.

Motivational Internalism Challenged

On what basis can one defend either motivational internalism or externalism? More often than not, moral philosophers on both sides rest their case on an intuition: an intuition about when an agent counts as having made a moral judgment. The claim

How Do Moral Judgments Motivate?

is usually that this is an intuition about the concept of moral judgment or about the concepts employed in moral judgment. On the basis of such an intuition, internalists claim that the thesis of weak motivational internalism has the status of a conceptual truth. Externalists contest this by designing thought experiments that introduce us to amoralists, people who make moral judgments but are not at all motivated by them. Internalists respond to such challenges by explaining away the intuition that externalists seek to trigger by these counterexamples. Their strategy is to argue that the purported amoralist either is not making a genuine moral judgment or is not as motivationally indifferent as externalists suppose. That is, internalists claim that we cannot really understand the examples as being of true amoralists for it is inconceivable that someone makes a genuine moral judgment without being motivationally affected by it. The purported externalist intuition betrays a conceptual confusion. Externalists respond in kind and argue that it is the internalists who are basing their case on a questionable intuition.

The dynamics of this debate is all too similar to that of other intractable philosophical disputes: a stalemate of conflicting intuitions accompanied by ingenious attempts to explain the conflicting intuition away. In an earlier work (Svavarsdóttir 1999: 176–83), I have attempted to break this deadlock by showing that the burden of argument lies squarely on the internalists' shoulders. I told a story of a woman, Virginia, who encounters a man, Patrick, who declares that he agrees with her assessment that he morally ought to help a politically persecuted stranger. However, Patrick appears to have no motivation to do so. I tell the story in purely observational terms that should be acceptable to both externalists and internalists. No claim is made about whether Patrick is in fact making a moral judgment and no claim is made about his actual motivational states. My strategy is to cast us in the role of observers trying to explain Patrick's observed behavior, both verbal and non-verbal. Several explanatory hypotheses are offered. Externalists should be able to accept them all as in the running, but internalists will have to dismiss one of them as badly formed: namely, the hypothesis that Patrick is making a moral judgment but is not motivationally affected. I argue that when there is a conflict of intuitions, among intelligent and sensible people, about which empirical hypotheses are in the running as potential explanations of some observable phenomenon, the burden of argument is on those who insist on a more restrictive class of potential explanations. I then argue that internalists cannot meet this burden by simply declaring that the hypothesis is conceptually incoherent. They have to lay bare the putative conceptual mistake. This is most straightforwardly done by identifying the concept or concepts that exclude as incoherent the explanatory hypothesis that the externalists favor and defend an account of them that yields the internalist thesis as a corollary.

I have no argument to the effect that this cannot be done. I rest my case with a challenge to internalists to give such a substantive defense of their position. Now, there are several accounts of moral judgments and of moral concepts in the metaethical literature which imply that moral judgments are motivating except in people with general motivational disorders. So, this challenge may seem easy to meet. There is, nevertheless, a problem. The problem is that these accounts have usually been defended by appealing to the thesis of weak motivational internalism. It has been treated as a constraint of adequacy on accounts of moral judgment. My argument, first and foremost, targets the assumption that this internalist thesis has unquestionable enough a status to play this methodological role in debates about the nature of moral judgments and of moral concepts.

I will not rehash my argument beyond the summary given above. I stand by it and have nothing of significance to add. I simply refer the reader to my "Moral cognitivism and motivation" (1999), especially section 3, for what I consider a conclusive case against conferring to weak motivational internalism the status of a conceptual platitude and of a constraint of adequacy on accounts of moral thought and language. What I propose to do in the remainder of this chapter is to defend my positive view of moral motivation, paying special attention to the worry that it cannot get right the normativity of moral judgments.

A Simple-minded Externalist Account of Moral Motivation

How do moral judgments motivate? Here is my answer. Moral judgments motivate by engaging a distinct conative attitude taken toward objects under the same mode of presentation as the judgment employs. In other words, they enter into motivation much the same way as other judgments do and we explain variations in how moral judgments enter into motivation much as we explain such variations with respect to the motivational role of other judgments. The mode of presentation involved in both moral judgments and the conative attitude central to moral motivation is a moral mode of presentation: i.e., moral concepts enter into the conceptual content of both the judgment and the conative attitude. I have and will continue to refer to the latter as the desire to be moral. I emphasize that any moral concept could figure into the conceptual content of these attitudes. Having the desire to be moral amounts to having a concern with doing what is morally valuable or required, when that might include what is just, fair, honest, etc.

I am committing myself to the view that the conceptual resources at play in moral judgment and in moral motivation are distinctively moral – a presupposition that I share with old intuitionists like G. E. Moore, H. A. Prichard, and D. Ross. Many have found this assumption problematic. Nevertheless, this should be the default hypothesis in an inquiry into the nature of moral judgments. Of course, it is (epistemically) possible that moral terms express concepts that are also expressed by other familiar terms, even non-normative terms, or that they have some entirely different semantic function like non-cognitivists claim. But we should not start an examination of moral discourse with the hypothesis that moral terms duplicate some other terms of the language rather than enhance its expressive power, or that they have some entirely different semantic function than terms that have much the same syntactic behavior. We should be long past the worry that admitting that there are *sui generis* moral concepts will lead to ontic or epistemic commitments on a par with those of moral intuitionists. It is quite possible that the concepts are *sui generis*, yet used to represent features of the social order or used to do something entirely different than represent features of the actual world. The right approach is to stick to the default hypothesis that we are dealing with unique conceptual resources and examine what is distinctive of the conceptual resources used in moral and other type of evaluation. If some special reasons arise for equating moral concepts with other concepts or for concluding that they are not genuine concepts, so be it. We should remain open-minded like in any theoretical inquiry, but I am unconvinced that such reasons have been uncovered in metaethical inquiry to date. This default hypothesis will be a background assumption in the following discussion.

In offering the above view of moral motivation, I am taking a stand on the mechanics of moral motivation as strong motivational internalists do. I am opposing their view that moral judgments motivate on their own, when they motivate, in addition to rejecting the thesis that strong motivational internalists share with weak motivational internalists, namely that an agent cannot be making a moral judgment unless he has the relevant motivation. My view of moral motivation is not the only one available to motivational externalists. Most externalists have traced moral motivation to conative attitudes whose conceptual content does not involve moral concepts, for example, a benevolent desire toward others or a desire to be able to justify one's conduct from an impartial standpoint. We should also note that my argument against motivational internalism targets only the thesis common to weak and strong motivational internalism. It is possible to combine the rejection of that thesis with the view that *when* moral judgments motivate, they motivate entirely on their own. Some of those who have been attracted to motivational internalism may think that this is the kernel of truth in the position, even if it is most commonly characterized as claiming that there is a necessary connection between moral judgment and motivation.

The view that I have offered of moral motivation has been attacked as "crude moral psychology" (Copp 1996). I plead guilty to the charge. My view is crude in that it gives us the most superficial understanding of why someone is motivated by his moral judgments, but that does not preclude it from being right as far as it goes. Undoubtedly, a deeper explanation of why people are motivated by their moral judgments is possible but, probably, the explanation will vary from case to case. There is hardly any unique psychology that sustains a disposition to be motivated by one's moral judgment. All I claim is that if we have an instance of genuine moral motivation – i.e., the person in question is not motivated by his moral judgment simply for the sake of appearances or other reasons of expedience – then the desire to be moral has a role to play in the motivational system of the person in question.

Defending the Simple-minded Account

But why presume that? Why postulate the desire to be moral to explain moral motivation? The variations that exist in moral motivation prima facie call for this explanatory hypothesis. The impact moral judgments have on our deliberations and actions vary a great deal. Some people almost always do what they deem morally right or good even when it is costly to their other concerns. Others have hardly ever the stamina to do what they deem morally right, even if they are not moral cynics. There is a whole spectrum between these two cases – a spectrum of people who are to a greater or lesser degree motivated by their moral judgments. Then, there are the cynics who acknowledge that their behavior has morally problematic consequences but who are indifferent to that. They have no moral scruples. And there are even moral subversives who intentionally and knowingly pursue what they acknowledge to be morally wrong, or bad, and do so for that very reason. There is also a great variation in how apt people are to think in moral terms both in deliberative and non-deliberative contexts and how these thoughts affect them not only motivationally but also emotionally. And finally, there are often such variations in moral motivation over time in a single individual: some people grow cynical about moral matters, others experience a moral awakening, although it is probably most common that people remain to some degree morally concerned throughout their lives while their level of moral concern fluctuates.

These variations need in part to be explained by differences in the overall mental state of these people or of the same individual at different times. Now, if we focus on people who make similar moral judgments, the difference has to lie in their motivational system. The most straightforward hypothesis seems to be that there is a conative attitude, engaged by moral judgments, which is present in most but not all of these individuals. Moreover, this attitude differs from individual to individual in that the motivation that ensues, when it is engaged by moral judgments, varies in strength. There are other associated differences in emotional and cognitive dispositions. Those who have this attitude are likely to pay attention to and emotionally react to moral matters – at least, more likely than those who don't have it. Moreover, how apt the individual is to pay attention to moral matters and how strongly he emotionally reacts to them correlates to some extent with the strength of the motivation that ensues from this attitude. (This is not to deny that there are other factors that affect these cognitive, emotional, and motivational dispositions, for example, temperamental factors such as absent-mindedness, depressive tendencies, emotional restraint, and so on.) Now, this is the sort of conative attitude that I have in mind when I speak of the desire to be moral.

It is easy to point to variations in motivation by moral or other types of judgment that do not seem to call for the postulation of a conative attitude or any other intentional state to explain the difference. Factors like exhaustion, overloaded attention, or depression, rather than a difference in conative attitudes, can explain many variations in the motivational efficacy of a judgment of a given kind in two people or the same person at different times (Skorupski 2001). However, my sense is that the above-mentioned patterns of variation in moral motivation (as well as in accompanying cognitive and emotional dispositions) are, at least partly, to be explained by postulating a conative attitude, which some people have but others lack and whose motivational strength varies a great deal from individual to individual. There is, of course, room for disagreement here. To settle the issue, close attention will have to be paid to variations in moral motivation (as well as accompanying cognitive and emotional dispositions), and they must be compared to the type of pattern that are commonly explained by postulating a conative attitude. Undoubtedly, general theoretical issues about the nature of motivation need to be discussed in this context. Indeed, it may seem like the issue is empirical and has to await further theoretical developments in scientific studies of our motivational system. It may seem that there are no a priori grounds on which philosophers can settle the issue.

Challenges to the Simple-minded Account

Is there really nothing that philosophers can validly say about the matter aside from empirical speculations? One interesting issue that seems to call for a distinctively philosophical investigation is whether there is anything in our everyday – especially normative and conceptual – practices that presupposes that the mechanics of moral motivation is one way or another. Michael Smith can be seen as employing such a strategy when he argues that the sort of view I have offered has the undesirable implication that those who are morally motivated suffer from the vice of moral fetishism (Smith 1994: 71–6). He is attempting to show that my view of moral motivation is at odds with entrenched normative ideas. A somewhat similar objection charges that tracing moral motivation to a *desire* debases moral motivation.

Smith's fetishism charge is, I believe, entirely unfounded. Moral fetishism is most appropriately thought of as the phenomenon of holding oneself and others to rigorous moral standards, while being completely unwilling to entertain any reflective question about their nature or ground. Morality is treated as sacrosanct, so sacrosanct that no reflective or critical questions are admitted about it. The desire to be moral is hardly bound to manifest itself in such a rigid attitude. Elsewhere (Svavarsdóttir 1999: 194–215), I have argued at length that Smith has not successfully identified any other vice that is bound to be manifested by those who are motivated by the desire to be moral. I cannot see that there is anything more to the debasement charge. Explanations of moral motivation must get the explanandum right: a person is motivated on account of his moral judgment and no ulterior motive lies behind that motivation. I cannot see that the fact that an explanation of this phenomenon refers to the presence or absence of a desire makes it less dignified to be morally motivated. (If the problem is just that the English term 'desire' has undesirable connotations, I'd be happy to give it up and use 'pro-attitude towards what is moral' or some other term of art to designate the conative attitude in question.)

True, one strain in ethical rationalism crystallizes in the assumption that human dignity is to be found in our rational nature and human weakness is to be found in our sensuous nature. This rationalist idea is questionable. First, there is not a sufficiently sharp distinction between our rational and sensuous nature for this assumption to make much sense. Even desires involve our representational capacities: they are attitudes taken toward objects or events under a certain mode of presentation. Second, certain sensibilities are arguably required for human dignity. I can sympathize to some extent with the awe in which rationalists hold our capacities for representation, reasoning, and reflection. They are truly astounding. These capacities are worth valuing and cultivating, but I see no cause to praise them at the cost of our sensibilities, which they infuse and, in turn, infuse them.

I have briefly considered and dismissed two attempts to show that my explanation of moral motivation is at odds with some entrenched normative ideas and creates tension in our overall practices that should be avoided if possible. Perhaps there are more serious ones lurking in the wings. The most serious charge, as far as I can tell, is that our conception of moral judgment as being normative or distinctively action-guiding is at stake. We conceive of moral judgments as evoking normative standards against which we and our conduct can be measured. They are normative in that they make a claim on us to be or act in a certain way; falling short of them opens us up to criticism. These are not standards we may take into account if we wish or that apply to us only if we have voluntarily submitted to them. They inescapably apply to all mature human beings. We conceive of moral judgments as guides: guides to action or, more broadly, guides to living. We do not think of this as an accidental feature of moral judgments but, rather, as their very essence. These are familiar claims and, I grant, platitudinous. If they could not be reconciled with the best account of the phenomenon commonly thought of as moral motivation, we would have a problem on our hands. This would not simply be an intellectual problem but also a practical problem. Our conception of moral judgments as normative guides infects not only how we think of moral thought and practice, it also affects our moral thought and practice. Perhaps, the most serious charge against my view of moral motivation is that if my view were right, we would be faced with such problems. The truth often creates intellectual and practical problems for us, so this could not provide a knock-down argument against my view. However, if there is something to the charge, we would have a good reason to hope that my view of moral motivation is wrong and try hard to find some support for that claim. In the remaining three sections, I will critically examine whether there is anything to this charge.

Guiding vs Motivating

Indeed, it may be thought that the case is so strong that a response to my challenge to motivational internalism can be built on the above platitudes concerning the action-guidingness of moral judgments. One way of understanding the claim that a judgment guides conduct is that it motivates the agent to act in one way rather than another. If the directional role essential to moral judgments is construed in this way, the fact that we conceive of moral judgments as guides to conduct implies that there is a conceptual connection between moral judgment and motivation. In that case, there is a strong case to be made for some version of motivational internalism. Thus, it may be thought that our conception of moral judgments as guides to conduct does not only sit badly with my positive view of moral motivation but, also, provides the resources for meeting my earlier challenge to motivational internalists.

However, this defense of internalism relies on an implausible understanding of the claim that moral judgments are guides to action: the directional role essential to moral judgments cannot be reduced to a motivational role. When a person ignores the moral judgment that it is bad to harass people and maliciously harasses an old lady, the moral judgment does not guide him in the sense of motivating him. Nevertheless, the judgment is action-guiding: it lays down guidelines that the person ignores and transgresses. There is room to argue that the judgment has some motivational impact on the scoundrel, even if other motivations clearly carry the day. However, it is silly to suggest that the action-guidingness of the judgment consists in this over-ridden motivational force. If that were true, the firmness of the moral guidelines against harassing people should vary from case to case depending on the motivational impact of the judgment on the individual involved. That is absurd.[1] Thus, my admission that moral judgments are understood as guides to action does not amount to a concession to motivational internalism. Moral judgments are guides to conduct. That is how they are understood by anyone who has any understanding of moral concepts and moral practice. Perhaps this is correctly characterized as a conceptual truth. But there is nothing strange in the idea that guides may fail to motivate even those who understand them. I can understand a recipe and pass it on to others without having any inclination to follow it and broil salted cod.

What is it to understand a piece of language as expressing a prescription, guidelines, or a directive? I am not sure what the right answer is, but it cannot be that such an understanding requires motivation to undertake the prescribed action. The recipe example demonstrates this. However, there is a difference between *understanding* something as a guide and *accepting* it as a guide, and the latter may be thought to be manifested in a motivation to follow its directions. This, however, cannot be right. I may accept the recipe as a guide to broiling salted cod, yet not be at all inclined to broil salted cod. Here, it might be thought, we have come to the crux of the matter: the only way of accepting something as a guide to a given project without being motivated to follow its directions is to opt out of the given project, but moral judgments are guides to living and we cannot opt out of living, yet continue to exist as mature human beings. This would imply that the guidelines laid down by moral judgments are inescapable and motivating to all who accept them.

This is a nice idea, but it does not work. I may accept the recipe as a guide to broiling salted cod and broil salted cod without being in the least motivated to follow the recipe. I may do this, even if I do not find any fault with the recipe. I just like to do things differently from how the recipe prescribes. In other words, it is possible to engage in a project and accept something as a guide – even a good guide – to such a project, yet not be moved to follow its directions. At this point, it is apt to point out the difference between accepting something as being *a* guide to broiling salted cod and accepting something as *one's* guide to broiling salted cod. Arguably, a person has not accepted something as *his* guide to broiling salted cod unless he follows, by and large (barring weakness of will), its directions when he broils salted cod. It seems reasonable that this holds generally for accepting *x* as one's guide to *phi*-ing. However, this does not help the motivational internalist. For although it is true that no one can adequately understand moral judgments and accept them without accepting them as being guides to action or, more broadly, to living, it is possible to understand adequately moral judgments and accept them without accepting them as *one's* guides to living. The cynics and the moral subversives do not accept moral judgments as *their guides* to living, even if they accept them as (being) *guides* to living. Of course, internalists will contest this claim, but they cannot appeal to the platitude that we conceive of moral judgments as guides to action in order to make their case. As I have argued earlier, they have to defend their position by giving a non-question-begging argument for an account of moral judgments that supports their position on moral motivation.

Admittedly, there is an important disanalogy between the guidelines provided by a cooking recipe and those provided by moral judgments. Only the latter are inescapable. But the thing to note is that this inescapability is normative rather than motivational in nature: there is no claim on me to follow the recipe – the directions of the recipe do not inescapably apply to me because I am a mature human being.[2]

They apply to me only if I intend to broil salted cod according to that recipe or if I have promised to do so. Otherwise I make no mistake when acting contrary to the guidelines of the recipe. Moral judgments, in contrast, make such an inescapable claim on me regardless of whether I wish to follow their directions or have committed to doing so. It is a deep philosophical question how to understand this normative inescapability of moral judgments. Motivational internalists seem to think that this can be done in terms of their motivational role. Here is, perhaps, the crux of my disagreement with them, for I question that the normative inescapability of moral judgments can be adequately illuminated in terms of their (non-normatively specified) actual or hypothetical motivational role. To anyone who thinks otherwise, I issue the challenge to provide such an illumination. Until that is done, my earlier challenge to motivational internalists also stands.

Is Moral Motivation Rationally Required?

The question remains whether there is anything to the charge that my positive account of moral motivation is at odds with our conception of moral judgments as being normative. Jay Wallace has argued so. The problem, he claims, is that I make the connection between moral judgment and motivation "seem altogether optional and arbitrary. Some agents happen to be moved to do what they judge to be morally right or good, while other agents are not so moved; but there is little in the view she advocates that would under gird the claim that those who are morally motivated are somehow responding appropriately or correctly to the moral distinctions they grasp" (2001: 7). His complaint is not that, on my view, moral motivation is psychologically contingent – this he accepts himself – but, rather, that I make it out to be "normatively contingent" (ibid. 8). Wallace is suggesting that there is a normative requirement to the effect that an agent be motivated by her moral judgments and that my view of moral motivation commits me to denying that there is such a requirement. He thinks that such a requirement rises out of the normativity of morality.

It is not an obvious truth that there is such a normative requirement and, at least, Nick Zangwill (2003: 150) has disputed Wallace's claim. The normativity of morality consists in there being inescapable claims on us to live like *correct* moral judgments specify – at least like those which speak of requirements, obligations, and duties. But is there a claim on us to live by our moral judgments regardless of their truth? As Zangwill observes, some people make dangerous moral judgments – for example, judgments to the effect that cruel behavior is justified in case it serves a morally important end. Are they somehow at fault if they do not live by these misguided moral judgments and do horrendous things? If there is a normative claim on the agent to live by his moral judgments, that claim conflicts in such cases with moral requirements that bid him not to commit atrocities. So, it is hardly obvious that there is a normative requirement that we be motivated by our moral judgments or that such a requirement is traceable to the fact that morality is normative.

Nevertheless, I am inclined to accept that, due to the normativity of morality, it is incumbent on us to do our best to discern moral distinctions and take our sincere moral judgments as guides to living. True, there is no guarantee that this will lead us to the morally right course of action, given our fallibility in moral matters. Even if we are in an epistemic position to discern moral distinctions, honest mistakes as well as culpable oversights are possible. However, it seems odd that there be a claim on us to live in a certain way but not a claim on us to take our sincere judgments about what that requires of us as our guide to living, even if there is always the risk that the judgments are radically mistaken and will, hence, lead us astray. If that happens, the correct moral evaluation of the relevant agent will be complex: he followed his sincere moral judgment as he prima facie ought to have done, but he nevertheless behaved horrendously because the judgment was mistaken. In such cases, the agent's culpability must be largely determined by what sort of failure led to his mistake in judgment and what sort of motivations had, or had not, to be overcome to do such horrendous thing. (The mistake in judgment may be rooted in a failure of sensibility as well as in a failure of cognition.) However, whatever the nature of the agent's culpability is, he did the wrong thing in behaving as he did. The evaluation of an agent and his actions, though intimately linked, can thus come apart. This is not to suggest that people who cannot bring themselves to act on moral judgments that bid them do cruel things should be judged harshly for they may be displaying a more important moral virtue than that of moral conscientiousness.

Is my concession that there is such a normative requirement somehow at odds with my account of moral motivation? I cannot see what the conflict is supposed to be, and find Wallace's charge that I make moral motivation out to be "normatively contingent" rather puzzling. In my earlier work, I proposed an explanation of how moral judgments motivate: a view of what is psychologically involved in moral motivation. This does not commit me to any position on whether there is a normative requirement to the effect that one be motivated by one's moral judgments. All it commits me to is that if there is such a normative requirement, it will not be satisfied (as a matter of fact) unless the agent has the desire to be moral; hence, having the desire will be as important as satisfying the normative requirement in question. It would be surprising if it counts against an explanation of how moral judgments motivate that it does not imply anything about whether there is a normative requirement that sanctions moral motivation. Thus, my view of the mechanics of moral motivation is not in tension with the normative view about moral motivation that I have just embraced. Jointly they imply that it is contingent whether any given agent is apt to be motivated by his moral judgment as he (prima facie) ought to be. This is not the same as it being contingent whether an agent ought to be motivated by his moral judgments.

The above normative requirement on motivation is, however, not identical to the one Wallace proposes: his *motivational requirement*. According to Wallace's requirement, those who are not motivated by their sincere moral judgments either have failed to appreciate, due to deficient deliberation, the normativity of moral distinctions or are suffering from practical irrationality. Nothing I have said implies that the defect of those who fail to be motivated by their sincere moral judgments lies in deficient deliberation or practical irrationality. But neither are my views, stated so far, inconsistent with that claim. Indeed, it will follow from the above normative view of moral motivation, provided that two assumptions are added: (i) that those who deliberate correctly will acknowledge that there is a normative claim on them to take their sincere moral judgments as their guides to living; (ii) that it is a condition of practical rationality that if an agent acknowledges that there is a normative claim on him to live by a certain type of judgment, then he must take such judgments as *his* guides to living and, hence, be motivated by them.

These assumptions mimic the assumptions from which Wallace derives his motivational requirement: (i) that we have an epistemic access, through deliberation, to moral distinctions and to the fact that they are normative (2001: n.4); (ii) that it is a condition of rationality that one is motivated in accordance with considerations that one acknowledges to have normative significance. Assuming that to acknowledge that moral distinctions are normative is to acknowledge that corresponding moral considerations (the correct ones) are normatively significant, Wallace's motivational requirement follows: "Agents are necessarily motivated to act in accordance with moral requirements, to the extent they are deliberating correctly and are otherwise practically rational" (ibid. 4). Wallace claims that this captures "what is worth preserving in the idea that moral judgments are somehow internally connected to motivation" (ibid. 6). In other words, the two above assumptions are his means to "undergird the claim that those who are morally motivated are somehow responding appropriately or correctly to the moral distinctions they grasp" (ibid. 7).[3] They are correctly acknowledging the normative significance of the moral distinctions they grasp and motivationally reacting to that acknowledgment as suits a rational person. Those who are not morally motivated are either missing a part of the truth due to poor deliberation or motivationally reacting to that truth in ways that are rationally inappropriate.

As noted above, nothing in my view of moral motivation prevents me from accepting similar assumptions and from embracing Wallace's motivational requirement. But are these two assumptions plausible? As for the first one, I suspect that a failure to appreciate the normative claim in question may, in some cases, be traceable to a failure in sensibility rather than in deliberation such that no charge of irrationality is warranted. As for the second assumption, I can appreciate the considerable intuitive appeal of the idea that it is irrational to fail to be motivated by considerations one acknowledges to have normative significance. However, on reflection, I have my doubts. It seems possible to acknowledge the normative significance, say, of legal considerations without being motivated accordingly. For example, I would not dispute anyone who faults me for ignoring traffic laws, and I would not object to being fined for doing so. For I acknowledge that it is incumbent on me to act in accord with the local traffic laws and, hence, to take my sincere judgments about these laws as a guide to conduct. Yet, I am not inclined to take them wholesale as *my* guide to action. For example, I have my own policy on jay-walking: jay-walk with caution except never jay-walk in front of young children, since they need to be encouraged to follow the traffic laws because of the limits on their perceptual and cognitive abilities. Even if I do not challenge the existence and the legitimacy of the relevant law, nor its applicability to me, I am not taking it as my guide to conduct for reasons that I will not go into here. Obviously, this shows my limits as a law-abiding citizen and, perhaps, it manifests other faults, but does it amount to a failure of rationality? It is far from obvious that the correct answer is in the affirmative. Pursuing this issue further takes us into controversies over the nature of practical rationality.

It is not quite right that Wallace simply assumes that it is a condition of rationality that one is motivated by considerations that one acknowledges to be normatively significant. He can be seen as deriving this claim from two assumptions that may seem trivially true: (i) to acknowledge the normative significance of a consideration is to acknowledge that it represents a reason for action; (ii) an agent displays irrationality if he acknowledges that a consideration represents a reason for action while not being in the least motivated by that consideration to take the action.[4] This defense of the rationality requirement puts much weight on the notion of reason for action without illuminating it. I worry that the term 'reason for action' can express an array of related but distinct notions, so that there is a significant danger of equivocation when it is used in statements of arguments. To give some substance to this worry, consider again the above example. What is it to acknowledge that the consideration that jay-walking is illegal represents, or is, a reason against jay-walking? Does it require that one take, other things equal, this consideration into account when deciding whether to jay-walk on a particular occasion? Or, does it suffice that one take it into account when deciding on one's policy on jay-walking? Or is it perhaps sufficient that one is apt to treat the consideration as relevant in arguments about whether one should ever jay-walk or about whether I can be faulted for jay-walking? Perfectly law-abiding citizens will meet the first condition, I meet only the last two, and a complete cynic about the law in question – who nevertheless acknowledges its existence and the authority of those who set it to do so – meets only the last condition. Do only some or all of us acknowledge that the consideration that jay-walking is illegal is or represents a reason for action? It is not clear that there is a single correct answer to this question regardless of context.

I accept that those who meet the first condition are irrational if they fail to be motivated by the consideration that jay-walking is illegal. Deliberation takes place with an eye to acting directly on the conclusion of that deliberation. If an agent takes, during deliberation, a consideration to count for or against the behavioral alternatives between which he is deciding, yet this has no resonance in his motivational system, something has gone amiss for him as a rational agent deliberating with an eye to acting directly on the conclusions of that deliberation. The charge of irrationality seems to be plausible in that case. I venture that this is because of this special feature of the context of deliberation that is missing in the context of deciding on a general practical policy and in the context of arguments about conduct that are divorced from decision-making.[5] If this is right, there are two options open to Wallace: (i) claim that acknowledging the normative significance of a consideration consists, at least in part, in taking, other things being equal, the consideration into account when deciding on how to act on a particular occasion; (ii) claim that if an agent is apt to take the consideration into account in setting practical policies or to treat it as relevant in arguments about how people should act, then he is irrational if he does not also take it into account in deliberating how to act on a particular occasion. The second claim is hardly right. If one has set a general policy on a certain type of conduct, surely one is not irrational in taking only considerations dictated by that policy into consideration when deliberating on how to act on a particular occasion and excluding considerations on which one based one's decision to adapt that policy. The first claim seems also implausible. I readily admit that I open myself up to legitimate criticism when I run foul of the law against jay-walking and do not object (in my heart of hearts) to being fined for doing so. Surely, this amounts to an acknowledgment that there is a claim on me to follow the law and that the consideration that jay-walking is illegal has normative significance.

I have been throwing out half-baked ideas about reasons for action, normative significance, and conditions of rationality. They have to be developed and defended in another place. All I hope to have done here is to cast doubt on the idea that Wallace's motivational requirement can be supported by platitudinous claims about the connection between normative judgments, acknowledgment of reasons for action, and the rationality of motivational responses. I am skeptical of Wallace's motivational requirement and the assumptions about practical rationality on which it is based. I suspect that this is what Wallace is onto when he claims that I make moral motivation out to be "normatively contingent" (2001: 8). What he means by this is that I do not take moral motivation to be rationally required. He happens to be right on this score, although nothing in my view of the mechanics of moral motivation commits me to this stance. As I argued above, the view that motivation by moral judgment is rooted in a desire is consistent with Wallace's motivational requirement.

The Intentional Perspective of the Morally Motivated

Wallace has another, related and more serious, challenge to my view of moral motivation. He argues that those who are morally motivated are not only responding appropriately or correctly to moral distinctions but are, also, conceiving of their motivational reactions in this way. My view of moral motivation, Wallace charges, cannot do justice to this feature of the intentional perspective of the morally motivated agent:[6]

> *Such agents characteristically take it that their actions are recommended or justified by the fact that they are morally required or otherwise morally valuable, and this in turn renders their moral motivation intelligible to them as a fitting response to the consider-ations that they take to have normative significance.* This is something that gets left out on the interesting reconstruction of the intentional perspective of the moral agent that Svavarsdóttir offers ([1999]: 202–3). That picture posits an "internal link" between the mental states of the person who is (say) motivated to help somebody because they believe that doing so would be morally right, insofar as the content of the agent's moral belief relates the object of their general desire to be moral to the more specific desire that moti-vates them to help. But *the internal link in this example is specified without use of any normative concepts* (202, note 60), and for this reason it fails to do justice to the inter-nal perspective of the virtuous agent. *Such agents do not simply find that they are inex-plicably drawn to doing actions which can be described as morally right or good. Rather, their being so motivated is connected to their own acknowledgment that the rightness or goodness of an action counts strongly in favor of performing it.* (2001: 7; italics mine)

I take Wallace's point to be that by postulating a desire to be moral to account for motivation by moral judgment, I am reconstructing the intentional perspective of a person who is morally motivated as being much like that of a person who, desiring something sweet, reaches out for something he thinks of as sweet. Wallace is right that there is an important difference between the intentional perspectives of these two agents. An agent who is morally motivated is acting on considerations that he sees as justifying the action. I doubt that the agent who reaches for the plum sees the consideration that the plum is sweet as justifying his action. In most circumstances, people will not see any need for justifying eating a plum. The consideration in question just makes it an attractive thing to do. Wallace is right that the intentional states that underlie the intentional perspectives of these two agents must differ.

Of course, they differ: judging that something is morally required or valuable expresses a very different belief from the belief expressed by the judgment that something is sweet. Understanding the content of the former judgment involves understanding it as presenting an inescapable claim on the agent judged. Moreover, accepting the judgment involves accepting that there is such an inescapable claim on the agent and likewise situated agents. It is baffling that Wallace claims that, on my account of moral motivation, normative concepts do not figure in the characterization of the intentional perspective of the morally conscientious. For moral concepts figure into the conceptual content of both the judgment and the desire that underlie moral motivation on my account of the matter. Surely, these are normative concepts. Mastering them requires that one understand judgments employing them as evoking normative standards and (competently) accepting such judgments involves acknowledging that these normative standards obtain and that they imply the specific guidelines that are laid down by the judgment. What I maintain is that such an acknowledgment of normative standards does not suffice for moral motivation. However, those who are motivated by moral considerations will see these considerations as presenting a claim on them to act or live in a certain way or, at least, as presenting a moral justification for such an action or a way of living. Moreover, this is what attracts them to this option (at least, those who aren't paying attention to moral consideration for ulterior motives). Indeed, they may be averse or indifferent to it under any other mode of presentation. Wanting to be moral is wanting to take the morally justified option.

Still, it may be asked whether I am depicting the morally motivated as finding themselves to be "inexplicably drawn" to actions they deem morally justified? Am I unable to depict their intentional perspective such that "their moral motivation [is] intelligible *to them* as a fitting response to the considerations that they take to have normative significance"? Notice that insofar as Wallace intends "finding oneself as being inexplicably drawn to" and "taking one's motivation to be intelligible as a fitting response to the consideration that" to describe the intentional perspective of an agent, he is describing the intentional perspective of a morally motivated agent who is reflective about his moral motivation. It is an intentional perspective that manifests the second-order intentional states of an agent who turns his gaze inward, reflects on his mental states, and takes a second-order stand on them. Admittedly, my account of moral motivation has nothing to say about the second-order intentional states of the morally motivated. It provides only the means to reconstruct the intentional perspective of the morally motivated in unreflective moments, when he is preoccupied with the moral considerations that are motivating him to act. Then, he will surely be thinking in terms of moral requirements or moral values rather than in terms of his motivational responses or the fittingness of his responses. The question raised by

Wallace's conjecture about the intentional perspective of the morally motivated is whether it is integral to moral motivation that the agent, in reflective moments, sees his motivational reactions to moral considerations as fitting responses to them.

Is the answer in the affirmative? There are some reasons to doubt that. We all know that the question 'Why be moral?' is apt to arise in reflective moments. Philosophical tradition has it that this question comes from the morally uncommitted – skeptics who challenge the morally committed to demonstrate that they rationally ought to shed their skeptical attitude and commit to morality. But the truth is that the philosophers who raise the question, and feel impelled to struggle with it, are typically morally committed: this is a question that grows out of a reflective stand on one's moral commitment – a stand that naturally leads to philosophical reflections on the nature and grounds of moral discourse and practice. When we step back and reflect on our moral commitment, we may come to wonder whether our allegiance to moral norms makes any sense. After all, their nature and grounds are not transparent to us. So, it is far from clear that it is integral to moral motivation that, in reflective moments, the agent will find that his motivational responses to moral considerations are warranted.

Nevertheless, there is something to the claim that, given *full* competence with moral concepts, the person who judges something to be morally required or valuable is apt to deem it fitting to be motivated by that consideration. This is, I submit, because the judgment that something is morally required or valuable is conceptually tied to the judgment that it is fitting to have various emotional and motivational responses to it: what is morally valuable does not only merit certain treatment, it also merits certain attitudes. This is, I believe, integral to our understanding of the normativity of moral considerations: they putatively refer not only to norms for conduct but also to norms for attitudes. But this does not raise problems for my view of moral motivation. On my view, the conceptual resources at play in moral judgment and in moral motivation are distinctively moral. If they are such that full competence with them requires that moral judgment is linked to a disposition to deem it fitting to have various emotional and motivational responses to moral considerations, then it is integral to moral motivation that the agent, in reflective moments, sees his motivational reactions to moral considerations as fitting responses to them. This conclusion can, indeed, be easily reconciled with the observations in the previous paragraph. The meriting or fittingness at stake is a moral notion and is not obviously connected to an evaluation of the agent as being more or less sensible or practically rational. The judgment about the merit of moral motivation that is conceptually tied to any moral judgment does not foreclose questions about whether our being morally motivated or, more broadly, morally committed makes much sense. Evoking that judgment would not provide a satisfactory answer to the reflective question, 'Why be moral?' Such a response reminds us that moral norms are norms for attitudes as well as conduct, and that does not address the question whether our allegiance to moral norms makes any sense.

I have claimed that any moral judgment is conceptually connected to a normative judgment about motivation. Perhaps, it will be objected that I cannot hold this without conceding that it is irrational to fail to be motivated by one's (fully competent) moral judgments because it is irrational to fail to have a motivational response that one

How Do Moral Judgments Motivate?

deems fitting to have in one's circumstances. In other words, I am committed to accept Wallace's motivational requirement. The person who addresses the reflective question 'Why be moral?' is – the objection continues – suspending all moral judgment and, therefore, the answer to his question cannot straightforwardly be: "Because you are committed to the judgment that your moral motivation is fitting, so you would be irrational if you were not thus motivated." However – the objection continues – this is the right thing to say to a person who genuinely accepts a moral judgment: a person is irrational if his motivations do not align with his judgments about what sort of motivational responses are fitting in his circumstances.

This is far from obvious. Take an individual who finds himself as having, due to racist upbringing, emotional and motivational responses that he deems unacceptable and lacking responses he thinks are more appropriate. He tries his best to eradicate or, at least, control the unacceptable ones and cultivate the appropriate ones. Is he irrational for having responses he deems inappropriate and lacking those he judges appropriate? My inclination is to answer in the negative. The problem of this man is not irrationality but, rather, deformed sensibilities. Again, my disagreement with Wallace boils down to questions about the nature of rationality and its relation to morality that will not be settled here. Wallace stands within the philosophical tradition that takes rationality to be the source of all normative requirements, while I doubt that the normativity of morality can be understood in terms of requirements of rationality. In any case, I hope to have convinced the reader that whatever the truth is in this matter, moral judgments motivate by engaging a conative attitude that employs a distinctively moral mode of presentation. Such a view of moral motivation is no threat to our conception of moral judgments as presenting normatively inescapable claims on us.

Notes

1 The problem cannot be fixed by proposing that the action-guidingness of a moral judgment consists not in its actual motivational force but, rather, in the motivational force that it would have under some (non-normatively specified) conditions. For this would make the firmness of moral guidelines vary from case to case depending on the disposition of the relevant individual to be motivated by them. True, there would not be any such variation if the relevant motivational disposition were the same in all of us. However, such a variation in the firmness of the guidelines should not be even an epistemic possibility.

2 Well, they apply to me in the thin sense of my being the sort of creature that can be thus directed, but they do not apply to me in the thick sense that running foul of these directions opens me up to criticism.

3 This claim is ambiguous and the same ambiguity plagues Wallace's entire discussion. The claim can be given either a *de re* reading (there are moral distinctions and those who are motivationally responsive to them are responding appropriately and correctly to their (successful) grasp of these moral distinctions) or a *de dicto* reading (those who are motivated by their moral judgments are responding appropriately and correctly to their assessment of moral distinctions). The statement of his motivational requirement suggests the *de re* reading, since it speaks of motivation to act in accord with moral requirements rather

than motivation to act in accord with one's assessment of moral requirements. The first assumption from which the requirement is derived suggests the same. However, the tenor of Wallace's discussion often suggests that he has the *de dicto* reading in mind and that his motivational requirement should be interpreted accordingly. Notice that the objection three paragraphs back applies to Wallace only if he is interpreted as intending the *de dicto* reading. This is Zangwill's interpretation of Wallace.

4   According to Wallace, the normativity of moral distinctions consists in their being reasons for action (2001: 4), and normatively significant considerations are considerations that "represent genuine reasons for action" (ibid.). Does this mean that only correct moral considerations are normatively significant (since, given the reasons there are, only correct moral considerations successfully represent reasons for action) or that all moral considerations are normatively significant (though some of them falsely represent normative reality, i.e., what reasons there are)? I myself think that normatively significant considerations *are* reasons for action: considerations that it would be rational to take into account in reasoning or considerations that represent values, requirements, or other things of normative significance. I don't think the disjuncts are equivalent, i.e., the term 'reason' is not a univocal expression.

5   I readily grant that it is likely (though not necessary) that an agent who takes a consideration into account in the two last contexts is motivated by that consideration. The issue on the table now is whether such an agent would be irrational, if he were not thus motivated.

6   Wallace actually says "of the virtuous agent." He seems to assume that moral conscientiousness is a part of every virtue. This presupposes a controversial Kantian take on the virtues, which is not required for Wallace's objection to my view.

References

Copp, D. (1996). "Moral obligation and moral motivation." In J. Coutrue and K. Nielson (eds.), *New Essays on Metaethics. Canadian Journal of Philosophy*, supp. vol.

Skorupski, J. (2001). "Comments on Svavarsdóttir." Brown Electronic Article Review Service.

Smith, M. (1994). *The Moral Problem*. Oxford: Basil Blackwell.

Stocker, M. (1979). "Desiring the bad: an essay in moral psychology." *The Journal of Philosophy*, 76: 738–53.

Svavarsdóttir, S. (1999). "Moral cognitivism and motivation." *The Philosophical Review*, 108: 161–219.

Wallace, J. (2001). "Comments on Svavarsdóttir." Brown Electronic Article Review Service.

Zangwill, N. (2003). "Externalist moral motivation." *American Philosophical Quarterly*, 40: 143–54.

Further Reading

Brink, D. (1989). *Moral Realism and the Foundations of Ethics*. Cambridge: Cambridge University Press.

Darwall, S. (1983). *Impartial Reason* (ch. 5). Ithaca: Cornell University Press.

Dreier, J. (1990). "Internalism and speaker relativism." *Ethics*, 101: 6–26.

Frankena, W. (1958). "Obligation and motivation in recent moral philosophy." In A. I. Melden (ed.), *Essays on Moral Philosophy* (pp. 40–81). Seattle: University of Washington Press.

Korsgaard, C. (1986). "Skepticism about practical reason." *Journal of Philosophy*, 83: 5–25

McDowell, J. (1978). "Are moral requirements hypothetical imperatives?" *Proceedings of the Aristotelian Society*, supp. vol. 52: 13–29.

Stevenson, C. L. (1937). "The emotive meaning of ethical terms." *Mind*, 46: 14–31.

Moral Motivation

R. Jay Wallace

Issues about motivation lie at the center of moral philosophy. They have helped to shape debates in metaethics, about the nature of the moral judgment, and about the objectivity of moral properties and distinctions. More broadly, normative ethical theories can be seen in part as attempts to characterize in substantive terms the objects of moral motivation and concern. One question that runs through these debates concerns the connection between morality and moral motivation. Arrayed on one side of this question are proponents of internalism in various forms, who maintain that morality is necessarily or non-accidentally a source of motivations to action. On the other side are externalists, who contend that moral motivations are at best contingently connected to moral judgments or to the moral properties and distinctions that those judgments record.

In this essay I wish to defend a version of internalism. To do so, however, it will be necessary to get much clearer about what might be meant by saying that morality and motivation are non-accidentally connected. The account I shall develop emphasizes the normative dimension of morality, its putative standing as a domain of reasons for action. Judgments about what one has reason to do give rise to corresponding motivations to action in agents who are not irrational. So if moral considerations constitute normative reasons, they will be motivating in those agents who are reasoning correctly.

Moral Judgment and Motivation

Let us begin by considering the connection between moral judgment and motivation. It has often been asserted that there is a non-accidental connection of some kind between endorsing a moral judgment and being motivated to comply with it. This thesis is commonly invoked in metaethical debates about the proper analysis of the mental act of moral judgment, as a constraint that such accounts must satisfy. Thus it is suggested that sincere endorsement of a moral judgment carries with it some tendency to be motivated to comply with the judgment. According to this view – which we might call moral judgment internalism (cf. Darwall 1983) – there is a distinctive psychological condition that must be satisfied if an agent is to count as accepting the claim expressed by a moral judgment.[1]

Moral judgment internalism has figured prominently in metaethical discussions during the past century. It has been appealed to by expressivists, for instance, who claim that moral judgments are not the kind of cognitive attitudes that aim to represent the way the world is, but involve instead desires or pro-attitudes of some kind, which moral assertions express or give voice to.[2] Indeed, it seems fair to say that moral judgment internalism in some form is the primary consideration alleged to support expressivist approaches – it is the expressivist's Ur-argument, if you will. The basic idea is that expressivism alone is able to account for the connection of moral judgment with motivation that is captured by the thesis of moral judgment internalism – the alleged fact that such judgments necessarily involve a motivation to action. One common argument for this conclusion starts by pointing out that motivation requires the presence of a psychological state with a distinctive direction of fit vis-à-vis the world, that which is characteristic of non-cognitive states such as desire, rather than such cognitive states as beliefs. If moral judgments are necessarily motivating, they must therefore involve essentially non-cognitive states with the peculiar direction of fit of desires. The expressivist claims that this condition can be made sense of only if we understand moral discourse non-cognitively, as involving the expression of such motivating states as desires.

Opponents of these approaches, for their part, need not reject moral judgment internalism. They can affirm the necessary connection between moral judgment and motivation, while developing a different motivational psychology to account for the psychological condition on sincere assent to a moral claim. The task is a challenging one, however. If moral judgment internalism is true, then either the state of sincere assent to a moral proposition must itself constitute a disposition to be motivated accordingly, or that state must be connected necessarily to such a motivational disposition, construed as a distinct psychological condition. Neither option seems especially promising.

If moral judgment and moral motivation are distinct psychological states, then any connection between them must be a causal one, and it is extremely hard to see why there should be a necessary causal connection of the required kind. The distinctness of moral judgment and moral motivation would seem to leave open the possibility of endorsing a moral judgment without exhibiting any motivation to comply. On the other hand, a cognitivist interpretation of moral judgment that renders the sincere acceptance of moral claims constitutive of motivation seems similarly elusive. Insofar as moral judgment is a cognitive state, it must be a propositional attitude that aims to fit the way the world is. But insofar as moral judgment is motivating, it must have the different direction of fit characteristic of desires. A state might satisfy these twin conditions insofar as it involves attitudes of the two different kinds toward distinct propositions (e.g. a world-guided attitude toward the proposition that x-ing would be wrong, and an action-guiding attitude toward the proposition that I will not do x).

But if discrete attitudes are in play in regard to distinct propositional contents, then it seems we are back to postulating two different psychological states that are necessarily connected, and the problem of defending this necessary causal connection reasserts itself.

These considerations suggest that, if the expressivist's Ur-argument is to be resisted, then moral judgment internalism will need to be scrutinized critically. But this is something that is independently called for. For one thing, there are basic difficulties that arise when we try to formulate the thesis of moral judgment internalism precisely.[3] Even if we set these difficulties to the side, however, a more fundamental problem remains. This is that it is very hard to see how one could defend moral judgment internalism against possible counterexamples to it in a way that does not simply beg the question.

Traditionally, opponents of moral judgment internalism invoke the figure of the skeptic about morality (see, e.g., Brink 1989). This is someone who understands moral language well enough, but who doubts or rejects the significance of moral properties and distinctions in reflecting about how to act. A person of this description might well be mistaken in thinking that morality has no proper authority to govern their practical deliberation. But, mistaken or not, the stance of the moral skeptic seems a coherent one, insofar as we can imagine a person who is competent at moral discourse, but who questions its significance for their own practical reflection. Yet moral judgment internalism appears to rule out the very possibility of adopting this stance, on grounds that seem questionably a priori.

Thus Sigrun Svavarsdóttir (1999) invites us to consider Patrick, a person who is to all appearances adept at moral thought and judgment, but who shows no tendency whatsoever to care about whether his behavior does or does not comply with the moral conclusions that he accepts and endorses.[4] Svavarsdóttir suggests that we should approach this example as a bit of observable behavior that we are called upon to investigate empirically. Moral judgment internalists, she concedes, may well be able to come up with explanations of the empirical data in a case of this kind. They may postulate, for instance, a motivational tendency on Patrick's part to comply with his moral judgments that is never strong enough to eventuate in observable moral behavior. She herself finds these explanations unconvincing, but her argument does not turn on intuitions of plausibility. Instead she offers a *methodological* case against internalism, contending that it violates more general principles on the proper explanation of observable phenomena.

Specifically, Svavarsdóttir (ibid. 180–1) contends that empirical theories carry a distinctive burden of proof when they rule out explanatory hypotheses that cannot readily be seen to be false (such as the hypothesis that Patrick has no motivation to comply with the moral judgments he is capable of endorsing). The burden is to justify the exclusion of hypotheses that would otherwise seem to be in the running, as accounts of the observable phenomena. In the particular case at issue, Svavarsdóttir suggests that there is no justification available that does not simply presuppose the internalist thesis, in a way that would obviously be question-begging in the context of the debate about that very thesis.

Svavarsdóttir's argument adopts the third-person perspective of explanation, asking how we might best make sense of the attitudes and behavior of an apparent moral skeptic. But her conclusion seems to cohere with reflection from the first-person perspective of practical deliberation. Thus, even if we are not moral skeptics ourselves, it seems that the outlook of the skeptic is available to be occupied. We can imagine, for instance, a trajectory that takes as its starting point our present commitment to moral ends, and arrives at the position of the skeptic. On this imagined scenario, we would retain our actual competence with moral predicates and distinctions, but lose any concern to comply with moral requirements, having come to doubt the significance of those requirements for our deliberation about what to do. The prospect of this imaginary trajectory in our thinking about morality will probably seem horrifying from our present point of view, and the skepticism in which it terminates may in fact be substantively mistaken. But it appears to be a perfectly intelligible scenario, and insofar as this is the case moral judgment internalism must be rejected.

But what exactly follows from the falsity of moral judgment internalism? Should we conclude that there is at best only a contingent causal connection between morality and moral motivation? Or is there some other way to defend the idea that morality is a non-accidental source of motivations to action? In what follows I shall attempt to develop the second possibility. The aim will be to formulate a version of internalism that avoids the problems with moral judgment internalism, giving adequate expression to the idea that morality is internally linked to motivation.

Morality and Normative Reasons

A number of philosophers who would agree with me in rejecting moral judgment internalism nevertheless affirm the motivating dimension of morality and moral thought. Consider the positions of Christine Korsgaard and Michael Smith. These philosophers concede that it is possible to grasp moral claims without in fact being moved to comply with them (see Korsgaard 1986; Smith 1994: sec. 3.1). They accordingly concede that internalism should not be understood as a general conceptual truth about the mental act of moral judgment. In the version of internalism that they favor, the conceptual connection between moral judgment and motivation can be formulated adequately only with the help of a rationality condition. The internalist thesis that results says that moral judgment necessarily gives rise to corresponding motivation in those agents who are practically rational.

To this it might be objected that it threatens to open up a can of worms, raising complex issues about the notion of practical rationality that render the internalist thesis useless as a constraint on accounts of moral thought (cf. Svavarsdóttir 1999: 164–5). I agree that the notion of practical rationality is potentially obscure and difficult, and for reasons to be explained directly I would prefer to formulate internalism in a way that differs somewhat from the version favored by Korsgaard and Smith. But cases such as Patrick's already suffice to call into question the suggestion that internalism functions as a general constraint on moral thought and judgment. Philosophers have introduced the rationality condition as a way of capturing the grain of truth in internalism, while leaving room for the kinds of examples that call into question moral judgment internalism. The question is whether an alternative formulation of internalism can be found that does justice to our assumption that moral skepticism of this variety is possible, and how we are to understand the role of internalism in our theorizing about morality if it does not function as a general constraint on moral judgment.

In thinking about these issues, we would do well to begin by focusing on the putative connection between morality and reasons for action. What is attractive about internalism regarding moral judgment, I believe, is the thought that moral considerations at least purport to have normative significance. They present themselves to us as reasons for action, in the basic normative sense of being considerations that count for or against courses of action that are open to us.[5] Thus it is not merely a brute fact about us that we tend to find ourselves drawn to actions that we judge to be morally right or valuable. From the first-person point of view, these moral characteristics strike us as considerations that recommend or speak in favor of the actions to which they apply. Furthermore, the fact that they strike us as normative in this way is connected to our tendency to be motivated in accordance with the moral judgments that we endorse. This strongly suggests that we can arrive at an adequate understanding of the internalist thesis only by attending to the putatively normative dimension of morality.

Those philosophers who have recently favored a rationality condition in their formulations of the internalist thesis can best be understood as responding to this normative dimension of morality. Korsgaard's suggestion that moral judgments are motivating in those agents who are practically rational, for instance, stems from a concern with the status of moral considerations as reasons for action.[6] Her idea seems to be that it is characteristic of rational agents to be motivated in accordance with their reasons for action. The normative dimension of morality does not entail that people will necessarily be motivated to comply with the moral judgments they sincerely endorse, but it does entail that they will be so motivated insofar as they are practically rational.

This suggestion cannot be accepted exactly as it stands, however. The problem is that it does not in general seem plausible to define rationality in such a way that rational agents perfectly comply with their reasons for action or belief. As T. M. Scanlon has observed, people may without irrationality fail to be motivated in accordance with their reasons if, for instance, they do not accept that those reasons obtain (1998: ch. 1, sec. 4). Thus it may be the case that there is reason to prepare in mid-career for one's retirement years. But if I do not accept this normative judgment, my failure to set aside sufficient funds in my retirement account will most likely be a sign of imprudence rather than irrationality – or so, at any rate, it would be natural to think. This suggests that we do best to reserve the term 'irrationality' to refer to cases in which people fail to act and think in accordance with the normative judgments about their reasons that they themselves endorse.

Now it might seem that this is a merely terminological point, with no deeper significance for our understanding of rational and moral motivation. But I believe this to be a mistake. The terminological insight reflects a substantive truth about the way in which reasons and motivation interact. Considerations that provide us with reasons do not have some kind of motivational power that is magically intrinsic to them. That a contribution to my pension fund would enhance my financial security in old age is, in itself, merely an interesting fact about that course of action. It is perfectly possible for a cogent (though possibly misguided) agent to concede that this fact obtains, yet lack any motivation to engage in the corresponding course of action. Motivation emerges through a further moment of acknowledgement that is logically distinct form the first: the acknowledgment, namely, that the fact in question speaks in favor of contributing to my pension fund.

If we accept this suggestion, however, we will need to understand in a different way the connections between moral considerations, moral judgment, and motivation. Here is one possibility that suggests itself. Assume, first, that it is a condition of rationality that one is motivated in accordance with the normative judgments that one endorses. It is presumably not impossible to fail to be motivated in accordance with such judgments – something like this happens, for instance, in cases of weakness of will and in some forms of self-deception. But when such cases arise, it is natural to say that the agents involved in them are irrational, insofar they fail to be motivated as they themselves judge that they ought to be. It is thus part of being a rational agent to have dispositions to action (and thought) that are in accordance with the normative reasons one acknowledges to obtain.

Assume, second, that moral considerations do in fact represent genuine reasons for action, having the status of considerations that, for any agent, count for or against that agent's acting in certain specified ways. If this is the case, then we can say that agents are necessarily motivated to act in accordance with moral requirements, to the extent they are deliberating correctly and are otherwise practically rational. The condition of correct deliberation rules out cases in which an agent does not acknowledge the truth of moral judgments, or does not acknowledge that such judgments have normative significance for practical reflection. And the rationality condition rules out agents whose motivations fail to align with their own verdicts about what there is reason to do, in the style of weakness of will.

The combination of these two conditions – which I shall henceforth refer to as the motivation requirement – provides a plausible (if rough) characterization of the motivating dimension of morality. The requirement combines a claim about the effects of a certain class of judgments, namely normative judgments about what there is reason for one to do, with a substantive thesis about morality, to the effect that it is itself a source of reasons in this normative sense. Before we explore the implications of this requirement, however, it will be helpful to address a few obscurities in its initial formulation.

A first issue concerns the notion of motivation. As stated above, the motivation requirement builds on the idea that rational agents are motivated in accordance with the normative judgments they endorse. But what exactly does it mean to say that someone is motivated 'in accordance with' normative judgments they endorse? It would be implausibly strict to interpret this as requiring that agents should have an occurrent desire for every normative reason they acknowledge to obtain, with the desire corresponding in its causal force or phenomenological intensity to the normative significance of the reason. It simply does not seem to be a sign of irrationality if I judge that I have some reason to go to a movie tonight, but fail to experience an occurrent desire to act on that reason. The reason I acknowledge to obtain may be defeated by other normative considerations, such as the importance of helping my daughter with her homework. Or it might merely render the movie option eligible for pursuit, leaving it open to me to choose to pursue other valuable but optional activities (such as staying home to finish the novel I am reading). In circumstances of this kind, the most that rationality might require of me would be a kind of conditional disposition to action. Rational agents will be motivated to act on the reasons they acknowledge to obtain, so long as they do not take those reasons to be defeated by other normative considerations, and so long as they have not resolved to pursue other eligible options (in circumstances in which there are competing reasons in favor of a number of alternative courses of action, none of which defeats the others).

Let us now consider how this interpretation of rational motivation intersects with morality. The thesis on the table is that rational agents will necessarily be motivated to comply with moral requirements, insofar as they are reasoning correctly. This thesis will follow from my interpretation of rational motivation only if moral requirements are not merely considerations that count in favor of the actions they specify, but considerations that count decisively in favor of those actions, *defeating* any reasons on the other side. For as we have seen, it is not irrational to fail to be motivated to act on reasons that one acknowledges if those reasons are either defeated themselves, or such as to render an action one of a plurality of eligible or valuable options for choice. On the other hand, it seems to me that we should not build into the motivation requirement the assumption that moral reasons are *always* so compelling that they defeat whatever reasons might count against the actions morality demands. Consider the view that some conflicts between morality and our most central personal projects and concerns have the structure of dilemmas, in which there are compelling rational considerations on both sides, with no clear answer to the question of what, all things considered, there is most reason to do. The idea that there is a non-accidental connection between morality and motivation remains in place even if we concede that moral requirements are, in rare and exceptional circumstances of this kind, not sufficiently compelling to defeat the competing reasons that might be in play. It will suffice if such requirements are *typically* supported strongly enough to defeat the other normative reasons with which they might conflict. I suggest that we understand the motivation requirement accordingly: as stipulating that rational agents who are deliberating correctly will normally be motivated to comply with moral requirements, where the 'normal conditions' clause is understood to exclude those exceptional circumstances in which moral considerations are not sufficient to defeat the competing reasons that may obtain.

It is assumed here that, if one is reasoning correctly, one will acknowledge the normative force and significance of the moral considerations that apply to the situation one confronts. Is this a fair assumption? It might seem that it is not. Moral requirements sometimes apply decisively in a given situation of action, without the agent in that situation being in a position to appreciate that the requirements obtain. To take an extreme example, a denizen of Europe in the Middle Ages might not have been in a position to grasp that all persons should be treated with respect and consideration (including women, Muslims, foreigners, etc.). Or again, a person subjected to a depraved and abusive upbringing might understand that it is morally wrong to hurt and exploit others, but be poorly situated to grasp that the wrongness of this behavior counts strongly against it. In cases of these kinds, agents may be making substantive mistakes in their practical deliberation, insofar as they are failing to acknowledge the normative significance of reasons for action that genuinely apply in their situation of action. But there is a familiar and respectable sense in which they are not reasoning incorrectly. Given the rest of what they believe about the world and are in a position to find out, for instance, it would not be reasonable for us to criticize their deliberations on account of their failure to acknowledge the (supposed) truth of the matter about what they have reason to do. In this subjective sense, they are not in a bad way in their reasoning about action, even though they draw a normative conclusion that is substantively mistaken.

We should distinguish, then, between this subjective notion of correctness in deliberation and the objective notion that is at work in my formulation of the motivation requirement. When we say that agents will be motivated in accordance with their reasons insofar as they are deliberating correctly, this must be understood in the objective sense that is fixed by the facts of the matter about what there is reason for a person in a given situation to do. It follows that an agent who fails to be motivated in accordance with their reasons might not deserve criticism of any particular kind on account of the substantive error of their conclusion.

Two Kinds of Error in Practical Reasoning

The motivation requirement, as presented in the preceding section, is very different from moral judgment internalism. To see how the two positions diverge, it will be helpful to recall the kind of agent whose possibility motivates the rejection of moral judgment internalism. This is a figure, such as Svavarsdóttir's Patrick, who seems competent at moral discourse, but who lacks any special motivation to comply with moral requirements, in a way that suggests an attitude of skepticism about the moral. The motivation requirement, by contrast with moral judgment internalism, seems to leave psychological space for attitudes or outlooks of this description. The distinctive thing about Patrick is the absence in him of any motives that align with the moral judgments that he himself sincerely endorses. But the motivation requirement, as I have formulated it, allows at least two ways in which a description of this kind might literally be true.

It could be the case, first, that Patrick accepts both the truth of some moral judgment and the normative significance of the judgment thus arrived at, without being motivated accordingly. He might believe, for instance, that one is morally obligated to help victims of political persecution in one's community, and that one's being so obligated speaks strongly in favor of acting accordingly, without really caring about whether he himself succeeds in providing such assistance when he is in a position to do so. In this development of the scenario, Patrick fails to be motivated in accordance with normative claims that he himself accepts. Insofar as this Patrick accepts the normative authority of moral principles for practical deliberation, however, it would not be very plausible to describe him as a skeptic about morality. He is more likely to be feckless or depressed, acting in ways that he himself would view as questionable or misguided.

In this respect our first Patrick exemplifies that paradigm form of irrationality in the domain of action, weakness of will. He not only acknowledges the immorality of the course of action that he is launched on, he grants as well that moral considerations of this kind are compelling reasons for action. Indifference to those in one's community who are politically oppressed is wrong, he might say, and for this reason one ought not display such indifference. To the extent Patrick fails to comply with normative judgments that he accepts, he is going astray by his own lights, and as we have suggested this amounts to a clear case of irrationality in action. It is fully on a par with other cases of weak-willed action, in which the acknowledged reasons that the agent fails to comply with do not have a distinctively moral dimension (as when one acts contrary to one's recognized prudential interests, out of laziness or lethargy or boredom).

In a different development of the scenario, Patrick might acknowledge the truth of moral judgments without yet accepting that conclusions about what is morally right and wrong have any normative significance at all for him (or perhaps for any agent). Thus he might accept that one is morally obligated to help the locally oppressed, without granting that this fact by itself counts in favor of his doing anything to provide such assistance when he can. This in fact seems to describe much better the outlook of a moral skeptic. Of course it would be possible to take a still more dismissive attitude toward morality, holding (for instance) that its central concepts are so incoherent that moral predicates such as right and wrong lack clear application. But more commonly skeptics do not go so far. Their challenge to morality does not consist in the denial that moral concepts have clear application, nor need they exhibit any deficiencies themselves when it comes to the ability to draw moral distinctions. What they doubt or challenge, rather, is the normative significance of morality – the idea (for instance) that one ought to help the politically persecuted in one's community, just because and insofar as the failure to do so would be wrong (or unjust or cruel or unkind).

Like practical irrationality, this second way of violating the motivation requirement does not seem restricted to cases that involve moral judgments in particular. Moral skepticism may be the most common or interesting form that the denial of normative significance can take, but other kinds of example are readily imaginable (if not quite so common in practice). Thus, for any consideration that is postulated to have normative significance for action, counting for or against a given agent's behaving in a certain way, we can suppose that the agent might accept that the consideration does in fact obtain, while questioning that it really counts as a reason. I might agree that it would be to my long-term advantage to invest in my pension account, but ask why I should care about my long-term advantage. In a still more extreme case, I might grant that it would be very painful to run barefoot over the hot coals, but deny that its being painful is really a reason not to perform the stunt. Stances of this kind might reflect a local skepticism analogous to that of the skeptic about morality, in which one denies the credentials of considerations about individual advantage or pain within practical deliberation, while continuing to think that practical reason has a genuine subject matter. Or they might reflect a more global position that is dismissive of the whole enterprise of practical reason, in the spirit of irrealism or nihilism about reasons for action of any description.

In leaving room for possibilities such as these, the approach I am recommending takes seriously a distinction latent in practical thought between moral judgment and normative judgment. Indeed, I see this distinction as a special case of a more general distinction between judging that a (reason-providing) consideration obtains, and judging that the consideration in question is a reason. In the deliberative processes that give rise to reasoned changes in an agent's motivations, there is an important role to be played by judgments of both kinds; the special roles of these two forms of judgment open up space for the two different kinds of substantive mistake in practical reasoning that I have been concerned to distinguish in the present section.

No doubt the distinction is often glossed over in practice. Someone who takes moral considerations to be reasons, for instance, will typically be moved straightaway by the consideration that x-ing would be wrong. There is no need for two separate acts of judging, involving endorsement first of the conclusion that x-ing would be wrong, and then of the conclusion that the wrongness of x-ing counts against doing it. Even if it is commonly elided in thought when we deliberate about what to do, however, it seems that a distinction between these two distinct classes of judgment must be possible to draw. In the moral case, it is the phenomenon of skepticism that brings this possibility into plain view. Moral skeptics grant that x-ing would be wrong, but deny that its wrongness is a reason for them to refrain from doing x themselves. If the motivation requirement is correct, of course, then the person who adopts this stance will be making a substantive mistake about what they have reason to do. But the intelligibility of the skeptic's stance reveals something important about the difference between moral and normative discourse, something that is overlooked by defenders of moral judgment internalism.

Motivation and Metaethics

This feature of the motivation requirement renders it useless as a constraint on philosophical accounts of moral judgment. As I have formulated it, the requirement tells us nothing much about the nature of the mental act of moral judgment. It presupposes, as I have just suggested, that there is a distinctive stance of *normative* judgment – the kind of judgment typified schematically by the belief that considerations of kind c recommend or speak in favor of x-ing – that is necessarily connected to motivation, at least in those agents who are rational. But there is no *conceptual* guarantee that moral judgments either constitute or entail normative judgments of this kind. I write this as someone who happens to believe that moral considerations have genuine normative significance, representing considerations that recommend or speak in favor of various of the actions that are open to us. Even if this is correct, however, it is not correct as a matter of conceptual necessity, and it is accordingly quite possible to endorse moral claims while denying that they provide one with reasons for action (or at least remaining noncommittal on the issue). As I suggested in the preceding section, this seems to me to be the natural way to think about what moral skeptics such as Patrick are doing.

What can perhaps be said about the connection between morality and motivation is that moral considerations *aspire* to the normative status of reasons for action. This is admittedly rather vague, but I mean by it to be gesturing in the direction of the following familiar facts. We typically cite moral considerations in discussion with other people, as factors that are of direct normative significance, counting for or against options that are under active consideration. We raise our children to treat moral considerations in this way, for example. Furthermore, many of us structure our (adult) deliberations on the supposition that moral considerations have normative standing, taking facts about rightness and moral value to have direct significance for our decisions about what to do. These aspects of our moral practice, already alluded to above, suggest that morality is widely viewed as a normative domain, insofar as moral considerations play the role in our individual and collective deliberations that is commonly ascribed to genuine reasons for action. Perhaps we are, as a matter of fact, wrong to view morality in this way. If that should turn out to be the case, however, it would come to many of us as a surprise, and force us to rethink assumptions about the nature and significance of morality that we had tended to take for granted. To the extent this is the case, it seems fair to say that morality aspires to the status of a normative domain.

Is this a conceptual truth, either about the concept of morality or about the moral concepts? I don't quite know how to answer that question. The facts to which I have just referred seem to indicate that it is quite fundamental to our understanding of morality that it should be taken by people to function as a normative domain. A person who rejected the normative significance of moral distinctions, but without any sense in doing so that they were going against widespread and entrenched assumptions, would certainly be missing something – if not about the concept of morality, then at any rate about common moral practices. On the other hand, even if it turns out that moral distinctions are in fact normatively significant, this won't be true in virtue of the concept of morality alone. I agree with externalists such as Svavarsdóttir that the Patricks of this world do not seem to be making a simple conceptual mistake when they deny that morality is something that they ought to be concerned about. So it seems the most we can say, sticking to the plane of conceptual truth, is that morality aspires to normative significance.

But the motivational requirement, in the version I have proposed, is distinct from this quasi-conceptual claim about the aspirations of morality. Even if morality was not widely taken to be a source of distinctive reasons for action, it might still be the case that it has that kind of normative status in fact. This, together with the further assumption that normative judgments are motivating in those rational agents who endorse them, suffices to yield the motivation requirement, which says that agents are necessarily motivated to act in accordance with moral standards, to the extent they are deliberating correctly and are otherwise practically rational. The requirement contained in this formulation derives neither from the concept of morality nor from the moral concepts individually, but from the substantive assumption – a version of what is sometimes referred to as 'rationalism' – that morality is a genuine source of reasons for action, together with further assumptions about what it is to be rational and to reason correctly about action. It is the normativity of morality that grounds the requirement, such as it is, that we should be motivated in accordance with moral standards.

Clearly a thesis of this kind cannot be appealed to as a neutral constraint in metaethical disputes, since it rests on a substantive claim about the standing of moral considerations as reasons. But the requirement, as I have formulated it, seems to me to capture what is worth preserving in the idea that moral judgments are somehow internally connected to motivation, tracing that idea to basic assumptions about the normativity of morality. It is a consequence of this that we cannot decide whether to accept or reject the motivation requirement without addressing messy issues about the nature and substance of reasons for action, issues that some externalist theorists might prefer to avoid (Svavarsdóttir 1999: 175). But I see no way to come to terms with the concerns that have led philosophers to postulate an internal connection between moral judgment and motivation without confronting these difficult issues head on. We need to consider on its merits the substantive thesis that morality is a normative domain, and we need to explain how normative judgments can reliably function as sources of motivation in those agents who are practically rational.

This latter issue, by the way, provides ample material for the ongoing disagreement between cognitivists and their expressivist opponents. It is open to expressivists, for instance, to contend that they alone are able to account for the effects of normative judgments on the motivational economy of rational agents who endorse them. I do not myself find this contention persuasive, but I would grant that it represents a real and important challenge, one that any theorist of practical reason will have to come to terms with. To the extent this is the case, the motivation requirement as I have presented it will raise issues that are important for metaethical debate. That requirement does not, however, function as a neutral or a priori constraint on metaethical accounts of the nature of the moral judgment.

Traditionally, philosophers have taken a different view about the role of motivation in relation to metaethical debates. In particular, proponents and opponents of motivational internalism have alike taken it to represent a conceptual claim about the nature of the moral judgment, a claim that – if true – should function as an adequacy condition on metaethical accounts of such judgments. If my remarks are on the right lines, however, then this is not the correct way to think about the connection between morality and motivation. The thesis that this connection is a non-contingent one has its place within a broader, substantive view about the normative character of morality, and there is no way to do justice to the thesis without going beyond metaethical platitudes, and engaging with difficult issues concerning the nature and force of moral reasons on their merits. That is simply where the action is in this area of moral philosophy.

The Non-contingency of Moral Motivation

The motivation requirement that I have developed in this chapter gives a sense to the idea that moral considerations and the motivation to act on them are non-contingently connected. The connection it envisages is a normative one, fixed in part by the rationalist thesis that morality is a source of reasons for all agents to comply with its requirements. There is not the space to defend this rationalist claim here. Nevertheless, it may help to convey the appeal of the motivation requirement if we consider briefly how moral motivation appears on an anti-rationalist understanding of morality.

Anti-rationalists deny that morality provides reasons for action to all agents. When people are moved to act as morality requires, their doing so cannot be understood as a response to the recognition of normative reasons that independently obtain. Moral motivation must be traced, rather, to basic desires or dispositions that are contingent or arbitrary from the standpoint of what there is independent reason to do. Thus Svavarsdóttir reconstructs moral motivation in terms of a desire to be moral, by which she means a desire directed toward objects that are conceived under a moral mode of presentation (ibid. 170, 215–18). In defense of this approach she appeals once again to the cases of moral skepticism that we have considered above. Her contention is that we need to distinguish sharply between cognitive judgments couched in moral terms and the conative attitudes that lead us to comply with such judgments if we are to account adequately for observed variations in peoples' patterns of moral motivation, such as those that distinguish Patrick from his morally committed friends (ibid. 216–17).

But there is something missing in this account of what moves us to comply with moral requirements. The worry can be put by saying that it makes the connection between moral judgment and moral motivation seem altogether optional and arbitrary. Some agents happen to be moved to do what they judge to be morally right or good, while other agents are not so moved, and that is pretty much all that can be said. There is nothing in this view to undergird the claim that those who are morally motivated are somehow responding appropriately or correctly to the moral distinctions they grasp. Perhaps we can explain, in social terms, why it is desirable that people should be brought up to have reliable dispositions to do what they believe to be morally right or good. We can also deploy the descriptive resources of morality to characterize those in whom moral motivations are present, calling them (for instance) virtuous, or kind, or considerate and just. But from the point of view of practical reason there is nothing to require that an agent who endorses moral claims should be motivated to comply with them. In this respect, the desire to be moral seems to be a mere optional extra, something some of us just happen to have – rather like a taste for clams or the color azure.

The motivational requirement, as I have formulated it, suggests a different understanding of the connection between moral judgment and moral motivation. In particular, it gives a sense to the idea that agents who have a desire to do what is right are responding appropriately to the moral circumstances, as they conceive them. This desire is not merely an optional extra, which an agent may or may not happen to have (as the case may be). It is rather a fitting reaction to the recognition that a course of action would represent the right thing to do. For if the motivation requirement is correct, moral facts of this kind constitute reasons for action, and this in turn makes it appropriate both to judge that they have normative significance, and to be motivated accordingly.[7] To the extent this is the case, the connection between moral judgment and moral motivation can be said to be non-contingent. It is not a *psychological* necessity that someone who endorses a moral judgment should be motivated accordingly; but by the same token it is not merely fortuitous that some of us happen to be motivated in this way, as it would seem to be on the accounts that anti-rationalists favor.

Furthermore, that motivation and moral cognition are connected in this way seems to correspond to the internal perspective on action of the virtuous agent. Such agents characteristically take it that their actions are recommended or justified by the fact that they are morally required or otherwise morally valuable, and this in turn renders their moral motivations intelligible to them, as fitting responses to the presence of considerations that they themselves take to have normative significance. The anti-rationalist account cannot do full justice to this dimension of the virtuous agent's point of view. It makes do with moral beliefs on the one hand, and desires to perform actions that fall under moral descriptions on the other. There is no normative connection between these desires and the moral beliefs that fix their objects, such as the virtuous agent characteristically takes to obtain.

We might put this point by observing that, in the absence of a normative connection between moral considerations and the desire to act on them, moral motivation becomes a kind of fetish. Here fetishism may be understood as the investment of interest and attention in objects that are not intrinsically worthy of such responses. Thus anti-rationalists suppose that moral motivation is due to a desire for moral ends that is arbitrary from the point of view of practical reason. If this supposition is correct, however, it becomes mysterious why those of us who find ourselves with such desires ought either to have or to act on them. Granted, we can perhaps account for moral behavior by supposing that virtuous agents are subject to a desire to be moral, in some form or other. But this pattern of explanation leaves it entirely open whether the considerations that move us are ones that *merit* our interest and concern; insofar as this is the case, morality starts to look like a collective fetish, involving the investment of emotional energy in objects that are not worthy of that response.

This is not by itself a conclusive argument. The anti-rationalist might deny, for instance, that we can make good sense of the notion of a normative reason upon which the motivation requirement depends. Or it might be argued that moral considerations do not possess the kind of *independent* normative significance that virtuous agents may be disposed to attribute to them.[8] And no doubt there are other possibilities as well. My point, at present, is merely that we need to come to terms with normative issues of this kind if we wish to do justice to the idea that there is a non-contingent connection between morality and human motivation.

Notes

1 Moral judgment internalism, as formulated in the text, raises large interpretative questions. To which moral judgments does it apply? How exactly is the notion of motivation to be understood? I shall bracket such issues in my discussion.
2 For two recent statements, see Blackburn (1998: ch. 3) and Gibbard (2003: 8–11).
3 Compare note 1 above.
4 Svavarsdóttir refers to Patrick as a cynic rather than a skeptic; I take moral cynicism to be an instance of the kind of skepticism identified in the text.
5 For this sense, see Scanlon (1998: ch. 1).

6 Korsgaard's interest in this question is pursued most extensively in her book *The Sources of Normativity* (1996), whose use of the term 'normativity' to refer to the status of a consideration as a reason I have followed.
7 The notions of fittingness and appropriateness at issue in this argument must be understood objectively rather than subjectively; for this distinction, see the end of "Morality and Normative Reasons" above (p. [235]).
8 Perhaps they are reasons, but only for those in whom the rationally contingent desire to be moral is present.

References

Blackburn, S. (1998). *Ruling Passions*. Oxford: Clarendon Press.

Brink, D. (1989). *Moral Realism and the Foundations of Ethics*. Cambridge: Cambridge University Press.

Darwall, S. L. (1983). *Impartial Reason*. Ithaca: Cornell University Press.

Gibbard, A. (2003). *Thinking How to Live*. Cambridge, Mass.: Harvard University Press.

Korsgaard, C. (1986). "Skepticism about practical reason." *Journal of Philosophy*, 83: 5–25.

Korsgaard, C. (1996). *The Sources of Normativity*. Cambridge: Cambridge University Press.

Scanlon, T. M. (1998). *What We Owe to Each Other*. Cambridge, Mass.: Harvard University Press.

Smith, M. (1994). *The Moral Problem*. Oxford: Basil Blackwell.

Svavarsdóttir, S. (1999). "Moral cognitivism and motivation." *The Philosophical Review*, 108: 161–219.

PART III

MORAL FACTS AND EXPLANATIONS

Is Morality Fully Factual?

Moral Factualism

Peter Railton

Introduction

Since the beginning, philosophers have puzzled over the nature of morality and its place in the world. Is morality objective, a realm of knowledge and facts? Or is it subjective, a projection of individual feelings or social norms? To be sure, talk of moral objectivity or "moral facts" will strike some ears as quaint. Even so, I think we all have an intuitive sense that a genuine issue is at stake in the question famously posed by Plato's dialogue *Euthyphro*: "Is something good because we favor it? Or, do we favor it because it's good?"[1] *Moral factualism*, as I will understand it here, is a way of viewing moral thought, language, and practice that seeks to capture the 'objective purport' that Socrates was trying to lead Euthryphro to see. This requires us to explain how morality can provide an independent, critical perspective on one's society and oneself, standing apart from one's own moral convictions and even, in principle, the opinions of one's gods.[2]

Moral philosophy took a decisive turn in the twentieth century when questions about the objectivity of morality and the possibility of moral knowledge were translated into metaethical questions about the analysis of moral concepts and language. Philosophers noted early on that moral ways of thinking could not simply be reduced to non-moral ways of thinking (Moore 1903: see Darwall et al. 1997). Moral judgments have not only a distinctive vocabulary, but also a distinctive character and function. Ordinary factual statements *describe* how things are, past, present, or future. Moral language employs directive and evaluative concepts, and moral statements make claims that *prescribe* or *commend*, saying what should or shouldn't be done, or how things might be better or worse. Moral language is therefore seen as *normative* or *action-guiding*. Could it nonetheless be factual? Could saying how things might be better, or what moral obligations an individual has, also be a way of saying how things *are*?

The terms 'fact' and 'factual' should not mislead us. Our familiar idea of a fact is something like a state of affairs that one might encounter directly in experience, such as the presence of a concrete object at a particular place and time. This idea does not seem to fit the moral case. However, it also does not seem to fit many other domains where we speak readily of facts: facts of arithmetic, facts about what is probable or possible, or facts about the meanings of words or the causes of cancer. The nature of moral facts, if there are such, will depend upon the sorts of claims morality makes.

Some Features of Moral Language

Moral claims have a number of characteristic features. For example, they have an important relationship to "ordinary" facts. 'Treat like cases alike' is a fundamental norm of moral thought and practice, and it requires us to give the same moral evaluation of persons and situations that possess the same non-moral features. This is one element of the objective purport of morality, since it brings with it a certain independence from personal preference or perspective. I might be tempted, for example, to excuse my own self-interested deceptions as morally permissible, while condemning as reprehensible essentially similar acts performed by others at my expense. But I am not free to do this if I aim to be taken seriously as expressing a *moral* judgment. Moral claims, then, are said to be *supervenient* upon the 'ordinary factual' or non-moral features of the world. Most philosophers agree that understanding this is part of what we learn when we acquire moral concepts.

Supervenience of this kind does not equate moral concepts with 'ordinary factual' concepts. Suppose that the 'ordinary factual' features of two acts are the same, and that two observers agree about this. Still, they can disagree about the moral character of the acts so long as each judges the two acts morally in the same way. There is, then, a distinctive shift in vocabulary and concept as we begin to express our views or feelings about what is good or bad, or what is to be done.

Ordinary language has many ways to express views and feelings, or issue commands, without resort to moral terms. We exclaim in anger or grief, exhort with cheers, command with imperatives. In such cases, we do not speak of truth or falsity. If I shout "Go Metros!" to express my support for the home team, and you favor their rivals, the Burbs, you will shout not "False!", but "Go Burbs!" By contrast, if I say that giving misleading directions to a stranger is innocent fun, you might say, "You're wrong – it's not innocent at all." What, then, are the special features we have in mind when we express ourselves using *moral* language rather than exhortations or commands, and why does this appear to involve us in some claim to truth, placing those who disagree into competition with us for correctness?

Whatever our moral particular disagreements, we appear to be in greater agreement concerning the sorts of consideration that count as relevant or irrelevant in moral deliberation and assessment. This enables us to talk *to* each other, rather than past each other, when we engage in moral discussions. We've already noted that making a moral judgment commits us to treating like cases alike. Moral claims involve a form of *impartiality* or *generality* that helps explain what sorts of likeness and difference have moral relevance. For example, morality need not exclude special obligations to oneself or to one's children, partner, or friends. But if I claim that my special relationship to my children gives me moral obligations to them that I do not owe to other children, I also have to recognize that other parents' relationships with their children ground similar person-specific obligations on their part. Moral claims should not be biased toward particular individuals or groups, and many believe this generality must indeed be universal – applicable in principle even to other species.

We also hold ourselves and one another to standards of logical *consistency* in moral thought and discussion, treating moral disagreements as contradictions. If you and I differ in our preferred pear, we can treat this as a matter of mere liking where neither side need be wrong. However, if I say that human cloning is permissible, and you are of the opposite view, we naturally assume that one or the other of us is in error. Moral claims, moreover, are to be squared with the "ordinary" facts insofar as we know them – a moral claim that is based upon 'ordinary factual' error thereby loses credibility. In this respect, moral judgments are much like 'ordinary factual' judgment in general, and call for similar kinds of responsiveness to evidence and logic.

Various *substantive* concerns distinguish morality from other normative domains. Moral thought has to do with acts and agents, with social practices and norms, and with matters of well-being and intrinsic value in a very general, encompassing sense. Prudential thought also concerns the well-being of agents, but is centered on the interests of a single individual and does not purport to be impartial. Aesthetic thought is impartial, but not linked to agency – we judge the aesthetic, but not moral, character of alpine meadows and driftwood. Epistemic thought is also impartial, but has to do with questions about what to believe, and issues of evidence and truth. Morality pays special attention to the conditions and principles needed to sustain reciprocal cooperation and mutual respect among agents in the pursuit of good lives. Moral disputes often concern tensions arising among these central considerations – how to reconcile considerations of well-being with questions of respect for individuals, fairness, or concern with the character and integrity of agents. The very persistence of such disputes tends to show that both kinds of question have moral relevance.

In addition to such questions about the subject matter and grounds of moral statements, we also think that morality has a *practical* point. We expect ourselves and others to put moral judgments into practice and not merely to pay lip service to them. Moral judgment is thus associated with certain attitudes and motivations: 'pro-attitudes' and positive motivation toward acts that fit with our moral judgments; and 'con-attitudes' and a tendency to sanction toward acts and individuals that violate them. This is so even in our own case, as when we feel pride at living up to a moral judgment we accept, or guilt at failing to do so. Here we encounter the "motivation problem" for morality. Almost all of us acknowledge that moral demands can run strongly contrary to powerful desires, and challenge our will power or motivational capacities. Such challenges manifest themselves not only in action, but in internal conflicts, guilt, excuse-making, and rationalization. There are also practical limits to what morality can demand. Morality cannot require us to do what is literally impossible, and the principle that '*ought* implies *can*' is central to moral reasoning in theory and practice. The loser in a championship fencing match can be obliged to shake hands with the winner, but not to like it.

Not only do we show considerable agreement or overlap in our views about the distinguishing characteristics of moral assessment, we also tend to converge in the vicinity of certain paradigmatic moral judgments: overcoming pain is a good; unprovoked assault, theft, deception, and disloyalty are wrong; honesty, fairness, and generosity are virtues, and so on. Still, moral disagreement on other matters is persistent, and we find striking moral differences among individuals within societies, and across societies and history. Moreover, we seem to lack definite ways of resolving such disagreements comparable to those found in more 'ordinary factual' domains. Of course, it is easy to overestimate the ease of resolving many factual disagreements, or to underestimate the extent to which persistent moral controversies draw upon such disagreements. However, some moral differences persist despite extensive agreement on the relevant "ordinary" facts. This should suggest that we often need to be self-critical and tolerant, but it need not lead us to 'moral relativism'. Indeed, in its simplest forms, moral relativism *removes* many disagreements by limiting the scope of moral claims to certain individuals or groups. And that seems to misrepresent how we understand ourselves and many of our moral disagreements.[3]

Somewhat metaphorically, we might understand ourselves as striving in moral judgment to assess things from *the moral point of view*, a perspective that unites the conditions of generality, impartiality, benevolence, supervenience, factuality, practicality, appeal to paradigm cases, and so on. We need not adopt this point of view explicitly whenever we make a moral judgment – most such judgment is intuitive. It is enough if we are disposed to treat our judgments as responsive to the considerations the moral point of view involves.

But what of individuals or cultures whose assessments reflect dramatically different constraints? We use the term 'morality' in a broadly descriptive sense for whatever norms play a role for an individual or culture akin to that of morality. I think we understand when someone says of Bert, a particularly egoistic person, " 'Bert First, Last, and Foremost' is his morality. But he hasn't had a *genuinely* moral thought in fifteen years." Similarly, consider a society that prizes military conquest above all and preaches ruthless violence and deceit toward all who are outsiders, using the term *Chal* as their term of highest and unconditional praise. They seem not to understand what we are asking when we question whether acts they call *Chal* really deserve such praise. "Everything *Chal* is praiseworthy," they say. Then we might say, in the broad sense, "Their morality is that of a warrior band at odds with the world." But it seems we would be ill-advised to translate *Chal* into English as 'morally good' or 'morally right' without qualification or comment. To be sure, *Chal* is like our moral terms in that it is a term of praise. Indeed, for them it seems a truism that everything *Chal* is praiseworthy, just as the connection between 'morally good' or 'morally right' and praiseworthiness is truistic for us. But the criteria or conditions for applying *Chal* differ so much from 'morally good' or 'morally right' that we are bound to misunderstand the point or content of one another's attitudes if we translate *Chal* into our moral terms, or if they think of us as claiming that our moral exemplars are *Chal*. They would, for example, admit that some warriors in other bands show ferocity and power equal to their own heroes, and equal success in battle, but they wouldn't call even these individuals *Chal*. They feel no pressure to treat like cases alike in a general or impartial way, and are simply puzzled when we ask whether members of another band could ever be *Chal*. *Chal*, then, appears to be an essentially parochial concept of glory in combat. So even though we disagree with their practices, and with the way they distribute praise, this is not because we think that we are the true experts on who is *Chal*. In the discussion of moral language and 'moral facts' that follows, we will be speaking of morality in the narrower sense, the sense in which *Chal* is not a moral concept, though it plays a similar social role in its home setting.

Our working idea of moral concepts, then, will be those species of directive and evaluative assessment tied to the "cluster" of distinguishing features that constitute the moral point of view. We manifest our appreciation of the distinctive character of moral judgments, and our commitment to objectivity and to shared meanings in our moral judgments, when we treat certain kinds of consideration, evidence, or argument as morally relevant, but not others. We need not all agree on exactly which features figure with which weight in moral assessment – a high degree of overlap is sufficient to begin mutual engagement. This in turn helps us to see how there can be persistent, substantive disagreement in moral theory despite shared understandings.

This cluster of features, taken as a whole, reflects what we aspire to capture in moral evaluation. It leaves open the question how thoroughly we can succeed – and therefore how much determinacy, factual character, or truth there is in moral assessment. In that sense, the cluster can be common ground for factualists and non-factualists, moralists and moral skeptics.[4] It certainly does not provide an analysis of the meaning of moral terms – at least, not if meanings are supposed to represent what speakers must "have in their heads" in order to use moral terms. It is a "job description" of the distinctive role of moral terms in our deliberation, discourse, and practice. Our understanding of its components has developed and become explicit only as moral discourse itself has evolved and distinguished itself from other forms of evaluation. Many elements in the cluster involve empirical presuppositions and substantive normative commitments, and none has guaranteed status a priori (cf. Putnam 1975). Therefore there is no incompatibility with Moore's "open question" argument.

A rather minimal and catholic factualism can be formulated by appeal to this cluster. Factual truth conditions for moral claims can be obtained by saying that moral terms refer to those (no doubt complex) "ordinary factual" properties of the world that have the "best overall fit" with this total cluster of features.[5] This view manifests our commitment to the objective purport of morality without reducing moral concepts to "ordinary factual" concepts, but also without requiring that the factualist embrace a special metaphysics of moral entities to answer to our moral concepts.

Moral Judgment and Motivation

An alternative approach to moral concepts takes as its starting point the claim that the chief function of moral thought and judgment is practical – discussing and resolving questions about what to do or how to feel, individually or collectively. This function is primarily *dynamic* or action-guiding rather than descriptive, since it merges such questions as 'What is morally right?' with actually deciding what to do or settling how to feel. A dynamic conception of moral meaning leads naturally to the family of views called *semantic non-factualism*, which have in common the position that moral meaning cannot principally or canonically be factual, descriptive meaning.[6] Instead, non-factualists variously interpret the meaning of moral judgments as "emotive" (a way of expressing emotion and influencing others emotionally), "prescriptive" (a form of generalized command or imperative, directed at oneself and others), or "norm-expressive" (an expression of one's acceptance of a norm concerning what to do or feel).[7] Non-factualist accounts promise to explain the meaningfulness of moral discourse without making special metaphysical posits or epistemological demands. And most importantly, they promise to help us understand the force of moral judgments in a way that factualists apparently cannot.

Consider Edgar, who says without any sort of qualification or irony, "Everyone ought to contribute a fraction of income to charity." Suppose that Edgar himself does not contribute to charity, and feels no particular compunction about failing to do so. Now Edgar's original assertion seems to be misleading – could he possibly have been sincere and speaking appropriately in his original judgment? Would we happily say that he has fully grasped the force of his original claim? If a necessary connection between making a sincere moral judgment and being motivated on its behalf were "built into" the very meaning of moral judgments, we could explain why Edgar's remarks seem anomalous. For evident reasons, this position has become known as *judgment internalism*,[8] and it sheds light on the "motivation problem."

Merely descriptive beliefs have a "mind-to-world direction of fit" – a believer seeks to fit her mental representation to the facts. But someone making a sincere moral judgment is, on the dynamical account, expressing a motivation-laden state of mind with a "world-to-mind direction of fit" – she aspires to bring reality in accord with what she thinks ought to be the case.[9] As Hume famously put it, moral judgments are meant to "influence the will." It is a distinctive feature of judgments of moral obligation, for example, that they are *categorical* or non-hypothetical, applicable independent of any other desire or incentive. If I am obliged to pay back a loan, I should do so whether I like it or not. If a moral judgment by its nature is a motivation-laden state, then forming a moral judgment will have motivational force in its own right, whatever one's other desires or goals.

Consider as well how dynamic meaning operates in moral discussion. If moral judgments express motivation, then sincere moral assertion would ordinarily signal something about my motivations to others – my willingness, say, to undertake or support a certain course of action, and my disapproval of doing otherwise. By venturing moral opinions as well as the facts used to justify them, we give our public discourse a capacity to influence one another it would otherwise lack. This helps us to understand the special role and urgency of moral deliberation and debate in our lives together (see Gibbard 1990). Indeed, a similar dynamic of conflicting pressures arises within one's own life when one makes moral judgments and yet feels pulled in other directions as well. Resolving these pressures involves pursuit of a kind of internal dynamic coherence or consistency, even though this may mean some sacrifice of other goals, indulgence in rationalization, or experience of guilt.

The Logic of Moral Language

The advantages of a non-factualist, dynamic account of moral meaning are striking. At least as striking, however, is the fact that the surface features of language show no visible linguistic or logical seams between moral and 'ordinary factual' discourse, which would be surprising if their fundamental character were so different. Suppose I believe that Geoff is over 40, actively involved in politics, and truly decent. I thereby conjoin moral and 'ordinary factual' statements freely. But if 'Geoff is truly decent' were really an expression of a feeling or an imperative, I could not do this: "Geoff is over 40, actively involved in politics, and 'Emulate Geoff!'" is ungrammatical, and lacks a clear sense. Exclamations, expressions of emotions, and imperatives can be sincere or insincere, appropriate or inappropriate, but they are not liable to truth or falsity, and cannot be substituted freely in grammatical and logical contexts where "truth-apt" expressions are found. Thus if they are taken as models for non-factualist accounts of moral meaning, it is far from clear how non-factualism can explain the logical appropriateness of freely intersubstituting moral and non-moral elements of language. Consider also:

(Veg)   True decency requires abstaining from eating meat.
        Geoff is truly decent.
        Therefore, Geoff does not eat meat.

We might disagree with either or both of (Veg)'s premises, but we can easily recognize the logical validity of this inference. Yet it draws a straightforwardly factual conclusion, readily attributable truth or falsity, by means of a logical inference from premises, each of which is a moral statement. If these premises couldn't qualify as fully truth-apt sentences, how could they suffice to entail a fully truth-apt conclusion by a valid process of reasoning? And if accepting the premises commits one to the conclusion, how could two states of mind that lack a mind-to-world direction of fit commit one to a state of mind that does? (See also Dorr 2002.)

An account of moral language therefore must be able to explain how moral and non-moral statements work together grammatically, logically, and rationally without a hitch. Though philosophers of language and linguists debate the best analysis of the various logical and inferential forms of ordinary language, the most straightforward way of explaining such behavior is via orthodox truth-functional logic. This straightforward explanation, however, is only available to those who allow moral statements like 'Geoff is truly decent' to be capable of truth or falsity. Non-factualist accounts therefore need to provide either (1) a way of assigning truth conditions to non-descriptive linguistic forms, or (2) an account of their logical and inferential role in ordinary language that need not appeal in this way – or more indirectly – to their truth.[10] Looking at language as a whole, its role in reasoning and thought, and the ways it functions for mutual understanding of one another, the simplest position – we might call it the *default* position – is to treat moral statements as capable of bearing truth values.

In recent years, however, a "minimalist" school of thought about truth has been revived, which denies that truth is a substantive relationship between language and the world (see Horwich 1990). Instead, minimalists claim, once an area of discourse exhibits certain logical and linguistic behavior in ordinary discourse – once predicates like 'is wrong' behave just like "ordinary" predicates, and moral statements like 'Geoff is truly decent' behave just like "ordinary" statements – it is appropriate to attribute truth and falsity to the sentences of this discourse. The following, after all, are equally acceptable and intelligible to speakers of English:

(1) 'Geoff is over 40' is true if and only if Geoff is over 40.
(2) 'Geoff is truly decent' is true if and only if Geoff is truly decent.

Would acceptance of this minimalist conception of truth permit the non-factualist to accommodate truth-aptness while still giving a dynamic interpretation of the meaning of moral expressions?[11] This might leave us as puzzled as ever. For we would be without even the first steps of an explanation of how an area of language whose primary function is to express emotion or give commands could have a perfectly logical surface behavior. Minimalism as such does not *explain* this surface behavior; it simply argues that such behavior is sufficient for truth conditions. So the real issue we face would appear to remain: if moral judgments have a dynamic, non-factual primary meaning, while 'ordinary factual' claims have a contrasting, e.g., descriptive, primary meaning, how do they manage to exhibit the same surface behavior across the wide sweep of language and context?[12] Some minimalists will insist that it is a mistake to ask for an explanation, since truth simply *is* minimal truth, and surface behavior is sufficient to secure it. But now the burden is on non-factualists to explain in what sense they are denying factualism. For surely we can say (3) with the same propriety as (1), and (4) with the same propriety as (2):

(3) 'Geoff is over 40' is a fact if and only if Geoff is over 40.
(4) 'Geoff is truly decent' is a fact if and only if Geoff is truly decent.

The Character of Judgment

So let's revisit the original question. Notice that a shift has taken place over the course of our discussion. We began by speaking of the meaning of moral *statements*, and now we are considering moral *judgments*. Is that harmless? After all, isn't our question: What sort of meaning must moral statements have in order to be fit to serve their primary linguistic functions? And surely moral judgment is the primary function of moral discourse. Since moral judgment seems so intimately connected to motivation on the part of the judge, mustn't this intrinsic link be sought in the meaning or content of moral terms?

That would be too hasty. For it is quite possible for a discourse to have as its primary function the making of judgments, and for these judgments to involve and express action-guiding attitudinal states, without building action-guidingness into the meaning or content of the terms of that discourse. Consider 'ordinary factual' language itself. Surely the primary thing we do with ordinary factual language is to make and share factual judgments. 'Ordinary factual' judgments bring to bear *belief*, a state of mind that commits the agent to the object of judgment in a way that a passing thought concerning the same object does not. This commitment is manifest in the dynamics of his thought and behavior. Here is Hume's characterization of that contribution (Hume 1888: 624, 629):

> [Belief] is something *felt* by the mind, which distinguishes the ideas of the judgment from the fictions of the imagination. It gives them more force and influence; makes them appear of greater importance; infixes them in the mind; and renders them the governing principles of all our actions.

Why is belief a "governing principle" of action, an *action-guiding* attitude? My beliefs *frame* my thinking and doing, influencing what I will attend to, priming what I will observe, shaping what inferences and associations I will make and what evidence or alternatives I will seek or ignore, and regulating what I will feel – e.g., whether I take an action with confidence, or whether a certain course of events surprises me. Indeed, variation in these cognitive dispositions, psychology has taught us, is among the chief determinants of conduct and affect. A functional account of the belief attitude enables us to understand how there could be an intimate relationship between making a factual judgment with a certain content, on the one hand, and a certain role for that content in the individual's tendencies to think and act, on the other, even though these tendencies are not part of that content itself.

The dynamics of belief, and therefore of factual judgment, operate not only in one's own mind, but also in interpersonal life. Suppose we have plans for a hike, and go to look out of the window. Seeing the clouds massing, I say, "A storm is on the way." Such an act of *assertion* is the characteristic way in which an agent expresses a belief publicly. An assertion ordinarily communicates to its audience not just the thought it contains, i.e., that a storm is on the way, but information about the speaker's own attitude toward this thought, signaling the speaker's confidence in it, and urging a corresponding claim upon the attention and credence of others. In effect, the speaker implicitly claims enough authority to make this statement, and puts it forward as relevant to the concerns at hand. He also places himself in the position of being liable to error and being called upon to defend the statement if others challenge it.

So intimate is the link between assertion and belief that, as Moore noticed, the following sort of remark would be very anomalous:

(5) A storm is on its way, though I don't believe it.

The first phrase of such a remark asserts a statement about the weather, while the second asserts a statement about what the speaker believes. Logically, the two statements are wholly independent – the one could be true and the other false – and so there is no evident logical contradiction in (5), despite its anomalous character. What puzzles us about someone who utters (5) are the questions: 'What is his state of mind? Why does he say a storm is coming if he doesn't himself believe it?'

We can use a term coined by H. P. Grice (1989), *implicature*, to distinguish the intimate connection of assertion and belief from logical implication. He developed a complex theory of how the norms that govern conversational exchanges – internalized by speakers as mutually understood intentions to be cooperative in communicating – make it possible for what we literally say to one another to convey spoken and unspoken information. Norms of conversation take into account what one takes one's audience to believe or seek, and include matters of the quality of what one contributes to a conversation (Say what you believe, Be relevant and informative, etc.) as well as its quantity (Avoid excess words, etc.). Because we hold ourselves to such norms and expect others to do so as well, and share a mutual recognition of these expectations, conversation can be richly informative and dynamic.

For example, if I respond to your question about the financial prospects of a colleague's investment scheme by saying only, "Jack is a lovely guy with his heart in the right place," you learn something about Jack's character, but also something about how I view Jack and whether (if you find me credible) it is wise to add your money to his. One way of showing the contrast with logical implication is that conversational implicatures ordinarily can be *canceled*: "Jack is a lovely guy with his heart in the right place – but incredibly shrewd financially." (Contrast, "Jack is a lovely guy with his heart in the right place – but unrelentingly cruel.")

Not all implicatures can ordinarily be canceled, however. In the case of the relation between assertion and belief, the matter is complex. Ordinarily, a confident affirmation implicates a confident belief on the speaker's part, and would be insincere or misleading otherwise, witness the oddness of (5). But suppose that you are sitting next to a friend, Mel, on a plane as it approaches take-off, and notice that he is gripping his armrests with white knuckles. You might well ask Mel: "What's up? Is this flight unsafe?" Mel can reply, "This flight is incredibly safe – virtually no chance it will crash. The statistics are overwhelming." But now you are puzzled by Mel's state of high anxiousness. He sees this, and adds, "Of course, I can't really convince myself to believe that – I fully expect it to crash in the next minute. But pay no attention. I inexplicably developed flight phobia last year." Based upon statistical evidence that he finds independently credible, Mel sincerely commends to you great confidence in the safety of the flight. But whether he can follow his own epistemic advice remains a separate question. The logical independence of the question of flight safety from whatever mental state Mel happens to hold enables him to assert an unequivocal claim sincerely despite his equivocal attitude – he recognizes the irrelevance of his phobic fear to actual safety, and speaks sincerely, though he risks misleading others about his state of mind unless he says more.

In the case of 'ordinary factual' judgment, then, a network of shared, internalized norms and expectations, and the human communicative, epistemic, and practical motivations that underlie and sustain them, make it possible for our remarks to have the force of assertions, communicating both facts and attitudes. At the level of individual psychology, it is only the fact that individuals have internalized epistemic norms and possess corresponding dispositions to expect or infer that makes it possible for them to form beliefs and make judgments in the first place. An attitude of belief is possible for me only if I can commit myself in certain ways, and for this I must be disposed to accord my thoughts and experience a certain epistemic authority, and to take certain mental representations as (what Hume called) 'regulative principles' in thought and action. The mental architecture of belief is complex, and the various parts need not always work together, as the case of the phobic flyer shows. But it would be radically implausible to think that individuals could acquire a shared language, or perhaps any language at all, in a world where these individual dispositions and shared communicative intentions were simply absent. With them in place, a "normatively loaded," dynamic understanding of factual judgment is compatible with attributing to such judgments 'ordinary factual' content. As *conditions* for the possibility of belief and communication, they are not thereby made part of the meaning of these beliefs and assertions themselves.

Moral Judgment and Moral Motivation

Might something like this be true in the case of moral language? Can a moral factualist argue that the "normatively loaded," dynamic character of moral thought and practice is attributable to the joint operation of an encompassing framework of individual and shared norms, dispositions, and intentions, on the one hand, and the particular factual content of moral statements, on the other? This would permit the factualist to link moral judgment and motivation while providing the most straightforward explanation of how moral judgment could be logically and linguistically integral with 'ordinary factual' judgment, possessing all the marks of truth.

At least some of the dynamic character possessed by moral judgment is attributable to the character of judgment and belief as such, quite independent of whether the content is 'ordinary factual' or moral. Thus, when we say that a moral judgment commits an individual, imposes a burden of defense and consistency, displays her acceptance of certain norms, involves an implicit claim to authority, makes a commendation to others, etc., we should be careful to notice that 'ordinary factual' judgments characteristically do likewise. Thus (6) is as anomalous as (5), above:

(6)   Failure to give to charity is morally wrong, but I don't believe it.[13]

Yet the forms of action-guiding and interpersonal force mentioned thus far as coming generically with the attitude of belief and act of assertion – the various epistemic pressures, dispositions to attend, infer, affirm, expect, etc. – nonetheless stop short of the sorts of motivational force needed for moral agency. Notice the distinction between (7), which seems unproblematic, and (8), which seems odd, even if it is less severely anomalous than (6):

(7)   A storm is on the way, but that doesn't matter to me. (I like hikes with or without storms.)
(8)   Failure to give to charity is morally wrong, but that doesn't matter to me.

What resources do factualists have to account for the association between moral judgment and motivation? We can divide factualists into two groups, those whose accounts in some way satisfy a condition of judgment internalism, and those who are judgment externalists.[14]

Internalist factualism

Rationalist forms of internalist factualism claim that certain features necessary for rational agency (i.e., the ability to act "for a reason") by their nature give motivational force to judgments with the formal or substantive characteristics of moral assessments. If so, then anyone exercising rational agency would be susceptible to motivational engagement on behalf of the moral judgments she makes. There would be a rational, not semantic, connection between moral assessment and the agent's own motivation. For example, Nagel rejects approaches to the judgment-motivation linkage that "build motivational content into the meaning of ethical assertions" (1978: 8) by interpreting them as expressions of a pro-attitude, and instead claims that the practical judgments of rational agents "include" acceptance of an objective justification, which he identifies with the judgment's "motivational content" (ibid. 65).[15]

An alternative form of internalist factualism locates the necessary link to motivation not in the conditions of rational agency as such, but in the conditions necessary for full competency with moral concepts. Those lacking certain sensibilities might as a result lack full access to a domain of concepts, e.g., color concepts, and be unable to see the world in their terms. To see the world in moral terms, it might be thought, requires a sensibility that includes not only ordinary cognitive and sensory capacities but also a motivating attitude – a capacity to find certain things simply "to be done." It would follow that those who master moral concepts will, when making moral judgments, have a tendency to act and feel accordingly. This, however, is compatible with attributing factual, objective character to moral concepts, much as we do to color concepts (see McDowell 1985).

Externalist factualism

Externalist approaches declare that the evidence in support of a connection between moral judgment and motivation is consistent with the idea that this connection is contingent, but nonetheless reliably present owing to certain widespread features of human psychology and social life.

The distinctive components of moral assessment tie it to matters of enduring importance to people and society – well-being, respect, reciprocity, cooperation, fairness. This enduring importance is reflected in the fact that the practice of moral evaluations is a pervasive feature in human life as we know it. The early emergence and long persistence of religion and of various social mechanisms for deciding and enforcing norms and laws testify to a tendency to accord authority to less personal, more general and enduring points of view. It is, indeed, a notable fact that humans appear so strongly interested in making judgments that bring to bear moral criteria, and that we hold ourselves as well as others to moral or quasi-moral standards. We can be outraged by the behavior of others, even when our own interests are not involved, and also guilty about our own conduct even when our own interests were served. The emotions and sensibilities that furnish the building blocks for moral attitudes – guilt and shame, a willingness to cooperate, empathy and a sense of fairness, a special concern for kith and kin, impartial anger, even vengefulness and a willingness to punish those who violate reciprocal understandings – are widely distributed in the human population.

The explanation for all this presumably lies in some combination of evolutionary history and human culture, but the result appears to be a highly robust set of conditions in which morality can take root and grow.[16] Hume observed that humans are "fitted for" society (1888: II.ii.5). This is not to say that we are born into the world with an innate, motivationally effective "moral sense" – an implausible claim given the diversity of human moral practices in the broad sense. Rather, in virtue of such features as empathy, reciprocity, and a capacity to recognize and follow rules, human psychology is "made for morality" in a sense akin to the way it is made for language.

It is commonly observed that virtually all human infants, even though born into a great diversity of linguistic communities, succeed in acquiring facility with the language around them, including the ability to understand and form novel sentences. This can be explained as the result of an inherent cognitive capacity for language and grammar allied to powerful and persistent motivations to communicate. An individual lacking these would find it difficult or impossible to acquire language, and if they were not widespread language would never have come to have the role it does in our lives. We might in a similar way say that humans are "made for morality" in the sense that children seem almost universally to develop a sense of right and wrong, a capacity for empathy, a notion of fairness, dispositions that make possible reciprocity and cooperation, and so on. They succeed in internalizing and applying a large number of complex norms and values, some specific to their family or community, but many that are found nearly everywhere. For this to occur, children must possess the capacities needed to represent norms and to apply them by assessing actions, conditions, and individuals in such terms as harmful or beneficial, fair or unfair. They must also possess the motives necessary for learning and in some measure conforming to such assessments.

Empathy, for example, is not simply the ability to form accurate beliefs about what others are thinking and feeling – it is a capacity to experience within oneself the felt character of others' states of mind, e.g., the discomfort of their pain. There is good evidence in the psychological literature that an empathetic capacity is part of our basic mental equipment, and that it is central to a wide range of cognitive and social skills, including language acquisition itself. If moral evaluation incorporates criteria of impartial or reciprocal concern with the well-being of others, then an externalist can cite the normal human capacity for empathy and reciprocity, combined with internalized norms, to explain how there can be a reliable connection between moral deliberation and judgment, on the one hand, and moral motivation, on the other. Perhaps the most elementary and effective form of moral reflection is the "Golden Rule," which engages these capacities by inviting us to use empathy to see and feel how our actions would affect others.

The psychological literature also amply illustrates the strong need of individuals to justify their conduct to others, and the discomfort they feel when this cannot be done. We are social beings, and how we see ourselves is seldom fully divorced from how we think others see us. Moreover, moral evaluation is an important component of mutual assessment, linked as it is to individual likelihood of keeping agreements, reciprocating cooperation, refraining from harms, and so on. Even the rationalizations we offer others and ourselves to portray our conduct as morally acceptable attest to the strength of this concern and the shape it takes. We all have a stake in sustaining a conception of ourselves in our own eyes and the eyes of others as beings with worth, whose lives have wider meaning and warrant respect.

The practice of making or expressing moral judgments could hardly occupy the important, even singular place it does in our lives if this were not so. And given this setting, our moral judgments will characteristically express and signal to others how we ourselves feel, and how we are likely to act or react. The implicatures of 'ordinary factual' assertions, we argued, depend upon the nature of belief and our standing motivation to be cooperative communicatively. In a similar way, the implicatures of moral assertions depend upon facts about the attitudes present in the typical contexts of moral evaluation. The most common context for moral evaluation is deliberation, and seeking or offering moral evaluations in such contexts would typically be irrelevant if the agent and her audience were expected to be indifferent to moral considerations.[17] Moral assertion in a conversational context thus goes with an expectation that the judgment made matters – to whoever makes it as well as to whomever it is made. An individual who blithely makes moral judgments without commitment to action on her own part runs the risk of being accused of pressuring others to act for reasons she does not herself take seriously, and her judgments would typically lack credibility. Can an individual who is not committed to playing her role in a general cooperative setting even be trusted to be faithful to the cooperative intentions that underwrite communication?

The externalist will maintain, however, that an individual who lacks moral motivation could nonetheless engage in genuine moral deliberation and judgment, and make sincere moral assertions. Is this plausible? Here are two examples.[18]

Consider first Brad. You know Brad to have had long-standing convictions on certain matters of social justice. Yet when you bring him news of an injustice committed in a Central American country and ask him to help with a petition campaign, you are surprised by his flat, diffident response. "Look," he explains, "please understand that I've been seriously depressed for some months now. I had already heard about this, and it *is* an injustice – an outrage, really. Something should be done. But the whole thought just leaves me cold." Has Brad changed his moral opinions – or lost them? That would seem odd. Depression drains motivation and affect, but Brad could retain his grasp of the conditions for applying moral concepts. Motivation matters in various ways in moral judgment, and we can in general take our own case as furnishing evidence about typical motives. Asking whether one's own or someone else's moral judgments manifest a real willingness to act can be a healthy discipline and an antidote to moral exaggeration. But Brad believes that his lack of interest has its origins in his own mood, not in features that would constitute evidence of typical motivation. Like the phobic flyer, he believes the relevant evidence warrants a particular moral conclusion, though he does not experience the usual dynamic concomitants of this conclusion.

The human psyche is complex, and motivation is a distinctive component. The externalist claims that an individual's ambition to be accurate and unbiased in judgment can lead him to an honest opinion that is dissociated from his own motivational engagement, even though such an individual clearly would lack the capacities of a fully effective moral agent.[19] In depression this condition is chronic, but I suspect we all know it from time to time, and it does appear to be a component of our capacity for objectivity in moral reflection.

Consider next Theresa, a highly talented philosophical logician. Like all of us, she learned moral language growing up, and has used it throughout her life. Theresa has wide interests and cares a lot about certain people, but her capacities for empathy and engagement on a universal scale are quite limited. This does not trouble her – "That's just how I am. Family and friends first. Other people? – Mostly I don't really care." She is not tempted by moral skepticism. She fully believes that people everywhere have genuine needs and interests, and that taking a general, moral concern for them is perfectly intelligible and coherent. Gifted in argument and constantly curious about facts of all sorts, she is highly motivated to challenge the moral claims of those she thinks have false, confused, or self-serving moral beliefs. She finds intrinsic enjoyment in spotting contradictions, fallacies, factual errors, and wishful thinking in morality as in any other subject matter, and she applies the same high epistemic standards to herself. Theresa has confident, well-developed beliefs about what is right or wrong, just or unjust, and she often challenges others with her moral views. Are her assertions then insincere? They do run the risk of misleading people about how she feels, given widespread expectations based on the normal psychological concomitants of moral judgment. But she could defeat this expectation. In the course of an argument over the fairness of substituting a sales tax for a progressive income tax, she might say, "Look, you're wrong. Whatever else you can say for it, a sales tax would *not* be fairer. That's easily shown. A sales tax is a boon to folks like us with high incomes, and I myself will vote for it. But unlike you, I don't feel the need to kid myself that it's really just." Whether she is right or wrong about the sales tax, is she misusing moral language? Or is she sincerely expressing a possible, if perhaps atypical, state of mind?

Examples can show only so much, however, and even the attempt to describe them can be question-begging. So I must leave it to readers to assess whether these examples seem credible as described, and whether an externalist account that leaves a potential gap between sincere moral judgment and actual motivational engagement affords a plausible representation of their own moral experience (see also Railton 1993b for further discussion).

The Euthyphro Contrast

Factualist accounts permit moral judgment to have standing similar to that of any area of 'ordinary factual' judgment, despite its distinctive character and role in our lives, including its normally close association with motivation. They account for the centrality and motivational force of moral evaluation in our lives in terms of the rational character or substantive importance of the elements of moral judgment.

Factualists of the sorts discussed here can offer an account of how our moral beliefs and practices might be seen as *responsive* to moral facts, much as our "ordinary factual" beliefs and everyday or scientific practices can be explained as responses to "ordinary" facts. Rationality, moral character, and empirical human psychology can function to attune us to those properties signified by our moral concepts. Factualists thus make a claim to capture morality's "objective purport" as brought bluntly into relief by the *Euthyphro* contrast. To the extent that we have moral knowledge, we could say, "We favor this because it is good."[20,21]

Notes

1 The original question was posed in religious terms – roughly, are acts pious because they please the gods, or do they please the gods because they are pious?

2 Moral factualism is quite compatible with the idea that moral facts by their nature involve or depend upon general facts about actual psychology and social-historical contexts. Moreover, factualism can take relativist or subjectivist forms that I will not be considering herein.

3 Relativism can, however, take more sophisticated forms. See Harman (1975), Harman and Thomson (1988), and Dreier (1990).

4 See, for example, the list of moral platitudes given by Horgan and Timmons (this volume, ch. 13).

5 This view focuses on sameness or difference in the functional roles of concepts in an overall account of thought, discourse, and action rather than on sameness or difference in the particular physical substances or relations that might realize these roles. For related discussions, see Boyd (1988), Horgan and Timmons (1992), Railton (1993b), Sayre-McCord (1997), Jackson (1998), and Gibbard (2003). Does the inclusion of substantive elements from our actual moral discourse and practice among the components of "best fit" introduce a kind of relativism into moral thought? In theory and practice, we have no choice but to work forward from where we now are, and how we actually use terms will contribute over time to their reference. However, an assessment of "best overall fit" need not take any particular moral judgments or practices as fixed points.

6 Such views are sometimes called 'non-cognitivist', since they treat moral claims as lacking ordinary truth conditions. But since 'non-cognitivist' carries the unwanted suggestion that our cognitive faculties (e.g., perception and reasoning) play no role in constituting the attitudes expressed in moral judgments, 'non-factualism' seems preferable.

   Non-factualist accounts of the meaning of moral terms need not exclude the possibility that moral discourse has other, secondary or indirect functions. For example, moral expressions can serve among people who share moral views (or at least know each other's moral opinions) to convey "ordinary factual" information.

7 We must be careful to distinguish them from *subjectivist* accounts of moral language, which in effect treat moral claims as *reporting* rather than expressing one's moral convictions or those of one's society. Subjectivsm renders moral judgments factual in character.

8 Steven Darwall (1997) introduced this term. A full taxonomy would distinguish this *motivational* form of judgment internalism from others. Moreover, it would distinguish motivational internalism about the *content* of judgment from motivational internalism about the attitude of judging. We will consider below forms of motivational internalism about the attitude of judgment that are also motivational externalists about the content of moral judgments.

9 See Humberstone (1992) and Smith (1994a).

10 This problem is often called the 'Frege-Geach problem'. Gottlob Frege and, much more recently, Peter Geach first raised it, and examples typically involve embedding moral state-

ments in non-assertive grammatical contexts, such as in 'if-then' statements or conditionals. We must recognize, however, that the problem arises even in such mundane logical and inferential operations as conjunction and negation. Moreover, the proper analysis of conditionals is controversial, and it is by no means clear that truth-functionality affords the most satisfactory way of treating conditional statements in ordinary language.

11 For related discussion, see Blackburn (1993), Stoljar (1993), Horwich (1994), Smith (1994b).

12 See Dreier (1996) and Sinnott-Armstrong (2000). Gibbard (1990, 2003) has offered a unified semantics for factual and normative areas of discourse, via the notion of a credal-normative world or hyperdecided state. What unifies these two domains of judgment is not truth and falsity as such, but something of which both are instances: they are dimensions along which attitudes can agree or disagree.

13 We must of course distinguish (6) from (6′), which is not at all anomalous:

(6′) People say that failure to give to charity is morally wrong, but I don't believe it.
There is nothing anomalous about (6′), just as there is nothing anomalous about:
They say that Geoff is over 40, but I don't believe it.
To understand (6) correctly, we must see it as involving a genuine assertion of the wrongness of failure to give to charity.

14 Note as well the possibilities of relativism or subjectivism, which can build a connection with moral attitudes into truth conditions, but in a manner that preserves factuality. If these attitudes include a motivational component, and if speakers are in general reliable judges of their own attitudes, then speakers who make sincere moral judgments will generally be motivated to act accordingly.

15 Such a view is internalist about judgment, and externalist about content. The connection between judgment and motivation is *rational* rather than *semantic*. Someone who makes an ethical or prudential judgment without being motivated is irrational rather than misusing language. Others more recently have pursued accounts of the norms that are deemed constitutive features of rational agency, and argued that these provide a connection between moral judgment and motivation *at least in agents who are rational* (see Korsgaard 1986; Smith 1994a). This connection between judgment and motivation is weaker than the strong form of motivational internalism ordinarily used to motivate non-factualism, which typically is meant to apply in all cases of moral judgment, regardless of the agent's rationality.

16 See Axelrod (1984), Skyrms (1996), and Kitcher (1998).

17 I am grateful here to suggestions from Jason Stanley.

18 See Brink (1986) for related discussion.

19 Damasio (1994) discusses some unusual cases in which moral cognition is separated from its ordinary connections to motivation and affect. For related discussion, see Roskies (2003). Various studies suggest that similar separation can be found between humor judgment and the experience of amusement (Moran et al., 2004).

20 Non-factualists have their own ways of rendering this aspect of the objective purport of morality. For example, Gibbard (1990, 2003) offers both rationalizing explanations and causal "quasi-explanations" of our moral judgments. These explanations are, however, downstream from normative or "plan-laden" commitments. Deciding whether non-factualism affords an adequate account of objective purport involves deciding whether this is objectivity enough. And deciding whether there is a genuine difference between a fully elaborated minimalist non-factualism and a metaphysically modest factualism of the sorts considered here involves deciding whether there is a genuine issue at stake. Neither answer seems to me entirely clear.

21 I am grateful for discussion with Jason Stanley and Allan Gibbard, and comments from Jamie Dreier, though they could not save me from my errors.

References

Axelrod, R. (1984). *The Evolution of Cooperation*. New York: Basic Books.

Blackburn, S. (1993). *Essays in Quasi-realism*. New York: Oxford University Press.

Boyd, R. (1988). "How to be a moral realist." Reprinted in S. Darwall et al. (eds.), *Moral Discourse and Practice*. Oxford: Oxford University Press, 1997.

Brink, D. (1986). "Externalist moral realism." *Southern Journal of Philosophy*, Suppl: 23–42.

Damasio, A. R. (1994). *Descartes' Error: Emotion, Reason, and the Human Brain*. New York: Putnam.

Darwall, S. (1997). "Reasons, motives, and the demands of morality." In S. Darwall et al. (eds.), *Moral Discourse and Practice*. Oxford: Oxford University Press.

Darwall, S., Gibbard, A., and Railton, P. (eds.) (1997). *Moral Discourse and Practice*. Oxford: Oxford University Press.

Dreier, J. (1990). "Internalism and speaker relativism." *Ethics*, 101: 6–25.

Dreier, J. (1996). "Expressivist embeddings and minimalist truth." *Philosophical Studies*, 83: 29–51.

Dorr, C. (2002). "Noncognitivism and wishful thinking." *Nous*, 36: 97–103.

Gibbard, A. (1990). *Wise Choices, Apt Feelings*. Cambridge: Harvard University Press.

Gibbard, A. (2003). *Thinking How to Live*. Cambridge: Harvard University Press.

Grice, P. (1989). *Studies in the Ways of Words*. Cambridge: Harvard University Press.

Harman, G. (1975). "Moral relativism defended." *Philosophical Review*, 84: 3–22.

Harman, G. and Thomson, J. J. (1988). *Moral Relativism and Moral Objectivity*. Oxford: Blackwell.

Horgan, T. and Timmons, M. (1992). "Troubles for new wave moral semantics: the 'open question' argument revived." *Philosophical Papers*, 21: 153–75.

Horwich, P. (1990). *Truth*. Oxford: Oxford University Press.

Horwich, P. (1994). "The essence of expressivism." *Analysis,* 54: 19–20.

Humberstone, L. (1992). "Direction of fit." *Mind*, 101: 59–83.

Hume, D. (1888). *A Treatise of Human Nature*, ed. L. A. Selby-Bigge. Oxford: Clarendon.

Jackson, F. (1998). *From Metaphysics to Ethics*. Oxford: Oxford University Press.

Kitcher, P. (1998). "Psychological altruism, evolutionary origins, and moral rules." *Philosophical Studies*, 98: 283–316.

Korsgaard, K. (1986). "Skepticism about practical reason." *Journal of Philosophy*, 83: 5–25.

McDowell, J. (1985). "Value and secondary qualities." In T. Honderich (ed.), *Morality and Objectivity*. London: Routledge & Kegan Paul.

Moran, J. M. et al. (2004). "Neural correlates of humor detection and appreciation." *NeuroImage*, 21: 1055–60.

Nagel, T. (1978). *The Possibility of Altruism*. Princeton: Princeton University Press.

Putnam, H. (1975). "The meaning of 'meaning'." In K. Gunderson (ed.), *Mind, Language, and Knowledge*. Minneapolis: University of Minnesota Press.

Railton, P. (1993a). "Non-cognitivism about rationality: benefits, costs, and an alternative." *Philosophical Issues*, 4: 36–52.

Railton, P. (1993b). "What the non-cognitivist helps us to see, the naturalist must help us to explain" (with comments and replies by David Wiggins). In J. Haldane and C. Wright (eds.), *Reality, Representation, and Projection*. Oxford: Oxford University Press.

Roskies, A. (2003). "Are ethical judgments intrinsically motivational? Lessons from acquired sociopathy." *Philosophical Psychology*, 16: 51–66.

Sayre-McCord, G. (1997). "Good on Twin Earth." *Philosophical Issues*, 8: 267–92.

Sinnott-Armstrong, W. (2000). "Expressivism and embedding." *Philosophy and Phenomenological Research*, 61: 677–693.

Skyrms, B. (1996). *Evolution of the Social Contract*. Cambridge: Cambridge University Press.

Smith, M. (1994a). *The Moral Problem*. Oxford: Blackwell.

Smith, M. (1994b). "Why expressivists about value should love minimalism about truth." *Analysis*, 54: 12–19.

Stoljar, D. (1993). "Emotivism and truth conditions." *Philosophical Studies*, 70: 81–101.

CHAPTER THIRTEEN

Morality Without Moral Facts

Terry Horgan and Mark Timmons

The title of this chapter refers to a project in metaethics that takes an austere approach to moral metaphysics yet attempts to remain faithful to moral phenomenology. It is austere because it denies that there are in-the-world moral properties like goodness and rightness to which moral terms like 'good' and 'right' refer. And so it denies that there are specifically *moral* facts that moral judgments purport to describe or represent. But our project also attempts to be faithful to moral phenomenology – faithful, that is, to the deeply embedded features of (the phenomena exhibited by) ordinary moral thought and discourse. The metaethical view that we defend in pursuing this project may be called 'cognitivist expressivism': cognitivist because it construes moral judgment as essentially a matter of *belief* rather than, say, a mere matter of feeling or desire, and expressivist because it claims that the beliefs expressed by moral statements are *non-descriptive* beliefs.

In order to understand our project, and the associated metaethical view that we defend, let us first explain some basic distinctions in metaethics.

Metaethical Taxonomy

Metaethics is primarily concerned with the semantics, metaphysics, and epistemology of moral thought and discourse. Here, we are going to focus mainly on issues of semantics and metaphysics. Let us begin with a basic contrast within moral semantics.

Consider a common-sense view concerning ordinary descriptive judgments about the external world. The claim that 'Jupiter is a planet' purports to describe or represent some factual state of affairs in the world – namely, that the astronomical object which we call 'Jupiter' is a planet. Whether the claim in question is true or false depends on two things: meaning and the facts. That is, the truth of the claim depends upon what the terms 'Jupiter', 'planet', and 'is' mean and upon whether as a matter of fact Jupiter has the property of being a planet. There are, out in the world, facts about Jupiter, and the claim in question is in the business of describing or representing certain of those facts. For convenience, let us say that judgments like the one about Jupiter are *descriptive beliefs*, and that statements expressing such beliefs are *descriptive assertions*.

Some philosophers think that moral judgments are also (primarily) descriptive – such judgments purport to describe or represent in-the-world moral facts. The idea is that moral terms like 'good', 'right', and 'ought' purport to pick out properties of some sort, and a statement of the form 'X ought to be done' is true just in case X has the property of ought-to-be-doneness (or, more simply, rightness). If it does, then the judgment is true; if not, then it is false. This position in metaethics is, for obvious reasons, called *descriptivism* and all rival metaethical views are called *non-descriptivism*.

Non-descriptivists, then, deny that moral judgments are primarily in the business of representing moral facts; rather, the idea is that such judgments play a non-descriptive role in our thought and language. As we shall see, non-descriptivists differ over what sort of non-descriptive role is characteristic of moral judgments.

In recent years, the term 'expressivism' has been widely used to refer to the view that moral statements are not primarily descriptive, but rather serve to express some non-descriptive attitude toward an object of evaluation. We will follow this trend. So the basic contrast in metaethical views about the semantics of moral judgments is between versions of descriptivism and versions of expressivism.

Turing now to questions of metaphysics, metaethical *factualism* is the view that there are moral properties such as rightness, goodness, and their opposites, and when an action or other object of evaluation possesses one of these properties there is a moral fact, such as the fact that some particular action is morally right. As we shall see, factualists can disagree about the nature of such properties. But all such views are opposed by metaethical *non-factualism* which denies that there are any moral properties possessed by actions or other objects of evaluation and so this view denies that there are in-the-world moral facts.

So, we have two sets of distinctions: the semantical distinction between descriptivism and expressivism and the metaphysical distinction between factualism and non-factualism. Metaethical positions can be sorted out, initially at least, in terms of how they stand on the semantic and metaphysical issues just described. You might initially think there are only two main positions: (1) descriptivism + factualism and (2) non-descriptivism + non-factualism. But this would be a mistaken. If one goes back to our definition of descriptivism which says that moral judgments *purport* to describe moral facts, one might take the view that although this is the business they are in, they systematically fail because there are no moral facts to which affirmative moral judgments might correspond. This position would combine descriptivism with non-factualism. What about combining non-descriptivism with factualism? This is a possible view, though it has not had many defenders. The idea would be that the primary role of moral statements is some non-reporting role such as prescribing an action, but that such statements also pick out moral properties and so they also have a secondary role of describing moral facts. See figure 1 for a visual aid.

	Descriptivism	Expressivism
Factualism	Realism Constructivism Relativism	???
Non-factualism	Error theory	Non-cognitivism (e.g.,emotivism) Cognitivist expressivism

Metaphysics (row label spanning Factualism / Non-factualism)

Figure 13.1 Metaethical views

So, in terms of the two sets of distinction, there are four basic positions. Within each quadrant on the chart, we have filled in the names of commonly discussed metaethical views, and also our own view – cognitivist expressivism. We will return to the chart and explain the various positions it contains beginning in the section below, "Troubles for Factualism." First, let us briefly outline some of the criteria that are often used in evaluating competing metaethical theories. Then we will be in a position to explain why we think our own, cognitivist, brand of expressivism is the best metaethical view going.

Evaluating Metaethical Views

How, then, are competing metaethical theories to be evaluated? The relevant standards have mainly to do with the central aims of metaethical theorizing. Of course, philosophers might differ over what these aims are, but if one looks at more than one hundred years of work in metaethics beginning with G. E. Moore's 1903 classic *Principia Ethica*, there are two very general aims (and corresponding criteria of evaluation) that characterize much metaethical theorizing. First, since metaethical inquiry is about the semantics, metaphysics, and epistemology of moral thought and discourse, it aims to characterize the deeply embedded phenomena of morality that bear on questions of meaning, truth, ontology, and knowledge in ethics. Here is a short list of some of the phenomena in question:

MP1 Moral judgments are typically expressed linguistically as statements in the indicative mood, and these statements appear to express genuine beliefs and to make genuine assertions. The moral judgment that apartheid is wrong asserts that apartheid is wrong.

MP2 Moral judgments are capable of being true or false, and indeed many such judgments are true and their contradictories are false.

Morality Without Moral Facts

MP3   There can be genuine, deep moral disagreements – including disagreements between people over fundamental moral assumptions and principles.

MP4   Moral judgments and statements are action-guiding; they typically are concerned with directing behavior.

MP5   Moral judgments are typically based on the authority of reasons. One bases one's moral judgments on what one takes to be good reasons in favor of the judgments – reasons that have a special authority.

MP6   Moral judgments are about matters of deep and fundamental importance to our lives, whereas, say, aesthetic judgments and judgments of etiquette are generally about matters of less importance.

Here, then, is one basic desideratum guiding much metaethical theorizing:

Moral phenomemology criterion: A metaethical theory ought, if possible, to account for and vindicate as many of the deeply embedded aspects of moral thought and moral discourse – the phenomena of morality – as possible.

This is not the only constraint, however. In addition, philosophers attempt to be systematic in the sense that they want their philosophical theories about a certain subject matter (in this case ethics) to fit with plausible assumptions and theories in philosophy generally and with the well-confirmed discoveries and theories of science. Talk of 'fitting with' is vague, and we won't try to explain it any further here. However, the idea is intuitive enough. If one holds the metaphysical view called *naturalism* according to which all the facts there are 'natural' facts of the sort discoverable through the empirical methods of common-sense observation and science, then if one also wants to defend moral factualism, one needs to show that moral facts are a species of natural fact. One might claim, for instance, that moral facts are sociological facts about the attitudes of groups. Since the latter sort of fact counts as a 'natural' fact in this context, the result would be that moral facts fit into the general ontological theory of a philosophical naturalist. So any metaethical factualist has some ontological work to do. She needs to defend an account of the nature of moral facts and connect her metaethical account with more general ontological commitments.

Again, as J. L. Mackie once noted, "Moral principles and ethical theories do not stand alone: they affect and are affected by beliefs and assumptions which belong to other fields, and not the least to psychology, metaphysics, and religion" (1977: 203). For instance, some philosophers claim that facts about deep moral diversity (facts discoverable through scientific means) do not fit very well with moral realism (a view to be discussed in the next section). They argue that if moral realism were true, there would not be as much variation in moral opinion as there is in fact. Empirical facts about moral disagreement lead some of these philosophers to embrace moral relativism (also discussed below).

We may formulate a rough but useful criterion guiding metaethical inquiry based on these observations:

Coherence criterion: A metaethical theory ought to fit with plausible assumptions and theories in both philosophy and other fields in inquiry including the sciences.

Defending a metaethical view, then, is a matter of considering the philosophical pluses and minuses of the various competing views in terms of how well they do in satisfying these two main desiderata. Let us now turn to the metaethical theories mentioned in the above chart. In the next three sections, we shall present and offer brief critical remarks about the positions we reject and then, in subsequent sections, we will turn to our own view.

Troubles for Factualism

Metaethical factualists differ over the status and nature of moral facts. The main basis of disagreement among realists, constructivists, and relativists has to do with the issues of the "independence" and the variability of putative moral facts. A moral realist claims that moral facts and truths are robustly objective. Moral facts are objective in the sense that their existence and nature is independent of beliefs, attitudes, and theories about them. In this way, moral facts are as objective as are facts about Jupiter. Thus, moral statements, when true, are true independently of what you or anyone might think about such statements – they are true in virtue of the objective moral facts.

Moral realism obviously contrasts with moral relativism. A moral relativist typically claims that there are moral facts, but such facts are both 'dependent' and 'variable' facts. They are dependent because their existence depends upon the acceptance of some set of norms by some group (where in the limit case a group might be a single individual).[1] And they are variable because there are or can be different groups with different norms and so what is true relative to one group's norms may be false relative to the norms of a different group. Thus, for the moral relativist, although there is moral truth, it is relative truth – true relative to some set of norms. If the moral norms of one group include a prohibition against eating meat, then it is a fact – a fact whose existence depends on the acceptance of that prohibition – that eating meat is wrong. If the moral norms of some other group do not contain this sort of prohibition, then it is a fact – again, a relative fact – that eating meat is not morally wrong. Facts about what is and is not morally wrong depend for the relativist on moral conventions or perhaps the attitudes of individuals.

In between realism and relativism are versions of (non-relativist) moral constructivism, according to which moral facts and truths are dependent upon a hypothetical set of basic moral norms – norms that all ideally rational agents supposedly would accept were they to engage properly in a process of moral reasoning. Like the relativist and unlike the realist, the constructivist claims that moral facts and truths do depend on the acceptance of some set of moral norms. But like the realist and unlike the relativist, she also claims that there is a single true set of basic moral norms – viz., those that ideally rational agents would accept – and hence there is a single true morality.

Our main objection to versions of realism and constructivism is that they end up committed to moral relativism – the very sort of view they seek to avoid. And our main objection to relativism is that it fails to accommodate some key aspects of moral phenomenology.

Moral realism rejected

In order for moral realism to work, two conditions must be met. First, basic moral terms like 'good' and 'right' must pick out certain properties, and moral judgments must be in the business of representing moral facts in which such properties figure. Second, the world must be such that moral properties are instantiated and, correspondingly, the world must contain such facts. But can these requirements be met?

Most contemporary moral realists are naturalists – they hold that moral properties and facts are a species of natural properties and facts.[2] How to define such talk of natural properties and facts is a difficult problem which we will not get into here. Suffice it to say that a natural property is one whose nature can be described without using moral or other normative terminology. What the naturalist realist needs to do, then, is give a convincing theory about the meaning and reference of moral terms that makes clear how terms like 'good' and 'right' refer to natural properties, and do so in a way that is compatible with moral realism. Following Frank Jackson (1998), we call this the 'location problem' – the problem of locating in the natural world the putative referents of moral terms. Here is where problems begin to arise for the realist. There seem to be two general approaches to the location problem in ethics which, as we will proceed to explain, result in a dilemma for the moral realist.

First, in attempting to solve the location problem, a realist might appeal to the various "platitudes" or common-sense truths involving moral terms like 'good' and 'right' that collectively seem to express at least part of what is meant by such terms in their ethical uses. The hope is that there are enough such platitudes of the right sort so that collectively they effectively pin down the referents of basic moral terms. Then the realist would be able to define a moral term like 'right' as referring to whatever natural property uniquely satisfies the set of platitudes. The basic idea behind this abstract proposal can be made more concrete with a non-moral example, inspired by David Lewis (1972).

Suppose you are a detective, investigating the murder of Professor Plum. You know that there is one and only one person guilty of the crime, and because at the outset of your investigation you don't know who the guilty party is, you refer to that person as X. Your task is to identify X. Suppose that early on you discover a number of clues which may be expressed as follows: X is a female; X is under 6' tall; X has red hair; X lives in Albuquerque; X drives a white Ford Mustang. But suppose also that there are six people who fit all of these facts. Because there are too many eligible referents, you don't yet know the referent of X. You need more clues. Suppose that later on you do discover more facts about X which can be expressed in the same form as the others – in terms of X having or being such and such. With all these facts about X available, suppose you now know that Miss Scarlet, and Miss Scarlet alone, fits all the facts of the case. Then you now know the referent of X: X picks out the unique individual of whom all of the facts are true and this turns out to be Miss Scarlet. The analogy with the attempt to fix the referents of terms like 'good' and 'right' is not perfect, but it should provide a sense of the kind of strategy a moral realist might use in attempting to solve the location problem. So, again, the idea is to take the platitudes involving terms like 'right' and 'good' (these represent the clues, as it were, about to the identity of the referent-properties of these terms) and then see whether the total information to be found in the set of platitudes enables you to specify a unique natural property that fits all the platitudes involving talk of rightness. Do the same for goodness.

So, what are the platitudes available to the moral realist? They would include formal platitudes that express conceptual connections among moral terms, such as: 'If an action is wrong, all things considered, then one ought not perform that action'; 'If an action is permissible, all things considered, then it is not wrong to perform that action'. There are also formal platitudes that represent the "logic" of moral discourse such as: 'If an action is right (or wrong) for one agent to perform in some set of circumstances, then it is right (or wrong) for any similar agent in similar circumstance.' The realist could also appeal to substantive moral platitudes such as: 'Right actions are concerned to promote, sustain, or contribute in some way to human flourishing'; and 'Right actions are expressive of equal respect and concern for individuals.' No doubt the list could be extended.

But the problem is that taken collectively these platitudes do not yield enough information to effectively pick out some unique natural property to which a moral term refers; there are too many eligible potential referent-properties. To see this, notice that competing moral theories about rightness are fully compatible with these platitudes. On a utilitarian theory (construed as telling us what natural property rightness is), rightness of an action is identical to the property of producing a maximum amount of happiness concerning all those affected by the action. But on one kind of deontological theory (again, construed as telling us what natural property rightness is), rightness of an action is the property of being from the motive of benevolence. Both accounts of rightness are compatible with the platitudes of ethics, and that means that these platitudes themselves do not provide enough information to pin down the referent of terms like 'right'. The result is indeterminacy of reference for moral terms: they fail to uniquely pick out natural properties. Hence, this strategy for the realist does not yield what she wants.

The other way to go would be to take the platitudes in question and add to them certain substantive moral judgments that identify actions that are right and traits that are good. The idea would be, for example, to make use of the widely shared and deeply held moral judgments about rightness of a community and use this additional information to help pin down the referent of 'right'.

But now the problem is that this way of understanding the semantics of moral terms like 'good' and 'right' commits one to moral relativism – a position at odds with realism. After all, suppose a community of utilitarians appeal to how they use moral language when it comes to judging right from wrong. Then, if one understands moral terms so that they refer to whatever natural properties guide the judgments of some community, one will conclude that for this group, the term 'right' refers to the natural property of maximizing overall happiness. But now if one considers a community of deontologists whose moral judgments about right and wrong are guided by properties having to do with an agent's motives, one will have to conclude that for this group the term 'right' refers to the property of being motivated by some desire. The implication of all this is that there are relative moral facts – facts about rightness that are relative to the substantive moral norms accepted by a given community. Since different communities do or might subscribe to different moral codes, what is right (the property rightness) for one group may differ from what is right for another group. This is relativism.

In our short discussion of moral realism we have not explored the various sophisticated semantic proposals by such moral realists as Richard Boyd (1988), Peter Railton (1993), David Brink (2001), and David Copp (2001). Doing so would require extended discussions of complicated issues which we have tackled in some of our previous writings.[3] But what we have said about the troubles for the naturalist moral realist amounts to a dilemma which we think besets the various versions of moral realism on offer. The dilemma is that in solving the location problem, either (1) a realist appeals to various relatively uncontroversial moral platitudes in an attempt to pin down the referents of moral terms, in which case the semantic theory fails to yield determinate referents for the terms in question, or (2) the realist appeals to moral platitudes plus a set of substantive moral claims about right and wrong, good and bad, in which case the result is relativism. We do not see any plausible escape from this dilemma.

Moral constructivism deconstructed

Moral constructivism, recall, is the view that moral facts and truths depend upon the outcome of some ideal process of moral deliberation. The hope of the constructivist is that all rational inquirers would converge in the basic moral norms they would accept, were they to undergo some method of moral reasoning. What are often called 'ideal observer' accounts of rightness and goodness constitute one kind of constructivism. In recent years, constructivism has been defended by such philosophers as John Rawls (1980), Michael Smith (1994), and T. M. Scanlon (1998). Rawls's own version of constructivism makes use of what he calls the 'original position' – a hypothetical position from which rational choosers are to deliberate about principles of morality. Rawls sums up his constructivist position nicely when he writes:

> The parties in the original position do not agree on what the moral facts are, as if there already were such facts. It is not that, being situated impartially, they have a clear and undistorted view of a prior and independent moral order. Rather (for constructivism), there is no such order, and therefore no such facts apart from the procedure of construction as a whole; the facts are identified by the principles that result [from the procedure]. (1980/1999: 354)

Constructivism is attractive because it promises to deny relativism and yet eschews the kinds of semantical and metaphysical difficulties that infect realism.

But it is hard to see how constructivism can avoid sliding into relativism. The main task of the constructivist is to characterize the conditions of ideal deliberation (the backbone of her metaethical theory) so that (1) the process or method of deliberation will yield definite moral norms with determinate moral implications and (2) do so in a way that yields one single set of "correct" or "true" moral norms. To fail at the first task is to fail to get any results, while to fail at the second task is to be committed to relativism. We do not think that any extant version of the theory satisfies both requirements, and we doubt that there could be one. The basic problem is very similar to the problem with realism. That is, in characterizing the conditions of ideal delib-eration, if the constructivist appeals to the relatively uncontroversial formal and sub-stantive platitudes associated with the concept of being an ideal moral judge, the result will be that there will not be enough constraints on what counts as "ideal" deliberation to yield determinate moral norms. So, to narrow the field of competitors, the constructivist is going to have to build in some substantive moral assumptions. What will guide the constructivist here? It looks as if the constructivist will have to allow ideal deliberators to fall back on their own deepest moral convictions. But this means that if a particular ideal deliberator happens to start the deliberative process with deep moral convictions of a kind best systematized by utilitarian principles, then the result of her ideal deliberations will be a utilitarian theory. Likewise, if another ideal deliberator instead starts the deliberative process with deep moral convictions of a kind best systematized by certain deontological principles, then the result of *his* ideal deliberations will be a deontological theory. Thus, different ideal deliberators would arrive at different moral norms via ideal deliberation, because of the differing deep moral convictions that would guide their respective ideal deliberations. In the end, one gets multiple and conflicting, but equally "correct" or "true," sets of moral norms. Once again, this is relativism.[4]

Moral relativism rebuffed

The issue of relativism in ethics is a confusing topic because of the many different ideas to which the term 'relativism' is applied. We are concerned with a metaethical view that makes moral facts and truths relative to some moral outlook or another, where (in contrast to constructivism) there can be many systems of moral norms, each conflicting with the others but all equally correct or true. There are moral facts on this view, but these facts are relative to some moral outlook.

Since we claim that descriptivists who are also factualists are committed to rela-tivism, why not be a moral relativist? The trouble with relativism, we maintain, is that it cannot make good sense of *moral* disagreements – disagreements that cannot be explained as disagreements about the non-moral facts of the case. Consider a case in which two persons, with different moral outlooks, are disputing the morality of euthanasia – one party claiming that active euthanasia is always wrong, the other party denying this claim. Let us assume that both parties here are in agreement about all medical facts concerning euthanasia, and they agree about the various effects of this practice on society generally and on the patient's family and friends. And let us suppose that they have considered the various arguments that have been made about the morality of euthanasia. Still, they disagree. One of them holds that any act that intentionally brings about the death of an innocent person is wrong, the other does not. This certainly seems to be a disagreement in basic moral principles about killing.

Now according to the kind of moral relativism we are examining, the apparently conflicting moral claims about euthanasia may both be true. When the opponent of active euthanasia claims that this practice is morally wrong, she is (we are assuming) judging in accordance with her basic moral norms governing killing humans. And when the proponent of active euthanasia claims that this practice is not always morally wrong, he is (we are assuming) judging in accordance with his basic moral norms governing the morality of killing. According to the relativist, both parties to the disagreement are speaking the truth; the disagreement is not really genuine. And this is deeply at odds with some aspects of moral phenomenology (recall MP3 from our list of assumptions regarding moral phenomenology). Indeed, for the moral relativist, there is a sense in which the parties to this dispute are just talking past one another. That is, for the relativist, person A and person B are both using moral language to correctly report (relative) moral facts; indeed, when A uses the term 'wrong', her usage is semantically governed by the moral norms she accepts, and similarly for B. But then aren't they using 'wrong' and other moral terms to refer to different properties? If so, aren't they just talking past one another? What happened to their moral disagreement?

This concludes our brief survey and critique of factualist descriptivist metaethical views. Let us now consider the non-factualist descriptivist option.

Why Not (Ontological) Error Theory?

Any metaethical theory that denies some elements of moral phenomenology might be called an error theory – error, because any such theory attributes to common-sense moral thinking some sort of mistake. We just saw that moral relativism is a kind of error theory in being deeply at odds with the assumption that there can be genuine moral disagreements. But the label 'error theory' in ethics is typically used to refer to the combination of descriptivism with non-factualism; hence the view gets its name from attributing an *ontological* error to common sense moral thought.

J. L. Mackie (1977) famously defended an ontological error theory in ethics. Mackie was a descriptivist who thought that a proper understanding of ordinary moral claims showed them to be claims that purport to state facts. More precisely, Mackie held that (1) moral thought and discourse purport to pick out objective moral properties and facts and, moreover, (2) such properties and facts would be "objectively prescriptive," that is, were they to exist then, unlike natural properties and facts, they would have normativity (to-be-doneness) as part of their intrinsic nature. However, as a committed metaphysical naturalist, Mackie further claimed that (3) there are no such properties and facts (they would be ontologically "queer" because of their built-in normativity), and so concluded that (4) affirmative moral judgments (as ordinary used) are all false – a claim at odds with MP2.

We limit ourselves to one observation about Mackie's view. If one can develop a metaethical view that avoids attributing massive error to ordinary morality, then so much the better. (This remark, of course, reflects commitment to the moral phenomenology criterion.)

Factualist Expressivism?

Given how we have defined factualism and non-descriptivism, it is not clear that any going metaethical view involves this combination of semantic and ontological claims. This category within metaethics is not often recognized because of the entrenched association of non-descriptivism with non-factualism. But the combination of factualism and non-descriptivism represents a coherent metaethical option, even if it hasn't had any defenders. For instance, one might follow non-naturalists and claim that there are simple, non-natural moral properties like oughtness and thus that there are non-natural moral facts. But in addition, one might claim that moral judgments mainly function to express prescriptions. So, judgments of the form 'S ought to do A' primarily function in thought and language to prescribe to S the doing of A. Again, one might embrace the non-descriptivist idea that moral judgments function primarily to prescribe, not to describe, but go on to claim that when one judges of some action that it ought to be done, one (at least tacitly) applies moral standards to the case at hand which pick out various natural properties that are the basis of one's moral evaluation. Thus, for example, if you are a utilitarian and judge in light of what you take to be facts about the effects of actions on the general welfare of individuals affected by the action, then it might be claimed that your judgment that action A ought not to be done by S is true – states a moral fact – just in case it is a fact about the action that it would fail to maximize general welfare. Here we have a relativist kind of factualism wedded to a non-descriptivist semantic view.

There are other possibilities, but they need not detain us, for if factualism is false, then metaethical views that embrace this ontological commitment are mistaken – including factualist expressivism.

The only general option left is the combination of expressivism and non-factualism: the general view *typically* called 'expressivism'. So let us turn to this metaethical position.

Expressivism

Unfortunately, there is a history of conflating expressivism with non-cognitivism. Expressivism, as we have defined it, is the view that moral judgments primarily function to express some attitude other than a descriptive belief. Non-cognitivism is a version of expressivism which makes the further claim that moral judgments are not beliefs at all. If all beliefs are descriptive beliefs, then an expressivist must be a non-cognitivist. But this is not how we see it. We claim that in addition to descriptive beliefs, which are in the business of representing the world, there are also evaluative beliefs; these are not a species of descriptive belief, but instead are in the business of reasoned action-guidance. As mentioned at the outset, our favored semantic view in metaethics is a version of cognitivist expressivism which we combine with non-factualism.

A word about non-cognitivism

Non-cognitivism in metaethics is the view that (1) moral judgments are not beliefs, (2) moral utterances are not genuine assertions, and thus (3) moral judgments and utterances are neither true nor false. For instance, according to *emotivism,* a moral judgment such as 'apartheid is wrong', thought or uttered by a person on some occasion, simply functions to express the person's negative attitude toward apartheid. What appears to be a genuine assertion expressing a belief is really a disguised expression of a subjective feeling. But emotivism, and non-cognitivism generally, are prima facie implausible because they deny some of the deeply embedded features of moral phenomenology, including the idea that moral utterances are genuine assertions that express genuine beliefs, and the idea the that some moral judgments can properly be evaluated as true and others as false (MP1 and MP2). But, fortunately, an expressivist can be a cognitivist.

Cognitivist Expressivism

We claim that moral thought and discourse do not purport to be factualist in any robust way. They are not in the business of representing or reporting moral facts (whether objectively real, constructed, or relative); moral terms and the concepts they express do not function to pick out moral properties. In short, moral judgments are not a species of *descriptive* beliefs. But as we have already said, we do maintain nonetheless that these judgments are indeed *beliefs*; we reject the view that all beliefs are descriptive beliefs. Moral-evaluative beliefs, whose primary role is action guidance and not description, do not purport to represent facts. We claim that this metaethical position can accommodate, better than any competing view, the various features of moral phenomenology listed above in our section "Evaluating Metaethical Views" (see above, p. 276).

We will not be able in the short space remaining to develop our view in detail, but we can accomplish two related tasks – which should give the reader a clear enough understanding of our view and its virtues. So, here are the tasks that we plan to accomplish:

Task 1: Articulate an independently plausible conception of belief that *does not require* evaluative beliefs to be a species of descriptive belief, and situate cognitivist expressivism within this conception as the *denial* that moral beliefs are a species of descriptive belief.

Task 2: Argue that cognitivist expressivism, elaborated in a way that draws upon the proposed conception of belief, is able to accommodate the various features of moral phenomenology.

Obviously the first task is crucial, given the very widespread semantic assumption that all beliefs are descriptive. We propose to challenge that assumption by setting forth a conception of belief that we claim has substantial independent plausibility, rather than being a mere ad hoc maneuver in the service of our own metaethical project. Also, since a metaethical theory is to be judged according to how well it is able to satisfy the moral phenomenology and coherence criteria, the second task needs accomplishing as well: explaining our theory, it satisfies these two criteria. In particular, since a non-factualist need not worry about the worldly location of moral properties and facts (and thus the coherence criterion is easily satisfied), our second main task will require showing that our view plausibly accommodates the various features of moral phenomenology set out above (see p. 276).

A Framework for Belief and Assertion (Task 1)

Speaking most generically, a belief is a kind of psychological commitment state, of which there are two main species: *is-commitments* and *ought-commitments*. Beliefs of both sorts involve taking an attitude toward an actual or potential state of affairs – a way the world might be. For example, the belief that 'John gave back to Mary the money he owed her' is an is-commitment with respect to a possible state of affairs, namely, John's giving to Mary the money that he owes her. By contrast, the belief that 'John ought to give back to Mary the money he owes her' is a ought-commitment with respect to that same state of affairs, viz., John's giving back to Mary the money he owes her. A non-evaluative belief is an is-commitment with respect to a possible state of affairs, while a simple (non-logically complex) moral judgment is an ought-commitment with respect to a possible state of affairs.

Both kinds of commitment state are beliefs, since they exhibit certain generic features that are characteristic of beliefs. For instance, both sorts of commitment state have the grammatical and logical trappings of genuine beliefs: in thought and language the contents of such states are declarative, and they can figure as constituents in logically complex judgments as in 'Either John has paid what he owes to Mary or he ought to do so'. As such, ought-commitments can figure in logical inferences. Furthermore, they can combine with other beliefs to yield new beliefs that are appropriate given prior beliefs. So, for instance, if Mary judges that one ought to help those in need and she believes that John is in need (and she is in a position to help him), then it is appropriate for her to form a new belief, namely, that she ought to help John.

In addition to such grammatical, logical, and functional characteristics, ought-commitments also exhibit certain *experiential* features that are typical of genuine beliefs. For instance, these states typically are experienced as psychologically involuntary (unlike voluntary commitments like intentions or promises), and as grounded in reasons. Thus, given the considerations that one takes to be reasons favoring or disfavoring various possible states of affairs, and given what one takes to be the net import of those reasons, normally one cannot help but accept certain is-commitments and ought-commitments. In the case of is-commitments, often one's reasons for the commitment are related to it in an experientially distinctive way: an awareness of those facts *as reasons* for the belief involves a *felt epistemic authority* that the reasons exert upon oneself – a felt authority in virtue of which the is-commitment arises involuntarily. One is aware of those facts in such a way that the facts are experienced as constituting rationally compelling *evidence* that a potential state of affairs actually obtains – and straightaway one finds oneself with an involuntary is-commitment vis-à-vis that state of affairs. One's reasons for an ought-commitment normally are related to the commitment's involuntariness in a similarly distinctive way, experientially: an awareness of those facts *as reasons* for a moral judgment involves a *felt moral-normative authority* that the reason exerts upon oneself, vis-à-vis a potential state of affairs – a felt authority in virtue of which the ought-commitment with respect to that state of affairs arises involuntarily.

All of these features that are typical of ordinary belief – their grammatical and logical trappings, their role in one's psychological economy, and their experiential aspects – strongly suggest that ought-commitments are indeed genuine beliefs. The idea that moral judgments are genuine beliefs is metaethical *cognitivism*. We are metaethical cognitivists: judgments expressing ought-commitments are beliefs.

But it seems very plausible to also suppose that moral beliefs are importantly different from ordinary descriptive beliefs – different enough that moral beliefs are not a species of descriptive beliefs. Whereas the job of ordinary descriptive beliefs is to represent how things are in the world, the job of moral beliefs is not descriptive but evaluative: one evaluates some potential state of affairs positively or negatively. In doing so, one's primary purpose normally is oriented toward action. Typically, anyway, moral judgments dispose one toward appropriate action in an especially direct way, independently of one's pre-existing desires and aversions. By contrast, non-moral descriptive beliefs only become action-oriented in combination with some prior desire or aversion. The belief that there is a fire in the vicinity purports to represent or describe some worldly state of affairs. But this belief alone does not seem to orient one toward any particular action or any action at all. Of course, if you have a strong aversion to fires, then together with the belief about the fire being in the vicinity, you will likely be motivated to flee the area. But, of course, if you have a fascination with fires and are not afraid of them, they you may be motivated to move closer to the fire. It all depends on one's prior desires and aversions. By contrast, the judgment that one ought not to put oneself unnecessarily in harm's way is directly action-orienting, independently of prior desires and aversions. And associated with this kind of direct action-orientation of moral judgments are certain notable experiential features: a felt demandingness, a phenomenological to-be-doneness with respect the action one judges to be obligatory.

So, ought-commitments are genuine beliefs whose primary role in human cognitive economy is reasoned action-guidance. Although they are indeed beliefs, they are not descriptive beliefs. Is-commitments are descriptive beliefs, whereas ought-commitments are non-descriptive beliefs. Furthermore, the same general points can be made about linguistic speech acts in which one utters or writes sentences that express one's moral beliefs. Such speech acts are genuine assertions. When one utters the sentence 'Apartheid ought to be abolished', one is taking a moral stance toward the practice of apartheid. In doing so, one linguistically expresses an ought-commitment toward a state of affairs. The typical role of such an utterance, in linguistic interaction with other people, is reasoned action-guidance. In judging as one does, one typically takes there to be features of apartheid that constitute good reasons for opposing this practice. One thereby enters the space of reason-giving, and so interpersonal discussion and debate over moral questions typically involves reason-guided linguistic stance taking.

To sum up: our metaethical view challenges the dogma that all genuine beliefs purport to represent or describe the world. Instead, one should acknowledge a kind of belief that is not primarily in the business of describing but, rather, serves to guide action on the basis of reasons. Such ought-commitments exhibit, we think, enough belief-like characteristics to count as genuine beliefs, but because they are directly action-guiding, they are distinct from ordinary descriptive beliefs. The kinds of features exhibited by moral beliefs are also exhibited by moral assertions as well.

This concludes our first task.

Expressivism Without Tears (Task 2)

We turn now to our second task of explaining how our view plausibly accommodates the various deeply embedded assumptions of ordinary moral thought and discourse. We are working with six key assumptions, MP1–MP6. So, let us now proceed to explain how our view accommodates each of them.

MP1: Moral judgments appear to be beliefs; moral utterances appear to be assertions.
Our view about moral ought-commitments as genuine beliefs directly accommodates the appearances.

MP2: Moral judgments are capable of being true or false.
The concepts of belief, assertion, and truth are tightly linked. To believe something is to take it to be true. Sincere assertions express beliefs. Truth and falsity are properly predicated of beliefs and assertions. So, if our view recognizes that moral judgments are genuine beliefs and utterances are genuine assertions, then it must make sense to say of a belief or utterance that it is true or that it is false. How, then, do we propose to understand ascriptions of truth and falsity?

On our view, the proper way to understand truth ascription in relation to moral beliefs and assertions is to focus on truth ascriptions as metalinguistic speech acts and ask about the nature of such acts. What is one doing when one predicates truth (or falsity) of a moral judgment? The basic idea is that when makes a claim like 'The statement that apartheid ought to be abolished is true', one is engaging in a *morally engaged* semantic appraisal: it is infused with one's own ought-commitment regarding apartheid. This can perhaps be best understood as involving two underlying ideas. First, ordinary uses of the truth predicate operate in accordance with the following schema, called 'schema T',

'S' is true if and only if S

where 'S' is some declarative sentence in a language. This means that in sincerely thinking or uttering a statement of the form, 'S' is true, one is committed to affirming S and vice versa. Second, when one predicates truth of a moral statement, one is engaged in an act of affirming "metalinguistically" the first-order moral claim in question (that is, affirming first-order moral judgment expressed by the statement one is calling true.) Such an affirmation, done metalinguistically by employing the semantic concept of truth, is a morally engaged "fusion" of semantic and moral appraisal. (Given that truth ascription normally accords with schema T, one should expect our non-descriptivist, non-facualist treatment of moral judgments and statements to extend, *mutatis mutandis* via schema T, to truth ascriptions concerning such judgments and statements.)

MP3: There can be genuine deep moral disagreements.
Moral relativists have problems with accommodating the idea that there can be genuine deep moral disagreements among parties who operate with conflicting fundamental moral norms. Recall that for a moral relativist, the truth of a moral

judgment is relative to some set of fundamental moral norms accepted by some individual or group. Since it is very likely that different individuals and groups accept conflicting fundamental moral norms, there will be cases in which, for example, one party to a dispute will claim that all instances of active euthanasia are wrong (and be judging in accordance with her fundamental moral norms), while the other party to the dispute judges that some instances of active euthanasia are not wrong (and be judging in accordance with his fundamental moral norms). If a moral judgment is made true by the fact that it follows from the judger's basic moral norms plus relevant empirical facts, then the relativist is committed to claiming that both parties to such disputes are speaking the truth. But if they are, then there is not a genuine disagreement between them, and this seems deeply at odds with certain aspects of moral phenomenology. One normally takes such disagreements to be genuine.

Our metaethical view is not a version of relativism, nor is it committed to relativism. Granted, on our view (on any metaethical view) a sincere moral judgment made by a judger at some time is, as we have said, morally engaged: the judger is morally judging in light of her or his own moral norms. But on our view, as we have said, there are no in-the-world moral facts that serve as truth-makers for moral judgments. And such putatively truth-making facts are exactly what the moral relativist is offering us – relative moral facts.

On our view, there can be deep moral disagreements which occur when parties working with conflicting moral norms come to disagree over the moral evaluation of some action, person, or institution. Such moral disagreements, although they do not involving conflicting *descriptive* beliefs, are a matter of conflicting *beliefs* nonetheless – that is, directly incompatible ought-commitments. What happens in such cases is an interesting and no doubt complex matter of interpersonal dynamics which we cannot pursue further here.

MP4: Moral judgments are action-guiding.

Again, our framework for belief and assertion allows us to make sense of this feature of moral phenomenology: as we have already explained, moral ought-commitments are genuine beliefs which, in contrast to non-moral descriptive beliefs, are more directly action-oriented. There is, of course, much more to say about moral psychology and the role that 'ought' judgments play in an individual's psychological economy. We believe we have said enough already to make clear how our view accommodates this feature of moral phenomenology, and we will not here explore the matter further.

MP5: Moral judgments are based on the authority of reasons.

As we have explained, moral thought and discourse is reason-guided evaluative discourse. Moral judgments purport to be grounded in reasons – considerations that count in favor of this or that moral judgment. But what about moral reasons? Is one to suppose that there are in-the-world normative-reason properties and, correlatively, in-the-world reason-facts? No. We think that the same considerations that defeat moral realism will defeat realism about moral reasons. And we propose to understand moral reason judgments in the same sort of way in which we understand first-order moral judgments.

Consider the moral reason judgment, 'You should refuse to give the terminally ill patient the huge dose of sleeping medication he requested, because doing so would kill him.' This judgment has the overall form 'Ought p because q', where q is some non-morally described reason. On our view, such ought-because judgments are a species of moral judgments themselves, and hence our non-descriptivist, non-factualist treatment applies just as much to them as it does to judgments of the form 'Ought p'. The judgment is an ought-commitment with respect to p, while also citing a fact q on which the ought-commitment is based.

MP6: The sorts of reasons that ground moral judgments are of particular importance in the lives of humans.
Of course, more should be said about moral reasons. Perhaps most significant is the fact that moral reasons typically have a special status compared to reasons of other sorts. Judgments of etiquette, for instance, are typically grounded on reasons of etiquette. But clearly there are important differences between reasons of etiquette and moral reasons, differences that we propose to understand in terms of the relative importance of reasons of both sorts. We propose to understand the importance of moral reasons in terms of the sorts of reason that count as moral. Moral reasons concern matters of vital interest to human beings; most generally, they concern fundamental matters of human well-being and respect. It is because they are reasons of this general sort and the role that such considerations play in our lives that we can explain their superior importance vis-à-vis non-moral reasons for action. And their role in our lives also explains why one should take morality seriously.

This concludes our presentation and partial defense of our brand of cognitivist expressivism. Let us now sum up and indicate further work to be done.

Summing Up

Our case on behalf of cognitivist expressivism has involved negative and positive strains of thought. Negatively, we have argued that competing metaethical theories, including versions of factualism and competing versions of non-factualism, have serious problems, and thus that one ought to look for something better. Positively, we have partially developed and defended our own view that combines non-factualism with a particular cognitivist brand of expressivism. After briefly articulating our position within a general framework for belief and assertion that allows the possibility of non-descriptive beliefs, we proceeded to explain how our metaethical theory accommodates deeply embedded moral phenomena – thereby satisfying the moral phenomenology criterion. Our position, as a version of non-factualism, also easily satisfies the coherence criterion: since our view does not countenance any moral properties or moral facts, we need not worry about how such properties and facts fit into a general metaphysics and epistemology.

In order to fully defend our view we would have to elaborate what we have said in this chapter. We would also have to come to grips with other challenges to our view that we have not broached in this chapter, including how our view allows for the possibility of moral error and how it treats logically complex judgments with moral constituents. In some of our other writings (Horgan and Timmons 2000a, 2006, and forthcoming; Timmons 1999) we have developed the position at greater length and have dealt with these additional challenges. We refer our readers to those writings. But in the end, we claim that the most plausible metaethical view going makes sense of morality without any need for a metaphysical anchor: in short, morality without moral facts.

Notes

1   A caveat about our taxonomy. In characterizing relativism and constructivism as factualist views, we only mean to be claiming that the versions of relativism and constructivism *typically discussed* are factualist versions. However, it is possible to combine a non-factualist moral metaphysics with relativism or with constructivism. But we think that the kind of problems that beset factualist versions of these views will, mutatis mutandis, undermine non-factualist versions as well.
2   For purposes of economy, we will not consider non-naturalist versions of moral realism. In the first half of the twentieth century, Moore (1903), Ross (1930), Ewing (1947), and Prichard (1949) were among the most prominent advocates of this kind of view. Having fallen out of philosophical favor for about 60 years, it is now enjoying a revival. See, for example, Shafer-Landau (2003).
3   See Horgan and Timmons (1991, 1992a, 1992b, 1996a, 2000b) and Timmons (1999: ch. 4).
4   For more details about how this objection applies to the constructivism of Smith and of Scanlon, see respectively Horgan and Timmons (1996b) and Timmons (2003).

References

Brink, D. O. (2001). "Realism, naturalism, and moral semantics." *Social Philosophy and Policy*, 18: 154–76.

Boyd, R. (1988). "How to be a moral realist." In G. Sayre-McCord (ed.), *Essays on Moral Realism*. Ithaca: Cornell University Press. Reprinted in S. Darwall, A. Gibbard, and P. Railton (eds.), *Moral Discourse and Practice*. Oxford: Oxford University Press, 1997.

Copp, D. (2001). "Realist expressivism: an overlooked alternative." *Social Philosophy and Policy*, 18: 1–43.

Ewing, A. C. (1947). *The Definition of Good*. New York: The Macmillan Co.

Horgan, T. and Timmons, M. (1991). "New wave moral realism meets moral twin earth." *Journal of Philosophical Research*, 16: 447–65. Reprinted in J. Heil (ed.), *Rationality, Morality and Self-interest*. New York: Rowman & Littlefield, 1993.

Horgan, T. and Timmons, M. (1992a). "Troubles for new wave moral semantics: the open question argument revived." *Philosophical Papers*, 21: 153–75.

Horgan, T. and Timmons, M. (1992b). "Troubles on moral twin earth: moral queerness revived." *Synthese*, 92: 221–60.

Horgan, T. and Timmons, M. (1996a). "From moral realism to moral relativism in one easy step." *Critica*, 28: 3–39.

Horgan, T. and Timmons, M. (1996b). "Troubles for Michael Smith's metaethical rationalism." *Philosophical Papers*, 25: 203–31.

Horgan, T. and Timmons, M. (2000a). "Non-descriptivist cognitivism: outline of a new metaethic." *Philosophical Papers*, 29: 121–53.

Horgan, T. and Timmons, M. (2000b). "Copping out on moral twin earth." *Synthese*, 124: 139–52.

Horgan, T. and Timmons, M. (2006). "Cognitivist expressivism." In Horgan and Timmons (eds.), *Metaethics After Moore*. Oxford: Oxford University Press.

Horgan, T. and Timmons, M. (forthcoming). "Expressivism, yes! relativism, no!" In R. Shafer-Landau (ed.), *Oxford Studies in Metaethics*.

Jackson, F. (1998). *From Metaphysics to Ethics*. Oxford: Oxford University Press.

Lewis, D. (1972). "Psychophysical and theoretical identifications." *Australasian Journal of Philosophy*, 50: 249–58.

Mackie, J. L. (1977). *Ethics: Inventing Right and Wrong*. Harmondsworth, UK: Penguin Books.

Moore, G. E. (1903). *Principia Ethica*. Cambridge: Cambridge University Press.

Prichard, H. A. (1949). *Moral Obligation*. Oxford: Oxford University Press. The papers in this book plus additional papers by Prichard on moral philosophy are contained in H. A. Prichard, *Moral Writings*, ed. J. MacAdam. Oxford: Oxford University Press, 2002.

Railton, P. (1993). "Noncognitivism about rationality: benefits, costs, and an alternative." *Philosophical Issue*, 4: 36–51.

Rawls, J. (1980). "Kantian constructivism in ethics." *Journal of Philosophy*, 77: 515–72.

Rawls, J. (1999). *Collected Papers*, ed. S. Freeman. Cambridge, Mass. and London: Harvard University Press.

Ross, W. D. (1930). *The Right and the Good*. Oxford: Oxford University Press.

Scanlon, T. M. (1998). *What We Owe to Each Other*. Cambridge, Mass.: Harvard University Press.

Shafer-Landau, R. (2003). *Moral Realism: A Defense*. New York and Oxford: Oxford University Press.

Smith, M. (1994). *The Moral Problem*. Oxford: Blackwell.

Timmons, M. (1999). *Morality Without Foundations: A Defense of Ethical Contextualism*. New York and Oxford: Oxford University Press.

Timmons, M. (2003). "The limits of moral constructivism." *Ratio*, XVI, ed. P. Stratton-Lake, pp. 391–423. Repr. in Stratton-Lake, *What We Owe to Each Other*. Oxford: Blackwell, 2004.

Further Reading

Bloomfield, P. (2000). *Moral Reality*. Oxford: Oxford University Press.

Brink, D. O. (1989). *Moral Realism and the Foundations of Ethics*. New York: Cambridge University Press.

Darwall, S., Gibbard, A., and Railton, P. (1997). "Toward *fin de siècle* ethics." *The Philosophical Review*, 101: 115–89. Reprinted in Darwall, Gibbard, and Railton (eds.), *Moral Discourse and Practice*. Oxford: Oxford University Press, 1997.

Hare, R. M. (1952). *The Language of Morals*. Oxford: Oxford University Press.

Harman, G. and Thomson, J. J. (1996). *Moral Relativism and Moral Objectivity*. Oxford: Blackwell.

Stevenson, C. L. (1944). *Ethics and Language*. New Haven: Yale University Press.

Stevenson, C. L. (1963). *Facts and Values*. New Haven: Yale University Press.

Do Moral Facts and Properties Explain Anything?

CHAPTER FOURTEEN

Moral Explanations Defended

Nicholas L. Sturgeon

Although the explicit debate about the acceptability of moral explanations is by philosophical standards a recent one, it is connected with deep issues about the metaphysics and epistemology of morals that have been discussed for a long time. The recent debate began on the epistemological side, with a challenge issued by Gilbert Harman (1977: 3–10). Harman intended to resuscitate, at least for the sake of argument, the positivist view that, when it comes to empirical testability, there is a sharp contrast between ethics and science: that whereas scientific statements can be tested empirically and are sometimes confirmed by experience, ethical statements are immune to empirical test and are never empirically confirmed. In its original positivist formulation this contrast had not fared well. It is true that many ethical views, taken in isolation, lack testable empirical implications; but, as came to be widely acknowledged, so do many respectable scientific hypotheses lack testable empirical implications, when taken in isolation. We do of course test scientific hypotheses empirically, but we do that by taking them not in isolation but instead against a background of complex scientific theory that is already assumed: for, if we take enough scientific assumptions together, they do then have the sort of empirical implications that we can test. But this is true in the ethical case as well: taken against a background that includes enough moral theory, ethical statements turn out to have empirical implications after all, and empirical information can certainly force us, on pain of inconsistency, to revise our ethical views.[1]

What Harman suggested was a different way of spelling out the contrast. It is as true in ethics as in science that we respond to perceived situations with what we may in a weak sense call 'observations', judgments that we form instinctively and without conscious reasoning. To stick to Harman's examples, a physicist seeing a track in a cloud chamber thinks, "There goes a proton"; seeing some hoodlums setting a cat on fire, you think, "That's wrong." The first of these judgments as much as the second depends on extensive training, on a socially inculcated way of looking at such situations. But there is in Harman's view a difference. This is that in the first case we need, in order to explain the physicist's making her judgment, to suppose that there really was a proton passing through the cloud chamber, and thus to accept a physical explanation of a physical judgment; but, he claims, there is by contrast no temptation to think that we need suppose that the hoodlums' action was wrong to explain why you would think it so – no need for a moral explanation of your moral judgment. We may need to assume certain facts about the situation you are observing, such as that the children really are setting a cat on fire, but we can explain your moral judgment without making any assumption about whether it is correct. As Harman says:

> It would seem that all we need assume is that you have certain more or less well articulated moral principles that are reflected in the judgments you make, based on your moral sensibility. It seems to be completely irrelevant to our explanation whether your intuitive immediate judgment is true or false. (1977: 7)[2]

And, he concludes, because of this difference about explanation, the physicist's observation confirms, or counts as evidence, that there really was a proton passing through the cloud chamber, but your thinking the hoodlums' action wrong in no way confirms that it really was wrong.

Harman's explicit target is thus a narrow one: he claims only that supposed moral facts or properties seem irrelevant to the explanation of a particular kind of moral judgment – intuitive judgments in response to perceived situations. It seems fairly clear, however, that if he is right about his examples, then his conclusion must apply more generally, to all moral beliefs: unlike non-moral beliefs, our holding them is never to be explained, even in part, by assuming them to be true. In fact, it appears that he must hold that moral facts are never relevant to the explanation of any non-moral facts that we have any reason to believe in. For if moral facts matter to the explanation of any non-moral facts at all, then it seems that there will also be situations in which they matter to the explanation of moral beliefs. Thus, to take an example that is in fact more difficult for Harman to handle, suppose we were to allow that Hitler's being morally depraved – a moral fact about Hitler's character – plays a role in explaining why Hitler did some of the things he did. Then if an observer, noting those actions, were to think, "What a morally depraved person," it seems that since the depravity helped produce the actions, and the actions helped to produce the belief, the depravity is relevant to the explanation of the belief. So Harman needs to deny that the depravity played any role in producing the actions. (In his contribution to this volume, Nick Zangwill appears to deny that Harman need be committed to this last extension of his thesis. I believe that he is committed to it, but I shall return to this question below.)

Harman's target is narrow in another way, in that his claim is explicitly only about moral judgments and moral explanations. When philosophers have investigated the epistemology of morals – how, if at all, moral judgments can be justified, and how, if at all, there can be moral knowledge – they have usually thought that moral judgments, though distinctive, have a lot in common with evaluative and normative judgments in other areas, such as aesthetics and epistemology itself. It is quite natural, therefore, that recent discussions of moral explanations have considered them as simply one kind of evaluative or normative explanation, and I shall follow that practice here. (And I shall usually refer to the whole category I am interested in simply as 'evaluative explanations'.) Of course, it might be that although there is no difficulty with normative explanations of normative beliefs in epistemology (such as that, sometimes, people come to think that there is good reason to believe some proposition precisely because there really is good reason to believe it), or in aesthetics (for example, that most careful listeners come to prefer Mozart to Bruckner because Mozart was the better composer (Slote 1971)), morality is still somehow different, so that there remains a problem with moral explanations of moral beliefs. But that would be a surprising position, and it would certainly require defense.[3]

Harman has pointed out one way in which whether there are reasonable moral explanations could matter to moral epistemology. If you hold, as he does, that perceptual knowledge requires a state of the perceiver that is explained by the very fact that is perceived, and also that there are, as he argues, no such states with respect to supposed moral facts, then you will have to hold that there is no perceptual knowledge of moral facts. But there are other implications as well, that are in my view more important. Many writers have thought that the justification of many of our beliefs, not just perceptual beliefs, derives from their explanatory role. Thus, for example, the justification of many scientific beliefs is said to lie in their contributing to good explanations of observed evidence. In a similar way, beliefs about the past may owe their justification to their helping to explain more recent evidence that we are aware of, and beliefs about others' psychological states may explain what we observe of their behavior. It is controversial just which beliefs must be justified in this way, but almost everyone agrees that explanatory coherence – the presence of explanatory relations among the propositions one believes – is an epistemic virtue in a set of beliefs, contributing other things equal to its being well justified. And this is thought to be especially so when there is explanatory integration across significantly different categories: beliefs about the past explaining evidence in the present, or beliefs about unobservables explaining what we observe, for example. Now, if evaluative beliefs play a plausible role in explaining other facts we have reason to believe in, facts that are not themselves evaluative, then they will be candidates for justification of a similar sort, by their integrative explanatory role. (Think again of explaining Hitler's actions by reference to his depravity: or, indeed, of many explanations of behavior by reference to moral character.) If all explanations of this sort are mistaken, however, then evaluative beliefs will lack this sort of justification. They might still play a more limited explanatory role, by helping to explain the facts postulated by other evaluative beliefs: for example, that an action deliberately and needlessly caused devastation to innocent persons might help explain why it is wrong. But they would not in this case contribute much to the explanatory integration of one's beliefs.

Even if we were to agree with critics that all evaluative explanations of non-evaluative facts are defective, skepticism about evaluative beliefs would not automatically follow. There are other ways in which they might be justified, and an argument for evaluative skepticism would have to eliminate those other possibilities as well. It would be an exaggeration, moreover, to think that Harman's provisional argument could show ethics to be immune from empirical test (1977: vii): for, whether or not there are perceptions of evaluative facts, evaluative views surely face the sort of empirical test I described in my first paragraph, as do scientific views, and people often change both sorts of views, quite reasonably, in the face of empirical evidence. Still, if our scientific views are sometimes causally responsive to the specific facts they represent, whereas our evaluative views never are, that does seem a striking difference; and this might appear to provide an opening for evaluative skepticism, even if the skeptical argument would require careful development. More seriously, if evaluative beliefs can never be justified by their role in the explanatory integration of our beliefs, then any non-skeptical epistemology for ethics will have to look quite different from the most plausible epistemology for other areas of thought.[4] It is not surprising, therefore, that Harman's argument has drawn criticism, and that one line of criticism has been a defense of the respectability and plausibility of many evaluative explanations.

So far I have focused on the relevance of the debate about evaluative explanations to evaluative epistemology, but there appear to be implications for metaphysics too. Many evaluative explanations of non-evaluative facts look like causal explanations: decency prevents people from doing certain things; injustice, like poverty, can provoke rebellions.[5] And it is hard to see how moral properties like decency and injustice could have these effects unless they were real features of the world. Many philosophers also find it hard to see how they could have such effects in the natural world unless they were themselves natural properties. It is not that miraculous intervention by the non-natural or supernatural in the natural order is inconceivable, but philosophers who take the scientific picture of the natural world seriously do not easily admit this sort of intervention.[6] So the acceptability of these explanations, if they are acceptable, would seem to provide an argument against skeptical views that would deny the existence of such properties,[7] and also an argument that the properties in question are natural ones. Not all will agree: just as empiricists wary of belief in unobservable things have attempted to show how scientists might cite electrons in explanations without really being committed to their existence, so some recent defenders of anti-realist views in ethics have attempted to describe a principled way in which one might deploy evaluative explanations without accepting their apparent metaphysical implications. It is highly controversial whether any of these strategies will work; I have criticized several of them elsewhere and will allude to some of their problems below, but will not attempt a survey. It seems worth noting, however, that the mere fact that anti-realists include evaluative explanations in their attempt to "save the discourse" of ethics, shows how central to that discourse they are taken to be.

What Standard?

As we have seen, Harman asks whether we "need" to appeal to evaluative explanations of non-evaluative facts; I have instead framed the issue as one about whether such explanations are acceptable, or are reasonable to believe. I believe that my formulation is preferable. If it is reasonable to believe these explanations, that is enough to insure the explanatory integration of evaluative with other beliefs, and to secure the appearance of a commitment to real evaluative properties. Whether we need evaluative explanations has usually been taken to depend on whether any non-evaluative explanation of the same facts might be better. But the comparative evaluation of explanations is difficult and seems context-sensitive, in that different explanations may be better for different purposes (see Wright 1992: 189–91). When different, plausible explanations are mutually compatible, moreover, it doesn't matter which is better: we can believe them both. And evaluative explanations are typically quite compatible with the non-evaluative explanations with which philosophers have compared them: comparing an evaluative explanation of the rise of opposition to slavery with a carefully non-evaluative one is often in this respect quite unlike comparing, say, religious with secular explanations of apparent miracles (Sturgeon 1992). Of course, we might still be suspicious of evaluative explanations if they never had distinctive insight to contribute; I shall say something about this below.

Evaluating Explanations

What, then, should we make of evaluative explanations of non-evaluative facts? They will of course all look implausible to anyone who is already skeptical about evaluation on other grounds. Just as explanations appealing to God's activity will be rejected by anyone who is already a convinced atheist, so moral explanations will be rejected by anyone who is already a thorough moral skeptic. But if our interest is in whether evaluative explanations are themselves the source of a basic, independent problem about ethics, a problem without a parallel in the scientific case – that is, if it is like Harman's interest – then the answer has to be that many such explanations strike most people as very plausible. It is commonplace to explain people's actions by appeal to moral states of character, good and bad, just as it is commonplace to hear social revolutions – some of them, at any rate – attributed to the combined effects of poverty and injustice. The characters in Plato's *Republic* argue about whether being a just person makes one's life go better or worse; though they disagree about what justice is, none of them doubts that justice is the sort of trait that could have this kind of effect. (Nor have I ever had a student encountering the *Republic* object that justice could not make this sort of difference.) Other plausible examples have been given above or will be considered below.

But what about Harman's example in which, recall, you see children setting a cat on fire and respond with the thought, "That's wrong"? It can certainly seem that he is right in this case that, to explain your judgment, we need make no assumption about whether your judgment is correct: that "all we need assume is that you have certain more or less well articulated moral principles that are reflected in the judgments you make, based on your moral sensibility." Your principles condemn as wrong, we assume, intense and pointless cruelty to an innocent victim; so, so long as the action continued to have that feature, you, with your principles, would have thought it wrong even if it wasn't. That's how Harman can seem right about the example. The problem, though, is that a closely parallel and equally plausible line of thought would lead to a similar conclusion about the case Harman intends to contrast with this one, involving the physicist and that proton. Given her training and the theory that she has internalized, the physicist would have thought, "There's a proton," at the sight of a vapor trail, whether the trail had been produced by a proton or not: so it looks as if assumptions about the proton are *not* needed, after all, to explain her observational judgment. Thus, we don't on this understanding of the examples get the contrast between the ethical and the scientific case that Harman was looking for, for we end up skeptics about both.

Here it helps to remember, though, that there are different reasonable ways of assessing explanations, for on one of them we can make the proton matter after all. If we are not primarily concerned with offering the *safest* possible explanation (that is, the one with the least chance of being mistaken), and if in the interest of fitting the physicist's judgment into a broad physical picture of the world we are willing to trust her theory about protons (which is after all a reasonable theory), then we may think as follows: if there had not been a proton there would not have been a vapor trail (since that is what her reasonable theory tells us), and if there hadn't been a vapor trail she wouldn't have thought, "There goes a proton." So the proton helps to explain her judgment after all. Now the problem for Harman is that we appear to be able to do a similar thing with the ethical case. If we are not primarily concerned with sticking to the safest explanation, and if in the interest of fitting your judgment into a broader moral picture of the world we are willing to trust the central features of your moral outlook (which, since we are not already moral skeptics, we regard as a reasonable outlook), then we may think as follows: for the children's action not to have been wrong, it would have had to lack the feature of being an act of intense and pointless cruelty to an innocent victim (since that is what your reasonable outlook tells us), and if it had lacked that feature you might well not have thought it wrong. So it is not true that you would have thought their action wrong whether or not it was really wrong, and so it is also not true that its wrongness is irrelevant to the explanation of your thinking it wrong. If like most people you are at least reasonably sensitive to the difference between right and wrong actions, then your views about which sort of action you are confronting will vary, often accurately, as you consider different cases.

Now, it is controversial whether this last reply, concerning the ethical case, is adequate as it stands: those who think that evaluative properties might be epiphenomenal have denied that the truth of the counterfactual judgment – that if the action hadn't been wrong, you wouldn't have thought that it was wrong – is sufficient by itself to show that the wrongness of the action influenced your judgment (Harman 1986: 63; Thomson 1996: 79–82). So I shall turn to the question of epiphenomenalism shortly. Notice, though, that what we have seen so far is that the only understanding of the ethical example on which it *clearly* leads to the skeptical conclusion Harman wants is one which, if applied to the scientific case, leads to a skeptical result there as well. This fact, combined with the initial plausibility of so many examples of evaluative explanations, certainly gives point to the question to which I now turn: What, according to the critics, is supposed to be wrong with such explanations?

Supervenience and Epiphenomenalism

Critics have raised a wide variety of objections to evaluative explanations, too varied in their details for me to consider them all here. Crucial to many of the published

Moral Explanations Defended

objections, however, is an argument that begins with an appeal to the widely accepted view that I shall call the supervenience thesis, that evaluative properties *supervene* on the natural properties of the things that have them, and concludes that the causal efficacy we attribute to the evaluative properties should really be attributed to those natural properties instead. (Sometimes the conclusion is, more cautiously, merely that we have not been given good reason to attribute causal efficacy to evaluative properties themselves, rather than to the natural properties on which they supervene.) So we need to examine this argument in detail (Quinn 1986: 525–37; Audi 1997: 112–28; Thomson 1996: 73–91).[8]

'Supervenience' is the technical name for a relation of necessary covariance among properties. A set of properties A supervenes on a set of properties B just in case, necessarily, no objects can differ with respect to A unless they differ with respect to B as well; or, equivalently, objects alike with respect to the properties in B are necessarily alike with respect to those in A. Although it is not an implication of this definition, it is often also assumed that the A properties, the supervening properties, depend on the B properties, the base properties, but not vice versa; although I think a different term should be used to mark this additional assumption (perhaps 'constitution' or 'realization'), I shall here simply take it to be part of supervenience.[9] The standard thesis about supervenience that concerns us, then, is typically put by saying that the evaluative properties of anything supervene on its natural properties. Intuitively, this means that things that differ in their evaluative properties must differ in their natural properties, and that things owe their evaluative properties to their natural ones. The problem for evaluative explanations is then supposed to be this. Whenever we have a case in which the presence of an evaluative property appears to lead to some natural effect – for example, in which injustice provokes a revolution – there are, the supervenience thesis assures us, natural properties sufficient to *make* the society unjust. (For example, there may be some specific distribution of benefits and burdens in the society that does this.) But these natural features, by themselves, seem sufficient to explain the revolution, along with any other effects we were attributing to the injustice; and the evaluative property, the injustice, seems unneeded for any causal or explanatory role of its own. The natural base properties make the society unjust, and they bring about the effects we were tempted to ascribe to the injustice, but the injustice itself does nothing. It is thus *epiphenomenal*, meaning that though it is produced by underlying properties that play a causal role in the world, it plays no such role itself.[10] So it is misleading to cite the injustice in our explanation of the revolution – *unless* doing so is simply shorthand for referring to the base natural properties on which the injustice supervenes.[11]

Supervenience?

What, then, to make of this argument that evaluative properties are epiphenomenal? I have several comments. The first is that the supervenience principle itself is more doubtful than commonly supposed. Writers usually introduce it as if it were obvious, but almost no one stops to defend it.[12] (In the past, this has included me.) I have come to think, however, that it is very hard to formulate an acceptable statement of the doctrine. At the very least, I believe, there is no version of the doctrine that is both (a) substantive enough to do the work that this argument requires of it and (b) neutral, in the sense of being dialectically acceptable to all of the metaethical views that are in fact taken seriously in philosophical debate. This claim requires more defense than I shall give it here, but here is an indication of the problem. First, if one thinks (as ethical naturalists do, and as I do) that evaluative properties are themselves natural, then the supervenience of evaluative properties on *natural* ones becomes obvious but trivial. It is obvious because any subset of the base properties of course supervenes on the whole set; it is trivial because it doesn't imply any of the conclusions usually associated with supervenience, and that proponents of this argument want to rely on, such as that evaluative properties depend on other properties or that we need to have reasons for ascribing them to things.[13] We can perhaps dodge this difficulty by noting that, when philosophers say that the evaluative supervenes on the natural, they are often using the term 'natural' in a way that is in one respect broader, but in another narrower, than one might expect (and than I have just done). It is used in a broader sense because 'natural' properties here include supernatural ones. Proponents of the supervenience thesis tend not to regard it as refuted, for example, by the possibility that an act, fixed in its this-worldly properties, might be right if permitted by God but wrong if forbidden. As context makes clear, however, what they typically mean by the supervenience doctrine is not exactly that evaluative properties supervene on all the natural and supernatural properties there are, either, but something more restrictive: namely, that evaluative properties supervene on all the *non-evaluative* properties, whether natural or supernatural. (This formulation will avoid the problem I raised earlier in this paragraph, since it guarantees that the evaluative properties cannot be a subset of the 'natural' ones – that is, the non-evaluative ones.[14])

So take this as the intended principle: that evaluative properties supervene on non-evaluative ones. (I shall now reclaim the term 'natural', using it henceforth as I have throughout this essay, to mean something that contrasts with 'supernatural', and certainly not as equivalent to 'non-evaluative'.) But then there will be another difficulty, unless we have ruled out the sort of reductive view according to which goodness is not just a natural property but a natural property for which we have a non-evaluative term: the view, say, that goodness is identical to pleasure. (G. E. Moore thought that he had shown how to refute such views; one reason they are still in contention is that his refutations are widely regarded as defective (1903: 1–27; for discussion, see Sturgeon 2003).) For, notice, for the proponent of this sample view our new version of the supervenience principle will have to be understood to imply that evaluative properties (including pleasure, which, being identical with an evaluative property, is of course evaluative) supervene on other properties that do *not* include pleasure (since it is an evaluative property, and so of course not a non-evaluative one). But it is far from obvious that this is true; why can't we imagine experiences otherwise exactly alike that differ in how pleasant they are?[15]

A way to avoid some of these problems, and thus perhaps a better bet to capture what proponents of the supervenience principle have had in mind, would be to avoid talking about non-evaluative properties and instead talk about properties that we represent by non-evaluative predicates. The principle would then say that evaluative properties (that is, the ones we represent by evaluative terms) supervene on properties that we represent by non-evaluative terms. This requires that evaluative properties, even if they are natural, supervene on ones that we can represent non-evaluatively; so it promises to make sense of the idea that we must have non-evaluative *reasons* for ascribing evaluative properties to things. Furthermore, it does not preclude evaluative properties from belonging to the supervenience base (though it does not require this, either). But it faces a different problem of its own. For now that we have brought language into the story, a lot will depend on the expressive power of our language. Consider a version of ethical non-naturalism that says that evaluative properties, which are not natural, supervene on a base that includes all the natural properties. *This* is of course not a neutral version of the supervenience principle, for no ethical naturalist would accept it. But from the point of view of someone who accepts this non-naturalist position, our latest attempt at a neutrally acceptable version of the supervenience principle could appear equally unacceptable. For there is no guarantee that we possess non-evaluative terms for all the natural properties that there are. And, if we do not, then this non-naturalist position could be correct even though our newest attempt is mistaken. For there could be natural differences that make an evaluative difference, but for which we have no non-evaluative terminology.[16]

Now, I have undoubtedly not exhausted all possibilities. So there may for all this be a version of the supervenience thesis that is correct and interesting. But I have indicated why there is room for doubt. At the very least, anyone who wants to rely on the thesis owes us an account of precisely which version she thinks is correct, and why. In the absence of such a defense, the supervenience thesis cannot be treated as obvious.

Proving Too Much?

Suppose, however, that we were to find a satisfactory version of the supervenience thesis. Even so, there would remain another problem for the epiphenomenalist argument, this time one of which a number of its proponents are aware (Quinn 1986: 528–9; Audi 1997: 117; Thomson 1996: 79–80n).[17] This is that the argument threatens to prove too much. For there are other kinds of properties besides evaluative ones that are commonly taken to supervene on properties of some other sort. For example, physicalists take psychological properties to supervene on physical ones; they furthermore take the base physical properties to be sufficient to produce the effects commonly attributed to psychological states (for example, a case in which someone winces, as we think, from pain); but they almost always resist the conclusion that psychological properties are epiphenomenal or that psychological explanations of physical effects are all mistaken. It is not that there is an agreed solution to this problem. There are instead a wide variety of proposals, all facing some objections. But almost no one is willing to conclude that psychological states are inefficacious. And there are many similar examples in other areas: social properties and biological properties, for example. So here is the problem. Any philosopher who wants to argue that evaluative properties are epiphenomenal, on the ground that they supervene on properties that are themselves sufficient to explain any effects we might be tempted to attribute to the evaluative properties, but who refuses to draw the parallel conclusion in these other cases, owes us a justification for what looks suspiciously like a double standard. (Furthermore, given the unsettled state of the debate about the causal efficacy of psychological properties, it cannot be a serious objection to the defender of evaluative explanations if she does not have, at this point, an obviously correct, widely agreed-upon account of *how* evaluative properties are efficacious even though they supervene on other properties that also look efficacious; for no one has an obviously correct, widely agreed-upon account of how that happens in the other cases, either.)

A Rejoinder

Critics of evaluative explanations have responded in more than one way to this challenge. I am going to focus on the reply that seems to have been the most influential.[18] It points out the following difference between the supervenience of the evaluative and the other cases. Although psychological properties may supervene on physical ones, we typically do not know what these physical properties are, and we certainly do not normally assign psychological properties to people on the basis of our knowledge or beliefs about the physical ones. In the evaluative case it is quite otherwise. We normally base evaluative beliefs on reasons, and those reasons typically point to features of the object evaluated that contribute to making the evaluation correct – that is, to features of the supervenience base. If we think a government unjust, that will almost always be because of some features of the government that we think *make* it unjust. Because of this difference, moreover, anyone who is tempted to offer an evaluative explanation – for example, that the injustice of the government helped to cause a rebellion against it – is in a good position to replace this evaluative explanation with a non-evaluative one, merely by replacing the reference to injustice with a reference to those non-evaluative features, whatever they are, that the injustice is thought to supervene on. As Warren Quinn puts it, our moral outlook, "in presupposing a rich supply of naturalistic concepts, contains the full-blown means by which its own explanations may be put aside" (1986: 530). By contrast, nothing like this is possible in the other acknowledged cases in which we appeal to supervenient properties in explanation.

A Complaint

I have two independent, and quite different, complaints about this reply. The first is that although it is true that we normally base our evaluative beliefs on reasons that cite features we think help make the evaluation correct, it is not true that this is obviously a route to non-evaluative explanations that can replace an evaluative one. For the reasons on which we base evaluative conclusions are often themselves evaluative. I suggested above that if the action in Harman's example, in which some children set a cat on fire, is wrong, this is because it involves intense and pointless cruelty to an innocent victim. So, instead of explaining your believing the action wrong by citing the action's wrongness, we could try explaining it by noting that the action is an instance of intense and pointless cruelty to an innocent victim (and that you think actions of that sort wrong). We would not by this maneuver have replaced a moral explanation by a non-moral one, however. For 'pointless' and 'innocent' here are themselves moral terms.[19] (As a first approximation, I take 'pointless' to mean 'lacking any point that could justify it' and 'innocent' to mean 'having done nothing to deserve this sort of treatment'.) A similar problem can be illustrated by one of Robert Audi's examples. He suggests that instead of citing injustice as the cause of a revolution, we might cite the factors we think make the society unjust: "say, government seizure of land, arbitrary curfews, and police brutality" (1997: 118). But which curfews are arbitrary and which police actions brutal are clearly still evaluative questions, so this is not yet an illustration of how to replace an evaluative explanation with a non-evaluative one.[20]

Audi is sensitive to this difficulty, for his sentence continues with a qualification that appears to be intended to deal with it. In our substitute explanation, he says, the seizure of land, arbitrary curfews and police brutality are to be "construed behaviorally in terms of, for example, soldiers' occupying farmland, clearing streets at night and clubbing non-protestors" (ibid.). But behaviorism is false and I do not believe that there is any purely behavioral account of brutality; when people resent brutality, in any case, part of what they resent is normally the perceived intent of the brutalizer. What Audi needs, moreover, is not that the account be purely behavioral but that it be purely non-evaluative, while at the same time – because supervenience is defined in terms of *necessity* – sufficient to guarantee that the society is unjust.[21] The account suggested here does not come close to meeting these conditions: soldiers can seize land as part of an enlightened and just program of land reform and can clear the streets of the enemies of justice. And when we add the detail needed to eliminate these possibilities, it is far from obvious that we will be able to do so without resorting again to explicitly evaluative terminology. What anyone pursuing this strategy needs to hold, therefore, is that whenever someone uses a piece of evaluative terminology in an explanation, there is, at least in principle, and at least for the speaker in question, a way of formulating a sufficient condition for the correct application of that terminology in purely non-evaluative terms. But whether this is possible has been widely questioned. It is often extremely difficult to accomplish in practice. And doubt about whether it is always possible even in principle forms part of the reasonable doubt I mentioned above, about whether we possess non-evaluative terminology adequate to represent all the natural properties there are.[22] Thus, there is no guarantee, and indeed there is considerable reason to doubt, that turning to the supervenience base of evaluative properties is always a way of locating non-evaluative explanations to replace evaluative ones.

This point can also help illustrate a question I promised to return to: how evaluative explanations can be not just credible, but in some cases especially illuminating. A good causal explanation needs to describe a cause at the right level of abstraction, including relevant detail while excluding the irrelevant.[23] That is why, even granting that slavery was unjust, it can be reasonable to ask whether the American anti-slavery movement is best described as responding to slavery's injustice or, instead, only to some specific way or ways that it was unjust. The answer presumably depends largely on how it did, or would have, responded to different forms of injustice: a fascinating question in this case, given its sometime alliance with other reform causes and especially its initial marriage to, and subsequent divorce from, the women's rights movement.[24] The answer might be that a more specific explanation is better, or it might be that the explanation that appeals to the injustice of slavery is better. And in *either* case, as we have seen, it may well be that the only terminology we have for characterizing the cause at the right level of abstraction is evaluative. *Neither* of these questions – about the right level of abstraction, and about what kind of language we have for capturing that level – is one that can be settled a priori. In my judgment, many evaluative explanations look promising in this regard. What I take to be even more certain is that we do not know a priori that they are not.[25]

Another Complaint

Suppose, though, that I am wrong in this first complaint: suppose, that is, that we can always find a way adequately to characterize the supervenience base for evaluative properties in non-evaluative terms. There is still another difficulty with the reply we are considering. It is that that it simply seems the wrong sort of suggestion to solve the problem. Our difficulty, remember, was that the argument for the epiphenomenality of evaluative properties appeared to prove too much. For there are many other supervenient properties as well, and it does not seem plausible to regard them all as causally inefficacious. The reply we are considering points to a difference between the cases: in the evaluative case, we typically know, or at least have a good idea of, what the base properties are, whereas in the other cases, such as that of psychological properties supervening on physical ones, we do not. But my question is: how is this difference in our *knowledge* supposed to make a difference to whether supervenient properties play a causal role in the world? Is the idea that if we came to know the base physical properties, and to ascribe psychological properties on their basis, then psychological properties, which are now causally relevant, would cease to be so? I do not find that believable. And if the difference in our knowledge does not make any difference to the causal roles of the supervenient properties in the two cases, I do not see how it can make any difference to the appropriateness of citing those properties in explanations.

My survey has been brief, and I have undoubtedly slighted considerations to which others would give more weight. On the whole, however, I do not think that anyone has made a plausible case for thinking all evaluative properties epiphenomenal.

Explaining Evaluative Beliefs

I will conclude with a few comments on the unusual position defended by Nick Zangwill in his contribution to this volume. Zangwill accepts evaluative explanations of many things, but denies that evaluative facts ever explain our beliefs in those facts.[26] Thus, he does not deny the reality of evaluative properties, since they are real enough to produce non-evaluative effects in the world. Nor, very importantly, does his view prevent evaluative beliefs from deriving justification from their integrative explanatory role.

Still, his seems a difficult position to defend. If Hitler's depravity could shape world-historical events, as Zangwill grants, it seems odd to think that it couldn't play any causal role in producing what is, by comparison, a much smaller effect, my coming to think Hitler depraved. Again, it is easy to think of cases where evaluative facts appear to play a role in producing false beliefs, so it is surprising to be told that they never help produce true ones.[27] On a larger scale, we can perhaps imagine or even find limited examples of the sort of situation Zangwill envisions, in which an object has an evaluative property, and people have many true beliefs about that property, but the property itself plays no role in producing the beliefs. But such cases seem rather special. Joseph Horowitz describes an approximation to one in his book on Arturo Toscanini (1987). According to Horowitz, Toscanini was a great conductor, and, in addition, a good part of the American public from the 1920s through the 1940s believed that he was – but his excellence as a conductor was no part of the explanation of their belief. Toscanini's fame, on Horowitz's telling, was instead due to such factors as the promotional skills of RCA president David Sarnoff,[28] the need of a culturally insecure New World audience for an Old World culture-god, and even Toscanini's relatively early and highly publicized opposition to fascism. In defense of his thesis, Horowitz cites a great deal of evidence about American cultural history during this period. Now, on Zangwill's view, it appears that we are *all* in the position, with respect to *all* evaluative facts, that Horowitz claims that some Americans were with respect to Toscanini's greatness: these facts obtain, and we often believe that they do, but their obtaining never plays any role in producing our beliefs. It also seems that, on Zangwill's view, Horowitz could have saved himself a lot of work, if only he had realized that a more general version of his thesis, and a less hedged one,[29] could be established a priori, without any of that hard research into cultural history. But this, again, is an implausible consequence. I am not persuaded that Horowitz could have saved himself work by consulting Zangwill's argument.

We can avoid these paradoxical implications, of course, if we hold, as I suggest we should, that evaluative properties can play a role in causing our beliefs about them, and in causing our knowledge of them, just as they cause other things.[30] But I believe that we should acknowledge, at the same time, an epistemological point that appears central to Zangwill's argument, and that he quite rightly sees as raising a question I need to address. This is that causal encounters with the world – whether or not we think of them as involving causation by evaluative properties – can have this sort of effect only on a believer who already knows, or believes, quite a bit about how the evaluative properties in question fit into the world. This point is simply the generalization of something Harman says, correctly, about moral "observations": that they are all theory-laden, in that they can only be made by someone who already knows, or at least implicitly believes, a great deal about evaluative matters. I believe that Zangwill thinks that I must deny this, but I do not deny it. When moral and other evaluative facts cause corresponding beliefs in us about those facts, on my view, they don't do it by reaching out and grabbing our minds in some ghostly way. Instead, they work through our ingrained moral and evaluative outlooks. And one consequence of this thesis is that the only way evaluative facts can act on us to produce *knowl-*

edge of those facts is for our ingrained outlook already to include a lot that is not just "outlook," but is in fact knowledge, what we might call background evaluative knowledge. Zangwill I and disagree about whether, when evaluative knowledge arises in this way, we should credit evaluative facts or properties themselves with a role in causing us to have knowledge of them. But I agree with him that this picture raises a pressing epistemological question, namely: where does that background evaluative knowledge come from? For me to say merely that it comes from other instances in which we have made evaluative observations, or more generally other cases in which evaluative facts have produced in us knowledge of those facts, seems just to push the problem back a stage. For, on this picture, we needed already to have background evaluative knowledge before we could gain knowledge from *those* encounters with evaluative facts, as well. So how do we even get started?[31]

This is a fair question – though, one might note, similar to questions that philosophers inclined to foundationalism in epistemology are always asking those whose approach to knowledge and justification is more holistic. Here is the sketch of an answer. On the view I favor, we begin with a wide array of evaluative views on many issues, and we refine them by playing them off against one another and against empirical evidence, in a search for what John Rawls calls reflective equilibrium (1971: §9). It may be that none of these views is initially an instance of knowledge: some of them are false, and the true ones may fall short of that title in being produced by a procedure that is too haphazard in its results to count as reliable. (Where do we – collectively – get these initial views? According to me, it doesn't much matter. Maybe we have innate tendencies to think in these ways, or perhaps there is some other explanation.) If, however, we are fortunate enough to start with views that, taken as a whole, are close enough to the truth, and in the right way, that refining them in this manner will bring us even closer to the truth, then at some point this procedure will become reliable enough in producing true rather than false beliefs that the true beliefs so produced count as knowledge. Evaluative observations and, more generally, cases in which (as I maintain) evaluative facts or properties play a role in causing our evaluative beliefs, are one element in this mix, but they do not have a privileged role. Precisely because they are theory laden, they can go wrong when they are based on mistaken evaluative theories, and we can always in principle question the theories. But when the whole procedure is working properly, they, and the background beliefs on which they rely, may count as knowledge all the same.

This is, as I say, a sketch: qualifications would be needed to address, among other things, familiar objections to reliabilist accounts of knowledge. But, the last point I will make, none of the qualifications would be special to the evaluative case. For I would defend the same general account of knowledge for the scientific case, and in response to the same problem. For, as Harman again emphasizes, and as I again agree, observation in scientific cases is also theory-laden. A physicist can't see that a proton is passing through a cloud chamber without already knowing a lot of physics. Zangwill emphasizes differences between evaluative and scientific examples, and it is true that in the evaluative case the theory a perceiver (or believer) has to know will normally connect an evaluative fact with its supervenience base, whereas in the scientific case this is not always so. But, despite that difference, the same epistemological problem arises. If scientific observation depends on background theory, and thus yields knowledge of what is observed only when the background theory is something we know, then where does that background knowledge come from? Saying that it comes from other observations we have made seems just to push the problem back a stage, if those observations too are theory-laden.[32] So the problem is much the same. And so is my answer. Scientific thinking consists in adjusting a wide array of theoretical views we already tentatively hold against one another and against empirical evidence in a search for reflective equilibrium.[33] If we are fortunate enough to have started with views that, taken as a whole, are enough in the neighborhood of the truth, and in the right ways, so that refining them in this way will bring us even closer to the truth, then this procedure can become reliable enough in producing true rather than false beliefs that the true ones count as knowledge. This knowledge can serve as the background to theory-laden observations, which can thus also count as knowledge. Such observations and, more generally, cases in which (as we think) physical properties play a causal role in producing our beliefs about those properties, are one element in the mix of views that we adjust against one another, but they do not have a privileged role. Precisely because they are theory laden, they can go wrong when they are based on mistaken physical theories, and we can always in principle question the theories. (As above, this is a sketch, but it gives the general idea.)

There is then the question of whether our procedures really *are* reliable. I believe that we have good reason to think that on the whole they are, in both cases, but that is an argument for another occasion. My conclusion here is just that, so long as we are not already evaluative skeptics, we do have reason for thinking of some of our evaluative beliefs as caused by the evaluative facts they represent – indeed, as perceptions of those facts – but that the epistemological implications of this view are not as simple as they might seem.

Notes

1 For illustrations, see Sturgeon (1988: 231–2).

2 Note that in some debates among historians, rather than philosophers, an explanation that attributed an important causal role to people's moral convictions might be called a moral explanation, just as an explanation that attributed an important role to religious convictions might be called a religious explanation. But that wouldn't count as a moral explanation for the purpose of Harman's challenge or in the subsequent debate. What is understood here by a moral explanation is one that appeals to the truth of some moral judgment as part of an explanation.

3 Harman appears initially to have thought that judgments about reasons and reasonableness are immune to the difficulties he alleges for moral judgments: for his proposed remedy for the apparent explanatory irrelevance of moral judgments is to reduce those judgments to judgments about reasons, which will then be explanatory (1977: 125–33). Many other writers have thought, however, that if there is a problem about evaluative explanations it applies equally to all judgments about reasons (that is, good or justifying reasons) and reasonableness. See, for example, Gibbard (1990: ch. 6).

4 Even here it is possible to ask just *how* different evaluative epistemology would have to be. I have suggested (Sturgeon 1998: 200–2) that even if evaluative explanations are mistaken because all evaluative properties are epiphenomenal – a view I consider below –

there might be an epistemic virtue in "epi-explanatory" coherence and integration in one's beliefs. But moral epistemology would certainly be more straightforward if there were no need for this expedient.

5   By contrast, my sample evaluative explanation of an evaluative fact – that an act deliberately and needlessly brought devastation on innocent persons helps explain why it is wrong – does not seems causal. That is an additional reason for focusing on evaluative explanations of non-evaluative facts. (For an attempt to assimilate even evaluative explanations of evaluative facts to causal explanations, see Pietroski 1993).

6   I speculate that this may help explain why some philosophers who accept the reality of moral properties (on other grounds) have wanted to deny the causal role of moral properties and the acceptability of moral explanations; they find the implied ethical naturalism implausible. (Of course, as we shall see, they offer other reasons as well). See Audi (1997: 112–28); Thomson (1996: 65–154).

7   Two points about my terminology in this essay. First, some nominalists reject evaluative properties not because they are evaluative but because they are properties. But standard defenses of nominalism maintain that it can through various devices accommodate all the useful things other philosophers are able to say by talking of properties: so I shall talk of properties and let others accommodate as they choose. Second, whenever I speak for brevity of a property's playing a causal role in the world, I have in mind the fact or event of the property's being exemplified at a specific time and place.

8   (Quinn (1986) does not speak specifically of supervenience, but his examples of how to replace moral explanations with better non-moral ones all appeal to properties the moral ones are taken to supervene on. When he considers the objection that his version of the "explanatory test" proves too much, by ruling out other things we believe, his examples are of other supervenient properties (e.g., colors).) This is also one line, but not the only line, considered by Blackburn (1993: 198–209). It is a crucial component in a complex view, quite different from the others mentioned here, proposed by Wright. Wright thinks that a minimalist, anti-realist account of truth in ethics can accommodate those effects of moral properties that consist in, or proceed by way of, our awareness of those properties, but he grants that there may be some effects of, say, injustice, that occur independently of anyone's being aware of an act or system's being unjust. These he proposes to accommodate by attributing them to the natural, non-evaluative features that make the act or system unjust (1992: 195–8).

I have not sharply distinguished here, because as a group these writers do not, between the view that (a) evaluative explanations are mistaken, and should be replaced with explanations that appeal only to the natural properties on which the evaluative ones supervene, and the view that (b) evaluative explanations are often correct, but should be understood to say no more than that certain effects are produced by the natural properties on which the evaluative ones supervene. Quinn comes closest to simply affirming (a). Audi thinks that moral explanations are acceptable when they are "naturalized in the (indirect) sense that they point us to explanations in terms of the natural base properties whose presence is their ground" (1997: 123). Thomson thinks moral explanations are mistaken (or, at least, that no one has shown that they are not), but proposes to accommodate much of the usage of those who offer such explanations by taking them to be appealing to the natural properties on which the moral ones supervene. Though she does not say, it may be that she thinks of this as a kind of "speaker's meaning" for such utterances, as opposed to their linguistic meaning (1998: 215–22). Blackburn's entire project is to accommodate, rather than reject, evaluative explanations within an evaluatively irrealist framework. Wright says of an explanation of a rebellion by appeal to injustice, that it is not "misplaced" (1992:

196), but adds about this "manner of speaking" that "without condemning [it] as wrong, we must at least acknowledge that it blurs a distinction" (ibid. 197).

It will not matter much whether one holds (a) or (b) if the implications are the same for the metaphysical and epistemological issues I mentioned above. Though none of these writers explicitly addresses the issue, those who waver between (a) and (b) appear to assume that the implications will be the same. There is some plausibility to this for the metaphysical issues: on either (a) or (b) we appear to lose the reason such explanations seemed to provide for taking evaluative properties themselves to be part of the natural causal order. As I have mentioned above, there is room for more doubt about whether the epistemological implications are the same, but I shall not pursue that here.

9   I pass over technical distinctions that do not matter to the discussion here; but I take the form of supervenience in question to be what Kim (1993: 53–78) calls strong supervenience.

10 There is an older understanding of the term 'epiphenomenal' that restricts it to events or facts that are *caused* but do not, in turn, cause anything themselves. Audi appeals to this understanding in denying that his view makes evaluative properties epiphenomenal: the natural properties of the society don't *cause* the injustice, even thought they are what make it unjust (1997: 122). But in recent debates the term has come to be used more broadly, to cover supervenient properties that are fixed (even if not caused) by base properties but are causally inert.

11 We can also see, now, why someone who regards evaluative properties as epiphenomenal will think it a bad test for the causal influence of such properties simply to ask whether, if the evaluative property had been different, the effect would have been different too. It might well be true in the kind of case we have been considering that, if the society hadn't been unjust, there wouldn't have been a revolution. For, since the injustice supervenes on natural properties, those properties would have had to be different in order for the society to be just; and that difference might have been enough to prevent the revolution. But, according to the epiphenomenalist, that merely shows that the truth of the counterfactual judgment is not enough to show that the injustice caused anything.

12 G. E. Moore (1959) defends a very special (and controversial) version of the thesis that applies only to intrinsic value (and not to other ethical properties), claiming that it supervenes entirely on the intrinsic properties of its bearers. For some reasons for doubting Moore's thesis, see Sturgeon (2003: 528–56). W. D. Ross argues that ethical properties are "consequential" (1934: 121–2). R. M. Hare argues for the supervenience of the evaluation expressed by "good picture" (1952: 80–6; cf. p. 145). Even these arguments are brief. Partly because they all assume that ethical naturalism can be dismissed rather easily, none of them addresses the sort of problems I mention here.

13 Audi refuses to count a subset of the base properties as supervening on the base (1997: 120–1). Obviously, this is primarily a verbal point – one can define supervenience with this restriction or without it. But readers of Hare will remember that he introduces naturalism about value – in his example, the idea that the goodness of a painting just is one among its natural properties – as a possible explanation for the supervenience of the painting's goodness on its natural properties. (Of course, he rejects this explanation. But he doesn't deny that this would be a case of supervenience (1952: 80–6).) Kim (1993) also defines supervenience without this restriction.

14 That is, it guarantees this so long as there *are* some evaluative properties, so that the set of them is not empty.

15 I believe that pleasure does supervene on properties other than pleasure (and so does that other candidate Moore considered, being what we desire to desire), because I accept the

physicalist view that psychological properties such as these supervene on physical properties. But, as is commonly remarked, this physicalist supervenience thesis is not a priori, and some philosophers reject it.

16 Why think that we might lack terms for some natural properties? Well, natural properties are usually understood to be the kind of properties dealt with by the sciences. But the sciences are always introducing terms for properties not previously recognized, and there is no reason to think that this process is or ever will be at an end. Some philosophers attempt to get around this difficulty by talking about the vocabulary not of, say, physics, but of 'ideal physics' or 'completed physics' (and so for other sciences). But they need to say more than they typically do about why we should think that any science could ever be "completed" in the way that they need. To mention just one problem, noted by Richard Boyd in an unpublished manuscript ("Materialism without reductionism: non-Humean causation and the evidence for physicalism") there are on the usual understanding only countably many predicates in any language, but according to the best physics we now have, there are some continuous physical parameters. So there are (it appears) more physical properties than there are predicates in any language.

. The idea that there may be natural properties for which we lack non-ethical terminology has recently become a familiar one for philosophers. It was a common idea among early non-cognitivists such as Charles Stevenson (1944) and Hare that there are some ethical terms that combine the action-guiding role that non-cognitivism takes as central with some descriptive, naturalistic content. It was also a common non-cognitivist assumption that these terms for what Bernard Williams has called "thick" ethical concepts (such as being honorable or brutal or courageous) could be factored into the two elements, one describing a natural property in non-evaluative terms, the other performing a purely non-cognitive function. But Williams agrees with John McDowell (1998: 50–73) that we may lack terminology subtle enough to carry out this factoring: he agrees, that is, that we may lack austerely non-evaluative terminology for representing the natural properties picked out by some ethical terms. This view has, moreover, been highly influential. See Williams (1985: 129, 140–2). (I have discussed this issue in "Moore and ethical naturalism" (2003) and in "Ethical naturalism" (forthcoming), from which I have here borrowed a few sentences.)

Kim also mentions problems with trying to describe any supervenience relation as a relation of linguistic predicates rather than of properties, because of a possible shortage of predicates (1993: 73). His reasons are different from the ones mentioned here, but they add to the problems for this last attempt at a neutral formulation.

17 (On Quinn, see note 8.) Wright may appear not to face this problem, since his proposal, for the special case in which injustice prompts rebellion, but not by way of anyone's perception of it *as* injustice, is not that we replace this evaluative explanation with one appealing to base properties, but that we replace it with one appealing to the properties by which we show (he says, "demonstrate") that the society is unjust. Of course, in this and other evaluative cases these properties we mention in such a "demonstration" typically *are* the base properties, but in non-evaluative cases they are not; so his proposal as worded does not appear to threaten the explanatory role of supervenient properties generally. However, it seems to me that he does face a problem. For the non-evaluative properties he mentions for contrast, such as the wetness of some rocks, do supervene on a physical microstructure. So we can surely ask him why the wetness should be thought of as having a causal role in the world, but injustice not, when both are supervenient. If his answer is simply that in the evaluative case, we appeal to the base properties in showing the society unjust, but that we do not (usually) show that rocks are wet by arguing from the microstructure of their surfaces, we may grant that this is true but ask, as I do below of

the proposals by Quinn and Audi, how it is relevant. How can this purely *epistemological* difference provide a reason for thinking that the wetness is really causally efficacious but that the injustice is not?

18 Thomson offers a different response. Her strategy is to describe a case of what she calls "paradigm epiphenomenality" in which, as she sees it, an evaluative property of a cause is clearly irrelevant to the effect produced, and then to ask, about the sorts of cases I have been presenting as plausible cases of evaluative explanations, how much they resemble that one. Her verdict is that the resemblance is close. I have doubts about her paradigm case, for reasons too complex to pursue here. But I also don't see the claimed resemblance. The plausible cases are, after all, ones in which many people *say* that injustice caused a rebellion, that decency kept someone from doing something and the like; on Thomson's own account of it, by contrast, her paradigm case of epiphenomenality is one about which no one would say such a thing. This fact suggests that the cases strike most people as significantly different.

19 Philosophers do not always agree about where to draw the line between the moral and the non-moral or, more generally, between the evaluative and the non-evaluative; but the phenomenon I am now pointing to is so pervasive that my case doesn't depend on any one example. My test for evaluative terminology is to remember the bad old days when philosophers thought that the central question of evaluative epistemology was whether evaluative conclusions could ever be deduced from entirely non-evaluative premises. I then ask myself: If I used this term essentially in what I proposed as the grounds for some evaluative conclusion, would I be accused of smuggling values into my premises?

20 Though neither Zangwill nor Thomson offers the reply I am criticizing, examples they give can be used to illustrate in different ways the difficulty of finding a non-evaluative explanation to replace an evaluative one. Zangwill says (this volume) that if we regard Isabella as a bad person, this will be because of her bigotry, intolerance, and resort to torture; but an explanation of our belief in her badness that appeals to her bigotry and intolerance is still an evaluative explanation. Thomson suggests that instead of appealing to the justice of Alice's giving Bert a banana to explain someone's belief that her act was just, we might just appeal to the fact that Alice's giving Bert the banana involved "her keeping her word on an occasion on which it cost her a lot to do so and she could have got away with not doing so" (1996: 77). This is perhaps not evaluative as it stands (though I suspect that what we count as a cost and, especially, as a lot of cost, varies with the other values at stake). But, as I expect Thomson would agree, neither is it sufficient to guarantee, as a supervenience base must, that Alice's action is just. For what if Alice had just stolen the banana from Charles, so that it wasn't hers to give? And once we add that the banana was rightfully hers, we are back with clearly evaluative terms in the explanation – unless, of course, we are prepared to state sufficient conditions for rightful ownership in entirely non-evaluative terms.

21 Someone might suggest that if we are simply explaining someone's belief (as in this example of Audi's we are not, but in others we might be), we do not need what is really a supervenience base for injustice but only what the believer *takes* to be a supervenience base. However, most believers are in fact sensitive to all of the considerations I claim that Audi's attempt at a non-evaluative characterization leaves out. If they really think that injustice caused the revolution, Audi's attempt to recharacterize their explanation is likely to strike them as highly inadequate.

22 See note 16. Audi (1997: 127, n.16) and Quinn (1986: 534–5) both recognize that they are committed to the possibility of such factoring, but they appear not to see their commitment as controversial. For additional discussion of the difficulty in tracing the reasons for

our evaluative beliefs all the way to purely non-evaluatively characterized reasons, one can see the recent debate on particularism: for a good sample, see Hooker and Little (2000).

23 See Yablo on locating "the cause," as distinct from causally relevant and causally sufficient factors (1992: 273–9). For a crisp application of the same general point to moral explanations, see Miller (1985: 526–7).

24 For a brief overview, see McFeely (1991: 265–9). Of course, this evidence has also been recognized as raising similar questions about whether the women's rights movement of the time is best described as responding to injustice or to something more specific.

25 Audi writes: "*given* an explanation of (say) a revolt by appeal to such things as police brutality and seizure of lands, it is not clear what explanatory element one would *add* to the explanation of why the revolt occurred by pointing out that these things constituted governmental injustice" (1997: 119; emphasis in original). One thing that one would add is generality – which might be the wrong thing to add, or might be just the right thing to add, depending on the case.

26 Though Zangwill's position is unusual, it perhaps has some affinity with Thomson's. Thomson offers two main arguments against evaluative explanations: a general argument, as I have mentioned, for the epiphenomenality of all evaluative properties, and a more specific argument (1996: 83–5) directed only against evaluative explanations of evaluative beliefs. A reader unpersuaded by the general argument but persuaded by the more specific one might thus end up with a position like Zangwill's. I have commented on the more specific argument (1998: 205–6). To the extent that there is an overlap between her concern and Zangwill's, some of my remarks below may also be relevant.

27 Quinn suggests, "A rather bad man might strike us as more or less decent because we see him always surrounded by villains who, by contrast, make him look better than he is" (1986: 529).

28 RCA sold Toscanini's recordings and also owned the NBC radio network, which broadcast Toscanini conducting a specially assembled NBC Orchestra.

29 Less hedged, because Horowitz's thesis, defended as he defends it (rather than as Zangwill would defend it) clearly does need hedging. For example, even if it didn't matter to Toscanini's fame whether he was actually a *great* conductor, it is hard to believe that the hype could have succeeded, over so long a period, if he hadn't been, in some respects, at least a pretty good one. So *something* about his merits mattered.

30 Another alternative would be to distinguish two senses of questions about the influence of evaluative properties on our beliefs about them, the philosopher's question (to which Zangwill thinks the answer, a priori, is that there is no influence) and the cultural historian's question (which is empirical, and to which the answer will depend on the case). But it is surely counterintuitive to have to distinguish questions in this way.

31 Thomson appears to share this worry (1996: 85–7).

32 Harman holds that *all* observation is theory-laden (1977: 4), and I am tempted to agree. In that case, my argument proceeds as stated. But since that claim may be controversial, I should point out that I can also defend my basic picture on the assumption that some observations are theory independent, so long as these privileged observations are limited in subject matter somewhat as traditional empiricists have thought, and so long, in particular, as they do not include observations of values or protons. For, in my view, the reasoning by which we base either evaluative conclusions, or conclusions about scientific unobservables, on this or any other base of non-evaluative, non-theoretical observations, is also theory-dependent: it depends on evaluative, or scientific, views we already hold. (On the ethical side, this is just an application of the doctrine of the

Moral Explanations Defended

autonomy of ethics.) So there is the same question of how, if this reasoning is to yield knowledge, we can ever get started; and my answer, with minor adjustments, is the one I give in the text.

33 For this account of scientific reasoning, and for comparisons to the evaluative case, see Boyd (1988).

References

Audi, R. (1997). "Ethical naturalism and the explanatory power of ethical concepts." In Audi, *Moral Knowledge and Ethical Character*. New York: Oxford University Press.

Blackburn, S. (1993). "Just causes." In Blackburn, *Essays in Quasi-Realism*. New York: Oxford University Press.

Boyd, R. N. (1988). "How to be a moral realist." In G. Sayre-McCord (ed.), *Essays in Moral Realism*. Ithaca: Cornell University Press.

Gibbard, A. (1990). *Wise Choices, Apt Feelings*. Cambridge, Mass.: Harvard University Press, 1990.

Hare, R. M. (1952). *The Language of Morals*. Oxford: Clarendon Press.

Harman, G. (1977). *The Nature of Morality*. New York: Oxford University Press.

Harman, G. (1986). "Moral explanations of natural facts – can moral claims be tested against moral reality?" *The Southern Journal of Philosophy* 24 (Supplement).

Hooker, B. and Little, M. (eds.) (2001). *Moral Particularism*. Oxford: Clarendon Press.

Horowitz, J. (1987). *Understanding Toscanini*. New York: Alfred A. Knopf.

Kim, J. (1993). "Concepts of supervenience." In Kim, *Supervenience and Mind*. Cambridge: Cambridge University Press.

McDowell, J. (1998). "Virtue and reason." In McDowell, *Mind, Value and Reality*. Cambridge, Mass.: Harvard University Press.

McFeely, W. S. (1991). *Frederick Douglass*. New York: W. W. Norton.

Miller, R. W. (1985). "Ways of moral learning." *The Philosophical Review*, 94: 526–7.

Moore, G. E. (1903). *Principia Ethica*. Cambridge: Cambridge University Press.

Moore, G. E. (1959). "The conception of intrinsic value." In *Philosophical Studies*. Paterson, NJ: Littlefield, Adams.

Pietroski, P. M. (1993). "Prima facie obligations, *ceteris paribus* laws in moral theory." *Ethics*, 103 (April): 489–515.

Quinn, W. (1986). "Truth in ethics." *Ethics* 96 (April): 524–44.

Rawls, J. (1971). *A Theory of Justice*. Cambridge, Mass.: Belknap Press.

Ross, W. D. (1934). *The Right and the Good*. Oxford: Clarendon Press.

Slote, M. (1971). "The rationality of aesthetic value judgments." *The Journal of Philosophy*, 68: 821–39.

Stevenson, C. (1944). *Ethics and Language*. New Haven: Yale University Press.

Sturgeon, N. L. (1988). "Moral explanations." In G. Sayre-McCord (ed.), *Essays in Moral Realism*. Ithaca: Cornell University Press.

Sturgeon, N. L. (1992). "Nonmoral explanations." In J. Tomberlin (ed.), *Philosophical Perspectives, 6: Ethics*. Atascadero, Calif.: Ridgeview Publishing Co.

Sturgeon, N. L. (1998). "Thomson against moral explanations." *Philosophy and Phenomenological Research*, 58.

Sturgeon, N. L. (2003). "Moore on ethical naturalism." *Ethics*,113: 528–56.

Sturgeon, N. L. (forthcoming). "Ethical naturalism." In D. Copp (ed.), *Oxford Handbook of Ethical Theory*. Oxford University Press.

Thomson, J. J. (1996). "Moral objectivity." In G. Harman and J. J. Thomson, *Moral Relativism and Moral Objectivity*. Cambridge, Mass.: Blackwell.

Thomson, J. J. (1998). "Reply to critics." *Philosophy and Phenomenological Research* 43: 215–22.

Williams, B. (1985). *Ethics and the Limits of Philosophy*. Cambridge, Mass.: Harvard University Press.

Wright, C. (1992). *Truth and Objectivity*. Cambridge, Mass.: Harvard University Press.

Yablo, S. (1992). "Mental causation." *The Philosophical Review*, 101: 245–80.

Moral Epistemology and the Because Constraint

Nick Zangwill

Metaethics and Explanation

Given some perplexing subject-matter or mode of thought, philosophers typically ask metaphysical and epistemological questions. They ask about the nature (if any) of the phenomenon, and they ask about our knowledge (if any) of it. When it comes to morality, many moral philosophers ask metaphysical questions like the following. Are there moral facts or states of affairs or property instantiations about which we are thinking when we make moral judgments, and which (when we get it right) are the truth-makers of those moral judgments? Or are there no such moral facts (or states of affairs or property instantiations)? Furthermore, if there are such moral facts (or states of affairs or property instantiations), what are they like? Are they in some sense 'mind-dependent' or 'mind-independent'? And how do moral facts (or states of affairs or property instantiations) relate to non-moral or "natural" facts (or states of affairs or property instantiations)? Those are the usual metaphysical questions. The epistemological questions tend be of the following sort. Assuming there are moral facts (or states of affairs or property instantiations), how (if at all) do we know about them? And what (if anything) would make our beliefs about them justified? These two epistemological questions make certain assumptions. One assumption is that our moral beliefs succeed in possessing the positive epistemic properties of being knowledge or being justified. But perhaps our moral beliefs fail to have these positive epistemic characteristics. Another assumption is that moral judgments are beliefs. But perhaps moral judgments are not beliefs at all, but are emotions or desires.[1] Or, to make the mental categories broader, maybe moral judgments are 'non-cognitive' rather than 'cognitive' states. We need to ask: what kind of mental state is forming or holding a moral judgment? This is not really an epistemological question, since epistemology is about a value that beliefs can have, not about whether the judgments in question are beliefs rather than some other kind of mental state. There is no standard label for this question. I shall call it the 'attitudinal' question. (This is not pretty, but I can think of nothing better.) These metaphysical, epistemological, and attitudinal questions are the classical questions to ask.[2]

However, there is another sort of issue that has come to the fore recently, which is not explicitly metaphysical, epistemological, or attitudinal. Philosophers have asked: what best *explains* our moral judgments? That is, what best explains our making either any moral judgments at all or else the specific moral judgments we make? These questions have perhaps a more empirical air to them. It seems that psychology and social science might be relevant to them in a way that is not usually thought appropriate to the more classical questions. It might be thought that the appeal to explanation raises new and perhaps better questions. Perhaps considerations of explanation give us a new source of argumentative leverage on the classical questions. Indeed, many philosophers have argued from explanatory consideration to conclusions about the metaphysics, epistemology, or attitudinology of morality.

For example, explanation bears on the metaphysical question in John Mackie's "argument from relativity." Mackie writes: "people approve of monogamy because they participate in a monogamous way of life rather than . . . participate in a monogamous way of life because they approve of monogamy" (1977: 36). He emphasizes that it is not merely the fact that moral codes vary with societies that is significant, but the fact that this variation can be explained solely in social terms without invoking moral facts. If so, Mackie takes it to follow that there is no need to posit a realm of moral facts or an epistemological faculty for detecting them. So, for Mackie, questions of the explanation of moral judgments lead at least to a metaphysical conclusion.

Explanation also bears on the epistemological issue – assuming that moral judgments are beliefs – in that to assert that moral facts can or cannot be known *empirically* is to assert a view about how moral judgments are explained: the empiricist about morality thinks that moral judgments are explained in part by the facts they are about, whereas the a priorist denies this. This is because belief–fact causal interaction is that which distinguishes empirical from a priori knowledge (McGinn 1975–6, 1982, 1984).[3]

Furthermore, explanation bears on the attitudinal question in that asserting that moral judgments are not beliefs at all but desires or emotions also means that they are not explained by moral facts. Explanations often figure in a more controversial way in the attitudinal debate as a way of giving meaning to debates between cognitivists and their non-cognitivist opponents. This need arises because of the possibility of a sophisticated kind of non-cognitivism that aspires to respect certain central and general ideas that govern ordinary moral thought. Ordinary moral thought, or what we might call 'folk morality', commits us to the following ideas: there are moral truths; whether something is good or bad does not depend on what we think; moral "propositions" can be unasserted; and whether something is good or bad depends on how it is in natural respects. Simon Blackburn's 'quasi-realism' is the project of finding ways to show that non-cognitivism can respect ordinary folk morality by showing that we have a right to these ideas, despite the non-cognitivist account of moral thought (1984, 1985, 1998; see also Zangwill 1993). If non-cognitivists can take morality as seriously as cognitivists, by respecting those ideas, then a question arises about what distinguishes the positions. The worry is that there is no remaining way to characterize a genuine debate. If quasi-realism is successful, then perhaps there remain only metaphors and images associated with the debate between cognitivism and non-cognitivism (Blackburn 1980; Zangwill 1992a). Quite a few objected to Blackburn that if his quasi-realism succeeds it undercuts itself (e.g. Wright 1985). But it is at precisely this point in the dialectic that Blackburn reaches for the explanation of moral judgments as that which gives sense to the debate, when conceptual features do not. Considerations of how moral judgments are explained may give sense to the attitudinal debate without those explanations being transparently available to those engaging in moral thought. Why should that explanation be transparent to us? Knowledge of the nature of perception or pain, for example, is not given free to those who have perceptions and pains or even to those who have beliefs about perceptions and pains. So why should knowledge of the nature of moral judgments be given free to those who make them? Perhaps ordinary moral thinkers have some kind of relatively transparent access to the conceptual features of moral thinking. But there is no reason to think that they should have transparent access to that which explains the fact that our thought has those conceptual features.[4] The surface conceptual features of moral thought may be explained by mechanisms of which we have no knowledge. The interesting issue is about which attitudinal theory best explains the conceptual features of folk morality.[5]

While it is true that explanation may be able to give sense to the attitudinal debate, when appeals to the notions of moral truth and the like do not, it is not clear that it is the *only* possible way to give sense to that debate. It may be sufficient but not necessary. We must be careful not to build in a prejudice against a priori knowledge. Where we have a priori knowledge, our judgments are not causally responsive (directly or indirectly) to their subject-matter (their truth-makers). One might want to be a mathematical realist, for example, without wanting to define the realism debate over mathematical entities and properties in causal-explanatory terms. Furthermore, it is possible that a particularly enthusiastic kind of quasi-realist might go beyond trying to capture the conceptual features I mentioned and also strive to capture the apparent efficacy of the projected property (Zangwill 1992a: sect. VIII); and if so, we will lack the explanatory means of characterizing the debate. Having "projected" a property onto the world, perhaps we also come to think of it as having causal efficacy.[6] I suspect that at some point we must simply concede that there is a very primeval and primitive notion of existence or fact which cannot be explicated in other terms (see McGinn 2000). If so, the notions of cause and explanation rest on this fundamental notion of existence or fact, rather than the other way round; and we can use this more fundamental notion to preserve the sense of the attitudinal issue even in the face of the particularly enthusiastic quasi-realist. Hence, the appeal to explanation may not be the only way to prosecute metaphysical, epistemological, and attitudinal issues. Nevertheless, where there *are* distinctive explanatory considerations, we should certainly consider their consequences.

I suppose I should mention that there are some philosophers who deny that we should seek to explain moral judgments (Dworkin 1996, 1997). This somewhat Luddite view says that all we can do is *describe* our moral practice; we cannot *explain* it. (The view has a Wittgensteinian ring to it.) We cannot ask what it is to make moral judgments and whether those judgments are beliefs about the world or are expressive of attitudes. We simply walk the moral walk and talk the moral talk. But this is ostrich philosophy. It is a refusal to see that there are questions that can be asked. Think about the holocaust. Some theorists have claimed that the holocaust cannot be explained. I agree with Daniel Goldhagen that this view is both obscurantist and irresponsible (see Goldhagen 1996; the papers by Goldhagen in Shandley 1998; Zangwill 1996b, 2003). The holocaust is a historical event and we can inquire into its causes like any other historical event. Similarly, the making of moral judgments by human beings is a phenomenon in the world like many others. We can surely ask what moral judgments are and about what explains them. Are moral judgments like alien beings from outer space? The real question is about what *kind* of explanation moral judgments have and whether they result from a causal sensitivity to their truth-makers (the moral facts) or whether they are well explained without positing such a causal route.

It has seemed to many philosophers in the last few decades that the project of explaining moral thought is not merely *one* way to prosecute the classical issues; it is also the best way to prosecute them (Harman 1977). They think that explanatory issues have a certain philosophical primacy. And along with this goes the idea that the metaethics should have more of an empirical component than is traditionally envisaged. These claims for what explanation can do may go too far. Nevertheless, the question of what explains moral judgments is certainly interesting and important and something we should consider, so long as we are cautious about the exact upshot of such inquiries. On the one hand, it is true that metaphysical, epistemological, and attitudinal questions about moral judgments can turn on explanatory considerations. For example, it is true that *if* there are moral facts *and* moral judgments are beliefs *and* are empirical *then* they have a particular fact-to-judgment explanation. On the other hand, if moral judgments are *not* explained in this way, it is not clear what it shows. What it shows is probably a disjunction: either there are no moral facts (Mackie), *or* moral judgments are not beliefs (Blackburn), *or* moral judgments are non-empirical (Moore). I particularly worry about the question being begged against a priori forms of knowledge when explanatory considerations are discussed. With these warnings in mind, let us now turn to the explanatory issue.

Sturgeon's Examples of Causally Efficacious Moral Properties

Many philosophers have thought that morality is not empirically knowable. This much is agreed between non-cognitivists (like Blackburn), who deny that moral thinking is a matter of any kind of belief or knowledge, and cognitivists (like Moore), who reach for a non-empirical epistemology. However, this consensus has been challenged by those known as 'Cornell realists'. Nicholas Sturgeon (1988) and David Brink (1989), for example, have sought to show that morality is after all known (and thus knowable) on empirical grounds. And they have sought to show this by establishing certain claims about the explanation of moral judgments.[7]

Let us consider some of the examples of moral explanations that Sturgeon gives, since these examples are made to do a lot of dialectical work. In his paper "Moral explanations," and in other places, Sturgeon gives various examples of which aspire to be common-sense cases of moral explanations (1988; see also Sturgeon 1986, 1991, 1996, 1998). My view is that these examples fall into two kinds. Let us call these *doxastic* and *non-doxastic* examples. A doxastic example is one in which what a moral fact is supposed to explain is a moral belief. A non-doxastic example is one in which this is not so. It is usually presumed that one either accepts both or neither. But this is disputable. The view of moral properties and our cognition of them to which I incline accepts non-doxastic examples but not doxastic cases. I am not against moral explanations in general; I am only against moral explanations of moral beliefs. With this in mind, let us turn to Sturgeon's examples. He writes:

> many died who might have been saved [because]...Passed Midshipman Woodsworth was just no damned good. (1988: 244)

> [The fact of Hitler's] depravity is relevant to an explanation of what he did. (Ibid. 249)

These are non-doxastic examples, and they are OK by me. They are moral explanations of natural facts, not moral explanations of moral beliefs. I would add that the instantiation of some moral properties can cause other instantiation of moral properties. The usual account of how this causal efficacy is possible would appeal to supervenience and constitution relations that hold between moral and natural properties (see Kim 1993 for discussion). Perhaps there are difficulties with such accounts, but if moral facts are doing as well on this score as psychological, chemical, and biological facts, then they are not doing too badly.

Sturgeon also gives examples of this sort:

> Hitler's moral depravity – the fact of his really having been morally depraved – forms part of a reasonable explanation of why we believe he was depraved. (Ibid. 234)

> [P]art of the explanation of [DeVoto's] believing that Woodsworth was no damned good is just that Woodsworth *was* no damned good. (Ibid. 244)

> [V]igorous and reasonably widespread moral opposition to slavery arose for the first time in the eighteenth and nineteenth centuries, even though slavery was a very old institution...and...this opposition arose primarily in Britain, France, and in French- and English-speaking North America, even though slavery existed throughout the New World ...[because] chattel slavery in British and French America, and then in the United States, was much *worse* than previous forms of slavery, and much worse than slavery in Latin America. (Ibid. 245)

These are doxastic explanations, and they are *not* OK by me. This chapter will focus on cases of this kind. My view is that moral beliefs are never causally responsive to moral facts. So I am committed to denying all Sturgeon's examples of such explanations. However, I think that folk morality *is* committed to the causal role of moral facts.[8] Sturgeon is importantly right about this. For example, the fact that an act is evil might explain why people suffered as a consequence of it. That's an example of moral-to-non-moral causal interaction. An example of a commitment to non-moral-to-moral causal interaction would be the accusation that Socrates corrupted the youth; for the idea was that what Socrates did cause the youth to become corrupt. He replied in the *Apology* that he would be irrational to do that since if he made them corrupt, their corruption would in turn corrupt him. This would be an example of moral-to-moral causal interaction. These are fairly common-sense sorts of examples of moral causal interaction. But the fact that ordinary moral thought is committed to moral explanations in *non*-doxastic cases does not mean that it is committed to moral explanations in *doxastic* cases. There is a lot to be said for the idea that non-doxastic explanations are common sense – part of folk morality. But the idea of doxastic explanations is not obviously part of folk morality. Either folk morality is neutral on this question, or at least what the folk think about this is controversial.

An ambiguous case is this: "Injustice caused revolution R" (Sturgeon 1998: 200). This might be a doxastic explanation. If *beliefs about injustice* are supposed to play a *mediating* causal role between injustice and revolutions, then we are assuming that injustice causes beliefs about injustice. That's not OK by me, even though I am happy to accept that beliefs about injustice cause revolutions. But if it is thought that there is some connection between injustice and revolution which is *not* mediated by moral beliefs, then it would be a non-doxastic explanation, and it may be acceptable. In an ambiguous case, we must disambiguate, and separate (acceptable) non-doxastic elements from (unacceptable) doxastic elements.

Before I go on to argue that moral facts and properties do not explain our moral beliefs, I want to say something negative, just to get it out of the way. Otherwise it will distract us. This is that we should not appeal to counterfactuals, at least in any simple way. For example, Sturgeon writes: "It [is not] plausible that we would all have believed [Hitler] was morally depraved if he hadn't been" (1988: 246). It is not at all clear whether such conditionals are true. It depends on people's background moral commitments. One certainly wonders who Sturgeon's "we" refers to. Does it include Germans of the pre-war years? If not, why not? We might lament: "If only Sturgeon were right about this counterfactual!"[9] But even if the counterfactual is true, it is not clear what it shows about the explanation of our moral beliefs. Not every counterfactual signifies a causal relationship, and the fact that this counterfactual obtains, if it does, does not show that the moral property is causally efficacious with respect to our moral beliefs. We do better to avoid appealing to such counterfactuals in this debate. Their interpretation is too controversial. (See also Thomson 1998: 220, n.3.)

The Realization Argument

Recall that lying behind this explanatory debate is the issue of the epistemic status of moral beliefs. If moral beliefs are, as Sturgeon says, the causal upshot of moral facts, we have the makings of a relatively unproblematic moral epistemology. Moral judgments turn out to be empirical. This is what I want to resist. However, the idea that we should take a different view about doxastic and about non-doxastic explanations may appear odd. If moral facts can cause other things besides moral beliefs, why can't they cause moral beliefs too?

Moral realists typically say that moral facts (states of affairs or property instanti-ations) are "realized" in natural facts (states of affairs or property instantiations) – where 'realized' means, very roughly, that every moral fact (etc.) obtains because of some natural fact (etc.). (I use the word 'realization' in order to retain a degree of neutrality about the exact relation between moral and natural properties.) Given that moral properties are realized in plain natural properties, about which there is no great explanatory (or epistemological) dispute, how can we deny that moral facts cause our judgments about them, especially when it is conceded that they cause other things?

One argument against Sturgeon and Brink would go as follows. Metaphysical nat-uralism says that instantiations of moral properties are realized in instantiations of natural properties. A substantive first-order moral question takes the form of the ques-tion whether X's having the (possibly conjunctive) natural property N realizes either X's being good to a certain degree or, on the other hand, X's being evil to a certain degree. But there is no natural difference between these possibilities. And if there is no natural difference, then there is no causal difference to which we can be sensi-tive. Empirical cognition implies that our cognition is causally sensitive to what we represent in its content, directly or indirectly (McGinn 1975–6). But the instantiation of the natural property N has the causal role it does irrespective of whether it real-izes good or evil. Hence there is no causal difference by which we could tell whether X is good or evil. The theory that something is N, and that it is N and evil, and that it is N and good, are all empirically equivalent.

Unfortunately, this argument will not do, because a parallel argument would label some uncontroversial examples of a posteriori knowledge as a priori. For example, a parallel argument seems to show that we cannot have empirical knowledge of water; for water has no causal role over and above H_2O. The same goes for rocks, snails, and chairs. Macro-physical, biological, and artifactual things are also realized in config-urations of micro-physical matter. Rocks, snails, and chairs are all physical objects. The same goes for psychological states if materialism is true. It looks as if any theory about upper-level properties, plus a physical theory of the same sector of space-time, will be empirically indiscriminable from the physical theory considered alone. So judg-ments about water, rocks, snails, chairs, and pains will come out as a priori. But we surely do have perceptual contents such as, 'That's water', 'That's a rock', or 'That's a snail', or 'That's a chair', and maybe 'That person is in pain'. And we are surely causally sensitive to these things. Beliefs about water, rocks, snails, chairs, and the pains of others are empirical. It looks as if beliefs about *some* properties that are realized in other properties are empirical. So why not moral properties too?

This is indeed a problem. But it should not lead us to abandon the argument alto-gether. For there still *seems* to be a difference between the moral case and these other cases. There is surely some difference that we can be empirically sensitive to, which is consequential on whether or not water is H_2O. This is why the identity claim is empirically knowable. A problem might be raised here. Perhaps we cannot say that if water were not H_2O then it would make an empirically discriminable difference (for example, if water were not H_2O then it would not boil at 100°C at normal pressure, and we could perceive that). For there are some philosophers who say that we cannot make sense of what would be the case if an impossibility obtains. Nevertheless it remains plausible that the identity of water and H_2O is something we know about empirically. One suggestion would be that we arrive at the identity belief by inference from the belief that water and H_2O uniquely share some contingent property (presumably some causal property). We then have an uncontroversially acceptable counterfactual: if water and H_2O had not shared this property, there would have been an empirically discriminable difference. Now compare [Goodness is what produces happiness] and [Goodness is not what produces happiness]; there seems to be no causal difference between these two hypotheses to which we could be sensitive. It seems that there is no observable difference that is consequential on whether or not goodness is what produces happiness. And if someone worries that these claims about goodness are necessary if true, then the claim we need is that it is not possible for us to find some contingent property that goodness and what produces happiness uniquely share that would supply inferential justification to the belief that goodness is what produces happiness. So our knowledge of the relation between moral and natural properties at least *seems* to be very different from our knowledge of the relation between natural kind properties and micro-physical properties. But – the problem is – how to *show* this?

The argument from realization needs repairing or at least supplementing. We need to say why we cannot know moral properties empirically in the way that we can and do know these other realized properties. The line of argument must be revised, but we should not give it up altogether. There is something intuitively right about it that we have not yet unearthed. We need to try again to say exactly how knowledge of morality is different from knowledge of water, rocks, snails, chairs, and pains.

The Because Constraint

Suppose I say that Barry is bad. You ask why. I reply that Barry is bad because he has blue eyes. You might with justice criticize this explanation on the grounds that being blue-eyed is not the kind of property that can (by itself) make someone bad. The idea is prejudiced because being blue-eyed is not by itself relevant to determining a moral property. Now suppose instead that I say that Billy is bad. You ask why. I reply, "No reason; he's just bad, that's all." This is utterly irresponsible and weird. This is like prejudice, except worse. In the case of prejudice, a person takes an irrelevant ground to be relevant, but at least he has some ground, albeit a bad one. But in the case of Billy, I have no ground at all. This is barking mad. For if Billy is bad, there must be something that *makes* Billy bad. We must think that Billy is bad *because* or *in virtue of* the way he is in other respects. Or to take a real example, if Isabella was bad in 1492, it was in virtue of bigotry, intolerance, torture, or whatever. Furthermore, if I judge that Isabella was bad in 1492, I must judge that she was bad in virtue of bigotry, intolerance, torture, or whatever. Too abbreviate: she is M because she is N; and if I judge her to be M it must be because I judge her to be M because she is N.

It is widely accepted that John Mackie's metaphysical queerness proves very little because of the possibility of a naturalist metaphysics (Brink 1989: 171–80). But Mackie was right to mention, if only in passing, the problem of this *because* ("Just what *in the world* is signified by this 'because'?" (Mackie 1977: 41)). Different theories are possible here. Cornell realists think that it is familiar Kripkean metaphysical necessity. Kit Fine (2002) thinks that it is a distinctively moral necessity. Blackburn (1985) has his non-realist surrogate, which looks superficially like metaphysical necessity for all conceptual reflection can tell, but in fact derives from the constraints on responsible combinations of attitudes. Nevertheless, everyone should agree on the existence and centrality of this *because*. Moreover, this *because* is not just metaphysical constraint on properties but also a constraint on our judgments (a "conceptual" feature of them). The slogan might be: not just *bad*, but bad because: we judge not that something is bad period, but that it is bad because of certain natural properties. It is a priori that moral properties depend. Let us call the requirement to judge that something is M because it is N the 'Because Constraint'.[10]

Three comments: First (a), there are two special cases of moral judgment that we should put to one side as derivative: authority and induction. In cases where we judge morally on the basis of authority or on inductive grounds, we judge without knowing anything *specific* about a thing's natural properties. Suppose I take Zak to be a moral authority, and he judges Zorro to be a man of impeccable virtue. I may well believe what Zak says even though I know nothing specific about Zorro's natural properties except that they are what Zak judges to be virtuous. However, if there are to be some secondary cases of knowledge by authority, there must be cases of primary knowledge where our knowledge does not depend in this way on other people. Those who gain their knowledge by authority are parasitic on those who do not. So we can put aside cases where one makes a judgment about someone on authority, in ignorance of the precise natural properties of the thing being judged. We also form beliefs on inductive grounds. It could be that so far everyone we have encountered who lives on Evil Street has turned out to have natural properties that realize badness. And so we might infer that Cruella, who lives there, is probably bad as well. But such inductive judgments are possible only because of non-inductive judgments. The non-inductive judgments are the basis for the induction. So we can also ignore inductive moral judgments. In authority and inductive cases, we do not know the *specific* natural properties of the thing judged, but we do know *something* about their natural properties: they are what Zak judges to be virtuous, or they are somehow bad-making properties like the natural properties of the others who live on Evil Street.

Second (b), some dependencies depend on others. Perhaps A depends on C because A depends on B and B depends on C. Moreover, perhaps we think that some dependencies depend on others. Thus, we might think that there is some more fundamental explanation of *why* it is that a thing is M because it is N. For example, perhaps someone thinks that an act is bad because it is a case of stealing, but he also thinks that stealing is bad because it produces disutility. Thus he thinks that one dependency depends on another; one *because* because of another *because*. A second person might agree that the act is bad because it is stealing, but instead think that stealing is bad because it transgresses rights. A third person might have no view about why stealing is bad, although he thinks that there is some such reason. He might be open to suggestion concerning the explanation of its wrongness. And a fourth person might think that the badness of stealing is fundamental and not to be explained in terms of some other dependency. Explanation has to come to an end, and perhaps the dependency of badness on stealing is one such bedrock dependency. Nevertheless, the

Because Constraint stands, because to make a moral judgment is to think that there is *some* natural feature that a moral property depends on. Whether or not that dependency relation is held to be ultimate or derived from another dependency relation is another matter. To take another example, we may think that cutting up one healthy patient to save five is wrong. One person may think that it is bad because it produces disutility; a second because it transgresses rights; a third person might never have reflected on exactly why it is wrong in the sense of thinking that there is some true moral theory that would explain it; and a fourth might think that the badness of cutting up one to save five is a bedrock dependency. All agree, however, that something makes the act of cutting up one to save five wrong.

Third (c), suppose we think that we should save a baby rather than an animal from a burning building. It might be objected that we might be surer of that verdict than we are of what made it the right verdict. We might be less sure of the natural base of the rightness than we are of the rightness. By way of reply, two things can be said. A harsh reply would be to say that if a person makes a judgment without having in mind some natural base, then he is irresponsible. So he really shouldn't hold the comparative judgment about the baby and the animal unless he has some reason for holding it. So he should retract the original judgment. On the other hand, I suspect that in this case, the person *does* think that being-a-human-rather-than-a-non-human-animal is morally significant, even if she has nothing *further* to say about why that natural feature is moral significant. So this case turns out to be like the stealing case in (b). One might condemn taking being-a-human-rather-than-a-non-human-animal as the natural basis for the moral property. But for better or worse this is certainly what much folk morality is like. Similarly a familyist, nationalist, or racist might say that someone's being from my family, nation, or race is moral significant and can mark a moral distinction from someone who is not. And he might either have nothing further to say about why that natural property is morally significant, or he might think that explanation stops there, and the moral significance of the natural property is fundamental and not explainable in terms of some other dependency.[11] Either way, the Because Constraint holds.

Hence, the Because Constraint is fundamental to folk morality. Indeed it is necessary and essential to it. But the Because Constraint vindicates, I believe, a claim that is fundamental to Moore's moral philosophy. Moore claims that it is a priori that a certain modal principle holds, which today we would call 'moral supervenience'. Although this wasn't Moore's phrase it clearly is the idea he had in mind. For example, Moore writes: "supposing a given thing possesses [intrinsic value] in a certain degree, anything exactly like that thing *must* possess it in exactly the same degree" (1922: 269). I would recast this slightly by saying that for every moral property instantiation there is some natural property instantiation that suffices for it (see Kim 1984). Moore's claim is that we know a priori that moral supervenience is of the essence of all moral properties (1922: 270–1). The Because Constraint is the idea that in moralizing we are committed to a certain kind of tight connection between moral and natural properties: the moral properties hold because of, in virtue of, as a consequence of natural properties. A priori moral supervenience is the idea that it is constitutive of moral thought that there is a certain modal connection between moral and natural properties: every moral property instantiation is such that there is some natural property the instantiation of which suffices for the instantiation of the moral property. The Because Constraint either is, or explains, moral supervenience. It might be thought that moral supervenience is like a rather complex, erudite claim; so it is not obvious that it is an everyday, common sense commitment of folk morality, which is a fundamental presupposition of the practice of ordinary people when they make moral judgments. But if the Because Constraint holds as a constitutive principle of moral thought, the same is true of moral supervenience. We conceive of moral properties as holding in virtue of natural properties, and so we conceive of natural properties as sufficing for them. The in-virtue-of relation explains the sufficiency relation. And our commitment to the former explains our commitment to the latter. (See further Zangwill 2005.)

The No-Independent Access Argument

How does this bear on the issues raised at the beginning of this chapter – the epistemic status and explanation of moral beliefs?

It might be argued that the Because Constraint and the a priority of moral supervenience do not mean that particular moral judgments are a priori. For the situation might be like the case of proper names (of individuals). As Nathan Salmon (1981) has well described, in both the case of natural kind terms and proper names (of individuals) we operate with a framework principle to the effect that if a claim holds it holds necessarily: in the natural kind case the framework principle is that if something is a natural kind then it has a certain molecular composition and it does so necessarily; and in the proper name case the framework principle is that if an object identity holds then it does so necessarily. A modal framework principle holds in both cases.

There is an important difference, however, which is that the principle is a priori for proper names but not for natural kind terms. As we saw, moral supervenience is a priori. By contrast, it is clearly *not* a priori that there is some molecular state that necessitates water. For all we knew a few hundred years ago, water might easily have turned out to have no molecular structure at all. Water might have been a pre-Socratic fundamental stuff with no composition. Thales might have been right! It is not a priori that something makes water water. But moral supervenience is a priori – something must make good things good. Moral supervenience is a fundamental a priori conceptual constraint governing all moral thought (Zangwill 1996a). That is, it is knowable a priori of moral properties that they are somehow necessitated by natural properties, whereas it is not known a priori that natural kind properties are necessitated by some molecular structure. (See Salmon 1981: chs. 5, 6, and appendix II, where he cites unpublished work by Donnellan; Putnam 1992; and Soames 2002: 271.) Kripke asserts the a priority claim for both proper name and natural kind framework principles (1980: 109), but at this rare point I think Kripke errs. This is a very important disanalogy between moral properties and natural kinds.

Even so, my opponent might concede this point and continue by replying that in both the cases of proper names and natural kind terms, the knowledge of the *embedded* object identity or composition relations *is* empirical. The suggestion we need to consider is that even though moral supervenience is an a priori modal framework principle, the knowledge of particular moral–natural connections is empirical. For example, perhaps we know that pain is bad empirically, and we then add the a priori framework principle that if pain is bad it is so necessarily. However, I shall argue that the moral case is not like the proper name case. Even though the moral case is like the proper name case in that their respective modal framework principles are a priori, and in this respect both are unlike natural kind terms, the moral case is unlike both the proper name case and the natural kind term case in that knowledge of particular moral–natural connections is a priori whereas the knowledge of both object identities and of natural kind-molecular compositional relations is empirical. Only in the moral case are *both* the framework principle *and* embedded claims a priori.

The Because Constraint is to blame. As we shall see, it is the Because Constraint that explains the fact that we cannot be causally sensitive to moral properties (such as badness) or to the connection between moral properties and natural properties (such as that pain is bad or that causing pain for fun is bad). By contrast, we can be causally sensitive to natural kinds (such as water) and to natural kind compositional relations (such as the relation that obtains between water and H_2O); and we can be causally sensitive to things (such as Cicero) and to the fact that identity relations hold between things (such as between Cicero and Tully). Crucially, this is because we have empirical knowledge of water and we have empirical knowledge of H_2O and we then infer the compositional relation; and we have empirical knowledge of Cicero and we have empirical knowledge of Tully, and we then infer the identity relation. But, as we shall see, the trouble – the fundamental trouble – with the moral case is that *we can have no independent knowledge of moral and natural properties.*[12]

The proper name case does not involve the idea of realization, so let us focus more on our knowledge of non-moral properties that are physically realized. How do we know that an instance of a natural kind has a certain composition? Or to take some other cases of realized properties that are probably not natural kinds, or at least are not natural kinds in the way that water is: how do we know that something with certain physical properties is a rock, snail, or clock? Answer: *not* by cognition of the connection between these upper-level properties and lower-level physical properties. Instead we start with *independent* knowledge that here we have a rock, snail, or clock. Next we investigate the physical properties that compose them. And we then infer the connection. (As with natural kinds, this may be done in the light of a framework principle to the effect that truths about composition are necessarily true.) But – crucially – it is *not* like this in the moral case. For our *only* access to the upper-level moral properties is *via* the lower-level natural properties plus knowledge of their connection. Hence the moral case is fundamentally different from the water, rock, snail, and clock cases. The crucial asymmetry is that in those cases we have independent knowledge of the upper- and lower-level properties, and we then infer the composition or identity relations, whereas in the moral case, we have knowledge of the lower-level natural properties and of moral–natural connections, and we then infer the upper-level moral properties. This is because moral ascriptions are subject to the Because Constraint, unlike water, rock, snail, and clock ascriptions. Proper name identities are also unlike morality. There is no a priori constraint on proper names according to which whenever we assert a claim about someone, such as Cicero, to the effect that he has a property, such as wisdom, then it must be because we think that there is someone, such as Tully, who is identical with Cicero, and he has the property of wisdom. Similarly, there is no a priori constraint on psychological ascriptions such that whenever we assert that someone is in pain, then we think that he is a pain because of some physical state (or even because of some soul state). We think Cicero is wise or that Martha is in pain, on the basis of evidence, to be sure, but not necessarily on the basis of an identity or composition claim. And similarly, there is no a priori constraint on color ascriptions such that whenever we assert that something is yellow, then we think that it is yellow because of some physical state. Morality is different from *all* these cases. (Yes, goodness differs from yellowness!) In all the other cases we have independent access to the properties or objects related and we infer the relation between them. Morality is not like this. Let us call this the No Independent Access Thesis. The Because Constraint leads directly to the No Independent Access Thesis. To give a homely illustration: morality is like a London double-decker bus. You have to enter on the ground floor. From there you can climb the staircase to the upper deck. And there is no other way to get up there.

Sturgeon and Brink seem to be committed to maintaining that knowledge of moral properties can be had completely independently of our knowledge of natural properties that generate the moral properties, in the way that we can know that something is a rock, snail, or clock without knowing about its constitution. But this is a fundamental error. The idea that we could know the moral properties of a thing while being ignorant of the natural properties in virtue of which is has those moral properties is incredible. Furthermore, it is alright to make rock, snail, clock, water, and pain judgments about things without a judgment about their microphysical composition, but it is not alright to make moral judgments about things without a judgment about the natural properties that determine the moral properties.

It is easy to show that it is *possible* for us to make rock, snail, clock, water, and pain judgments about things in ignorance of their microphysical composition, since people actually *do* make these judgments in ignorance of their composition; and actuality implies possibility. By contrast, apart from authority and inductive cases, people do in fact make moral judgments only given natural beliefs. What is more important than this general truth about people is the normative point that we encountered before: to make a moral judgment about a thing in ignorance of its natural properties is to be *irresponsible*. Surely it is a common and uncontroversial thought that one has no right to judge if one is ignorant of the thing judged. This sin is like that of prejudice, only worse. Prejudice in judgment is something that we should avoid. Moral prejudice is taking some irrelevant natural feature of the person judged – such as having blue eyes or red hair – and letting one's moral judgment turn on that rather than on the relevant natural properties (qualities of action, motive, and character). But if that is something we should avoid, then how much more so is judging something morally in complete ignorance of its natural features. By contrast, in the water/rock/snail/clock case, judging in ignorance of composition is not irresponsible. Moreover, we can make a stronger point than the negative point that it is *irresponsible not* to have beliefs about natural properties. The positive point is that we have a *positive duty* to make moral judgments on a natural basis. The Because Constraint means that we take moral properties to be *consequential* or *dependent* properties. If we think that something has a moral property, we are duty bound to think that it has the moral property as a consequence of certain natural properties. One could not make a moral judgment without that idea. And happily this is a norm that is well respected. But the natural kind model cannot respect this idea.[13]

So far we have seen an important disanalogy between moral thinking and thought about water, rocks, snails, chairs, and pains. The Because Constraint holds of moral judgments but not of these other judgments.

Epistemological Consequences

Given the above, what follows for the epistemology of moral judgments about actual individuals, such as the judgment that Queen Isabella of Spain did many evil things in 1492? The structure of the argument so far can be put like this: (1) The Because Constraint holds. The Because Constraint means that knowledge of moral properties depends on knowledge of natural properties plus knowledge of moral–natural connections. So, given knowledge of natural properties, we cannot arrive at knowledge of moral properties without knowledge of moral–natural connections. (2) The No Independent Access Thesis holds. The No Independent Access Thesis means that knowledge of moral–natural connections cannot be derived from knowledge of moral properties plus knowledge of natural properties. (And obviously, it cannot be derived solely from either of these.) It follows that knowledge of moral–natural connections is *sui generis*. It must have an independent source. (Schematically: (1) knowledge of A depends on knowledge of B and knowledge of C; (2) knowledge of B does not depend on knowledge of A and knowledge of C (and obviously not from knowledge of A or C alone). It follows that knowledge of B must be *sui generis*.)

Now Moore steps in at this point and says that this independent source is a priori. The argument thus far, however, only shows that knowledge of moral–natural connections has *some* independent source. But is it perhaps an independent *empirical* source? No, for the following reason. Add the uncontroversial claim that we have empirical knowledge of natural properties (by causally interacting with them). That is, we are causally sensitive to natural properties. From the No Independent Access Thesis we know that however it is that we come by our knowledge of moral–natural connections, it is *not* by combining independent knowledge of moral properties and knowledge of natural properties. How then could we be causally sensitive to moral–natural connections? Being causally sensitive to the natural properties is not enough. So how, starting from empirical knowledge of natural properties, with no independent knowledge of moral properties, are we to conclude that there is a connection between those natural properties and one moral property rather than another moral property? There is nowhere else to look. Moreover – if we are worried about counterfactuals with impossible antecedents – the No Independent Access Thesis also tells us that we have no independent access to contingent causal properties of moral or natural properties, from which we could infer moral–natural connections. Hence knowledge of moral–natural connections is non-empirical.

From this point it is easy to show that particular moral beliefs about individuals have a crucial a priori component. (Of course, we know that Isabella did what she did empirically, but our knowledge that she was evil because of what she did is a priori.)

To recap: moral supervenience is a priori. And the cognition of specific moral–natural connections is also a priori. But if moral supervenience is a priori and our cognition of specific moral–natural connections is a priori, it means that having some natural property and some moral property, and having that same natural property and a different moral property, are empirically indistinguishable. There is no difference between them to which we could be causally sensitive. And this means that particular moral judgments about individuals, assuming that they are beliefs, involve a priori moral knowledge. This is the full-blown Moorean conclusion.

With this in hand, let us return to the issue of explanation that I raised at the beginning of this chapter. How does the Moorean epistemology impact on the original question of whether moral judgments are caused by moral facts? Considerably! It remains true that moral facts have causal efficacy. But they don't have causal efficacy with respect to our moral beliefs such that the formation of our moral beliefs is causally responsive to moral facts. Moral facts have a ghostly quality as far as our moral beliefs are concerned. This means that the issue of causal efficacy and the issue of epistemic status come apart, at least in moral philosophy. While it may be true that moral properties have causal efficacy with respect to many things, our moral beliefs are not sensitive to that efficacy. Note that I am not rejecting the idea that moral judgments need to be explained. Only the Obscurantist Ostrich philosopher does that. What I reject is just the particular explanation that is characteristic of empirical judgments. I have argued that moral beliefs should not be explained by appeal to moral properties. What explains moral beliefs is the natural facts, plus our natural beliefs about those natural facts, plus our beliefs about moral–natural connections. Hence moral beliefs can be explained without moral facts, as philosophers like Mackie rightly said. But this negative explanatory claim can be shared by unlikely bedfellows. In particular, Moore should be happy to get into bed with Mackie.

Consider an example, which is parallel except that it involves objects instead of properties. Imagine someone with a strange theological belief: Paul believes that Elvis Presley is God. Suppose that the incarnation of God is not conceptually or metaphysically impossible; and suppose, amazingly enough, that God is in fact incarnate in the person of Elvis Presley. The overall situation is then this: there is Elvis, God, and the incarnation relation. And then there is Paul's beliefs about Elvis, his beliefs about God, and his beliefs about the incarnation relation. Question: is Paul causally sensitive to the presence of God? Obviously not! For Paul has no independent access to God and to Elvis. So the incarnation relation is empirically inscrutable. Paul's God beliefs are arrived at inferentially from his ordinary natural beliefs plus his belief about the incarnation relation. So even if God *is* incarnate in Elvis, God plays no role with respect to Paul's God beliefs. The situation with moral properties is parallel.

In sum, the Because Constraint makes a great difference to the content of ordinary moral judgments. When we judge that something has some moral property, we are constrained to judge that the thing has that moral property because it has some natural property. By contrast, in the case of natural kinds, colour, and proper names, there is no such principle at work. We can judge simply that the thing is water, not that it is water because it has such and such molecular structure. We can judge simply that a thing is yellow, not that it is yellow because it has such and such reflectance properties. We can judge that someone is in pain, not that he is in pain because he has such and such brain or functional states. And we judge that someone is Cicero, not that he is Cicero because he is Tully. Yet in morality we cannot just judge that something is bad; we must judge that it is bad because it is such and such. This is fundamental, and it has profound consequences for the epistemology and explanation of moral judgments. Moral thought is very different from science or ordinary empirical judgment. Moral judgments, if they are beliefs, are a priori. Moore was right about that.[14]

Notes

1 I use the word 'judgment' so as to be neutral between different kinds of mental act.
2 In a past era philosophers would have raised semantic questions about what we mean by moral *words* or *sentences*, but such issues are derivative from the above metaphysical, epistemological, and attitudinal issues. Moreover, it is crucial not to cast these three issues in terms of *moral truth*, since that results either in the failure to address any of these three issues or in a grand confusion of them all.
3 I agree with Colin McGinn that causal accounts of the empirical/a priori distinction are superior to experiential accounts.
4 The objection that successful quasi-realism undermines itself is likely to seem persuasive only to those who think that philosophy is limited to conceptual analysis.
5 I configure (or reconfigure) the debate over unasserted moral propositions ('the Frege-Geach point') in these explanatory terms in Zangwill 1992b. I believe that this is Blackburn's approach. This is missed by many of his commentators. The issue is not simply one of finding a formalization of the non-cognitivist construal of complex contexts that yields the correct inferences, but of explaining, on a non-cognitivist basis, why ordinary thought displays complex propositional constructions, and complex propositional constructions of specific sorts. The task is to show why they might be expected and why they might be a needed development of moral thinking, given the function (or functions) of moral thinking. A corollary of this approach is that there are no non-complex moral contexts. By this I mean that even the step from a simple attitude of approval of a thing to a judgment that it is good (or to the linguistic expression of such a judgment) is a step that implicates other attitudes and the systemization of attitudes. *All* contexts are complex contexts, for the quasi-realist.
6 The bad news for such an enthusiastic quasi-realist will be that along with the benefits of capturing the common-sense idea of the causal efficacy of moral properties, the quasi-realist will also incur the cost of an error theory about their spatial location. Moral properties are not really in the objects, but we think of them as if they are. Hume describes our sensibilities "gilding and staining all natural objects with the colours, borrowed from internal sentiment, raises in a manner a new creation" (Hume 1975: 294). But if we think of wrongness as in the objects, we make a mistake. However, that news is not *very* bad. While it may be true that the quasi-realist has to swallow an error theory about this aspect of moral thought, he can still hold a non-error, or vindicationist, theory about a great many other aspects of our moral thought.
7 I shall not discuss Brink and Sturgeon's idea that moral claims plus auxiliary hypotheses logically entail observable states affairs (Sturgeon 1988: 232; Brink 1989: 184). The fact that moral claims entail observable claims when combined with auxiliary hypotheses no more shows moral claims to be empirical than "The absolute is lazy" is shown to be empirical because, in combination with the "auxiliary" claim "If the absolute is lazy it will rain

Moral Epistemology and the Because Constraint

tomorrow," it logically entails the empirically knowable conclusion "It will rain tomorrow" (Berlin 1950: 19).

8 Hence there is a reason for the quasi-realist to have the extra ambition of seeking to secure the idea that moral properties are causally efficacious.

9 See Goldhagen (1996) and Zangwill (2003) for arguments to the effect that many of the German perpetrators morally endorsed Hitler's policies.

10 In this chapter, I remain neutral about various difficult issues about the modality of this *because*.

11 Consider the extraordinary near-encounter between Churchill and Hitler in 1932. They both turned out to be staying in the same hotel, and they arranged to meet. Churchill remarked to the intermediary "What is the sense of being against a man simply because of his birth?". This was reported to Hitler, who cancelled the meeting (Churchill 1948: 65).

12 It is relatively uncontroversial that truths about particular moral–natural property connections are not conceptual or analytic truths (Zangwill 2000).

13 This major flaw in Sturgeon's and Brink's account is shared in spades by those of the English Perceptual School (e.g. McDowell 1998). Their view is that we are perceptually aware of moral properties (perhaps "directly"). But the idea of a form of immediate perceptual access of the mind to moral properties is extraordinarily implausible. It means that we have some kind of direct confrontation with a thing's moral properties, without any need for knowledge of its natural properties. This is both incredible and irresponsible. Moral thinking, as described by those of the English Perceptual School, is worrying akin to the kind of thinking involved in traditional English class snobbery and prejudice. What masquerades as the perception of important subtle nuances is in fact a system of baseless distinctions. See Nancy Mitford (1959) on 'U' and 'Non-U'. For example, saying 'horse-riding' is 'non-U' whereas saying 'riding' is 'U', since, after all, what *other* kind of riding is there (Ross 1959)?

14 Material in this chapter was presented in talks at the universities of Oxford and Cambridge, where there was some interesting discussion. Thanks to Jamie Dreier and Ralph Wedgwood for written comments.

References

Berlin, I. (1950). *Concepts and Categories*. London: Hogarth Press.

Simon Blackburn (1980). "Truth, realism, and the regulation of theory." Repr. in Blackburn 1993.

Blackburn, S. (1984). *Spreading the Word*. Oxford: Oxford University Press.

Blackburn, S. (1985). "Supervenience revisited." Repr. in Blackburn 1993.

Blackburn, S. (1993). *Essays on Quasi-realism*. Oxford: Oxford University Press.

Blackburn, S. (1998). *Ruling Passions*. Oxford: Oxford University Press.

Brink, D. (1989). *Moral Realism and the Foundations of Ethics*. Cambridge: Cambridge University Press.

Churchill, W. S. 1948. *The Second World War, Volume 1. The Gathering Storm*. London: Cassell.

Dworkin, R. (1996). "Morality and objectivity." *Philosophy and Public Affairs*, 25: 87–139.

Dworkin, R. (1997). "Reply to Blackburn, Otsuka and Zangwill." *Brown Electronic Article Review Service*, ed. J. Dreier and D. Estlund. <http://www.brown.edu/Departments/Philosophy/bears/homepage.html>. Posted September 4, 1996.

Fine, K. (2002). "The varieties of necessity." In T. Gendler and J. Hawthorn (eds.), *Conceivability and Possibility.* Oxford: Oxford University Press.

Goldhagen, D. (1996). *Hitler's Willing Executioners.* London: Abacus.

Harman, G. (1977). *The Nature of Morality.* Oxford: Oxford University Press.

Hume, D. (1975). *An Enquiry Concerning the Principles of Morals.* Oxford: Oxford University Press

Kim, J. (1984). "Concepts of supervenience." Reprinted in Kim 1993.

Kim, J. (1993). *Supervenience and Mind.* Cambridge: Cambridge University Press.

Saul Kripke (1980). *Naming and Necessity.* Cambridge, Mass.: Harvard University Press.

Mackie, J. (1977). *Ethics.* Harmonsworth: Penguin.

McDowell, J. (1998). *Mind, Value and Reality.* Cambridge, Mass.: Harvard University Press.

McGinn, C. (1975-6). "A posteriori and a priori knowledge." *Proceedings of the Aristotelian Society.* Repr. in McGinn, *Knowledge and Reality.* Oxford: Oxford University Press, 1998.

McGinn, C. (1982). "Modal reality." In R. Healy (ed.), *Reduction, Time and Reality.* Cambridge: Cambridge University Press. Reprinted in McGinn, *Knowledge and Reality.* Oxford: Oxford University Press, 1998.

McGinn, C. (1984). "The concept of knowledge." *Midwest Studies in Philosophy.* Reprinted in McGinn, *Knowledge and Reality.* Oxford: Oxford University Press, 1998.

McGinn, C. (2000). *Logical Properties.* Oxford: Oxford University Press.

Mitford, N. (1959). "The English aristocracy." In Mitford (ed.), *Noblesse Oblige.* Harmonsworth: Penguin.

Moore, G. E. (1922). "The conception of intrinsic value." *Philosophical Studies,* London: Routledge.

Putnam, H. (1992). "Reply to Alan Sidelle." *Philosophical Topics,* 20: 391-3.

Ross, A. (1959). "U and Non-U." In N. Mitford (ed.), *Noblesse Oblige.* Harmonsworth: Penguin.

Salmon, N. (1981). *Reference and Essence.* Princeton University Press.

Shandley, R. (ed.) (1998). *Willing Germans? The Goldhagen Debate.* Minnesota, University of Minnesota Press.

Soames, S. (2002). *Beyond Rigidity: The Unfinished Semantic Agenda of Naming and Necessity.* Oxford: Oxford University Press.

Sturgeon, N. (1986). "Harman on moral explanations." *Southern Journal of Philosophy* supp. vol. 24: 115-41.

Sturgeon, N. (1988). "Moral explanations." In G. Sayre-McCord (ed.), *Essays on Moral Realism.* Ithaca: Cornell University Press.

Sturgeon, N. (1991). "Contents and causes." *Philosophical Studies,* 61: 19-37.

Sturgeon, N. (1996). "Evil and explanation." *Canadian Journal of Philosophy* supp. vol. 21: 155-85.

Sturgeon, N. (1998). "Thomson against moral explanations." *Philosophy and Phenomological Research,* 58: 119-206.

Thomson, J., (1998). "Replies to critics." *Philosophy and Phenomenological Research,* LVIII: 215-22.

Wright. C. (1985). "Review of Simon Blackburn's *Spreading the Word.*" *Mind,* 94: 310-19.

Zangwill, N. (1992a). "Quietism." *Midwest Studies in Philosophy,* 17: 160-76.

Zangwill, N. (1992b). "Moral modus ponens." *Ratio,* 5: 177-93.

Zangwill, N. (1993). "Quasi-realism, justification and explanation." *Synthese,* 97: 287-96.

Zangwill, N. (1996a). "Moral supervenience." *Midwest Studies in Philosophy,* 20: 240-262.

Zangwill, N. (1996b). "Zangwill reviews Dworkin." *Brown Electronic Article Review Service,* ed. J. Dreier and D. Estlund, <http://www.brown.edu/Departments/Philosophy/bears/homepage.html>. Posted February 12, 1996.

Zangwill, N. (2000). "Against analytic moral functionalism." *Ratio*, 13: 275–86.

Zangwill, N. (2003). "Perpetrator motivation: some reflections on the Browning/Goldhagen debate." In E. Garrard and G. Scarre (eds.), *Moral Philosophy and the Holocaust*. Aldershot: Ashgate Press.

Nick Zangwill (2005). "Moore, morality, supervenience, essence, epistemology." *American Philosophical Quarterly*, 42: 125–30.

Are There General Moral Principles?

CHAPTER SIXTEEN

Ethical Generality and
Moral Judgment

Robert Audi

Ethics is commonly considered a realm of inexact standards, unpredictable exceptions, "grey areas," and subjectivity. Even those who believe in moral rules tend to
think that they admit of exceptions or should be stated with qualifiers such as 'normally', 'for the most part', and 'other things equal'. Aristotle formulated a major point
underlying this view when he said, regarding the mean between excess and deficiency,
that it is "relative to us" (*Nicomachean Ethics* 1107a). The influence of this point in
his presentation of the "Golden Mean," especially taken together with Aristotelian
virtue ethics in general, has been enormous. The point does not depend on virtue
ethics, though any virtue ethicist is likely to accept it and to hold that what we ought
to do on a given occasion depends on what virtue requires in the circumstances. To
say this, however, is not only to relativize obligation to circumstances, as nearly every
moral theorist would, but, in effect, to interpose the complex and controversial
concept of virtue between circumstance and action. Is there a better alternative that
enables us to determine our obligations more directly?

In seeking to avoid excessive relativity, it is natural for philosophers to search for
basic principles. For many philosophers, and particularly for those constructing
an ethical system, only principles that are both clear and highly general will suffice.
Quite apart from any theoretical concerns, it is also natural for moral agents to seek
clarity and generality in ethics. Ethical generality facilitates the teaching of ethics to
children, the guidance of moral decisions, the justification of moral judgments, and
the formulation of laws and social policies. Examples of general moral principles
abound; recall those corresponding to the prohibitions of lying, stealing, and killing
that are expressed in the Ten Commandments. Among those put forward by philosophers, there are probably none more widely cited than Kant's categorical imperative
or Mill's principle of utility (though, to be sure, in varying formulations). The
central question I want to pursue is what kind of generality moral principles may
exhibit.

If there is any position in the history of ethics that stands out for its attempt to capture both ethical generality and the kind of relativity to context that Aristotle described, it is the intuitionism of W. D. Ross. He formulated general principles, but treated each as in a sense admitting of an indefinite range of exceptions; he also gave special emphasis – and perhaps treated as in some way basic – singular moral judgments, those to the effect that a particular person (including oneself) should do a particular deed. On the first count, he is a kind of generalist, on the second, a kind of particularist. My aim here is to explore the varieties and prospects for both kinds of position in ethics. A moderate Rossian intuitionism, and especially the kind of generality it embodies, will be my main focus.

Types of Ethical Generality

It is doubtful that there is any philosophically interesting notion of ethical generality that can be specified in a purely formal way. Mere universality, at least, in the sense of having the form of 'All *F*s are *G*s', will not serve. Consider the principle that all lies not excusable by considerations of confidentiality, self-protection, non-injury, self-development, or impact on human welfare are wrong. This is universal, "perfectly" general, and arguably true; but it is not a good moral guide. There is too much lack of clarity about the nature of the exceptions and indeed about how tradeoffs among them might be accommodated, say where self-protection would be well served by a given action but confidentiality breached. There may be other problems, but the vagueness and the tradeoff problems, as I will call them, are serious and recurring difficulties in any plausible ethical framework.

The systems of Kant and Mill each have resources one might use to deal with these problems. Exploring their systems in detail would be a major task that is impossible here, but let me make just a few points to suggest why these systems do not readily solve the problems.

In the case of Kant, let us focus on the intrinsic end formulation of the categorical imperative: *"Act in such a way that you always treat humanity, whether in your own person or in the person of any other, never simply as a means, but always at the same time as an end"* (1961: 96).[1] Even if we ignore the controversy concerning how to interpret this imperative, we must grant that there can be a tradeoff between treating one person as an end and treating someone else as such (say, where one's time and resources are limited); and it might be argued that treating some people as ends might conflict with avoiding treating others merely as means, as where the only way to save a large number of people is to sacrifice one. It is true that once we have a proposed moral principle, the universality formulation of the imperative commends itself as a *test* of its adequacy; but even then, there remain problems concerning what counts as *rational* universalizability.[2]

As to Mill, he was specific enough in *Utilitarianism* to enable us to make a more explicit appraisal of his success with the two problems of special interest here, the vagueness and tradeoff problems. On one interpretation of his principle of utility, it says that an act is obligatory if and only if it has at least as much utility as any alternative available to the agent, where utility is understood in terms of contribution to the happiness of sentient beings, measured by the ratio of pleasure to pain caused by the act, with quality as well as quantity taken into account.[3] Difficulties with this formulation are well known, and here I make no attempt to appraise its ultimate plausibility. For our purposes, it is enough to note two points.

First, the principle has significant vagueness. This holds regarding the notions of pleasure and pain, the concept of the *quality* of a pleasure, and the *scope* of the reference to sentient beings – for instance, concerning how animals figure in the calculation (for instance, how various species count in relation to pain and pleasure), and concerning how readily an agent should be able to perform an action in order for it to count as available: roughly, as a genuine alternative. (I leave aside the question how far into the future consequences matter for moral decision – I assume that, strictly speaking, it is for ever and that vagueness is perhaps not a problem here, whatever may be the difficulties of calculation.)

Second, as to the tradeoff problem, there is the difficulty of weighing quantity against duration of pleasures and pains; and Mill himself recognized the further difficulty of measuring quality against quantity. He proposed a formula for dealing with it; but he left us with an indeterminacy.[4] He did not even address the point that moral reflection reveals a greater obligation to reduce pain rather than enhance pleasure, other things equal. This point is unavoidably vague, but is highly plausible and widely taken into account in moral thinking.

Mill was aware of the sorts of difficulty I have described. His response, above all, was to suggest that in practice we can usually be guided by what he called "secondary rules," such as the rule that one should not lie. We do not need to appeal to the principle of utility except when we encounter a conflict between duties that we have under two or more secondary rules.[5] There is much plausibility in the idea that usually we can be guided by secondary rules. These are, however, vague; and as Mill would grant, reliance on them does not free one from the tradeoff problem.

Are there any moral principles that are at least largely immune to these problems? One might hope to frame some that are so definite as to avoid the vagueness problem by their clarity and so selective in their requirements as to put them beyond the tradeoff problem. This aim would force us to set aside certain kinds of principle that might be true, say that one should never do an absolute injustice. A word like 'absolute' is significantly vague to begin with and conceals such tradeoff problems as occur in wartime, where collateral harm to innocent people is inevitable and must be weighed against the value of victory. Qualifiers like 'absolute' and 'unconditional' conceal rather than solve our problem.

We might hope, however, to frame exceptionless, fully general principles by anticipating the relevant conditions in which the kind of obligation in question does not apply (or is overridden) and building them into its content. Call this a *conditionalization strategy*. With this strategy in mind, consider a reply to the claim that we need not always do what we promise to do (as where we miss a dinner appointment in order to prevent a serious accident). "To any relatively trivial promise there are a host of tacit conditions, all of which will normally be satisfied, which promiser and promisee must and do understand, and when, as occasionally happens, such a condition is not satisfied, the promiser treats his obligation as annulled" (Donagan 1977: 93).[6] I have four points about this tacit conditionalization strategy.

The first point concerns the content of promises. It is essential to keep in mind that *what* we promise to do is what we specify in saying 'I promise to . . .' (the specification may be indirect, e.g. where we say 'yes' to 'Do you promise to . . .?'). Most commonly, this is an action, though we may only indicate a range of actions, as where we promise our support for a project. We do sometimes cite conditions that must obtain before the obligation "takes effect," for instance in promising 'to pay a bill *if* he doesn't'. But here we make a *conditional promise*; this is not putting conditions *on fulfilling* a promise. I could promise to defend you *if* your life is threatened even where I see nothing whatever as a condition for my defensive action in case the threat materializes.

Second, though promising takes place against a background of understanding of *excusatory conditions* – the kind whose presence absolves one of moral guilt for non-performance – normal contexts of promising do not require that there be a definite list of these assumed to be absent, nor can we in general specify them *all* even with effort. Third, it would not be morally advisable for us to try to internalize the suggested excusatory list standard even if we could; for then we would be loath to believe we had been promised anything significant unless the excusatory conditions (or others warranting non-performance of the promised deed) were specified or – as it quite unlikely – clear enough not to need specification. Finally, the occurrence of excusatory conditions does not *annul* the promise in question; otherwise there would be no obligation, or a different kind of obligation, to explain the non-performance to the promisee by appeal to such a condition. I conclude that the tacit conditionalization strategy fails as an attempt to show that some (sound) moral principles are absolute (and in that sense perfectly general), and that if it is improved by allowing a blanket clause such as 'so long as nothing of greater importance requires non-performance', it would still only conceal the kinds of problem we are addressing.

It might seem that some acts are utterly impermissible. This would imply that there are absolute generalizations of narrow scope. Isn't it always wrong to torture an infant? We recoil at the mere thought of this. But is it impossible that an infant be afflicted (perhaps by brain manipulation) with a condition curable only by torture? In that case, the kind and amount of torture relative to the kind of life we can secure for the child becomes crucial. This is a tradeoff problem. We might now try the principle that it is always wrong to torture an infant *for fun*. But here another problem arises: 'for fun' is not part of an act-description but an indication of motivational underpinning. Adding it to a report of what someone does tells us *why* the agent did it; it is explanatory of the action, not an indication of a different or further act. If the action is not absolutely wrong, does *it* become wrong if performed for a reprehensible reason? This is doubtful. A permissible act can be performed with shameful motivation.

Perhaps we may say, however, that there are some absolute conditional obligations, for instance, *given* the regrettable necessity to torture an infant, to avoid doing it for fun (this is not avoiding an "act" of doing-it-for-fun, but avoiding torturing an infant in any case in which one *would* be doing it for fun, something one may well be able to anticipate). But what if the only way one could bring oneself to torture the child, and thereby meet one's regrettable obligation, is to cause oneself to be motivated in such way that one does it for fun? There are many questions here. I will not pursue them now. Enough has been said to make it clear that the suggested *specificity approach* to achieving moral generality without serious vagueness or difficult trade-off problems is not promising.

Apparently, the vagueness and tradeoff problems are unavoidable in ethical theory. Ross saw that, and his strategy was to integrate a kind of particularism (a term to be clarified shortly) with the highest level of ethical generality he thought it reasonable to seek. He did this by appeal to Aristotelian practical wisdom as our only good resource for dealing with the tradeoff problem and, regarding the vagueness problem, with the presupposition of Aristotle's judicious point that one must not demand more precision than the subject admits. Ross seems to me to have been on the right track on both counts. The next section will briefly set out his position on ethical generality. We can then consider some important challenges to it.

The Rossian Integration Between the Particular and the General

Ross took obligatoriness (actual duty, in his terminology) to be a consequential attribute of action: roughly, to belong to an act in virtue of certain of its other properties. Among the most important are the grounds of obligation he cited in his famous list of prima facie duties in chapter 2 of *The Right and the Good* (1930).[7] He also used the word 'resultant', and he treated obligatoriness – *final duty*, as I shall call it – as a "toti-resultant attribute," on the ground that it belongs to an act in virtue of its "whole nature," whereas being a prima facie duty is a "parti-resultant attribute" (see e.g. ibid. 122–3). His view was that its whole nature is something we can never know for certain; and it is apparently at least partly for this reason that the most general moral principles he proposed are phrased in terms of prima facie rather than final duty. We have prima facie duties of fidelity (requiring promise-keeping and avoidance of lying), of reparation, gratitude, justice, self-improvement, beneficence, and non-injury.

Ross's principles are general not in the sense that they specify types of acts that *must* be performed on pain of moral failing – call that *generality as exceptionlessness* – but roughly in the sense that there is *always* a moral reason to observe them – call that *generality as universal applicability*. In being defeasible, they are, to be sure, not "absolute" but *prima facie,* as is apparent where one duty is overridden by another. Here 'prima facie' is not epistemic: its force is not to indicate that what may seem to be a duty is not one, though Ross saw that this is true. Its force is to indicate that what *is* a duty-if-not-overridden can be overridden and thereby fail to be a (final) duty. Universal applicability, moreover, does not mean bearing on conduct for all persons at all times, but rather having such bearing *given* a person's satisfying the grounding conditions. If I promise nothing, I have no promissory obligation; but *given* my promising, I have a prima facie obligation in any kind of situation. To be sure, there may always be someone I can benefit, so the prima facie duty of beneficence may apply to me at all times and places regardless of what I do.

On the plausible assumption that obligatoriness is a consequential property, one might think that Ross stopped short of the strongest form of generality he might have captured: the kind expressed by principles that are universal in scope but, unlike the principle of utility and the categorical imperative, specific as to the act-type they demand. A rationale for this idea might be that, *given* an exercise of practical wisdom in which we determine our final duty in a context of moral decision, we may retrospectively formulate such a generality by describing the situation in sufficient detail. If I can see that nothing overrides my obligation to keep a promise, surely I can frame a generalization listing the relevant considerations – obviously finite in number since I take them all into account in a reasonable amount of time. Surely, it may seem, I can frame an informative principle to cover the type of action in question. But is this so?

Granted, if we know that we have a final duty to *A*, we may infer that in exactly similar circumstances anyone would have this final duty. But similarly, if we know that a Modigliani sculpture is graceful, we may infer that any sculpture exactly like it will also be graceful. This is an aesthetic generality of quite limited significance. In particular, it does not by itself help us significantly to *identify* what counts toward beauty in sculpture or how to create it in a non-imitative way. Let us explore how far some major ethical theorists have gone in enabling us to formulate significant moral generalizations.

Suppose, as Mill, Kant, and apparently Ross as well believed, we always have duties of beneficence (for at least most of us, there is virtually always something significant we can do to help others). To be sure, one might (as Ross and others have taken Kant to do) regard promissory duties as invariably overriding those latter duties; and one might, as Mill presumably did, think that in some cases it can be obvious that utility is best served by keeping one's promise. But even supposing one can know that one's promissory duty overrides any duties of beneficence one has, putting such an overridingness clause in one's guiding moral principle gives it generality at the cost of both vagueness and a tacit acknowledgment of the tradeoff problem. It would not do to try to teach the duty of beneficence to our children by saying that one should do good deeds for others unless one has a stronger (an overriding) conflicting duty, for instance to keep a promise.

Ross would say that we can never know whether such overridingness obtains, and even that we cannot know the related (and arguably equivalent) proposition that no other duty overrides the promissory one, say a duty of justice or non-injury. For one thing, there is commonly injustice to which we should attend; for another, whether we may cause injury in keeping a promise (even injury to the promisee) may be difficult to predict. I do not share Ross's rigorism about knowability. I believe we often know what our final duty is. Still, even on the assumption that we do know a singular moral judgment to be sound, this is *because* we presuppose something which is both highly vague and itself presupposes that there are possible tradeoffs.

Should we conclude, then, that (as Ross may have thought) the kinds of prima facie principle he articulated are the most general ones close enough to action to be a practical guide to moral judgment? I believe that conclusion would be too strong. What counts as a practical guide to judgment is, in a certain way, relative to the capacities and experience of the agents whose guidance is in question. Moreover, the Rossian principles themselves are not equally applicable to everyday action. Even a young child can tell right off that saying a certain thing would be a lie; and the promising rule applies to deeds that, having been promised, have antecedently entered consciousness and so, when the time comes to keep the promise, can commonly be reidentified without reflection.[8] But some kinds of injury are not readily identifiable. Some psychological damage, for instance, is highly injurious, but not readily perceptible.

As to the duties of justice, some of these may, even for morally sensitive agents, be as difficult (or as easy) to identify in practice as are acts that treat someone "as an end," in a broadly Kantian sense. Some moral agents are extraordinarily perceptive and have great facility in moral reasoning; some situations straightforwardly demand a given action which, like pulling a drowning child from deep waters, any normal person can see to be obligatory.

What is practical for one agent, or for one kind of situation, need not be practical for another; and even if we can find clear cases of the generally impractical at one end of the moral spectrum and clear instances of practical ones at the other, we cannot determine, a priori, just what contents will or will not yield practical moral principles across all moral agents and in all contexts of moral decision. There may be moral principles far more general than Ross's that are practical for some agents in some contexts, perhaps including *principles of action* like the categorical imperative and *principles of character* such as the injunction to be just, honest, loyal, and kind.

To be sure, principles of character may be argued to count as moral principles only insofar as they "point" to action. But virtue ethicists would deny this; and, more important for the issue here, these principles are in any case capable of being both general, and, in some cases, practical. It should be added that directly guiding moral decision is not the only function a moral principle can have. It can also unify and provide understanding of less general principles, as may be held for the categorical imperative and the principle of utility.[9]

To say that there can be true moral principles that are both of great generality and have potential value in guiding action is not to posit any principles that bypass the vagueness and tradeoff problems. Suppose (as Ross apparently thought) these problems are inevitable. Was Ross right in thinking that we may at least bring to the effort to surmount these problems the kinds of prima facie principle he articulated? Or are practical moral problems so particular that even Rossian principles may not apply to them in the way he thought? One way to frame the question I have in mind is to ask if there is any ethical generality at all *before the fact*, i.e., apart from a context in which judgment is to be made. This brings us to the sense in which Ross was a particularist and to questions about whether we should prefer a version of particularism that is inconsistent with his ethical generalism.

Five Types of Particularistic Intuitionism

I have so far represented Ross as formulating the most general moral principles that he considered both true and sufficiently practical to represent the moral standards, or at least moral presuppositions, of mature moral agents as such, i.e., conceived as "plain men" not committed to an ethical theory. Since the principles are highly general, one might wonder in what sense Ross could be regarded as a particularist at all. His intuitionism may at least be considered epistemically particularistic. Specifically, he held that at least some intuitions about concrete cases are epistemically more basic than, or in any event indispensable to, intuitive knowledge of the corresponding generalizations. Indeed, in the course of moral development, it may be only when one thinks of a deed concretely and sees that it is wrong that one can see (or be justified in believing) that all deeds of that kind are wrong.[10] This is doubtless the kind of thing C. D. Broad had in mind in holding that experience of fittingness in particular cases is required before one can "rise," by intuitive induction, to general knowledge of the kind of case in question (1930: 282).

In calling Ross's intuitionism particularist, I use a term that applies to many domains, but my concern here is mainly with the notion of duty. I have already suggested that Ross's intuitionism is an *epistemological particularism*, which (putting it in more general terms) is roughly the view that cognitions (including intuitions as a special case) regarding duty in a concrete instance, such as a situation in which one must aid an injured person, are epistemically prior to cognitions regarding duty in general, particularly to knowledge or belief of a general principle of duty. Intuitive induction is one kind of epistemic process in which knowledge of something particular yields knowledge of something general that the particular instantiates.

A related view is *conceptual particularism*, roughly the position that cognitions concerning such concrete cases are conceptually prior to cognitions concerning duty in general. On this view, one can acquire (or at least possess) the concept of duty only on the basis of acquiring (or at least possessing) the concept of, say, a duty to do a good deed for someone who has gone to great trouble to help one paint a garage. It is from one's understanding of such a concrete duty that one acquires a concept of duty as such. This is not the view that *knowledge* of particular truths about a case of duty yields knowledge of something general about duty; that epistemological point, which an epistemological particularist like Ross is likely to accept, could hold where the former kind of knowledge embodies a general concept of duty. Conceptual particularism requires that one have a concept of a particular duty as a basis for a concept of duty in general.

Conceptual particularism should be distinguished from an empirical thesis we might call *genetic particularism*, the position that in the normal order of learning of concepts and propositions, exposure to concrete cases is prior to understanding general deontic concepts and general principles of duty. This view does not entail conceptual particularism, since the *content* of what one learns initially through exposure to concrete cases can be conceptual and general: a child who genuinely learns what it is to have a duty to keep a particular promise may at some level be both acquiring the concept of a duty to keep *promises* (this is conceptual learning) and learning that promising implies such a duty (this is propositional learning). Ross, like Broad and others, was apparently a genetic as well as an epistemological particularist. But it is not clear that he held conceptual particularism, and in any case a moderate intuitionism can hold the former two views and not the third.

Genetic particularism does not entail that any specific method of moral thinking is preferable to the others, but it naturally goes with a kind of *methodological particularism*. This is the thesis that moral reasoning, whether about individual cases calling for moral judgment or in theoretical matters, should give some kind of priority to reflection on particular cases, such as those in which one person owes reparation to another or does an injustice to another.[11] This view can take various forms, depending on the kind of substantive priority that a proponent assumes, say temporal or, more likely, epistemological. I mention this view for the clarity it adds by contrast with the other kinds of particularism. Many intuitionists have implicitly held some version of it, but as a methodological view it might be held by non-intuitionists and is not of major concern in evaluating substantive particularist views or in determining the respects in which sound moral principles can be general.

A fifth kind of (ethical) particularism – *normative particularism* – is more controversial among intuitionists. I refer to the view that the deontic *valence* of a consideration (such as one's having promised to do a deed), i.e., the consideration's counting for or against the action in question (or neutrally) is determinable only in particular cases and is not invariant across different cases. This differs from the counterpart ontological view on which the valence of any element is *determined* by factors that vary from case to case. It is clear that different sorts of thing can underlie an injury or an injustice; our question is whether the valence of, say, injury or lying varies, not whether the basis of what has the valence can vary.

A stronger normative particularism has it that even the *relevance* of a consideration to determining duty is ascertainable only in particular cases.[12] If this view is sound, then not only could lying count negatively or positively in different cases; in some it could also be irrelevant. Ross was not a normative particularist in either sense. He held, regarding the grounds of basic prima facie duties, an *invariant valence view*: the valence of, say, an action's being an injury of another person is always a prima facie reason against it. Let us explore this view.

Moderate Intuitionism and Normative Valence

A moderate intuitionist can (with Ross) maintain epistemological and genetic particularism, leave open conceptual particularism, and reject normative particularism in favor of the invariant valence view. It is natural to call this position a *moderate particularism*, by contrast with the strong particularism that endorses all four particularist theses. But at least the invariance thesis, as in a sense generalist, may seem inappropriate for any particularist view and perhaps even for ethical intuitionism as such. Let us explore this.

Suppose I promise to pick a friend up at a certain crowded place at ten and I discover just as I am about to drive off that a third party intends, when I get there, to detonate a powerful bomb he has concealed in my car. Is my promising to pick up my friend even relevant to deciding whether to do so, much less a consideration favoring it? We might also imagine the man who promised Macbeth to kill Lady Macduff and her children. This is a morally outrageous act. Does he have even a prima facie obligation to do it? Should we not adopt a thoroughly contextualist view here, as a strong particularist would?[13] A great deal can be said on this issue. I have space for only a few of the major distinctions a moderate intuitionism can bring to bear.

First, it is essential to distinguish the *deliberative relevance* of a consideration, roughly its relevance to making a decision regarding what to do, from its *normative relevance*, its valence (positive or negative) in relation to the action(s) in question. My promise to pick up my acquaintance is not deliberatively relevant; I would be at best foolish to bring it into my thinking about whether to do something that would kill dozens of innocent people. It does not follow that it has no normative relevance. To say so would be like saying that because it makes no sense to wait for a penny in change at the cost of missing one's flight, the penny has no value. Granted, to *say* that a promise like the one in question has normative relevance is odd. But that may be owing to the pragmatic point that it is highly misleading to call a consideration normatively relevant when in the circumstances any normative weight it has is far below the threshold of deliberative relevance. That it is misleading or even in some way wrong to assert a proposition does not imply that it is untrue.

A further point supporting the normative relevance view (and indeed the invariant valence view) is that despite how obviously my promissory obligation is outweighed, it is important to offer my friend an explanation of my non-appearance. This bespeaks a normative factor that was overridden rather than eradicated. The case of Macbeth's hired killer is perhaps more complex than the other example. It is not clear that he would owe Macbeth an explanation if he failed; still, that could be not because he had no such prima facie duty but because it is massively overridden by a duty not to cooperate with someone who would have one kill innocent people (other negative duties toward such a person may also come in). Nonetheless, the man's feeling such a duty would be a positive element in his character; compare him with a man who would be quite willing to do the killing but accords no weight to the promise and instead breaks it in order to perpetrate an exactly similar killing for which he is paid more. The best explanation of the even more negative assessment of the second agent is that, with the first, the promise retained some moral weight despite its outrageous object; in acknowledging that weight, the first man showed himself likely to be at least one step closer to reformation than the second. The first needs a moral transformation that may include everything except whatever element of fidelity is implicit in his sense of fiduciary duty; the second may need a complete moral transformation.

Another point emerges if we imagine the bomb case differently. Suppose I later discover that I can get the bomb defused in time to pick up my friend up a bit late. I should then do this rather than not appear at all. This point also suggests that a positive reason has been overridden in a way that generates a duty of substitution, rather than that in the context the promise had no force at all. The promise remains as a ground on which one should try to build something, even when it is clear that one should not do the promised deed.

This brings us to a second major distinction that must be observed here. Just as we can distinguish considerations above and below the threshold of deliberative relevance, we can distinguish considerations above and below the threshold of ordinary discernibility in the context of decision. A flashlight beam is not visible in bright sunlight; promising to pick up my friend at ten is not readily discernible as a reason to do so in the special case in question. But just as we can conceive blocking the sun-

Ethical Generality and Moral Judgment

light, we can conceive removing the bomb; and there seems no better reason to say that the presence of the bomb changes the force of the promise than to say that the presence of the sunlight changes the brightness of the flashlight.

Indeed, suppose I am certain that the very same people (including my friend and me) will be killed by a different terrorist if I do *not* pick up my friend at ten. For those to whom promising is a serious matter, it may seem better to keep the promise than not: at least I fulfill one more obligation before the end. I say 'may seem' because in this case I allow myself to be *used*, and there is prima facie reason to avoid *that*. To get a good analogy to the flashlight we may have to remove this element. In principle, however, a consideration's being below the level of ordinary discernibility does not entail its being below the threshold of deliberative relevance (and conversely). A similar point might apply in mathematics. Given a clearly cogent proof of a theorem, competent testimony that it is a theorem may add so little to one's justification as to seem negligible; but given a plausible attack on the proof, such testimony might become an important reason to retain belief of the theorem. Deliberative relevance varies with changes in context.

These points about promising should not be allowed to create the impression that it is easy to say just what constitutes a promise. The notion has an element of vagueness. For instance, can one promise under duress, as where one is forced at gunpoint to say 'I promise to vote for you'? I am inclined to say that so speaking in response to a *threat* does not suffice for promising, but that if one is forced to promise something because (say) one has a debt of gratitude, then (in at least some cases) one's promise can be genuine.[14] Imagine that, in gratitude, I owe you a great deal and you are a good candidate. If you insist, I presumably may promise to vote for you. Granted, I might have stronger moral reasons to vote for someone else. But suppose the only other candidate is equally good (hence not better) and that I have in mind another way to discharge my debt of gratitude to you. Even if I prefer the other way of discharging my debt, I am not free to choose that and vote for the other candidate, but should keep my promise. Genuine promises seem to retain weight not only when massively outweighed but also in some cases when they are infelicitously made.

A third distinction pertinent here is between the intrinsic valence of a consideration and its overall normative role in the context of a given decision or action. A major case in point is *Schadenfreude*, roughly taking pleasure in the suffering of another. Can the prima facie duty of beneficence, for instance, provide any reason at all to give someone an opportunity to take pleasure in sadistically beating another person? Plainly, this is the wrong kind of pleasure. Does the invariant valence view allow us to say this, at least if it endorses promotion of pleasure for someone as a (prima facie) reason for action? (It may, of course, deny that beneficence is manifested in promoting just any kind of pleasure.) The view does allow this.

To see how, we might focus on the closely related case of pain. Is it not at least in part because of the invariant badness of pain (at least of the kind in question) that the pleasure in question *is* the wrong kind? That an act produces pain is a reason to abstain from it. Moreover, we may plausibly hold that the overall state of affairs, someone's taking pleasure in paining another, has a negative value vastly outweighing the positive value of the pleasure in question. This point may allow us to say, in some cases, that whatever positive value promoting pleasure may have is below the threshold of deliberative relevance and perhaps even below that of ordinary discernability.[15]

The fourth distinction relevant here is between a kind of *holism regarding judgments of final duty*, roughly the view that where two or more conflicting considerations bear on a prospective action one can discern one's final duty only in the light of an overall assessment of them, and *holism regarding judgments of prima facie duty*, which is roughly the strong particularist view that the same point applies to judgments of prima facie duty. Moderate intuitionism (including Ross's, apparently) is committed to the first but the not the second kind of holism.

Holism regarding final duty might be called *bottom-up holism*: the identity and interrelations of the particular elements having a constant valence are the main basis of the overall judgment. On this view, final duty is compositional. Holism regarding prima facie duty – a position that goes with a normative particularism – might be called *top-down holism*. On this view, only the overall assessment of the whole – roughly, of the act in its full context – can indicate the valence of the elements in question, such as promising, lying, and injury. Suppose one faces a conflict of duties, with considerations of fidelity and familial beneficence favoring an expenditure for one's children and considerations of both rectification and beneficence favoring an incompatible expenditure for a special charity. Determination of final duty can be a holistic matter involving a huge variety of considerations even if the relevant prima facie duties are grounded in factors having a constant valence.

A constant valence, moreover, does not entail a constant *weight*. Promising, for instance, can invariably be a normative reason to do the thing in question even if some promises provide better reason for action than others and even if, as circumstances change, the overall weight of a promise in the context of decision can change. A change in weight tends to carry with it a change in moral significance; other things equal, the less weighty a consideration, the less significant. Moral significance is perhaps a threshold concept, like discernibility; and just as a consideration may be below the threshold of ordinary discernibility without being irrelevant or without its appropriate moral valence, it may be below the threshold of moral significance relative to a given decision without irrelevance or a change in its appropriate valence. Moral significance, like its close relative, deliberative relevance, does vary with context. Both notions help to show that one can be a holist about final duty and not about prima facie duty.[16]

A nice analogy to express the idea of holism about final duty is the role of a dab of paint in the whole artwork: "Natural features carry their contribution to an action's moral status in the way that a given dab of paint on the canvas carries its contribution to the aesthetic status of a painting: the bold stroke of red that helps balance one painting would be the ruin of another" (Little 2000: 280).[17] This is true, but, aesthetically, much depends on what aspect of the paint we consider, just as, morally, much depends on the aspects of an action in a social context, say that of being the making of a promise or of causing pain. Color can be invariant. The paint can retain its color regardless of the painting to which it belongs; but its effect on one may be good, on another bad. Similarly, the pain caused by a slap on the face is bad, and there is reason to avoid causing it, whether the context is an angry attack or a needed reversal of a dangerous drowsy condition that threatens a car accident. But the one can be inexcusable as an assault and the other morally right as a protection necessary in the context. A major difference is that there is no sound generality giving a particular color or shade invariant aesthetic positive or negative significance, whereas there are sound generalities giving certain kinds of acts invariant moral positive or negative significance. The aesthetic domain is not rule-governed in the way the moral realm is, but both are organic in that the value of the whole is not necessarily the sum of the values of the parts or aspects.[18]

It would be misleading, however, to say that in the slapping case the *contribution* of something prima facie wrong and intrinsically bad is to make something larger right and good, as if some element or aspect of the pain or the causing of it were transmitted to the whole and perhaps mysteriously transformed in the process. We must distinguish in such cases between the contribution of a part or aspect to a whole and its *effect* on that whole.[19] The effect of the pain that the slapping causes is to induce wakefulness; but the pain does not contribute to wakefulness, as the pleasures of conversation may contribute to the enjoyment of a dinner.

To be sure, for a strong coherentist theory of justification, *any* kind of justification is a holistic matter. For coherence is never linear, but always determined by how all the relevant elements (usually taken to be numerous and most commonly conceived as cognitions) fit together. One may, however, embrace a coherence theory of the acquisition and functioning of concepts – *conceptual coherentism* – without holding *epistemological coherentism*, which is roughly the view that the justifiedness of beliefs and other cognitions (including intuitions) is grounded in the mutual coherence of the relevant items.[20] We apparently do not acquire concepts one by one, and understanding any of them is essentially connected with understanding certain others. But it does not follow from this conceptual coherence constraint that there are no considerations which, even by themselves, provide us with prima facie justification.

Indeed, just as it is doubtful that we can account for justified belief without giving experience *some* role in generating prima facie justification, it is doubtful that we can even be in a position to decide what action is our overall duty without giving some role to independently accessible considerations, such as fidelity and veracity, generating prima facie duty. Note, too, that appeal to such considerations always has some measure of both explanatory and excusatory power. If, for instance, we wonder why someone said something evasive, some degree of explanation can be provided by saying that it avoided lying. Similarly, if I fail to keep a promise, say to preserve a confidence, I may excuse – or at least mitigate – the prima facie wrong by saying that I was asked direct questions and would have had to lie to preserve it. The invariant valence view explains such points better than alternative views.[21] This is not to imply that every non-performance of a duty *calls* for excuse or mitigation; it may be quite clear (as in the terrorist case) that a promise should be broken. A type of duty, such as a promissory one, can have an invariant valence without all its non-performances needing excuse or mitigation. The point here is that *performing* it can always provide some mitigation (or at least a morally relevant counter-consideration) where a wrong has been done.

It should be plain from a number of points made in defending the invariant valence view that it does not imply a *subsumptivist conception* of our knowledge of singular moral judgments, the idea that these judgments are knowable only as applications of generalizations, such as Rossian principles of prima facie duty. This conception may also arise from the correct point that in many cases, before we can answer the commonly encountered question of what, overall, we should do we must be able to see that two or more conflicting (prima facie) generalizations apply to our options. But the applicability of several generalizations to a case does not imply that one's final obligation therein is determined by applying a further, reconciling generalization. That point holds even if such a generalization is in principle formulable after the fact.

Moral Character as an Element in Ethical Generality

Moral generality need not be understood along Rossian lines. I have already indicated that a virtue theorist might take the bearing of moral traits to be the basis of any general moral standards with significant practical application. It is noteworthy, in this connection, that in specifying the grounds of prima facie duties, Ross emphasized certain virtue notions. The duties to keep promises and avoid lying are called duties of fidelity; and there are also aretaic duties of gratitude, justice, and beneficence. It is difficult to find virtues so closely linked to the duties of self-improvement, reparation, and non-injury, but what we need to discover here can be seen from the other cases.

The suggested view might be called *aretaic generalism*: the only basic kinds of ethical generalizations that are significant and useful are certain kinds in which virtue is central, such as 'We ought to be honest'. Applying this to promises and lying, one might hold that the basic moral reason not to break promises or lie is that such conduct bespeaks infidelity to one's word. We could even go so far as to say that the latter is our primary moral reason for the relevant act, and the fact that an act is a lie is only a derivative moral reason: operative only when the act is suitably connected with a virtue.[22] This would account for varying valence on the part of the latter kind of reason. In the game of contraband, for instance, the point is to lie and get away with it, and so lying is not even prima facie wrong in this context.[23] I have two sorts of question here.

First, if it is true that certain virtue concepts (and perhaps other "thick" moral concepts) carry invariant valences, how is that to be explained? Deontologists like Ross and presumably Kant will likely respond with either or both of two points. One is that virtues may be viewed as above all internalizations of moral principles (where this involves, of course, a sense of how to deal with tradeoff problems). The other, which is suggested by Ross's emphasis on intuitive induction as a basis of moral understanding, is that moral concepts are basically tied to certain act-types, and understanding what constitutes a virtue is at least in good part a matter of seeing what types of act are appropriate to expressing it: keeping one's word, helping others, making reparation for harming others, and so forth. Arguably, if there were not basic moral reasons to perform acts of these kinds, there would not be the associated virtues. There is much more to be said on this issue.[24] My point here is simply that a great deal of argument would be needed to show that the strategy in question provides as good an account of the relevant data as a deontological intuitionism like Ross's.

The second point concerns concrete cases. It should be granted that when a person does something wrong, we can, given information about the context and motives of the deed, find terms connected with virtue that apply to the act or the agent or both. The language of virtue is immensely rich, and it can also apply in cases of fulfillment of moral obligation. But this does not show that the moral reasons operating in the context are *grounded* in the relevant virtues. The point is compatible both with the view (which an intuitionist like Ross might well hold) that virtues are internalizations of moral standards of a Rossian kind and with the axiological view that both aretaic (virtue) reasons, such as 'It is dishonest', and deontological ones, such as 'It is a lie', are grounded in (even if not only in) values, such as the kinds essential in human flourishing.

A related point should be made about the intriguing case of a game in which lying is part of the point. It is essential to distinguish here between two kinds of overrider, those that apply to an entire series of acts of a certain kind and those that apply to a single one. Consider the moment at which we agree to play the game. This agreement overrides the obligation not to lie for the entire game; it is a *diachronic* (temporally extended) *overrider* of indefinite scope. By contrast, the need to break a promise to do a single thing given a sudden stronger obligation to put out a fire is a *synchronic overrider*. The plausibility of the example seems to me to rest at least partly on our picturing the individual acts of lying. These are unexcused by any overrider at the time; there is no synchronic overrider. Their apparent disconnection with anything outside the game may also contribute to the impression that there is no overrider at all. But should anyone think that there would be no prima facie moral reason not to lie to someone who is not in the game, who happens to ask the relevant questions about the contraband, who cares about the answer, who knows nothing of the rules or spirit of the game, and who could be given the information without detracting from the game? I doubt it.

Final Duty and Overall Moral Judgment

So far, I have defended the invariant valence view and affirmed the kind of ethical generality that goes with it. But it may be reasonable to claim something more specific. Suppose that (all) moral properties are consequential on (supervene on, in one sense of 'supervene') some finite set of natural ones and that the relevant natural ones and their grounding relations to the moral ones are discernible by ordinary kinds of inquiry. Then, given a sound moral judgment in a case of conflicting obligations, it would seem that one can in principle formulate a generalization that non-trivially applies to similar cases. For the overall obligatoriness one discerns will be based on natural properties each of which one can in principle discriminate and appeal to in framing a generalization. Still, this kind of generalizability in principle is not a necessary condition for one's forming a justified judgment (or one constituting knowledge). One can achieve a sound result whether or not one generalizes on it or is even able to do so. It could be, for instance, that overall obligation is *organic* and that given the sense in which it is, there is no guarantee that in every case of sound moral judgment we can specify just what properties are its basis. Recall the example of a painting: we can justifiably believe a painting to be beautiful even though we would need both new observation and reflection even to begin to point to the elements in it that render it beautiful. Even if prima facie obligation is entailed by certain natural properties (a view that intuitionists commonly hold), overall obligation apparently requires a more complicated account.

One might question whether final obligation *is* consequential on natural properties. Consider having a final obligation to tell the truth, where this obligation prevails over a conflicting obligation to protect a friend. What might be the natural base of the relational normative property of (moral) *prevalence* or *being weightier*? As a moral pluralist, Ross would insist that there is at best no one dimension, such as the hedonic, determining the finality of the duty of veracity. There is no reason to doubt, however, that a counterpart prevalence will occur in any exactly similar case of conflicting duties. This does not entail that final duty is consequential on natural properties, but how are we to explain this generalizability except on the assumption that final obligation *is* grounded in natural properties of the relevant case? I see no good alternative explanation.

It is, moreover, at least in the spirit of a rationalist intuitionism to say that *if* we could formulate and understand all of the relevant variables, we might thereby achieve knowledge of the resulting – presumably consequential – final duty. Suppose, however, that there simply is no closed list of relevant natural properties. If not, then first, the consequential character of final duty is difficult to establish, since the overall basis of the duty may be inaccessible, and second, the epistemic organicity of final duty is to be expected, since one should not expect knowledge of final duty to be determined in any quantitative way by fewer than all of the variables underlying that duty. Such consequentiality may yet hold. Compare again the beauty of a painting: should we not consider it consequential on such elements as the colors and shapes and their relations because we cannot close the list of relevant factors? Responding to all of the relevant properties does not entail an ability to list them.

Suppose, by contrast, that in some cases we can formulate and understand all of the variables relevant to determining the finality of a duty. The generalization we could then articulate might be (and, on sufficient reflection, could to seen to be) self-evident or otherwise a priori. One might now plausibly argue that the comparative weights of the relevant duties in the kind of case in question are an a priori matter. This not only would not undermine the idea that final duty is consequential on natural properties, but would in fact extend the scope of intuitionist moral principles beyond the range anticipated by Ross and other intuitionists. Although there would still be no a priori hierarchical ranking that places some general duties, such as those of fidelity, over others, such as those of beneficence, some judgments of final duty could be instances of more specific comparative moral principles; and there would then be more such principles available to us in proportion to our skill at generalizing on the use of practical wisdom.[25]

A further point concerning the epistemic resources of the intuitionism I am defending is that in many cases of a singular judgment settling a conflict of duties, there is the possibility of reaching a reflective equilibrium between this judgment and various moral principles and other singular judgments. This equilibrium may contribute to the justification of that judgment, as well as provide, in some cases, justification for a second-order belief that the judgment is justified. It may even make the difference between a judgment with only some degree of justification and one sufficiently well justified to be both a good guide for action and a candidate for knowledge. Here, then, is one way a judgment that begins as a tentative assessment can graduate to the status of justified belief or even knowledge.

There is another aspect of the question of how general practically useful moral principles can be. It concerns possible conflicts, and hence apparently the need for tradeoffs, between moral and non-moral values. This problem can affect any plausible ethical theory. To be sure, Kant treated ethical considerations as basic in the theory of practical reason and regarded the categorical imperative as grounding absolute moral obligations. But suppose for the sake of argument that it does ground some absolute obligations. This does not entail that there is no possibility of anyone's ever rationally doing something that morality does not permit. Even apart from the (disputed) possibility of doing this knowing the act is morally impermissible, one can rationally hold a mistaken view, such as the view that a deed is permissible, and rationally holding this belief can render rational an action based on it.

Regarding consequentialist theories, if (as I shall assume) they ground all reasons for action in whatever they posit as having intrinsic value, then unless (implausibly) a utilitarian view considers *only* one quite specific kind of value to be basic, something like an incommensurability problem can arise. Consider a hedonistic utilitarianism. Even if, contrary to the view of Mill and others (almost certainly including Aristotle), no one kind of pleasure is better than any other, there would still be difficulties in weighing promotion of pleasures against reductions of pains. The trade-off problem is apparently inescapable in ethics. Radical particularism is in part a response to it, but its resources are inadequate to the task.

On the basis of this explication and partial defense of a moderate particularism and the kind of ethical generality it provides for, I conclude that a Rossian intuitionism is a plausible basis for an account of ethical generality. There is a significant kind of ethical generality: some moral principles are both wide in scope and useful in day-to-day moral thinking. The application of general principles must, however, be balanced by attention to concrete cases understood in the light of a multitude of facts about them. Moral knowledge can occur at either level. Some of it is quite general, some highly particular. At either level, moreover, certain kinds of consideration play an important role in our moral attitudes and judgments. Ross and other intuitionists have apparently been right in taking certain kinds of element to have a constant valence; but those intuitionists (and other moral theorists) who take the valence of such elements to vary with context are surely correct in emphasizing that moral judgment must be highly sensitive to particular facts that differ from one case to another.

There is, then, a holism concerning final duty that constitutes common ground between Rossian intuitionists and ethical theorists who believe in a stronger particularism. On either kind of view, I believe that we can find more room for a rationalist moral epistemology than is generally realized. Once it is seen how to eliminate mistaken assumptions that neither Rossian intuitionism nor rationalism need endorse, we can clear away some of the major obstacles in the way of a rationalist account of the foundations of ethics. There is much to commend a fallibilist, intuitionistic moral rationalism that countenances both ethical generality and moral intuitions about concrete cases as prima facie justified inputs to ethical theorizing.[26]

Notes

1   Some translators use 'merely' rather than 'simply', and I follow their practice as preferable in capturing the relevant notion as expressed in English.

2   For extensive critical discussion of how to interpret and appraise Kant's categorical imperative (in more than one formulation), see Parfit (forthcoming).

3   One can also formulate the principle in terms of *expected* utility; but there is no need to add that complication explicitly. We can assume that a utilitarian will in any case have a theory of excuses; hence if one does something wrong, one may be excusable provided one was justified in taking the utility of the act to be optimal.

4   Mill spoke of "the rule for measuring it [quality] against quantity, being the preference felt by [all or almost all?] those who in their opportunities of experience, to which must be added their habits of self-consciousness and self-observation, are best furnished with the means of comparison" (1863: ch. 2). He left indeterminate whether a simple majority suffices here or whether a stronger consensus is needed. Sidgwick's version of utilitarianism does not encounter this problem. He says, e.g., that "by Greatest Happiness is meant the greatest possible surplus of pleasure over pain . . . of course, here as before the assumption is involved that all pleasures are capable of being compared quantitatively with all pains . . . so that each may be at least roughly weighed in ideal scales against any other" (1907: 413). As Sidgwick's use of 'roughly' suggests, however, the vagueness problem is not eliminated; and although Sidgwick's formulations are superior to Mill's on some points, tradeoff problems also remain.

5   The view is also expressed by Mill in ch. 5 of *Utilitrianism*. It is among the passages in that book that lead to a reading of him as representing rule- rather than act-consequentialism. For a defense of the former and a detailed contrast between it and the latter, see Hooker (2000).

6   The principle Donagan is defending by such a tacit conditionalization strategy is that it is "*impermissible for anybody to break a freely made promise to do something in itself morally permissible*" (1977: 92–3).

7   For Ross's list of prima facie duties see *The Right and the Good* (1930: 20–1). A difficulty with the list as a candidate for a comprehensive self-sufficient set of moral principles is that some of its elements employ moral terms, e.g. 'wrongful'. I have indicated a strategy for dealing with this problem (2004: ch. 5).

8   Since one can promise to do something rather indefinite, say give psychological support, it is not always the case that when the time comes to perform, one need not reflect on what one promised but only remember it.

9   This unifying and explanatory function of certain comprehensive moral principles is explicated in Ross (1930: ch. 3).

10   Ross says, of "insight into the basic principles of morality," that it is not based on "a fairly elaborate consideration of the probable consequences" of certain types of acts; "When we consider a particular act as a lie, or as the breaking of a promise . . . we do not need to, and do not, fall back on a remembered general principle; we see the individual act to be by its very nature wrong" (1939: 172–3). Speaking approvingly of Aristotle, Ross said of right acts that, while first "done without any thought of their rightness," when "a certain degree of mental maturity" was reached, "their rightness was not deduced from any general

principle; rather the general principle was later recognized by intuitive induction as being implied in the general judgments already passed on particular acts" (ibid. 170).

11 Methodological particularism and other kinds are distinguished by Walter Sinnott-Armstrong (1999). A strong version would hold that adequate moral reasoning *must* properly attend to particular cases.

12 Jonathan Dancy holds both forms of normative particularism (e.g. 1993: 60–2, 66–8).

13 For Dancy, "The leading thought behind particularism is that the behaviour of a reason ... in a new case cannot be predicted from its behaviour elsewhere.... I borrow a book from you, and then discover that you have stolen it from the library.... It isn't that I have *some* reason to return it to you and more reason to put it back in the library. I have no reason at all to return it to you" (1993: 60). One might think this view is supported by an argument of Sidgwick's: "[A] promise to do an immoral act is held not to be binding, because the prior obligation not to do the act is paramount ... otherwise one could evade any moral obligation by promising not to fulfill it, which is clearly absurd" (1907: 305). But notice that not only does he implicitly recognize some promissory obligation by calling the prior, conflicting obligation *paramount*; he also says the former is not *binding* rather than, e.g., eliminated or never generated by promising in the first place. The validity of his reasoning, moreover, requires only that prior obligations *outweigh* any promissory obligation arising from the promise (where 'prior' means roughly 'antecedently existing' rather than 'having priority'–that reading would make his point trivially true).

14 Cf. Hooker's claim that a promise extracted under duress has no force (in Hooker and Little 2000: 9).

15 I discuss the problem of *Schadenfreude* and the related organicity of intrinsic value in some detail elsewhere (1997: ch. 11; 2004: ch. 4).

16 Cf. Dancy: "Since I recommend a particularist understanding of the rightness or wrongness or the action [public executions of convicted rapists if the event would give pleasure both to the executioner and to the crowds], I recommend a particularist approach to the rightness or wrongness of any resulting pleasure" (1993: 61). This is not quite to deny that one can be a holist about final duty and not about prima facie duty, but Dancy seems to think it at least unnatural to hold the former without the latter view. I cannot here do justice to the richness of his discussion of the overall question of particularism. For a later statement of Dancy's views, see his "The particularist's progress," in Hooker and Little (2000: 130–56) (which also contains many other positions concerning particularism).

17 I hasten to add that Little's intention is apparently to use the analogy to support the view that "the very 'valence' of a feature is context-dependent" (2000: 280). As I see it, however, valence is like color in that it need not change in order for the element in question to have different effects in different contexts.

18 I explore the nature of organic unities and the non-additivity view just stated in some detail elsewhere (2003).

19 My view here contrasts with that of Jonathan Dancy in his critical study of Moore (2003).

20 I develop this distinction elsewhere (1997: ch. 4), where I defend a moderate foundationalism that incorporates what I consider the most plausible elements in epistemological coherentism.

21 If coherence is the only standard we bring to holistic moral assessment of an action, we cannot adequately distinguish between right and wrong. Wrong-doing can be supported by as coherent considerations as doing what is right. This is not the place to assess the prospects for a coherence theory of justification, but detailed critical treatments are offered in Audi (1997: ch. 4) and Plantinga (1993). Ross is clearly a foundationalist about the grounds of duty, and a moderate intuitionism is most plausible when placed within a carefully qualified foundationalism regarding prima facie duty.

22 In defending a Rossian account of the kinds of moral principles he formulates and in the moral concepts he works with as at least as basic as virtue notions, my view contrasts with that of David McNaughton and Piers Rawling in their wide-ranging "Principled Ethics" (2000). See, e.g., pp. 267–73.

23 For instructive discussion of the contraband example (and of the views of Dancy, from whom it comes), see McNaughton and Rawling (2000).

24 I have discussed this issue in some detail elsewhere (Audi 1995).

25 For discussion of the resources of Rossian intuitionism regarding comparisons of duty, see McNaughton (1996).

26 Earlier versions of this paper were given at the University of Helsinki and Wake Forest University. I benefited from the discussion on both occasions, and would also like to thank Derek Parfit for helpful comments on an earlier draft.

References

Audi, R. (1993). *The Structure of Justification*. Cambridge: Cambridge University Press.

Audi, R. (1995). "Acting from virtue." *Mind*, 104: 449–71.

Audi, R. (1997). *Moral Knowledge and Ethical Character*. New York: Oxford University Press.

Audi, R. (2003). "Intrinsic value and reasons for action." *Southern Journal of Philosophy*, XLI (Supplement): 30–56.

Audi, R. (2004). *The Good in the Right: A Theory of Intuition and Intrinsic Value*. Princeton: Princeton University Press.

Broad, C. D. (1930). *Five Types of Ethical Theory*. London: Routledge & Kegan Paul.

Dancy, J. (1993). *Moral Reasons*. Oxford: Basil Blackwell.

Dancy, J. (2000). "The particularist's progress." In B. Hooker and M. Little (eds.), *Moral Particularism*. Oxford: Clarendon Press.

Dancy, J. (2003). "Are there organic unities?" *Ethics*.

Donagan, A. (1977). *The Theory of Morality*. Chicago: University of Chicago Press.

Hooker, B. (2000). *Ideal Code, Real World*. Oxford: Oxford University Press.

Kant, I. (1961). *Groundwork of the Metaphysics of Morals*, trans. H. J. Paton. London: Hutchinson & Co.

Little, M. (2000). "Moral generalities revisited." In B. Hooker and M. Little (eds.), *Moral Particularism*. Oxford: Oxford University Press.

McNaughton, D. (1996). "An unconnected heap of duties?" *Philosophical Quarterly*, 46: 443–7.

McNaughton, D. and Rawling, P. (2000). "Principled ethics." In B. Hooker and M. Little (eds.), *Moral Particularism*. Oxford: Oxford University Press.

Mill, J. S. (1863). *Utilitarianism*. London.

Parfit, D. (forthcoming). *Climbing the Mountain*.

Plantinga, A. (1993). *Warrant: The Current Debate*. Oxford: Oxford University Press.

Ross, W. D. (1930). *The Right and the Good*. Oxford: Clarendon Press.

Ross, W. D. (1939). *The Foundations of Ethics*. Oxford: Oxford University Press.

Sidgwick, H. (1907). *The Methods of Ethics*, 7th edn. London: Macmillan.

Sinnott-Armstrong, W. (1999). "Some varieties of particularism." *Metaphilosophy*, 30: 1–12.

Defending Moral Particularism

Mark Norris Lance and Margaret Olivia Little

Introduction

Moral particularists like exceptions. At any rate, they regard exceptions as ubiquitous to moral principles; more importantly, they view them as friend rather than foe. This is of course simply to state their philosophical intuition. We believe, though, that it's the right intuition; and in this paper, we try to say why.

In doing so, we will argue more to the second point than the first. We'll be concerned less with demonstrating that the right moral principles in fact irreducibly admit of exception, and more with demonstrating that, if such exceptions do (as we suspect) exist, they should be tolerated and indeed embraced. This distinction points to two quite different bases for objecting to the type of moral particularism we'll be developing. The first, about which we'll have less to say, stems from *substantive moral* commitments. One might well believe that, all things considered, the best moral theory is one that in fact ends up cleaning up all exceptions; if so, one certainly won't be a particularist. Resistance to particularism thus sometimes reflects commitment to a view such as Kant's about lying, say, or the utilitarian's about pain, on which it turns out that lying is always wrong-making and pain always bad-making. This is a stance we respect (though we do not agree with it). After all, even those who believe that exceptions can be important must agree that not all realms admit of them. Physics, for instance, may well be a system susceptible to a codifiable structure of exceptionless laws (though its exceptionless laws may ending up having statistical quantifiers embedded in them); and even those who are particularists about physics would agree that we could, at any rate, make up a game whose every move is governed by a finite set of exceptionless rules.

For many people, though, resistance to moral particularism stems not from any *ex ante* commitment to a given normative theory. It stems, instead, from commitment to an extra-moral view about the nature of *explanation*. It stems from a conception of the way in which reasons and explanation must function in any realm – namely, by subsumption under strict theoretical generalizations or laws. According to this view, exceptions stand in the way of genuine explanation. Those committed to such a picture will regard the presence of moral exceptions as an embarrassment to the theoretical task of moral understanding and justification: morality had *better* be secured by a structure that doesn't admit of exception, on pain of morality's demotion to second-class epistemic status.

The answer to this sort of resistance is provision of a different model of explanation. We believe that, while reasons and explanation can travel by way of subsumption under strict laws, it is a deep mistake to think they always do – a mistake which, unless resisted, will obscure some of the richest views available. For some realms, ethics included, understanding and expertise is, at its heart, a matter of understanding, not eliminating, exception.

Exceptions and Explanation

Few people believe that lying is always wrong. After all, there may be some contexts in which another moral duty or principle – relief of terrible suffering, say – proves more important. Except where we are prepared to be absolutist, then, claims about the *all-things-considered* rightness or wrongness of following a given duty will have exceptions.

Amongst those who concur with this rather innocuous statement, some believe we can recover a tractable calculus governing the interactions of the various duties or principles that come our way. Perhaps justice is lexically ordered over utility maximization; perhaps we can find a way to render duties' strengths that will allow us to recover a calculative procedure for balancing them; perhaps specifying the duties to specific roles will allow us to set forth a once-and-for-all ordering of them. Others have set this aside as a misguided project. There is no algorithm or quantitative method, they urge, for deciding when justice should trump mercy rather than the other way round, no setting out a way to order or balance the virtues, principles, or duties (take your personal favorite) independently of context. Instead, it takes qualitative judgment or phronesis to make the comparative judgments in individual cases.

Whichever side of that debate one comes down on, though, the vast majority of contemporary philosophers believe that relevant moral duties or features always make the same *sort* of contribution to a moral situation. Like the forces of physics, but without the vector calculus, we can isolate various moral forces that always push, as it were, in the same moral direction as telling for or against an action. We could put it by inserting a 'ceteris paribus' or 'prima facie' or 'pro tanto' qualifier in front of the claim that 'lying is wrong', where those qualifiers function to abstract away possible competing moral considerations. Such a claim is in essence equivalent to asserting an exceptionless connection between lying and a milder moral property: lying may sometimes be morally justified, but it is always wrong-*making* (see, e.g., Pietrowski 1993).

It is here that moral particularists part company. Pain is always bad-making – well, except when it's constitutive of athletic challenge; intentionally telling a falsehood is prima facie wrong – well, not when done to Nazi guards, to whom the truth is not owed, or when playing the game Diplomacy, where it's the point of the contest. Pleasure always counts in favor of a situation – well, except when it's the sadist's delight in her victim's agony, where her pleasure is precisely part of what is wrong with the situation.[1] It is always wrong-making not to take competent agents at their word; well, not in the S&M room, where 'no' precisely does mean 'yes'. Considerations that in one context tell in favor of an action can in another go neutral or flip directions entirely, and all in a way that cannot be codified in any helpful concrete way.

The central core claim of particularism, then, is defense of a radical holism of moral reasons: the considerations that count as good- or bad-making, right- or wrong-making in one context can count in just the opposite way in another context, and all in a way that can't be helpfully cashed out in concrete terms. Moral considerations can "switch valence." The claim is not just that other considerations can override the import the first brings to the situation, but that a change in context can actually switch the contribution it brings itself, the moral direction that contribution pushes toward.

Many will disagree. In particular, many will argue that the examples above don't actually evince valence-switching: in each case, it's just that the relative contribution of the relevant feature is so small, so swamped by the vastly more important overriding considerations, that it's hard to see. A simple counterfactual test will reveal the residue: when thinking of the pain suffered by a needed inoculation, for instance, one will see it as justified even as one admits that if the medicine could be administered without pain it surely should be.

But the examples given in fact point to a different phenomenon. It is not just that the moral contribution of the specified features is easily overlooked: quite to the contrary, it may be significant. That one takes pleasure in torturing an innocent victim, for instance, makes the action substantially worse. (As Dancy (1993: 61) puts it, the sadist's pleasure is not the "silver lining" of the situation.) The counterfactual test here, that is, goes the other way, and in large measure; better that the torturer felt appropriate discomfort. In other cases, it isn't even clear that one can perform the counterfactual test because the feature in question seems constitutive of the case at hand: certain types or levels of pain are what make athletic endeavor the endeavor it is.

Once again, though, this isn't to deny that one *could* read the cases as involving constant valence overridden by other moral features. After all, whether or not one believes a consideration right- or wrong-, good- or bad-making is a function of the moral framework one holds: those who believe, for instance, that lying to autonomous agents is necessarily violative will think it is in the Nazi case, too. In our view, the examples themselves do put pressure on such first-order normative theories; nonetheless, one might believe the pressure can be resisted at the end of the day. Our primary concern, however, is with a different motivation for resisting the valence-switching interpretation, namely, one that stems from a commitment to a certain picture of how reasons and explanation must function.

Reasons, of course, are supposed to be the sort of thing that explains something else, and explains it in a robust sense (as opposed to a woolley, entirely open-textured notion of 'anything that answers a why question'). On a standard picture, explanation is said to proceed by at least tacit subsumption under strict (that is exceptionless) theoretical generalizations. On this model, genuine reasons *can't* valence-switch. If a consideration here leads to, or constitutes, or carries a given moral import, but does not do so elsewhere, then the consideration itself cannot constitute a complete explanation. Only when we find something univalent do we have a reason. Of course, since that reason may well be joined by others in different situations, its *relative* strength will change from situation to situation, which is why we always need to be attentive to context. Nonetheless, to understand it as a reason is to understand that it always makes the same sort of contribution to a situation. If we had the time, we should be able to fill in our description of any reason to produce a set of conditions that is everywhere sufficient for pushing in the direction of the right.[2]

Now here we must be careful. For *everyone* can agree to one sense in which the 'conditions can be filled in'. Just so long as the domain supervenes on the physical, for instance, we could fill in the conditions by providing an infinite disjunctive description of the various physical states of the universe with the relevant moral predicates tagged on. Such 'supervenience functions', as we might call them, though, are not explanatory for they have no projectible shape.[3] The 'filling in' or 'enthymematic' strategy, then, can't simply be a matter of offering to fill in the conditions in which the conjunction holds; it must claim to do so in a tractable, illuminating way that fully retains the explanatory power contained in the original claim (see. e.g., Lipton 1999). It is this that the particularist finds doubtful. Anyone who has succeeded is, of course, welcome to present her case; in the absence of seeing the goods, though, the particularist will have her doubts.[4]

Now there is a different way, attractive to some, to agree that exceptions beset the moral import of familiar moral concepts like pain and lying, while staying loyal to the enthymematic picture of explanation, namely, by insisting that genuine explanation must not be found at this level. The reason that lying is wrong-making, where it is, is that it's a case of *dishonesty*; the reason that promise-keeping is right-making, where it is, is that it's a case of *fidelity*, and these are properties that always count in the same direction. Considerations that valence-switch, then, are simply contingent bits and pieces that come together, in a given case, to constitute a reason, but do so only in virtue of coming to instantiate a more abstract, and univalent, moral property. Genuine moral explanation resides, that is, at a more abstract level.[5]

Of course, it will be admitted, understanding what *counts* as a case of fidelity or dishonesty takes interpretation and wisdom. One cannot expect someone untutored in moral matters to pick it up, any more than one can expect someone ignorant about fine wine to discern the oak from the earthy in the chardonnay. Nonetheless, it is claimed in good Aristotelian fashion that education can develop the ability to read a situation and see in it these more abstract moral properties. On this view – what we might call the 'pure discernment' view – we proceed by mastering the deep concepts of morality such as fidelity, justice, honesty (one may insert one's favorites from virtue theory or deontology) and then discern their instances directly in the situation at hand: here a cruelty, there a fidelity.

Now we're fans ourselves of Aristotelian phronesis – as indeed any good particularist must be. Moral discernment forms a more important, and less mysterious, part of the epistemological repertoire than structuralists often admit.[6] Nonetheless, the present view is highly problematic. The problem is not just that it requires a huge wallop of Aristotelian mojo to make any respectable moral move, but that it ends up denying the explanatory connection that does exist between, say, lying and wrong-making, or again promising and good-making. According to the pure discernment view, all elements – from infliction of pain to shoelace color – are simply details to be apprehended; the former exhibits no more theoretically intimate a tie to bad-making than the latter. Here's what we have in mind.

There is a key difference between discernment and explanation. When the presence of certain details allows us to apprehend something, the details need not themselves function as premises in an inference. In contrast, to treat some aspect as explanatory, one is adducing it as a premise in inference – even if one draws the conclusion immediately. To treat some aspect A as explanatory in a given situation of feature B involves commitment to the claim that simply knowing that another situation exhibits A gives at least *some* grounds to believe that B obtains there as well. That something's being a lie here is a reason not to do it *just is* a reason to think that something else's being a lie over there is also a reason not to do that. There is, then, a crucial difference between adducing reasons for a conclusion, and merely providing our audience enough scattered features of the situation to allow them to discern that truth on their own. The former requires commitment to some sort of generalization – just what the pure discernment theorist denies of familiar factors such as lying and promising.

According to the pure discernment theorist, then, morality would (in this respect) have to be like aesthetics: while we can *thematize* or *conceptualize* the aesthetic realm – helpfully classifying paintings according to aesthetic concepts such as balance and composition, there are no genuinely *explanatory* connections between a given type of paint dab and those more abstract properties such as balance. Such dabs can in a given case help constitute balance; those trained in aesthetics (a group which unfortunately excludes the present authors) can discern the balance in the dabs. But there is no explanatory connection, no more intimate connection, between the placement of the dots and balance in general.

Promise-keeping, lying, inflicting pain – these elements that make up the everyday stuff of morality *do* seem to sustain an intimate connection with moral import, whatever we might want to say about the likelihood of exceptions. They are genuinely explanatory of why something was right or wrong, carry explanatory weight in a way that extraneous details of the situation do not. To render them mere dots in a moral gestalt, one more detail among many in a narrative, is strongly at odds with everyday moral practice (see Little 2001).

To preserve this central feature of morality along with a commitment to the presence of exceptions requires another conception of principles, one that allows them to be both explanatory and porous.

Defeasible Generalizations and Privileged Conditions

Defeasibly, matches light when struck; other things being equal, fish eggs develop into fish; in standard conditions, red ties look red; as a rule, the future is like the past; generally, people say what they believe. Aristotle called them "*hos epi to polu*" (literally, "for the most part") generalizations. Despite the expression, Aristotle did not mean to describe such qualified generalizations as simply making assertions about what usually happen.[7] (Fish eggs, after all, usually get eaten before turning into fish.) Rather, they in some way are meant to capture the nature of the object in question. For Aristotle himself, such generalizations in biology, for instance, pointed to a reified potential by reference to which other things count as interfering factors (thus acorns are potential oaks even though they rarely turn into one). Those unconvinced by Aristotle's metaphysics may look askance at this particular view. But the structure of the generalizations itself, and the lesson to take from it, is broader.[8]

To illustrate, take a thoroughly conventional case. Defeasibly, soccer is played with eleven members on a team. Only defeasibly, for there are any number of variations – pick-up soccer with three-on-three, "little league" soccer with twenty-on-twenty and no goalie: the list goes on. It's doubtful we could specify in any concrete terms when a game counts and when it doesn't. (We can codify in boring detail the structure of FIFA soccer, of course; the claim is that there is no codifying which means that pick-up games count as soccer rather than a different game.) The variants, indeed, probably statistically predominate. Nonetheless, it would be quite wrong to think the play with eleven members is just one among many. The other games are, crucially, understood by reference to the first. Games may count as soccer while deviating from this standard, but it is nonetheless the standard. Eleven-member soccer stands in no need of explanation, while other versions do and the explanations reside in appropriate relations to the standard case.

Further, coordinate revisions in the rules are justified in terms of the ways the number of players deviates. Five-on-five soccer typically involves a smaller goal. Why? Because otherwise, given the smaller number of players and consequent increase in open space, there would be too many goals – that is, enough to constitute an unacceptable deviation *from standard soccer*. That is, it's not that there exists some Platonic norm opposing games with lots of goals (one needn't eschew basketball to motivate a smaller goal in soccer). Rather, one sort of soccer is functioning as a standard, and acceptable variations are motivated by their relation to this norm. In this sense, then, even non-standard soccer games carry a "trace": they each defeasibly involve eleven-membered teams, in the sense that their deviations from eleven-membered soccer must be justified and shown to be acceptable as variations.

In this case, we are not using the qualified generalization to say that soccer *usually* has the features highlighted. Nor, though, must we think we can exhaustively specify the conditions under which it in fact would. One needn't specify the conditions in which a connection does obtain in order to say that *where* it does it counts as informative in a certain way that allows the generalization to explain why we make certain other changes.

Sometimes, then, when we issue a generalization to the effect that something has a certain feature, what we really want to say is not that such a connection always, or even usually, holds, but that the conditions in which it *does* hold are particularly revealing of that item's nature, or of the broader part of reality in which the item is known. We might put it by saying that we're asserting what happens in "normal" conditions, except that the notion of 'normalcy' is so freighted with misleading connotations. Better put, then, we are taking as *privileged*, in one way or another, cases in which the item has the feature specified. Such generalizations can tell us about the nature of something, not by eliminating exceptions to the connection, but by maintaining and demarcating their status *as* exceptions.

As we've argued elsewhere, we think the best semantics is given in terms of embedded privileging maneuvers, which themselves form a complex typology.[9] Sometimes, as with soccer, it's the relatively simple case of paradigm-riff, or theme and variation. The pick-up soccer game is, if you like, a riff on the theme of soccer; and one can't understand a riff without understanding the theme to which it stands as variation. In that case we have a single concept, the extension of which was given via some notion of acceptable variation from a paradigmatic theme. But paradigm-riff privileging often comes in a richer form.

Consider irony. An ironic use of a sentence is a speech act in which what is meant is roughly the opposite of that which is usually meant by the utterance of that sentence. But irony is not simply a species of ambiguity, in which a sentence said in one tone of voice has one meaning and in another the opposite. For irony to function as it does, it must wear its reversal of semantic valence *on its sleeve*. It presents itself explicitly as being a non-standard use. Not, again, in a statistical sense: we could, in principle, turn into a society of Oscar Wildes, using irony more than literal speech. The point is that the speech acts nonetheless function by *carrying a trace* of that standard use. Utterances of P, we might put it, *always* have the property of defeasibly meaning P, even when used ironically to mean not-P. To use a sentence ironically is thus to use it in a way that can be understood only as derivative upon literal uses. Irony is essentially a riff on literal use, but a riff whose character as a riff is essential to it. (Compare kitsch in art.)

At other times, the privileging move is more complex, involving a structure that involves not conceptual, but justificatory, dependence. To illustrate, imagine having a perception as of a red cup. Having such a perception typically has a positive epistemic valence vis-à-vis the belief that there is a red cup; put into our language, defeasibly, appearances that P are justifying of beliefs that P. But sometimes, of course, having the appearance pushes in the direction of not believing its content – as when you know the evil demon is playing with your eyesight in a particular way. Epistemological holists will argue that there is no spelling out once and for all, in any relatively concrete terms, the conditions under which the perceptual experience is justifying. Nonetheless, it seems natural to think there is some sort of intimate connection between appearance and justification. For when appearances *are* unreliable – when seeing as P, or appearance that P, is not justifying of P – one's knowledge of this fact itself relies on justification provided by contexts in which one *can* rely on appearances (as when, say, we see the evil demon at work). Cases in which one is justified in taking one's appearances at their word stand as epistemically unproblematic; it is cases in which one is not so justified that demand explanation – and an explanation precisely that appeals to cases of the former type. Appearances, then, can mislead, but the relation between an appearance that P and a justified belief that P is deeper than the connection between, say, a justified belief that P and a justified belief that Q – *even* when P and Q happen to be tightly evidentially related; and this is so even if, given one's own background beliefs, the second actually holds more often in your vicinity than the first. For while the belief that P may in fact provide evidence that Q, it's of the essence of an appearance that P that it is defeasibly connected to justification of P. Appearances, we might put it, are necessarily *defeasibly* trustworthy. They carry this feature – the property of being defeasibly trustworthy – as a trace even into situations in which their justificatory import changes from trustworthy to non-trustworthy.

And sometimes, the justificatory dependence embedded in the privileging move is more specific yet: a counter-valence story must also make essential reference to something that has gone wrong. Think again about the epistemic case. Amongst the exceptions we can encounter to being able to take appearances at face value, some are cases in which we can nonetheless reach, as it were, as much justification as those in privileged conditions. If we have available a clear translation manual to our circumstances, after all, we can make adjustments that preserve justification (think of the quick inferential adjustment we do every time we see a bent stick in the water). Often, though, cases in which one cannot take appearances at face value indicate that one is in a worse situation, by knowledge's own lights: someone who's just entered the Hall of Holograms is in a situation which, however much fun, is epistemically deficient. Sometimes, then, non-privileged conditions are not just *deviant*, they are *defective*.

Across these various species, our understanding of defeasible generalizations involves two parts: understanding what happens in circumstances that are in some sense privileged, and, second, understanding where one is in relation to privileged conditions and what compensatory moves are necessitated – or again, which deviations acceptable.

Note that both pieces are needed. If all we knew were what happened in the privileged conditions – conditions, note, we often don't inhabit – we would have no idea whatsoever of the import something carried elsewhere. The generalizations would simply be a description of what exceptionlessly happens in a highly circumscribed and often unusual scope of possible worlds, with no relevance whatsoever outside that scope; life beyond the privileged conditions would be a black box (Dancy 1993: ch. 6; Lange 2000: ch. 6). The claim, then, is not simply that some circumstances are privileged, but that our understanding of the property's import *everywhere* is informed by how one's situation stands in *connection* to those circumstances. In soccer, for instance, one must know not only what counts as paradigmatic, but also what counts as an acceptable riff. Five-on-five soccer might, but eleven-on-eleven kickball does not. Even more important, one must understand not only *that* a given variant is an acceptable riff, still within the realm of soccer, but also which things follow from the *particular ways* that a deviant riff deviates from the normal. If we move to five-on-five, we ought to make other commensurate adjustments in the field, the goal, etc. so as to be true to the spirit of the game. One needs to understand, then, what counts as a paradigm example, what counts as an acceptable deviation from that paradigm, *and* what follows from the way that an acceptable deviation deviates.

Moral Defeasible Generalizations

Defeasible generalizations, we want to argue, offer a way of recovering exception-filled yet genuinely explanatory moral connections. The exceptions pointed to by particularists need not stand in the way of genuinely explanatory generalizations; they can, instead, be marks that the explanations in question are ones offered by defeasible generalizations. The features of an act that are genuinely explanatory of its moral status – as opposed to random details of a narrative, or again contingently relevant features – are precisely those governed by defeasible explanatory generalizations. Pointing to the fact that an action is a case of lying is explanatory in a way that pointing to surrounding detail is not (and this even though the world is rife with exceptions to lying's wrong-making status) because lying is defeasibly wrong-making. It's not that lying always, or must, or even usually has that status, but wrong-making is the valence it has in conditions that are privileged in certain ways, and whatever status it has in deviant circumstances is given by the relation of those circumstances to the privileged conditions and the compensatory moves called for by that relation. Where lying lacks this valence, as it sometimes or even often does, it is in virtue of the way the context deviates from privileged conditions.

Shoelace color and the infliction of pain can both be bad-making, but shoelace color isn't explanatory in the way painfulness is: while the former can have various moral imports (good-making, bad-making, indifferent) in various contexts, it has none of them defeasibly. Lying, in contrast, not only often has a negative moral import, it also always has the import of being defeasibly bad-making.

Moral defeasible generalizations, we believe, exhibit the full range of the privileging typology. Sometimes, the privileging is meant to mark out a paradigm-riff move. Pain, for instance, is paradigmatically bad. Sometimes, as when the pain contains a phenomenological element of pleasure ("it hurts so good"), it is plain variation – a permitted extension of the category, akin to treating pick-up soccer as part of a genus paradigmatically defined by the FIFA game. At other times it bears the more complex relation to the paradigm that irony does to non-ironic speech: the good-making pain wears its non-standard meaning "on its sleeve" as constitutive of its meaning. In athletics for instance, it is only because pain is paradigmatically something to be avoided that the notion of physical challenge has the meaning, and the status of constitutive good, that it does. It is only *because* pain is normally bad-making, then, that we can understand its good-making instances.

Similarly for claims that we are motivated "under the guise of the good." As many have urged, an unqualified version of this claim is far too strong: it seems possible to love evil and despise the good. A proper understanding of the claim, though, is not that such exceptions cannot occur, but that such cases, on analogy with irony, cannot be understood except *as* perversity. One can understand attraction to evil only parasitically on attraction to good; more specifically, one can understand rational motivation towards evil only as a non-standard reversal of good's normal valence. Pursuit of the good cannot be a perversity, though it can be a statistical anomaly; for what gets counted *as* the good is precisely what one is non-perversely attracted to.

And again, for motivational internalism: the claim, roughly speaking, is something like 'all things equal, if one judges there is overall best reason to phi, then one will be motivated to phi'. There are, as many have pointed out, all manner of exceptions to the generalization itself: weak will, ennui, and other forms of practical failure. What matters, though, is that one cannot understand what action is without categorizing these *as* failures. They may be frequent occurrences – in some agents, indeed, outnumbering cases of rational motivation. But, just as biological classifications privilege fish eggs turning into fish, so too classifications of practical reason privilege motivation following from some notion of best reason. Something counts as an action just in case, defeasibly, it is normatively responsive to the agent's best reasons. Thus, while Michael Stocker (1979) may continue to lie on the couch despite his all-things-considered judgment that he has most reason to get up and discuss philosophy, such episodes contain a trace: if he does not understood his situation as problematic, he has an inadequate understanding of himself as an agent. It is essential to categorizing an event *as* an action that it is governed by this defeasible generalization.

At other times, the privileging involved in moral defeasible generalizations involves justificatory dependence, with all its attendant complexity. Lying, for instance, can be good-making; but justifying that status often makes essential reference to contexts in which it has its classically negative valence. Exceptions, we might put it, are justificatorily derivative. They call for explanation, and their explanation makes essential reference to the more explanatorily basic or "unproblematic" case in which the actions have their more familiar valence. Thus imagine lying while playing the game Diplomacy. Lying is morally neutral in the game because of agreements that people make to play the game. More specifically, it is neutral because of agreements that must be seen as having been made in a context in which the normal moral valence of lying holds. Understanding lying's good-making status relies on invoking a notion, consent, that itself cannot be understood without invoking a framework in which the normal case is not to lie. The "defeasibly bad-making" nature of lying, thus, leaves a trace: a proper moral understanding of one's situation in Diplomacy includes an awareness of the fact that one is in a non-privileged situation.

Or again, consider the following general norm: defeasibly, not taking people's statements about what they want as expressing their desires is bad-making. There are contexts, such as certain practices of S&M, in which this norm is routinely violated: it is not wrong-making to interpret "Oh, please stop!" as expressing a desire that one continue. Here, too, though, there is a sort of justificatory dependence. It is *because* people have freely agreed to take part in this practice in a context governed by a commitment to the defeasible norm, 'take people at their word', that *not* taking them at their word gets here to enjoy positive valence. If a practice of ignoring statements of desire like this were to arise not in any way grounded in open statements of desire to participate, they would remain morally problematic in the usual way. The authority of not taking people at their word in the S&M room, then, is somehow grounded in open statements of desire to participate taken freely in a privileged situation. We have, then, a clear norm – namely, 'take people at their word' – and a clear sense of the justificatory dependence of contexts in which this norm is defeated upon contexts in which it isn't.

Note, again, that it's highly unlikely that we can codify out the content of what folks have consented to, other than some trivial principle such as 'one should take people seriously in a different manner in here than outside'. For there is, we are told, no blanket moral entitlement to ignore people's statements of desire while in the practice of S&M. The norms that capture the contours of interpretation are ones that develop, evolve, and gain in complexity with the evolution of the practice itself. There is an asymmetric moral dependency between the privileged context in which we take people at their word and the S&M context in which we routinely don't, but the game has its own evolutionary trajectory. Justificatory dependence is quite a different matter from codifiability.

Finally, sometimes, as in the epistemic case, the moral valence-switch indicates not just deviance, but *defect*: the situation is worse by morality's own lights. If it is honorable to tell a falsehood to the Nazi guard, for instance, it's because something has gone awry: there is something badly amiss (namely, the Nazi's evil) from the moral point of view. It is, if you will, a bad-making feature of the situation that lying is now a moral plus (*would* that it weren't honorable here to lie). In these sorts of cases, the connection between lying and the bad leaves a very particular kind of trace. To exhibit moral understanding in the Nazi world – to navigate its moral terrain – requires that one understand one's situation, not just as deviant, but as thereby morally *defective*. Even here, then, when one occupies a world in which most lies are in fact honorable, one must still appreciate that lying has an intimate tie to the bad.

Where the Laws Are

If the above is correct, then explanatory connection can persist in the face of – indeed, via a structure of – exceptions. Nonetheless, some will say, this is only a partial victory. Explanations themselves may be porous, but their success is parasitic on the existence of further, deeper *laws* that are themselves exception-free. In much the same way that defeasible explanations might be said to exist at the level of 'phenomenological physics' but only if backed by strict laws at the ultimate level, so, too, with moral generalizations.[10]

Here, that is, we see a more sophisticated version of the move to secure explanation by ascending to a higher or more abstract level. The concept of defeasible generalizations, it will be said, allows us – in contrast to the discernment theorist – to recover the idea that everyday moral features such as lying and the infliction of pain are explanatory of moral status in a way not true of shoelace color. It allows us, that is, to recover the idea that promise-keeping is explanatory, rather than merely constitutive, of a given moral status. Perhaps it will even be granted that the best semantics of this is rendered in terms of privileged conditions. Nonetheless, some will insist, all of these defeasibility explanations must depend on the existence of exceptionless laws stated in more abstract moral terms, such as 'honesty is always right-making'. If promise-keeping is defeasibly related to right-making – if, that is promise-keeping is right-making in privileged conditions, but not in many others – it is in virtue of the fact that promise-keeping is, in privileged conditions, a case of honesty, and one of the moral laws is that honesty is always right-making.

Such a view is certainly understandable against a certain traditional logical model of laws, such as Hempel's classic deductive-nomological model (1966). It's also reinforced by certain metaphysical views on what is specifically law-like about laws (what the 'nomological' bit means). Views such as those of David Armstrong (1980), for instance, regard laws as assertions of *identities* between special kinds of properties known as universals.[11] On any such views, laws *can't* admit of exceptions; they simply wouldn't be laws if they did.

If we agree that there are ineliminable exceptions to the wrong-making import of inflicting pain, we do so on pain of acknowledging that law-likeness lies elsewhere.

In contrast, the particularist – at least the interesting version to our mind – is one who insists that such considerations nonetheless function as laws – function as explanatory in as deep a way as any generalization does. For the above is not the only sort of approach to what law-likeness consists in.

Those attracted to contemporary inferentialism – the view that semantic content is to be understood, at least in large part, in terms of various sorts of inferential propriety[12] – can illustrate the intuition in particularly powerful ways. According to inferentialism, the semantic function of conditionals is to make explicit various inferential proprieties. But not all inferences are decisive. Adducement of something as a reason necessarily involves a commitment to an inferential propriety in other contexts, that is, but some inferential proprieties are 'non-monotonic' in that they can be overridden by additional premises. Putting this general point into the inferentialist framework, Robert Brandom argues that *ceteris paribus* qualifiers serve to make explicit the non-monotonicity of the underlying inference.[13] Of course, non-monotonicity is a broad genus, which includes, for instance, enthymemes and the inferential structure of epistemic defaults, but for all that can include the defeasible generalizations we described above.

Working in the same tradition, Marc Lange (2000) has urged an account of law-likeness that distinguishes law-like statements from other universal conditionals in terms of the former's special role in inference. Law-like statements are a sort of inference license which is necessary, supports a particularly broad range of counterfactuals, and provides special confirmability: to treat a generalization as a law is to treat each instance of it as confirming every other instance. (I need only test one sample of sugar to confirm the claim that all sugar dissolves in water; in contrast, I would need to look at each item on my shelf separately to confirm that all of them dissolve in water.)

But the scope of relevant counterfactuals supported by a given law is determined by the methods, goals, and aspirations of a discipline. What counts as a law for evolutionary biology, thus, may not count as a law of developmental biology, or again medicine. For Lange, then, to claim that something is a law is, roughly, to take the inference expressed within it to be applicable not only in actual circumstances, but across a set of possible worlds whose contours is set by the goals of the relevant discipline whose inferential proprieties are at issue.

When we put these two insights of inferentialism together, we have a rendition of defeasible conditionals fit to play the role of genuine laws. For we can use conditionals that meet *both* inferentialist criteria: they are both irreducibly porous – shot through with exceptions – and robustly law-like. Exception-filled conditionals, that is, can do more than merely reflect contingent regularities or locally warranted epistemic defaults; they can function as genuine explanatory laws.

It is common in the philosophy of science to suppose that the presence of genuine kinds is coordinate with the existence of genuine laws. A kind is a sort, each instance of which is governed by a group of laws, and a law governs the nature of a kind. Thus, if the defeasible nature of a discipline's principles does not rule out their functioning as laws, we remain in a position to maintain that there are genuine kinds in that discipline as well – just kinds governed by defeasible laws. Some such instances are thoroughly conventional, as with soccer (though even here, note, one is dealing with a practice whose contours of privilege and compensatory moves, far from being purely subjects of fiat, are governed by a deep notion of the "point" of the game). At any rate, when we turn to disciplines, such as biology, which institute an investigatory (rather than recreational) practice, kinds will emerge that are sufficiently objective to deserve, if anything does, the title of 'natural'.

Without returning to Aristotelian metaphysics, then, we can recover the idea that it's of the essence of the kind 'fish egg' that defeasibly they develop into fish. One classifies the fish egg as being the kind of biological organism it is by reference to its "standard" or "normal" development. There is of course an infinite number of trajectories that fish eggs could take, from developing into fish, to being ennucleated with sheep DNA and becoming a sheep, to breaking down into nutrients for a turtle, to being irradiated and turned into a strange and horrid swamp monster. Nonetheless, we elevate one such trajectory as a "natural" one, viz. one that does not call for explanation (at least at this level of theory); and in this sense we circumscribe some developments as expressions of an organism's "nature." In this way, we can – and should – regard a fish egg as a *potential* fish, and a salamander egg – which could in some possible world be turned into a fish by laboratory machinations – as only thereby a *possible* fish. Fish form a natural kind, then; but it is a kind governed by defeasible laws.

Similarly, there are, on such a view, moral kinds governed by defeasible moral laws. It is of the essence of lying that it is defeasibly wrong-making: such a connection to the wrong is part of what it is for a speech-act to be a case of lying. (A society in which being misled is known to be in principle impossible would not classify the act of stating a falsehood as a lie.[14]) Or again, the Good is, necessarily, defeasibly such as to be pursued. Or again, an agent is, necessarily, defeasibly to be motivated by what she believes she has most reason to do. One need not say that all moral connections are on a par; some generalizations mark intimate ties - if you like, moral natures – for they are *necessary* defeasible generalizations.

Such defeasible generalizations bear all the marks of an inferentialist understanding of laws. They are inference licenses – albeit non-monotonic ones. They support counterfactuals, though unlike the case of strict laws in which the same regularity holds in each relevant world, here the regularity holds in privileged worlds and varies in epistemically discernible ways in worlds deviating from the privileged. That is, as we saw in the discussion of soccer, *what* one projects with a defeasible generalization is not only what happens in a set of privileged circumstances, but also the specific compensatory ways that other situations differ in virtue of deviation from privilege in one way. So the law 'soccer goals are x feet wide' supports not only the conditional 'if it were raining, the goal would be x feet wide', but also 'if a game were played with five on a side, the goal would be substantially less than x feet wide'.

Finally, we have a correlate of the confirmation condition, one which exhibits just the same emendation. For strict laws, each instance of x being F is a reason to believe of every other x that it is F. In the case of a defeasible law – defeasibly pain is wrong-making – one's understanding of the way that pain contributes to the wrongness of an action in one case is itself a reason to think that pain will contribute in the way determined by the defeasible law in all others. Just what that contribution will be is variable, but again the shape of variation is discernible. Because an understanding of pain requires a grasp of the structure of privilege and compensatory deviation, one's understanding of the way that the pain of being assaulted here contributes to the wrongness of the assault does count as a reason to believe that pain in the context of athletic endeavor would be right-making.

What then to make of the ascension move? Here, as with the enthymematic move, we must proceed carefully. *Everyone* will agree that we can recover exceptionless moral generalizations if we ascend high enough in abstraction: after all, everyone can agree we should always "do the right thing." Beyond these sorts of commitments, though, things get interesting.

For one thing, those friendly to exceptions are likely to find them everywhere short of the above aphorism's triviality. Sometimes one must be cruel to be kind; fidelity to some causes would be constitutively evil; some commitments are not worthy of respect. (As Elijah Millgram [2002] puts it, the "defusing move" works on just about anything.) This isn't to deny that cruelty is related in a law-like way to wrong-making; again, once one allows laws that admit of exception, one might happily say that cruelty sustains just such a connection, and that the defeasible laws involving both cruelty and pain inter-illuminate one another. It's to say, rather, that deep illumination should not be thought necessarily indicative of expunged exceptions.

To be sure, ascending to more abstract moral language can be explanatory. After all, one of the marks of explanation is to unify what are otherwise disparate phenomena, and the more abstract language of virtues, duties, or principles (again take your pick) seem to do just that. We say what giving someone the benefit of the doubt has in common with sending money to a charity by reference to the concept of *generosity*. One needn't think generosity univalent, though, to think it capable of unifying other phenomena which are themselves precisely marked by defeasible generalities.

But what if one *does* believe cruelty and the like to be univalent? The first thing to say is that, even if there are exceptionless moral generalizations functioning as higher-order laws in morality, this doesn't itself obviate the (now lower-order) law-likeness of the generalizations concerning our old friends lying, promise-keeping, and the infliction of pain. Higher-order laws, it turns out, can't do all the heavy lifting. To give an example of Lange's, it might be the case that all the phenomena of island biodiversity can be unified as instances of Darwinian survival strategy; pointing to laws at that higher level, that is, may unify and constrain patterns of behavior at the level of islands. Nonetheless, there are inferences – the *raison d'être* of theoretical principles – we can make only by invoking the lower-level laws. Laws of island bio-diversity allow us to predict with fair accuracy, for instance, the population of a species given only the size of the island, something that cannot be done within Darwinian theory, which makes no mention of islands. Higher-level laws, in short, even where they exist, often fail to capture the content of laws at a lower level. Lower-level laws retain autonomous value.

Second, once we realize that genuine laws admit of exception, space opens for a more radical rejoinder. For once we realize this, pressure is placed on why one should believe that exception-filled laws *must* be backed up at some higher level by a strict one. It places pressure, that is, on any *ex ante* commitment to the claim that exception-laden laws depend, for their existence, on exceptionless ones.

Again, one may have a particular view about morality – here, about its metaphysical backing rather than its first-order normative structure – that implies the existence of strict higher-order moral laws. A Natural Law theorist, or again a Platonist about morality, is committed to the existence of strict moral laws that determine everything's ethical nature, in much the same way the laws of physics determine all physical nature. But for those who have an essentially organic, practice-based notion of morality, according to which morality is objective but not transcendent, there may be no hidden "scientific moral image" lying behind the manifest one.[15] Given the practice we find ourselves engaged in – and only from the perspective of such engagement – we have a sense of the point of that practice, and an understanding of our goals and purposes that allows us to amend that practice. But apart from our skillful involvement with it, we could not formulate any conception of its point, much less produce a codified theory of it that could be used to determine appropriateness within the practice.

Moral understanding, while drenched in exception, is understanding of a structure, not merely a series of instances. What one comes to understand is a complex whole, in which intuitions about cases, privileged conditions, and compensatory moves all exert leverage on one another.

Notes

1 The pain example is from Millgram (2002), the Diplomacy example a variant from McNaughton (1988), and the pleasure example from Dancy (1993).
2 For invocation of this view to moral particularism, see, for instance, Crisp (2000).
3 For more on this point, see Dancy (1993: ch. 5), McDowell (1979, 1981), and, in contrast, Jackson et al. (2000). Even more trivially, note, we could fill in the *ceteris paribus* with anything that logically entails right-makingness – a move that clearly sacrifices explanatory shape.
4 The example of pain is particularly difficult. It's hard not to think that pain genuinely constitutes the wrong-makingness of many actions, but difficult to see how to eliminate exceptions to the claim that it is always wrong-making. Athletic pain lacks cruelty, but so does negligent pain.
5 For a sophisticated version of this 'abstraction' strategy, see Crisp (2000).
6 For defenses of moral discernment's bona fide, see for instance McNaughton (1988), McDowell (1979), Nussbaum (1985), Murdoch (1970), Blum (1991).
7 See Irwin (2000) for more on Aristotelian conditionals – and an argument for why Aristotle should not be regarded a particularist.

8   Much of this section is taken from our forthcoming "Particularism and anti-theory."
9   See our forthcoming "Particularism and anti-theory."
10 Such a view seems behind McNaughton and Rawlings (2000).
11 A view which would argue that the examples of 'defeasibility' given above will come to naught: after all, talk of fish eggs "defeasibly" (not just possibly) turning into fish will seem suspect to those who leave behind Aristotelian substances; and soccer is a game, for goodness' sake! But keep reading.
12 See especially Brandom (1994, 2000). (The latter is a much easier introduction to inferentialism, while the former is Brandom's official and more thorough development of his version of the view. There are, of course, many other views that go under the name, but this one is most congenial to the ideas we develop here.)
13 It's just wrong to remain hobbled by the thought that useful conditionals must be exceptionless – a thought grounded in the supposition that principled reasoning must ultimately be deductive. For an example from the philosophy of science, consider the following characteristic statement, made by no less pre-eminent philosophers of science than John Earman and John Roberts in considering Nancy Cartwright's claim that there is an irreducible and theoretically unspecifiable context dependence to physical laws:

> Consider what would follow if it were true: none of our theories, and not even all of our theories taken together, would suffice to make a reliable prediction of any course of observable events ... for any deviation from what one might have expected given those laws could be explained away as a result of context specific factors not captured by the net of theory. Given this, it is difficult to see how laws, as Cartwright understands them, can be used for making predictions or giving explanations, and it is far from clear how such laws could be confirmed. (Earman and Roberts 1999: 456)

Clearly this makes sense only if one assumes that the only mode of inference is deduction. Since we deny this, we hold that it is a central error to think that dependence is the same as codifiable dependence.
14 Our thanks to Pekka Vayrynen for pressing us on this issue (see his 2004: 77).
15 The manifest image is the conceptual space of ordinary objects, properties and relations, most of which are non-inferentially observable. The scientific image is the conceptual space of theoretical posits and the laws that govern them. This image is populated by purely theoretical entities – that is, by entities belief in whose existence is justifiable only inferentially. ('Scientific' in this sense need have nothing to do with 'science' understood as a naturalistic enterprise.)

References

Armstrong, D. (1980). *A Theory of Universals*, vols. 1 & 2. Cambridge: Cambridge University Press.

Blum, L. (1991). "Moral perception and particularity." *Ethics*, 101: 701–25.

Cartwright, N. (1999). *The Dappled World*. Cambridge: Cambridge University Press.

Crisp, R. (2000). "Particularizing particularism." In B. Hooker and M. Little (eds.), *Moral Particularism*. Oxford: Oxford: Oxford University Press.

Dancy, J. (1993). *Moral Reasons*. Oxford: Oxford University Press.

Dancy, J. (2004). *Ethics Without Principles*. Oxford: Oxford University Press.

Earman, J. and Roberts, J. (1999). "Ceteris paribus, there is no problem of provisos." *Synthese*, 118: 439–78.

Hempel, C. (1966). *Philosophy of Natural Science*. Prentice-Hall.

Irwin, T. H. (2000). "Ethics as an inexact science: Aristotle's ambitions for moral theory." In B. Hooker and M. Little (eds.), *Moral Particularism*. Oxford: Oxford University Press.

Jackson, F., Pettit, P., and Smith, M. (2000). "Ethical particularism and patterns." In B. Hooker and M. Little (eds.), *Moral Particularism*. Oxford: Oxford University Press.

Lance, M. and Little, M. (forthcoming). "Defeasibility and the normative grasp of context." *Erkenntnis*.

Lance, M. and Little, M. (forthcoming). "Particularism and anti-theory." In D. Copp (ed.), *Oxford Handbook of Ethical Theory*. Oxford University Press.

Lange, M. (2000.) *Natural Laws in Scientific Practice*. Oxford: Oxford University Press.

Lipton, P. (1999). "All else being equal." *Philosophy*, 74: 155–68.

Little, M. (2000). "Moral generalities revisited." In B. Hooker and M. Little (eds.), *Moral Particularism*. Oxford: Oxford University Press.

Little, M. (2001). "On knowing the 'why': particularism and moral theory." *Hastings Center Report*, 31(4): 32–40.

McDowell, J. (1979). "Virtue and reason." *The Monist*, 62: 331–50.

McDowell, J. (1981). "Non-cognitivism and rule-following." In S. Holtzman and C. Leich (eds.), *Wittgenstein: To Follow a Rule*. London: Routledge & Kegan Paul.

McNaughton, D. (1988). *Moral Vision*. Oxford: Blackwell.

McNaughton, D. and Rawling, P. (2000). "Unprincipled ethics." In B. Hooker and M. Little (eds.), *Moral Particularism*. Oxford: Oxford University Press.

Millgram, E. (2002). "Murdoch, practical reasoning, and particularism." *Notizie di Politeia*, 18: 64–87.

Murdoch, I. (1970). *The Sovereignty of Good*. London: Routledge & Kegan Paul.

Nussbaum, M. (1985). "Finely aware and richly responsible: moral attention and the moral task of literature." *Journal of Philosophy*, 82(10): 516–29.

Pietrowski, P. (1993). "Prima facie obligations, ceteris paribus laws in moral theory." *Ethics*, 103: 489–515.

Sellars, W. (1956). "Empiricism and the philosophy of mind." In H. Feigl and M. Scriven (eds.), *The Foundations of Science and the Concepts of Psychoanalysis*. Minnesota Studies in the Philosophy of Science, vol. I. Minneapolis: University of Minnesota Press.

Stocker, M. (1979). "Desiring the bad." *Journal of Philosophy*, 76: 738–53.

Vayrynen, P. (2004). "Particularism and default reasons." *Ethical Theory and Moral Practice*, 7: 53–79.

Index of Subjects

error theory 221–2, 229
ethical statements
    testability of 241–2
Euthyphro (Plato) 201, 216
expected value 8–10, 12, 16
    vs. actual value 8–9
explanation
    context-sensitivity of 244–5
    deductive-nomological model of
        315–16
    exceptions and 316
    subsumption model of
        generality 305–6
        valence switching 307–8
explanation, evaluative
    causal explanation and 253
    commitment to evaluative properties
        and xxii, 244–5
    of evaluative beliefs 252–4
    of non-evaluative facts xxii, 243–5,
        250–2
        vs. non-evaluative explanation xxii,
            250–1
explanation, moral xix–xxiv, 241–319
    'Because Constraint' xxii, 270–8
    causal explanation and 244, 251–2
    confirmation of 242
    counterfactual conditionals 267
    defeasible generalizations and
        313–15
    doxastic vs. non-doxastic 267–8
    epiphenomenalism 246
    as evaluative explanation 242–3
    explanatory coherence 243, 246
    levels of 308, 315–19
    of moral belief 266–7
    moral epistemology and 243, 267–8
    moral laws and 315–19
    safety of xxii, 246
    scientific explanation and xxi–xxii,
        241–2, 244–6, 254–5, 315–19
    truth/correctness of 242, 245–6
    vs. discernment 308–9
expressivism 148, 183–4, 206–8, 220
    'cognitivist expressivism' 231–7
    'factualist expressivism' 229–30
    non-cognitivism vs. 230
    non-descriptivism vs. 221
    truth-aptness of moral claims and
        207–8

externalism xviii, 46–7, 163–4, 182
    desire to be moral and xviii, 166–8,
        194
        appropriateness of 177–8
        arbitrariness of 172–3, 194–5
        fetishism and 169–70
        normativity of morality and xviii,
            172–6
        practical desire and 176–7
        rationality and 173–9
    innate moral sense 213–4

factualism, moral xix–xxi, 201–15,
        220–2
    argument from relativity 264
    constructivism and *see* constructivism,
        moral
    'externalist factualism' 212–15
    factual judgment *see* judgment, factual
    'factualist expressivism' 239–40
    'internalist factualism' 212
    moral facts vs. ordinary facts 202–5
    moral realism and *see* realism, moral
    moral relativism and *see* relativism,
        moral
    motivation and xx–xxi, 211–15
    naturalism and 223, 269
    non-cogntivism and 264
fetishism 169, 195
folk morality 264–5
free agency 65–8, 70–1

generality of moral principles xxiii,
        285–302
    'aretaic generalism' 298
    conditionalization and 287–90
    exceptionless 289
    scope of 288
    specificity of demand and 289–90
    tradeoffs and 286–8
    universal applicability and 289–90
        see also duties
    vagueness and 286–8
    virtue and 298–9
    see also particularism, moral
goodness
    agent-neutral conception of 7
    as independent of the right 7, 43
    as a matter of degree 42, 44
    utilitarian conception of 10

rights 29–30, 50–1
  choice-protecting vs. interest-protecting
    30
  negative vs. positive 51
  see also separateness of persons

satisficing xi, 21–23, 28, 40
  vs. maximizing 21, 23, 28
semantics of moral terms 220–2
  inferentialism 316–7
  reference-fixing 225–7
sentimentalism xvii–xviii, 129, 134–58
  blame and 139
  categorical imperatives and 134–8, 141
  causal efficacy of moral properties and
    278n6
  charity and justice for the dispossessed
    154–5
  civility and 134, 137, 141–2
  common point of view, the 134–7,
    141–2, 155
    counterfactual conception of 136
  evaluation of moral scenarios and
    147–53
  explanation and 265
  folk morality and 264–5
  foreign office knaves xvii, 135–9, 141,
    145
  mind-dependency of morality and
    148–9, 152–3
  moral obligations and xvii–xviii, 135,
    137–9, 144–7, 153–6
  reason and 144
  resentment 155–7
  response-dependency and 152–3
  sympathy 155–7
  two-dimensional logic and 146–52
  universal obligations and xvii, 129
separateness of persons xi, 29–32, 38,
    49–51, 62
  respect for persons 62–3, 70–1, 73, 78
  treating people as equals 64
skepticism, moral 178, 184–5, 189–91,
    244
social contract *see* contractarianism
strength of will *see* enkrateia
supervenience of moral facts on non-
    moral facts 202, 246–52, 256n8,
    266, 270, 272–3
  a priority of 272–3

epiphenomenalism and 247–52, 256n8,
    258n16, 258n17
evaluative belief and 250
naturalism and 248–9, 256n8, 270–1

A Theory of Justice (Rawls) 100
truth
  minimalism about xix–xx, 207–8, 234

Utilitarianism (Mill) 286–7
utilitarianism 10–12, 59–65, 68
  act vs. rule 287
    see also consequentialism: act vs.
      rule
  as 'esoteric' theory of morality 63–4, 66
  as impersonal conception of morality
    61–6
  philosophical *see* welfarism
  respect for persons and 62–3
  utilitarian conception of the good 10
  vagueness of 287
  weighing values on 287, 301, 302n4
  well-being and 10–12

value
  fine-grained vs. complete theories of 26
  permissibility and 22
  plural vs. singular 10–11, 23
virtue xvi, 101–12, 118–20
  Aristotelian theory of 101–12
    right action and 106–12
  character and 102–3, 111–12
  demandingness, objection to 120
  fundamental attribution error 102
  guiding action 106–12
  the obligatory and 111–12, 119–20
  phronesis see phronesis
  practical wisdom *see phronesis*
  rationality and 104–5
  reductionist accounts of 101, 107–8
  right action and 106–14, 116–18
    virtuous person as advisor 118
  supererogation and xvi, 111–12, 119–20
  as threshold concept 105
  tragic dilemmas 108–11, 115
  unity of the virtues 105
  virtues of ignorance 102–3
    modesty 102–3
  virtuous action and 102
  v-rules 106–15

as cross-cultural 107
as guides to action 107–12, 114–15
reductionism and 107–8
vs. *enkrateia* (strength of will), in
    Aristotle 104
as well-functioning 118–9
virtue ethics xvi–xvii, 91, 99–112, 285
application problem xvi, 106–12;
    113–19
indeterminacy worry xvii, 116–19
messiness worry 115–16
consequentialist and deontologist
    criticism of 99
reductionism of moral concepts and
    xvi–xvii, 101

as teleological/consequentialist moral
    theory xvi, 100–1
tragic dilemmas 108–11, 115
virtue theory and 99, 113
virtue theory 99, 113

welfarism 59
wrongness
ideal circumstances and 81–4
impersonal 84–5, 89–90
interpersonal 78, 81, 84–5, 89–92
reasonable complaint and 92–5
    in ideal situations 81–3
    in real-world situations 81–3
as unjustifiability to others 78–9, 81

Index of Names

Moore, G. E. 11, 15, 19, 166, 205, 209, 222, 248, 266, 272, 276–8

Nagel, T. 212
Nietzsche, F. 120
Norcross, A. 19
Nozick, R. 17

Peacocke, C. 147–52, 157
Pettit, P. 70
Plato 57, 201, 245
Prichard, H. A. 166

Quinn, W. 250

Railton, P. 227
Rawls, J. xi, 16, 49, 60–1, 71, 77, 100, 227, 254
Raz, J. 70
Ross, W. D. 16, 166, 286, 289–93, 296, 298–301
Rousseau, J.-J. 58, 153

Salmon, N. 273
Scanlon, T. M. 59–60, 77–90, 95, 186, 227
Scheffler, S. 28
Sidgwick, H. 46, 62–3, 72
Slote, M. 114, 121
Smith, A. 134, 154–7
Smith, M. 85, 169, 185, 227
Stocker, M. 164, 314
Sturgeon, N. 266–70
Svavasdóttir, S. 184–5, 189, 192, 194
Swanton, C. 101–2, 112, 114, 120–2

Thomson, J. J. 7

Wallace, J. 172–9
Watson, G. 113, 119
Wilson, M. 158n4

Zangwill, N. 172, 242